EMILIA BRESCIANI was born in Peru of Peruvian and Italian parents. At the age of eighteen she travelled to Australia on a journey of adventure and later graduated as a journalist from the University of Technology, Sydney. For fifteen years she worked in radio and television, dedicating her time to the promotion of cultural diversity and the fight for social justice. Her vision and commitment to work for a harmonious society earned her a series of highly regarded awards. Emilia lives in Sydney and is now writing her first work of fiction. This is the story of her spiritual journey.

The Raw Scent *of* Vanilla

A Memoir

EMILIA BRESCIANI

MACMILLAN
Pan Macmillan Australia

First published 2000 in Macmillan by Pan Macmillan Australia Pty Limited
St Martin's Tower, 31 Market Street, Sydney

National Library of Australia
Cataloguing-in-Publication data

Bresciani, Emilia.
The raw scent of vanilla: a memoir.

ISBN 0 7329 1065 X

1. Bresciani, Emilia. 2. Mothers and daughters – Biography.
3. Mythology, Peruvian – Biography. 4. Journalists – Australia – Biography. I. Title.

070.92

Typeset in 12.5/15 pt Bembo by Post Pre-press Group, Brisbane, Queensland
Printed in Australia by McPherson's Printing Group

Cover and text design by Greendot Design

The events in this book are true but some names have been
changed for reasons of privacy.

To my mother, whose smile lives in the colours of the rainbow;

to my father, who showed me that love is eternal; and

to Richard, whose soul guided me into a more meaningful world.

CONTENTS

PROLOGUE

MY HUSBAND CAME back to say goodbye two weeks after his death. He came before dawn when the scent of his breath was still fresh on my pillow, reminding me of pure love. He was coming with a message that I could not possibly understand, because the symbols of the dead can be mystical and bewildering. I had to live through a series of nightmares to finally interpret the significance of his farewell. However, his visit filled my heart with hope and convinced me that the essence of those who pass away, the ones who have touched us with genuine love, can continue to relate to us even from the Other Side, as long as we choose to let them in.

I could have sworn I was awake. I was lying in bed when I heard a soft noise on the other side of the door, and I began to sense an eerie presence in the house. Outside on the streets, the air was calm, there was no traffic on the road, not even a distant whisper. 'Who is there?' I asked. My eyes tried to pierce a curtain of shadows, eager to find a sign, to see a familiar face. Then I heard a strange whistle in the lounge room next door, like the echo of a breeze blowing across the floor. My skin tingled, blood rushed to my face and my muscles tightened. There was an alien energy in the air; some kind of entity that was not from this world. A ghost? My mother had seen ghosts. They had come to her to announce things before they happened. A friend from Peru had once told me that the dead always came back to say goodbye when they have been prevented from doing so before they transcended. I had chosen to believe her. I had it within me to believe her.

The murmur came to a halt and a sweet scent streamed under the door, towards my bed, like ripples of a good omen. It soothed my anxiety. Then I heard the door opening, and I saw him, bathed in the light that shines from the other side of pain. He glided across the room, a luminous apparition, dressed in the wedding clothes in which I had buried him. The same calypso blue silk shirt we had bought together to match the colour of the Caribbean sea, next to which we had been married early that year. My eyes opened even wider as I saw his head covered with a mane of long, thick red curls. His beautiful head that only days before had been hit by a lethal blow in the Blue Mountains.

'Richard, you have come back,' my heart spoke and I was filled with warmth. He sat on the edge of the bed and offered me a look of love.

'Yes,' he said softly. His gaze fused with mine and I felt as if I was floating in the same two deep pools I had recognised eighteen months before, when I had first met him. My heart pounded with exhilaration. I wanted to ask him so many questions, I wanted to touch him, I wanted to beg him to tell me the whole story. Why had he left me so soon, so early in our marriage? What had possessed his soul? Was it all my fault? But something prevented me. I wondered how painful it had been, and I wanted to know whether his soul had been conscious at the moment of his tragic death. Perhaps it had fled in time, as I had been told by a spiritual adviser. I hoped that this had been the case.

'You are here!' I was bewildered but too scared to move and blow his image away with my breath. He looked ethereal.

'I came to get my computer.'

'It's not here, it's at work,' I said. We had both worked for the same broadcasting station.

He pulled me by the hand and my body glided behind him, moving through walls and windows with ease, flying over the roofs to the station. The city was calm, and I swung into the fantasy of my own dream, happy to be with him again. How silly, I thought. Why does he need his computer on the Other Side? He is not going to work there, is he? He looked at me and smiled, and I realised he could read my thoughts. Perhaps he needed it for some other reason. Perhaps there was something he had failed to complete? I was only to discover his reasons much later. We stopped in front of a large white temple crowned by a crystal dome. I had never seen it before, but it looked familiar.

We waited in silence until the lift doors opened and we stepped inside. In my excitement I wanted to clasp his body against mine, but I felt intimidated by his presence, so I just stared at him, at his gentle eyes. Again he read my mind and wrapped his arms around me and hugged me with the love that knows no beginning and would never end. My body melted into one large bursting tear and he dissolved inside it.

'Did you understand what he wanted to tell you in the dream?' asked Caroline, my therapist, who was sitting in the green armchair across the room.

'Well, it was obvious. I got into trouble because of a computer disk,' I replied, referring to the legal battle that had incriminated me with the murder of my husband. The incident had left me traumatised.

I went to see Caroline in the midst of a crippling depression. Despite my legal victory I had become the prisoner of my mistrust and emotional alienation. I had cleared my reputation, and had undergone a series of spiritual purifications in South America, but I knew there was a deeper wound somewhere in my heart. A wound that was turning my feelings into ice.

She wanted to take me back to the source of the trauma. To the

xii THE RAW SCENT OF VANILLA

scene of the 'trial': the inquest session. I had been reluctant to let go because of a disturbing experience which had happened just before Richard died. But Caroline said that this therapy was necessary to help me take control of my emotions and to thaw my frozen feelings.

I learned to trust Caroline. I believed she was the only person who understood me, who recognised my entangled emotions. She had a serene smile and a gentle disposition. Her voice was affectionate and imbued with husky undertones. And she often smelled of lavender, a scent that made me feel safe. I finally agreed to the treatment because Caroline also reminded me of the women of my land and my legends.

In the softness of her gaze I found the soul of Latin American women, the strength of their spirit and the smile of innocence. Those who walked through the valleys of the Urubamba River, gathering corn and chanting odes to the Sun. As I told her my story I thought of the women from the Amazon, the seers of time and the shakers of sin, the priestesses who searched deep into the darkness of distressed minds. Those who teased the rivers with mysterious tales and bathed wicked souls in holy waters, smoking away the evil eye with a hundred lashes of fresh *ruda*. Entranced by the aromas of eucalyptus and lavender, or sometimes rose and lemon, that wafted from her oil burner, I let my mind travel through time where all moments became one. Using hypnotherapy of a dissociative approach, as Caroline called it, we decided to go to the past in an attempt to unlock the trauma.

On the day of the session I sat on the green couch, and closed my eyes and listened to the tick of the clock. I began to descend into the days, weeks, months and years to the rhythm of tick . . . tock . . . tick . . . tock . . .

A scene appeared in my mind. I found myself at Sydney's Coroner's Court, February 1996. In the foyer I was greeted by the man who had found Richard's body lying by the edge of a cliff in the Blue Mountains. He had been bashed, robbed and left to die. As I saw the scene in my mind a cold shiver ran through my body.

There were lots of reporters inside the courtroom. I began to feel cold, very cold.

A senior detective stood up and read a long piece. He read and read. His mouth seemed to dribble every word as though he had trouble speaking. He kept reading and chewing on the gory details of where Richard had been struck, how he had been hit, how much he had been punched and kicked until he was finally killed. He dismissed this and that, assumed one thing, rejected another, and all I wanted was for him to stop. To end the nightmare.

'My heart is pounding,' I said to Caroline.

'OK, go on.' She wanted me to delve into the moment, crack the bubble of ice.

My body was bathed in perspiration, my heart pounded even faster, then suddenly the pounding stopped. A feeling of relief came over me. I felt as if my soul had left my body. If not the soul, then something very powerful. Next I was outside the feeling but my body was still standing in the courtroom, listening to the painful details of that sinister day. I sat in the front row clutching a Buddhist book I had carried for protection. I was eager to find out what had happened, then I heard the senior detective say something like: 'Therefore, Your Honour, Emilia Bresciani is the only person who had a motive to kill Richard Diack.'

His words sliced the silence of the room. I heard them but could not make sense of them. In a flash my status was reinterpreted. With one sentence my reality had been shattered. I had moved from being Richard's widow to being his most likely killer.

The reporters began to scribble in a frenzy. I felt all alone.

From where I sat in the therapist's couch I saw the whole room move away from me. A slab had lifted off the ground, shifting me, detaching me from the woman in the cream suit who was clutching a book against her heart. She looked around too and a tear fell from her pain. Then she screamed, 'You are wrong. You have always seen me as a killer. Never as a widow.' And a part of me flew away, leaving her to fight her own battle.

That night I meditated deeply into the meaning of my circumstances. I spread salt around my bed, drank the last of my chamomile tea, put the candles out, and went to sleep with a lavender twig under my pillow. As I slept, the scent of forgotten memories began to filter through my dreams, and I saw myself travelling down a luminous tunnel. During the following days flashes of my life appeared before my eyes. I saw the image of a child in pink taffeta with a piece of vanilla cake in her hand; then I caught a glimpse of a sobbing young woman kneeling in the middle of a lonely park, drenched to the bones, her blouse torn open and her innocence shattered. I cried for hours as I had not thought about this for a very long time. I had touched a place that held the meaning of my memories. I came to understand then that the tower of my life as I knew it had to collapse before I could put together the pieces that made up my true story.

Perhaps my life, like a movie, could be re-edited. Perhaps if I understood the meaning of the script and of the scenes that made up the story, the punch line could be changed. As a filmmaker I had learned to create realities by juxtaposing scenes of my own choice and writing meaning around them. My life was made up of scenes in which I was the protagonist, produced by the choices I had made, lived by meanings I had given them. So, if I looked at the scenes of my past under a different light, perhaps I could see something else in them, find a reason for the pain, a meaning to my tragedy.

The more I thought about it the more I realised that the flashes of my past were signposts that life was placing along my path. Something was tapping from behind my chest, telling me that to take this journey, the one that I now share with you, I had to write the book of my life. I had to look at the past in all its nakedness. To smell the scent of my raw essence and to understand the meaning of the episodes that made up my life became my mission in this new age of resolution.

THE SCENT OF VANILLA

MY DREAMS BEGAN to reek of vanilla. The first sign had emerged, like a raw scented petal that fluttered out of the labyrinth of my memories. It was my mother's scent, the sweet smell that shrouded our storytelling afternoons, the rich aroma that rose from the cake on the dining table as we rode into her fantasies, mounted on her unbridled imagination. The spirit of my mother would guide the first steps of my journey back into the past. Hers was the voice that came from beyond time, the sound that lived in between my thoughts. I felt guided and protected by her presence. Armed with resolve, I hugged my pillow at night and inhaled the scent that impregnated my life before I was even born, for surely she craved vanilla biscuits as I floated in the waters of her womb. There is a reason for it, I know, a very good reason for my mother's sugar cravings, which have now become the cravings of my heart. She said that vanilla was good to spice our thoughts and give life a meaningful dimension. Perhaps she was right. So to get the initial glimpses of my story I closed my eyes beneath the covers and tucked my anxieties under the pillow. Then I let the scent lead me down into the dark chambers of my underworld. I pushed through the first web of shadows that blocked my way as I entered my memories and followed the scented path, a step here and a step there, slowly, and with care. The scent of vanilla was beckoning my soul to read the genesis of my life.

The scent takes me to the time when I was a child, when I used to sit on a tiny stool by my mother's side and watch how she embroidered white damask pillowcases to give as gifts on special occasions. Not because she was a brilliant embroiderer, but because she believed that a gift made at home carried a piece of the giver's heart. I would often visualise a piece of her red heart pinned on the pillowcase as she slid her soft fingers along the winding line on the white linen, breathing life into the stitches, filling the landscape with green cotton, and then with orange, and then with pink. It was during those times that she filled my head with her stories about our past. The exuberance of her mood seemed to draw sparks out of thin air. And I, with eyes wide open and a heart full of expectations, would watch how her crimson lips relished every piece of vanilla biscuit that she put in her mouth, keeping the thread of her own imagination alive. One side of her mind followed the patterns on the linen, while the other carried me through the doorway of the In-between, the place where all time became one. The place where she visited the past in order to restore her present. That is how I came to know about the legends of my ancestry.

Sometime during the early part of the nineteenth century, on an enchanting island near Manaos, a city in the Amazon region, lived a young girl who became the fount of our legends. The island was indeed enchanting. And enchanted, for it had been pulled away from the mainland during an ancient cataclysm that had closed the passage between our world and the realm of the spirits, and had penetrated the space Mama called the In-between. This was the place where all souls rested before they moved into other lives, and where the jungle gods reconciled all sins. This island was visible only to people imbued with good intentions and could not be reached by those possessed by wickedness. From the In-between came all things good and unexpected, and to it all souls were returned once they had completed their journey here. A bridge built by the love and collective belief of most of the locals brought the inhabitants of the ethereal island down to the mainland every so often so they could do some shopping, check the new imports, and mingle with the rest of the population to whom they told stories of extraordinary value and wisdom.

No one knew for sure the origins of these enchanting inhabitants, although tales had it that they were related to ancient gods who had arrived from the stars at the beginning of time. Most people had forgotten their source or did not care much about it, for in the Amazon there were many villages that existed in the realms of the In-between, perceptible only to those who truly wanted to see them and had the courage to do so. Old people said that some of these islands had been vast and exuberant territories bathed in golden auras, for they were immersed in the light of the sun and golden awareness, entrusted with the true secrets of nature. Large and primeval trees grew on these islands, trees that possessed human heads and fed from exotic flowers in the darkness of the night, and sipped the early morning dew to refuel their fertility and vigour. These jungle giants also provided relief for tormented souls and protected all forest pets from clandestine attacks by heartless men.

'The maiden of our story lived on one of these enchanted islands,' said Mama with intimate passion and a deep sigh, her eyes filled with fascination. The name of our feminine past was 'Sarinha', a girl with endearing grace and unquestionable purity. Her virtue attracted the admiration of most villagers, for the air in the jungle had been impregnated with many spells, powerful enough to bewitch even the purest of souls, and fiery enough to ignite in its heart a torrent of uncontrollable desires. The island had been marked by destiny, for it had been so written with the quill of prophecy. Some old villagers knew deep in their minds that one day the island would disappear, immersed in the oceans of its own source.

Sarinha, whose name means 'Princess of the jungle', loved taking walks through the green and golden forest, greeting the spirits who lived in every tree, hid in every shrub, swam in every droplet of rain, and roared in every wild animal that crossed the enlivened jungle. She was slender and agile, with long legs and extended neck, and undefined hips that at times made her look like a boy. But one day she woke up and saw that she had developed the beginnings of a womanly bosom. It was also the first time she noticed a Blue Cat in the distance. It did not stop her from running through the jungle on balmy afternoons, and wading like a young heron through the thick vegetation, eyes shining and glee in her heart.

Sarinha could connect with almost everybody and everything that moved in the jungle because she possessed strange attributes. Her almond-shaped eyes could see in the dark, her refined nostrils could distinguish the smell of fear in all creatures, and her thick long hair, always waltzing in the wind, had the remarkable power of alerting her to danger. She trusted the jungle would never hurt her because she believed she was part of it. As she walked she often hummed a bouncing tune that her family had taught her in order to connect with the main Spirit of the Jungle. Filled with such a belief, she traversed walkways ingenuously, crushing leaves and pushing shrubs in order to collect fruits and nuts for the family meal. Sometimes she would stop by the river to catch fish brought to her by small alligators, and there she would often chat to Bufeo Colorado, the famous Pink Dolphin, the spirit of the mother river with whom she had a special relationship.

But there was another side to the jungle. The treacherous and dark side, the face of the Spirit in anger who only manifested when the collective soul of the island was weak. However, as long as Sarinha's hair was shining clean she did not have to worry about dangerous beasts that lurked behind trees or emerged from the bottom of poisonous swamps. Or about savage felines that stalked her as she walked in the afternoon, or slimy reptiles hungry for her soul, or dangerous plants ready to bite her unsoiled flesh and infect her with guilt-ridden nightmares. Sarinha believed that the big boa, the Sachamama, primordial serpent and holder of ancient secrets, would always protect her. Sarinha had always respected the power that lay in the folds of the past. The giant boa with her powerful body was indeed one of the layers of the forest on which life balanced.

Aware of the islanders' premonition, Sarinha's parents lived with anxiety in their hearts. They had noticed a mysterious Blue Cat, believed to be a messenger from the underworld, following Sarinha at all times. Particularly on the occasions she went to see Bufeo, the wise dolphin who lived in the waters of the Amazon River and often lay on the edge, basking her iridescent body and alluring those willing to listen to her tales and advice. Legend has it that Bufeo Colorado had once been a woman with a broken heart whose beloved partner was devoured by the torrid passions of the jungle. One balmy afternoon when Sarinha came to sit by the edge of the river, Bufeo Colorado told her that a shining knight with golden skin and feathers on his head was on his way to meet her. The wise dolphin added that this 'most handsome creature' was coming down from the far northern lands, a place of tall pyramids and glistening lights where the sun shone even brighter and the moon was twice the normal size. The knight was bringing a gift that would be good for her own growth. Sarinha's heart swelled with joy; she believed every word that Bufeo said because she knew her friend was a knower of all things, wise and dangerous. But Bufeo warned her to handle the gift with care, and the foreigner with discretion, for his intentions were not very clear.

Mama's tales often came on Mondays. The days when she did the laundry, and cooked beans with smoked pork ribs, and onion and tomato salsa. She taught me that even doing the laundry could be turned into a ritual. All white linen should be soaked in soda salts to clean the 'impurities of the flesh'. Our school uniforms were always boiled in a copper with herbal soaps and disinfectant and a touch of lavender, to invite good fortune. She taught me to use creativity in everything I did, including the hanging of laundry on the line, placing every garment under the sun in aesthetic balance. 'For even the stars like to see our world as a piece of art,' she would hammer on the wall of my forming brain.

So, as my ears awaited the next chapter of the story, I would hand her the wooden pegs one by one to place my brothers' socks next to Papa's socks, my pants and underwear next to her underwear, and white napkins next to bleached linen. The beans were often cooked in a wrought-iron pot so we would get stronger, and she put in chunks of smoked pork to add punch, and a bay leaf to enrich the aroma and nurture our passion for life. Every Monday the atmosphere in our cement-floor kitchen was impregnated with her love for nostalgia, the aroma of smoked pork and the ardent flavour of her voice as she penetrated the thicket of her jungle tales.

Bufeo's prophecy had swung from tree to tree and every leaf breathed the story into the wind, to be carried to every corner of the island. Even the mosquitoes, always thinking of themselves, helped carry the story in their nib, and when every living soul was finally aware of the forecast visit, quietness returned. Hush reigned and the butterflies became transparent. The fervent pulsations came to a lull and drums toned down their rumbles for a while as Sarinha waited for the gift with pubescent anticipation. Then one early morning a heavy downpour fell from the sky to signal the moment. After the rain passed, the air in the forest was spiced with a strange animation and the life force again pulsated with excitement. Every leaf and pebble in the forest was pregnant with exhilaration. After breakfast Sarinha went out on her daily errands, but this morning she wore a crown of feathers and a silky tunic hung over her shoulders. It was a gift from her mother, a delicate gown made out of butterflies' wings and good wishes. As her slender frame disappeared behind the giant ferns, the large Blue Cat followed, moving sinuously, his mind alert. Her mother watched silently in the background, aware of a strange premonition and unable to stop destiny.

Sarinha crossed the jungle freely and unconcerned, without much thought about her Mama's anxieties, wrapped in the whims of her adolescence and inhaling the scent of fresh walnuts and ripe banana. Suddenly a strange sensation snapped from the bottom of her belly and her skin began to glow with unprecedented radiance. She whirled round and round, skipping and dancing to the tune of her Amazon's lullabies. She hopped and skipped under the spell of tropical enchantment, reaching with the tip of her fingers the leaves that hung over her from giant ferns. Then, as she was about to take a rest on a fallen tree, she noticed the expected knight in the distance. The boy moved majestically through the foliage with a certain glow around him. He carried the aura of a dignified being, like an emissary from the luminous gods of the past, those who spoke the language of the universal heart.

Sarinha's eyes, speared by curiosity, marvelled at the apparition as it approached her, slowly. With the sun sketched on the firmament above his head, the handsome creature from the northern land emanated strength and magnetism. His eyes glistened with vigour, and his golden skin shone with the brilliance of his solid race. He smiled as he stepped closer, touching her presence with his radiance, filling her heart with new-found joy. An air of familiarity engulfed her. She knew she had seen him somewhere before. Of that she was sure. Perhaps in a dream? Or in the mirror of her own soul. A head-piece of colourful feathers adorned the boy's hair, and a solid pendant of emerald and lapis lazuli hung against his hairless chest. He wore a cotton-silk wrap around his waist, and on his well-defined feet he wore sandals made of soft hide and brown leaves. As he reached her, he bowed and lifted his right hand, his palm facing her. She looked at him with wonder and noticed he carried something wrapped in a silk cloth. It was as the dolphin had forecast. Somehow she felt very comfortable with the stranger. He gazed at her with friendliness and nodded a greeting smile. She smiled back, with timid eagerness, experiencing the blushing of her cheeks. An odd tingling sensation pricked her skin. An omen.

After the initial courtesies had taken place, both teenagers found a clearing with dry leaves close to the edge of the river and began their acquaintance. He came from a kingdom in the northern peninsula, far away from her island. A territory that could always be reached when the heart was truly open, he said, and she listened with bewilderment. The boy had brought a liquid from his lands, a fluid from a sacred pod that his people used in ceremonies to taste Life's different flavours. He said that the liquid was called 'Vanilla', and that this essence had the power to align the past, present and future so changes could be made when necessary. He lifted the cloth that covered his gift, revealing a beautiful bowl. He handed it to her. Her eyes sparkling with fascination, she praised the smooth contours of the skilfully adorned chalice and the drawings on it. It was a most delicate piece. A set of symbols had been drawn on its smooth outer surface, a string of carefully aligned geometrical motifs of perfect angles and waving lines. Inside, the figure of a serpent was etched across the bottom. A tiny bottle of dark liquid was sitting inside the bowl. The knight lifted it out, opened it and offered her a taste of the liquid.

'Try it, you may get a glimpse of life as it is,' he said.

She was filled with curiosity. The boy added that the key to true happiness was in swallowing the right amount. But Sarinha was far too excited to register any other details and remained hypnotised by the candid nature of her friend and the contents of the bottle. She thought of the Bufeo's words 'the present had come for her growth', and with a burst of impulsiveness, she lifted the tiny jar up to her face, fully inhaling its hypnotising scent. The intriguing aroma travelled into her nose, taking her mind to distant places, unknown territories of magnetic fascination. The Blue Cat stared, quietly perched on a hidden branch of a tree, watching the scene with voracious confidence, aware of its imminent unfoldings.

Moved by her desire to remain suspended in timelessness and keen to watch how the past fused with the present, Sarinha fell prisoner to her own extremes. Temperance had never been a virtue of hers. She threw her head back and poured the entire bottle of liquid down her throat as if to experience the whole of life in one swallow. As if the moment would never end. And as prophesied by her friend, the feathery knight, happiness was not experienced because the measure was out of moderation. Indeed, it totally exceeded life's necessary equilibrium. Once the liquid was in her being, Sarinha's soul fragmented into sparkling dots and she experienced her body evaporating into a gaseous breath, melting in the fluids of the sweet potion. In horror she also saw the handsome knight fragment into glowing pieces, bubbling in the same fluids that now poured out of her; and she lost consciousness. The alchemy had not worked.

Soon after the lethal drink had been consumed, a bolt of lightning appeared in the sky, thunder was heard in the jungle and the blow of an earthquake roared under the ground. Cold rain pounded on the earth, and the Blue Cat, that terrible feline with a gleaming gaze and an ominous mission, hid behind a giant leaf, staring at the unseen, searching in the void, and swallowing the images in the transparency of nature. The boy disappeared and Sarinha became confused. Suddenly she was violently jolted by a loud uproar, a clamour that came from outside the forest. She recognised the voices of her family. The shrieks and roars made her shiver with fright for she now felt guilty. Her father and other villagers yelled and moved into the thicket with machetes, sticks and sharp knives, chopping down everything that moved with the frantic rustle of the wind, looking into the night, searching for the lost maiden. Even the slimy reptiles, ancient beings from the underworld, were frightened for they knew that the earth would shake before its final collapse.

I never ceased to be frightened when Mama narrated her version of the first sign of collapse in our family history, when the thread of innocence snapped and suffering made its way into our lives. During those occasions Mama lowered her voice to a whisper and I watched the restless jungle loom inside her eyes, and in the disquietude of her breath I could perceive the events that stirred the terrifying prophecy of the enchanted island.

Above the Amazon island the sky turned dark blue, and the reptiles slithered along the ground, rattling their tails in apprehension, hiding from the wrath of destiny and the inclemency of fate. The virgin jungle was in danger. The girl, now fully conscious and recognising the familiar voices of the search team, dashed towards her father in blind despair, her heart filled with a newly acquired emotion. She ran and ran but reached nowhere, and to her horror she saw a sharp machete hurtling towards her, landing almost at her feet. 'Oh no!' She realised that the search team could not see her. She had become invisible, sucked into her own dream. In sheer terror, she darted to the edge of the river to bring an end to her shame, for it was at that moment that she remembered the warnings of her friend Bufeo Colorado. Before plunging into the water, determined to wash away her nightmare, she turned to take a last glimpse of her beloved island. Sadness descended upon her with full force and she saw her island slide away from her, moving further and further, slowly disintegrating into the dark sky, entering the realm of emptiness. Returning to the In-between. Tears flooded her and a newly found remorse invaded her spirit. In the distance the big Blue Cat gazed at her with an air of intimacy. She sank deep into her sorrows, her grief so heavy that it pulled her to the bottom of the river.

But not all was despair. Her genuine repentance persuaded Bufeo Colorado to look upon her with compassion and turn a school of silver cod into a shining vessel to carry her to a faraway land where her sad memories would be rinsed away. As she floated off, the girl cried and cried in anguish, touching with her deep sorrows the sacred force of the Amazon. So much so that her tears filled the vessel, overflowed and managed to raise the waters of the river. All beings of the underworld began to cry with her. With such an emotional outpouring, a misty foam spread over the water until, finally and miraculously, tiny droplets soared up out of the river, transforming themselves into crystals. As they reached the limits of our sky, and in divine alchemy, they came down as floating feathers, gliding like tender blessings filled with raw vanilla scent. Sarinha's sadness subsided for a while and she fell into a deep sleep.

As she lay exhausted in the swaying vessel that drifted along the river, a playful wind blew a kiss towards her, brushing past her navel, parting her tunic and allowing one of the feathers to enter her belly. The subtle prick brought a sweet smile to her face and her cheeks shone a bright red. With a flutter of her eyelashes she emitted a golden glow into the air, and a taste of pure ecstasy filled the atmosphere as she let loose a big moan. The silver cod watched her with astonishment, unable to understand the strange episode, wondering whether this was a symptom of tropical madness.

After a long journey, the vessel arrived at the other side of the river where she was greeted by a delegation of zesty women and young girls bathing. Helped by the female clan, Sarinha, who arrived with a swollen belly due to all the vanilla petals she had eaten, gave birth to a honey-coloured child. Her name would be Sarita, a variation of her own, for she was born on a land that spoke a different language. The instant the baby took her first breath, her mother's soul flew back into the sky, led by the remaining petals, following the dream image of the feather boy who had brought her the syrup of Life. The vanilla toddler grew into a young woman and learned the ways of her adoptive clan and, later as the time was ripe for the clan to enter the In-between, the girl crossed over to the real world and moved to a nearby village called Yurimaguas, which means 'City of women'. This town is not too far from Iquitos, the main city near the Amazon River, and it was there that the female line of my ancestors settled.

My mother discovered her personal legend with the tip of her tongue as she nibbled a vanilla bar she had bought from a travelling merchant one steamy afternoon. The sweet flavour became the tool that rattled her memories and the quill with which she would write the tales of her life on the enthusiastic attention of her audience. One day when she was already an adult, she narrated the tale to her father, and he, fascinated by the coincidence, confessed he had heard the same tale from Mama's mother. Her life in the land of the Amazon was not a fairytale; however the memories of her vanilla line and fertile imagination made it richer and more endurable. Her mother had inherited the name of the family clan, Sarita, a name I also carry.

Sarita Davila, my mother's mother, grew up in Yurimaguas as a quiet and practical woman who knew exactly what she wanted and waited until the time was ripe, and competition scarce, to get it. Her strength lay in her discretion, for she knew that a woman who reveals little holds power. In the early part of the twentieth century, a woman had to proceed with guile and moderation, and Sarita Davila followed all the rules of life in order to safeguard her existence and keep unnecessary dangers at bay. She was slender and flexible as if made of rubber, with almond-shaped eyes which glowed as she smiled. A gesture she seldom made, for she was forever vigilant, as she felt deep in her heart she was stalked by a restless spirit. She treasured prudence and acted always with temperance, for in the back of her mind she was aware that extremes only lead to trouble. She always moved about the streets with agility, appearing here and there like a ghost, sudden and enigmatic as a nimble spirit. Her long, dark brown hair was often plaited over her shoulders or pulled up in a bun, but was never loose, unless she was in the intimacy of her own company. She did not speak of magic nor of her legendary beginnings, although she knew about the fount of her own power. She grew up as a lonely child, feeding her own needs, learning from the signs of life and the voice of the great mother that lived within her.

One day she realised she had already come of age and did not have a partner; she decided it was time to search for a loving and durable companion to walk with her the green path of fertility. A few weeks later she met a musician. She saw him as a free-spirited knight whose air of congeniality and smell of seduction convinced her to cast her net upon him, in the way only Amazon women can, and invest her feelings on the emotional enterprise. With her mysterious power, she recognised the sound character behind the bohemian smile of the happy troubadour. The scent of vanilla came her way and she appreciated the alchemy of the moment, when certainty is so strong that it dissolves inhibitions and time. For the statement by the northern knight about life's measures was written in my Grandma's cells, as it is in all of us who came after her. Sarita Davila remembered well how to brew a potion of green seduction.

Desiderio Lujan, my mother's father, was a man who came from a respected middle-class family, well known in the region for their musical talent. His soul was possessed by a rebellious spirit and he was always uncomfortable with keeping up appearances or following the rigorous map of tradition. His talent for playing the clarinet had earned him wide popularity in bohemian circles. His tunes often bedazzled his audience, which included the four-legged ones, the gnomes of the jungle and the mischievous Shipibos, the ferocious children of the wild forest who shrank the heads of jungle infidels. So the day he discovered the perfect opportunity to escape from the stuffiness of his family, he left home perched on the back of a cart, bound to chase his own fortune in the womb of the jungle, following the path of many adventurers.

The Amazon was a region known to provide fabulous riches to those who dared ride on the wings of uncertainty and sweat their fear out with courage. Rubber was the precious fluid that had turned a few audacious men into wealthy lords whose courage was measured in coins and machetes. But it had not been easy. A dear price was often paid and unfortunately it was not paid by the big lords but by their workers. For the jungle had its own wild and unpredictable ways to defend itself. Shrunken heads, poisonous insect bites and snake hugs would ferociously hit back at the machos who attempted to dig out its treasures; lethal fevers and leprosy sores pulled the kingdom of hell up from down below. The jungle was no place for the feeble or the treacherous. Either you carried courage under your sleeve, or you fastened it around the sharp blades of your machetes. Or your head was shrunk, your tongue pulled out and your heart chewed at mealtime.

The clarinet minstrel had been hired by a mob of rubber prospectors to appease the Spirits in the jungle, and he became deliriously happy with the prospect of unfolding his talent in the heart of the fertile wilderness. But soon my grandfather realised that the jungle was not the place where he would meet his destiny. He became convinced of it on the day when, after he finished playing a tune about the Green Spirits in the sky, he noticed a huge boa – watching him with attentive mood and undulated pleasure, her skin glistening like prime silk, her tongue flickering in true delight – wrapped comfortably around a tree, only a metre away from him. His heart nearly stopped and the earth shook beneath his feet. Half hypnotised by the giant reptile and half terrified, his brain melted and his blood began to turn to ice. His waters flooded down his legs, but he did not notice. Nor did he notice his clarinet dropping to the ground. My grandfather was convinced that the boa apparition signalled his final hour, for in the Amazon all things are symbolic of the journey we take in life. But instead, the boa was far more scared of him and of his jittery reactions, for she was a good boa, the Keeper of the Forest, and had made not even a tiny move to scare him. On the contrary, this awesome reptile had enjoyed his music and had been enchanted by his melodies. Saddened by the incident and feeling pity for the feeble minstrel, the huge boa moved away to search for help.

After this initiation Desiderio decided to search for happiness in less perilous surroundings and became a troubadour of happy tunes and auspicious tales, travelling from town to town exchanging his rhapsodies for smiles. When the elders in his family discovered his adventures and his performances as the troubadour for the Shipibo Indians, they ordered his immediate return home, under threats of disowning him and locking him in a madhouse forever. Disheartened, Desiderio returned with his head down and a feeling of defeat, but with a pouch full of funny tales that 'made even stones crack with chuckles'. Finally, his family convinced him to join the army, explaining to him that perhaps he could earn an honorary rank in the service and give his family pride and honour. It was the tradition and at the time the army was actively keeping invaders from the border. Young recruits were being enlisted to block the passage of intruders eager to reach the Amazon River because of its riches and access to the Atlantic. 'You could inspire the soldiers with your tunes,' his family told a rebellious Desiderio. The argument convinced him and Grandpa joined the army with more enthusiasm for musical adventure than patriotism.

Rosita, my mother, took after her father and was proud to describe him as an attractive man with the looks of one who knows how to please people and is always happy to do so. Average in height, with a seductive presence, thick black hair and a mischievous pair of brown eyes, Desiderio Lujan possessed a romantic tongue, and a weakness for good food. He had a cosy friend in every town, whom he would regale with serenades of love every time he visited. A thin moustache outlined his upper lip, giving his mouth the appearance of an 'elongated heart'. He was always prompt to recite pearls of passion, as some Latin men can do so well with sonorous elegance and affected sincerity. It was during a music tour to Yurimaguas that Desiderio's heart was pricked by the spear of love, not from Eros but from Sarita Davila, whose purposeful heart lurked in the crowd to launch the arrow of her intentions. And it was not Sarita's beauty that pricked Desiderio's skin and conquered his heart, but the solidity of her presence and a degree of invincibility about her, which he recognised as pillars for a healthy future. Once bewitched by Sarita's spell he saw the brown-skinned girl as a genuine inspiration to contemplate the highly improbable and realise the totally impossible.

How could a bohemian of hearts, accustomed to soft and silky touches, notice such wise features in the image of an unadorned girl? After all, she was a humble figure of plain constitution with hardly any embellishment on her skin, or decoration on her dress, and no rouge on her lips.

'No rouge on her lips?' I asked Mama.

'No, no rouge on her lips,' she replied.

Most unusual in our family.

But Sarita Davila had the unsurpassed strength of her youth and her legendary mysteries. Her love potion was contained in a single bowl of *masato paco*, a special banana porridge she prepared for him, to be served the moment the Amazon spirits came into 'emotional alignment'. According to Mama, a person is in emotional alignment when one's heart surrenders to the dictates of life. Women of the Amazon are known for their secret love potions, and that's how it worked with my *abuelo*, my grandfather. After one swallow he was convinced that Sarita Davila would become the name of his destiny and the ambrosia for his delight.

The story emerged from the river where the fish tell the future under the moonlight and mosquitoes carry an aphrodisiac in their bite. This exotic aphrodisiac is picked from a voluptuous serpent whose sole purpose in life is to tease men unable to control their desires. These are the passengers of the night who step out of their boundaries, searching for the devil that looms in the obscure passages of their souls. The banana of the *masato paco* contains a potent aphrodisiac and comes from a luxuriant tree, known as *El paco banano*, fertilised by the local and exuberant Huallaga River. It is believed the *paco* is able to intoxicate anybody who dares to eat its golden fruit without taking the protective antidote. The fruit is said to excite its victims with insatiable and erotic cravings, intensifying all senses to such hedonistic levels that a man could explode in delight. But beware those who eat too much of it! And this is important advice: too much *paco* porridge can lead its prey to enter the lower chambers of the unseen world. There they get lost in the labyrinth of unpronounceable pleasures, able only to come out at night to wander in delirious craving and swollen membranes, unable to consummate any sexual yearnings; for these men are no longer of the flesh. So the *masato paco* should never be eaten raw and should be served only in small portions, unless the daring Romeo wants to be arrested for indecent exposure.

After a wild and successful concert, Desiderio was invited by 'love alchemist' Sarita to enjoy a small portion of *masato paco* mixed with cream and vanilla essence. This was an important detail: Sarita had presented her original dish in a ceramic bowl which had etched on the base of it a silver snake, the symbol of wisdom. She served a small enough portion that the love recipient could savour the porridge with ease, thus allowing the warmth of her formula to enter his body, glide into his heart and make him contemplate her attributes from the essence of his soul. After savouring the scrumptious porridge, young Desiderio Lujan felt renewed and jollier than ever, a sense of trust for natural law and a strong feeling of responsibility suddenly possessed him, and, recognising the wisdom of the unadorned girl, decided he should marry her on the spot. His family, who lived in the capital, breathed a sigh of relief when they discovered that there was now a strong woman to 'handle the reins of Desiderio Lujan's wild horse'. The young couple settled together with the blessings of all the people around them. Those were the happiest of all times in Desiderio's life because for the first time he felt the strength of unconditional love around him, even though to bring the couple together, the wisdom of the underworld had to be summoned.

My mother was born out of such love under a Leo star, the sign of courage and leadership. Her name was Rosa, but her family came to call her Rosita. She was a pink ball with straight black hair, rosy skin, a mischievous spark in her eyes, and a strong determination to see the invisible, explore the improbable, push down barriers and make things real. The three of them formed a silent alliance of mutual love and protection, a sentiment that Mama stored somewhere in her chest, in a glowing rosy chamber close to her heart, for the episode of happiness was not to last long.

Her blissful years ended abruptly when the large Blue Cat of the island of Manaos visited Sarita Davila in her dreams to tell her that her purpose in this life had already been fulfilled. It happened one tenebrous night when Sarita Davila went to sleep with a touch of fever, complaining of a sore throat. As she fell into a deep sleep she met the Blue Cat, who told her about her past, her fate and her predicament. A wave of despair flooded the young woman's dreams, for her daughter was still a toddler, and her own life so short. However, with strength in her heart she told her husband of the dream of the Blue Cat, instructing him to pass the story of her lineage to her daughter when the time was right. The descendant of the vanilla lineage, who had once promised never to reveal her secrets to men, knew that it was the only way. Desiderio Lujan was struck by sorrow but refused to accept her version of fate. With clarinet in hand he struggled to convince her to set such fantasies away. 'Life is not a legend,' he claimed, but Sarita Davila replied, 'We all come from a legend, and the story in it lives in the depths of our soul.' Sarita Davila knew of her final hour, with the knowing of those who have read their life's mission in their hearts. Soon her fever turned into a bronchial infection that no city doctor nor jungle healer could alleviate. The next evening, unable to avoid her own prophecy, Sarita Davila mounted the Blue Cat and rode into the dark sky, and never woke up. She had entered the In-between.

Mama never recovered from her grief, and for the rest of her life sought the company of women, mainly strong ones, to fill the gap her mother had left. I became one such woman, for I learned from a very young age that the fibre of my soul was strong and enduring, and able to help her heal. As the calendar renewed its pages, she managed to transform most of her grief into fortitude. She was still a toddler when Sarita Davila passed away, and during her own sixty-six years she revered the legacy her mother had left, because included in it was the source of our imagination. And as her soul began to record her experiences in the Book of Life after the passing of her mother, she also learned to accept what she could not change, and celebrate the gifts she received. But that took a long time.

Unsure of her future, Rosita would dangle her adolescent legs by the edge of the river, trying to connect to her legendary wisdom. She sat on the jetty, her eyes fixed in the centre of the radiating circles that she made as she threw pebbles in. The image on the flowing waters was like a fluid mandala, and she watched it with intensity, pondering how her life would unfold and how her story would be carried by the wind to the horizon. 'Perhaps this fortitude will be necessary in the next millennium,' she once said when she came to visit me on the other side of the ocean.

Mama grew up in Iquitos, the capital of the Peruvian Amazon, and a magic word for me. It encapsulated every fantastic story she narrated over lunch or afternoon tea to an audience made up of my family and neighbours. My cousins would often book spots on the wooden floor of our lounge room, drunk with curiosity and bewitched by Mama's mysterious tales, sucking the ice blocks she made with purple corn and sugar syrup. Bunched up around the table, and inebriated by raw sugar, we would ascend to the In-between riding on Mama's wondrous imagination, bound to the realm of the spirits, flying with her surreal ability to enliven meaningful details. But her audience was more than just children. Against the three-door wardrobe sat my father, my aunties and uncles, our neighbour, Doña Panchita, and even some friends of my father who enjoyed her ghostly love stories, particularly the tale of seduction between a voluptuous woman and a melancholic foreigner.

It was a story of torrid passion in which a sailor savoured desire with a most seductive temptress to be later horrified to discover that she was a wandering spirit, and that the bed on which they had ignited their flaming passion had, in fact, been a cold and spooky tomb. 'Oooohh!' would cry the mob on the floor. Probably the foreigner had not followed the rules of the jungle and had eaten too much *masato paco*. Mama often giggled, and only the adults would understand. She entertained us until we grew up and television captured most of the children's attention and split our imagination. However, I remained her loyal spectator and learned to carve the sound of her voice into the walls of my own imagination.

Mama's life bubbled in the early twenties in Iquitos, a town bustling with raw energy, duty-free trade, gorgeous women and intriguing visitors, seekers of magic potions to heal emotional and physical sores. The atmosphere in the town was enlivened by exotic animals such as the mischievous 'Capuchin' monkeys, named after the Franciscans because the ruffs of hair on their heads resembled the cowls worn by the monks, and because of their devotion to humans. In Iquitos one could find the biggest pineapples and paw paws on the planet, which grew on spirited trees under surreal skies, along vibrant rivers where young maidens rubbed their skin with alligator oil to keep their sensuality alive and their fertility strong, for the children of the civilised jungle were always at risk.

Everyone who was interested in the mysterious and the profane visited the Amazon, particularly at a time when Europe was being torn by struggles of all kinds. From workers against aristocrats, to Germans against the rest, tensions brewed, seeding anxiety in the hearts of many and filling the coffers of a few. Many of these casualties flocked to the peaceful Amazon jungle, spreading their seeds across the southern continent. They knew they had come to a land so nurturing and virginal, a place that was as much alluring as it was aloof, a paradise that rotated in the rhythm of its own seasons to gestate new varieties of life force. The healing secrets of this land were much sought after, for mysterious diseases had become famous in the Northern Hemisphere. In the Amazon, herbal concoctions could settle any psychotic, arouse the impotent, repair mortal wounds, annihilate bacteria and revitalise the chronically fatigued. It was known as 'The Magic Hospital', and it honoured this name for generations.

Along with those looking for magic had come the Christian missionaries who tried to transform the children of the Amazon, 'sinners of the underworld', into followers of the suffering Christ. Some of them were generous of heart, but some were guided by religious arrogance; together they hooked the children of the jungle to a God that offered them misery and sacrifice. Some of the population respected the Christian God and prayed to Him in their own style, but others resented His representatives fiercely.

Rosita was a product of religious diversity. She carried her own spiritual connection to the Green Spirit of the jungle in her genes and watched others pray to natural idols and sacred effigies. In the past, Iquitos had not been a religious place, not one of the Christian kind. It was hot and sensual, often teasing the prudish and titillating the obscene. Most of the trade was done at the Bethlehem markets, a large floating bazaar spread on the bank of the river, half on the water and half snuggled in the luxuriant land. The extravagant market pulsated daily with the slyness and dexterity of local traders, many of whom lived on the grounds and were accustomed to waking up on floating mattresses cruising the river after torrential downpours. In Bethlehem you could find your way to heaven, and you could also discover an orifice to hell. From crocodile skins for the ostentatious, cat's tongue for the lecherous and tortoise's heart for divine inspiration, it was all there, to please the most demanding eccentric. Fish of the freshest quality and fruit of the sweetest taste were always available from the baskets of young women as tender as the harvest they picked, but who knew how to juggle the tricks of life, and how to tickle your appetite. Together with fine linen, floral silks and French cottons, you could find oriental spices, Italian leathers, Egyptian fragrances and toiletries from distant lands whose smell invoked ancient spells of Arabian delights; there were also pots and pans, and all types of liquor and tobacco. No duty was applied because Iquitos was a free port and the lifeline of the region.

These were the grounds where Rosita grew up, hiding under giant ferns like a lion cub, meandering with the spirits of the forest, concocting imaginary potions, and chasing gypsy children who had appeared with their families one day on the shores of the mother river, as if purged by the bowels of the Earth. The gypsies settled where the woodland and the birds played tricks on you, where it was hard to distinguish the real from the imaginary. With Sarita Davila gone, Desiderio Lujan's family wanted to take custody of Rosita and be in charge of her education in the proper tradition of the family, and to prevent her from developing the natural rebelliousness of her father. To let the child have what she deserved. But Desiderio would not hear of it and refused to give her away. He argued that Rosita was the only link he had to the woman he loved, if only for a short time in the physical world. Desiderio did not believe in what he couldn't see with his own eyes. Therefore he did not believe his wife had gone to the In-between, so he grieved for a long time, and this grief affected his formerly exuberant lifestyle.

Rosita learned to play alone by the river and often walked along the tropical gardens near the family home, trying to catch enchanted butterflies, singing to frogs and christening naughty monkeys with kinky names. She grew into a lean and light girl with a contagious laugh, and an agility on her feet. She loved dancing and often practised charleston steps on the edge of the river, watching her own reflection. When she turned six years old, Desiderio Lujan formed a duet with her and performed in the town square. He played, she danced, all in the name of innocent fun. For Rosita they were some of the most hilariously memorable times in her life. With clarinet in hand and rapture in his heart, Desiderio played bouncy charleston tunes while Rosita tapped in criss-cross lines, showing a flair for fancy footwork and a penchant for business as she would often claim her share of the enterprise.

The public display and street business affair provoked the fury of the Lujan clan, who threatened my grandfather to take custody of Rosita if he did not place her under 'decent' care. To please his family, he put young Rosita in a boarding school run by Anglicans, where she learned the ways of the people from the north – the *gringos* who lived above the big lake and spoke English. The missionaries endeared themselves to her with a less strict church than the Catholics and seeded warm memories in her heart, for she was a girl who also treasured refinement and starch. After she had helped in the kitchen and changed into her white and blue uniform she would strut across the patio feeling like a princess, proudly bound to the students in her English class. She was delighted with the new girls she met, the daughters of foreign merchants and some of the non-Catholic well-to-do. She learned to speak a different language and treasured it like a bosom friend. It was this experience that nurtured Rosita's desire to travel and to explore new horizons, later instilling in me the belief that 'knowledge is the key to survival'. At boarding school she also learned embroidery and ballroom dancing, trying always to excel in whatever she did, for the school principal had promised her a scholarship to go abroad. But again destiny showed its ugly claws and disrupted the unfolding of a fairytale. Desiderio Lujan, who had been sent to the border to repel the intruders, was taken prisoner. His new partner, Rosita's stepmother, pulled Rosita out of boarding school and sent her to work in the markets, to help support her father's new family. Definitely a culture shock for Rosita, who at the time was beginning to greet people in English.

With a mournful face, she was forced to farewell organza frocks, starched petticoats, flowery hats and candied fruit for tea. Rosita Lujan, the teenager with the gifted tongue and transparent butterflies in her heart, returned to Bethlehem markets, to the smell of fried fish and banana porridge. Her new reality threatened to rip her heart to threads, but Rosita chose to grow a transparent skin to protect it. Barefoot, grief-stricken and with eyes filled with sour melancholy, the long-legged adolescent fitted a pot of cooked bananas inside a basket, placed it on top of her head, and with the air of those who accept life's resolutions for there is nothing else they can do, strode market-bound to help feed her new family. It was her first real taste of private enterprise.

The conflict on the border intensified and the number of casualties increased but the government would not give in. The border struggle was becoming more and more ferocious but the modern authorities had realised that the Amazon basin was a paradise of natural wealth and future income. They would not let one blade of jungle grass go, even if in the process they let their soldiers be swallowed by the forest or shredded by the bullets of the invaders. There was no word from Desiderio Lujan and his family feared the worst. Confusion sprouted gloom and cynicism in town. Wild invaders seized on the moment and moved in against defenceless villages, raiding locals' properties, pillaging and abusing women. A deep-seated anger exploded against the villagers, the people lost control and were sent into total chaos. In a horrifying display of the most wretched features of human nature, soldiers and locals alike discharged their frustrations upon the feeble, the vulnerable and the defenceless. Against this backdrop, and shut within her protective sheath, Rosita would still head down to the markers and continue her trade in cooked bananas, sell the few beads and necklaces left from abroad, and exchange perfumed soaps and talismans meant to clear bad luck. She saw the horrors take place before her eyes and felt them under her skin, but she had learned to transfer her feelings into a bubble she had built out of fragments from the past to shelter her from the violations of her personal reality. It was her way to protect herself and not collapse.

When Desiderio Lujan returned from the war he was a broken man. Sores from insect bites and poorly healed wounds covered his skin; his inner glow had been shadowed by war hardships and the atrocities he had seen. Instead of playing, he would mumble strange words, a dialogue with beings from the unseen. His brain followed its own direction as though it was responding to the call of the jungle pixies, creatures in whom he had never believed. His condition shocked his family, for he had lost all desire to live, or compose or play music. Poor Desiderio, he had been traumatised by war, his spirit had retreated inside to protect itself, unable to deal with the crude and gruesome atrocities he endured as soldier and as a prisoner. There was not a shadow of the dandy minstrel from days gone by. All that was left was a dependent carcass with a tear in his eye and pain in his heart. His superiors, who knew little about depression, described his condition as 'Fifi's', or 'poofter's' disease and ordered him to re-enlist immediately. But it could not be. The man was sick, his soul was hidden and his spirit debilitated. Eventually he was charged with desertion and made to face public shame in the eyes of those who once had cheered him and enjoyed his music. Now, people scorned him and his heart retreated even further. But, as life takes away, so does it return, when patience fertilises the mind to wait for new shoots.

Desiderio Lujan earned back his name and was pardoned, because, in his delirious trip with the green pixies, he had been linked again with his tropical Muse. She, who filled his songs with joy and led him to new grounds of musical possibilities, had returned to his heart, and he regained his passion for music, composed his best pieces and founded the Great Brass Band. To his amusement, the band became the town's most popular attraction and the pride of all who attended the plaza every Sunday afternoon to enjoy the tunes that returned to the locals their joy in life. But all gifts have a price, even if they are given by a spirit: Desiderio remained distant from his family, and from his elder daughter.

While he recovered from his emotional ills, Rosita was pregnant with her first son. The child was the fruit of a relationship that could not be. The sort of love that is written with the ink of intensity and the pen of enthusiasm.

The women in my family received a bag full of unexpected predica-
ments when it came to romantic liaisons. It was a sad legacy that some
of us inherited, a force that led love to fall out of the window and hit
the grounds of disenchantment. Once, as a child, while helping Mama
do the dishes in the kitchen, she whispered in my ears her own con-
fessions of unrequited love and disillusionment. It was the first time
she let me touch the core of her emotions. It was then, when charged
with conspiratorial whispers and enraptured sighs, we let our hearts
connect. Amid mincing and chopping and the clackety-clank of pots
and pans, she hummed into my ears the story of her first love.

It was a moment of emotional alignment. When two pairs of eyes
meet and recognise that they have to watch a romantic landscape
together. For Rosita it was the reaching of a summit. He was her first
feathered knight, as well as her first villain. The love prince who ele-
vated her spirit to a high plateau, to later push her into the abyss of
cruel disenchantment. Mama never mentioned his name but the way
she referred to him made me realise she had adored him with the
innocence of love that knows no boundaries. They had met during a
lemonade party at a relative's house. She was spending a short vacation
with a dear cousin with whom she shared her name, Rosa. On that
particular afternoon, her cousin was to give a piano recital for a group
of family friends accustomed to piña coladas, siestas and coteries.

Mama would often recall one particular room in the house framed
by tall palms on the wooden verandah. It was warm and blue, with a
powerful and shiny grand piano that rested proudly in the centre, and
a cedar and glass cabinet crowded with multicoloured china. Music
overflowed into the four corners of that room. Probably even ghosts
had parties after everyone went to bed, for the old gramophone was
often heard softly during the night. Her cousin Rosa had been
encouraged to follow the family musical tradition and she had done
well. Mama was her dearest admirer, 'She played with exquisite sensitivity and deep emotions.' I remember how Mama used to hum and
relive the tunes her cousin had played during her adolescence, as she
spoke with her hands pressed against her heart. 'What your Aunt

Rosa did not get in looks, she certainly made up for with musical talent,' she would say, 'and that is much better, for talent never leaves you. Even if you do not see it, your talent will always find you.' She was sure of it and I always looked behind my right shoulder to see whether it was after me.

When the young people's paths crossed, it was love at first sight. At least for Rosita, who had believed that passion was the driving force in life. A flutter of an eyelash, an innocent smile and a keen feminine curiosity captured the emotions of the young man. He came from a 'good' conservative family with a snobbish flavour and a disdain for the less privileged. Rosita fascinated the boy with her ability to charm her audience with tales of transparent beings who lived in the jungle and teased clean souls with enchanted syrups. They talked music, pets and future wishes, and their penchant for adventure took them deep into lush gardens eager to explore each other's secrets and exchange sensual rhapsodies. Their friendship grew and their illusions intertwined like creepers, urgent to cross over the boundaries of time. One afternoon, as they followed the sinuosity of life's path, lost in the jungle's voluptuousness, they unlocked each other's inhibitions and discovered the taste of genuine seduction. As the young lovers, inebriated with desire, swallowed the prohibited syrup from the luminous jar of passion, they fell into an ecstasy that no word could verbalise, because the bliss of pure love is indescribable.

When Rosita discovered the gift that the boy and his luminous jar of passion had left in her womb, she panicked. And to her dismay, salt was added to her agony. The boy's family had already made arrangements to send him to the capital to join the navy. So Rosita found herself drinking her tears with vinegar to purify her soul and cleanse herself of bitterness. Again she was left alone. Snubbed by the Lujans, she returned to her stepmother to confess her 'shame'. The stepmother, whose harsh life had turned her into a severe woman, was not at all impressed. 'So much for the Anglican school,' she said. Rosita did not even weep. Her anger at life had found a spot deep inside, far hidden where no one could find it. And the strict stepmother found a soft spot in her heart and took pity on Rosita, agreeing to assist in the birth rites just as long as Rosita forgot her 'crazy illusions' of learning English and travelling abroad. That was not for girls like her. Not with a baby. Oh no. 'One had to know one's own place.'

The baby was born a happy little boy with the joy of life inherited from his musical grandfather and with the lightness of those who touch this world for only a brief season, as though they came here to bring a short message. His name was Hernancito and his company made Rosita the happiest girl in the village. It also gave her a touch of maturity, for she stopped dreaming the dreams of a seventeen year old and became a single mother in charge of the affairs of the market and of a large household.

Another big war had just broken out on distant shores, the source of the gorgeous goods found in large mansions and the key for active trade in the villages of the Amazon. Sorrow cast shadows on the population, who felt God was again abandoning them. Song and dance in town became sourness and abuse. Local people, although far from the war and recovering from local conflicts, felt the pinch of global scarcity. They were forced to work long hours to produce supplies and provisions required abroad. Rubber barons became richer and their rule became stronger as the authorities bowed to their mighty power. It was the doorway to the nineteen-forties in Latin America, a decade that would usher further pain and injustice, as victims arrived from war-torn lands carrying bitterness in their withered souls.

Rosita returned to the markets to the smell of fried fish, sandalwood soap and the fear of the pigs bound for the slaughterhouse. One day, her young sister Techa brought ominous news to her. Hernancito was very sick. The boy, who had just celebrated his first birthday, had been affected by a lethal virus unseen in the area before. It was a viral poison against which there was no known antidote in the jungle. Prayers were invoked, but the gods were not listening. No motherly love potions, nor prayers to the Jungle Spirit, nor medicine from the

old worlds, could kill the virus and alleviate the baby's condition. The
sinister bug had poisoned his lungs and blocked his bronchial cavities.
As the clouds marched through the sky, a sheer veil covered his tiny
eyes, and, like a withering petal, Hernancito dissolved out of this
world forever. As the baby's last breath reached the sky, Rosita recognised the shadow of the Blue Cat carrying her boy back to the
In-between. This time, the dark feline, messenger of death, looked
somehow apologetic. After the funeral Rosita poured her heartache
into the river until she ran out of tears. Then she opened the box of
her memories and carefully placed the story of Hernancito inside it.

Her life went on in nostalgic acceptance, as the lives of many girls
who are forced to find the antibodies of tragedy in the core of
tragedy itself. One day, as she walked past a large department store a
Chinese gentleman standing at the door greeted her.

'Good morning, Rosita. Happy are the eyes resting upon your
beauty.' The man bowed to the lean girl with the long legs and cute
face.

'Hello, Don Ramon,' she said smiling demurely.

'Would you like to try some of the chocolates I have just received
from overseas?' He offered her a box covered in silver wrapping paper
and cellophane.

'No thank you, Don Ramon.' He's a nice gentleman, she thought,
but too old.

'Perhaps your Mama and your little brothers would like some?' he
insisted.

'No thank you, Don Ramon. We'll get some later perhaps.'

She walked away, sensing the pressure of his gaze and his attentions.

Don Ramon was a successful and respected Chinese businessman
who had moved to Iquitos from T'aipei many years before. It was
obvious he was looking for a wife, the future mother of his children.
He was generous with those he wanted to please and from whom he
wanted favours. Discreet and cunning in business, as family tradition
dictated then. To procure Rosita's affections the Chinese man, long
past the pinnacle of his youth, would often send large fruit baskets,

jars of conserve, smoked fish and chocolates to her family. The neighbours speculated on how long it would take for the merchant to
catch Rosita's heart, how many more baskets and generous signs of
his intentions would have to arrive at the door of the modest adolescent with a shadowy past and a pragmatic stepmother. Don Ramon
did not mind about Rosita's romantic past, for he was different from
those males who were bonded to the strict tradition of protected vir-
ginity. He was a man of business who spoke the universal language of
money, and no one dared to disapprove of his actions or intentions.
But Rosita was not interested in him. The most she could do was to
grant him a smile of thanks for the gifts and jams his keen heart provided. Never had she given him a sign that could encourage his
intentions, but Don Ramon would not give up. No, he was relentless
in his enterprise. As he was with everything that could be traded or
exchanged. He knew that perseverance would always work. And he
waited for the right moment.

One afternoon, his heart fuelled by rejection, Don Ramon decided
to try a more direct approach. Armed with silk fabrics, lace ribbons
and jars of sweet conserves, he marched towards the bungalow where
Rosita lived with the stepmother and her children. Rosita was in the
backyard feeding chickens with fresh corn and lettuce hearts. She
would do this every afternoon before she packed a basket ready for
her early morning market rounds. Her sister and brothers had gone
to play by the river so the stepmother was able to receive the important visitor in style and in private. When Rosita saw Don Ramon
approach her door she sensed the tone of his visit. Placing the bowl
of corn and lettuce hearts on the ground she quickly tried to jump
over the back fence to spare him the embarrassment of her rejection.
But the escape was not to be, for as soon as she started climbing over
the fence the stepmother caught her, slapped her backside with a
banana leaf and ordered her to get ready immediately for the visitor.

Inside the humble hut, after two glasses of vermouth and a few
canapés of fresh sardines, Don Ramon spoke of his intentions. He
wanted to take her to live with him. She would be well looked after,

of course. The whole family would. The stepmother listened carefully, ruminating on every word with keen attention, exploring every possibility with feminine calculation. Rosita sat listening with a blank face, distant from the plans about her future. All she wanted to do was dissolve into the ground and meet her maker. The stepmother promised Don Ramon that she would give him a definite reply the day after. Affably, she accompanied him to the door, chitchatting about the latest fabrics in fashion and how Rosita 'would love to work in the shop'. She waved at the merchant courteously, hinting that she'd make sure the decision was positive. A few minutes later, Rosita stamped her feet on the ground, banged her head against the wall and pleaded to the stepmother to leave her alone. She argued with the stepmother, tried to convince her she could no longer love. Her refusal did not reflect the quality of Don Ramon's suitability, but more a heart filled with melancholy, she claimed. She was still waiting for her knight in feathery armour. The stepmother would not hear of it, insisting a woman was better off in a marriage, that she had nothing to lose and so much to gain: 'This gentleman would return to you the respect you lost with your irresponsibilities.'

Rage began to brew in Rosita's veins for she had been refused the right to choose, but what could she do? In the end she agreed to discuss it with her father, hoping he would come to the rescue.

Sadly, her father was away in his own world of music, communicating only with his clarinet and the spirit of his wife Sarita, leaving all women's business to the inclement discretion of the stepmother. Rosita's dreams stopped and the transparent butterflies closed their wings behind her sadness. After a chat with the river she came to the conclusion that the best alternative was to agree to the proposal, for leaving the house alone was not an option. She prayed that one day she would learn to love this gentleman.

Three years later, two sons had enriched the life of Don Ramon, the stepmother's lifestyle and comfort had improved, and Rosita had learned to play the dutiful wife. Her mood gradually changed as her hormones settled with childbearing. She became a mature woman, more elegant in her attire, with rounder hips and a poised step. However, some nights her young heart pounded with nostalgic emptiness, still sensing the past and its tyrannic stream, still longing for another chance. Staring at the sky during summer's tropical nights she often pondered how it would have been had her soul chosen another option in life.

THE COLOUR OF EMOTIONS

ROSITA SOUGHT REFUGE in the spirits of the green forest. Although her mother had not had a chance to introduce her to the spirituality of the Amazon, this intangible legacy was recorded in her genes, and she came to experience it the first time she cried from her heart. Her intuition had grown fatter since she'd left the Anglican school. She spent hours watching the river and reading the iridescent lines the sun's reflection made over the water. She also liked reading the shapes of the clouds and the messages she found in the depth of their shadows before the rain. And she was often accurate at predicting rain long before it fell, and finding rare herbs for healing sores.

Most afternoons around sunset she would leave the large timber house she shared with Don Ramon and head towards the river, traversing a tropical landscape imbued with the smell of ripe bananas and virginal dreams. She paced herself with the rhythm of the flowing palms, her feet strapped into brightly coloured raffia sandals, her chest up and proud, and a straw basket on her forearm. In the solitude of her moments by the edge of the river, her gaze would penetrate the gap that existed between two worlds, where she found the balm that mitigated her sadness, where her soul touched the very essence of the raw fruits and rare flowers. During those moments she

chatted with Bufeo Colorado, with whom she communicated telepathically, for the legendary dolphin no longer sat on the river bank
to avoid running into jungle infidels. With the advent of the missions
and the border conflicts, the Green Spirits had resigned themselves
only to living in the In-between, touching the hearts of the few who
still believed in their power. From these encounters Rosita received
fruitful consolation and the seeds of wisdom that lay hidden in
ordinary life.

Whilst Iquitos, the inscrutable rubber town, was also described as a
green dump on the boundaries of civilisation, more intrepid adventurers saw it as the grand entrance to the unseen dimension, the place
where my mother learned to let her imagination gallop unbridled,
and search within our ancestors' memories. It seemed that she had
inherited a powerful receptor. Some invisible wiring was connected
at the centre of her heart that linked her with a paradise, where the
spirits roamed wild. This realm, she'd often say to me when I felt the
burden of gloom on my shoulders, was the dimension from where all
dreams came to life. Such revelations always brought happiness to my
heart, and a huge sense of relief would lift all the weight from my
shoulders. I liked knowing that Mama was in touch with such a
world, for I hoped that one day it would also be my world. She said
that the unseen dimension, the In-between, was a sphere that mirrored our yearnings as well as our most horrifying fears.

It was during her strolls through the green forest that she learned
to interpret the colours of the rainbow, a revelation that she applied
fruitfully and with finesse at the store of Don Ramon, where she
acquired a reputation as the Lady of the Rainbow.

The store had everything the town required to fulfil their basic
needs, plus some luxuries of European and Asian extraction that
arrived from the other side of the Atlantic: bric-à-brac for the rich
mansions, perfumes, electrical appliances, imported liquor, creams and

cosmetics, stuffed animals and rice. It also sold lavish silks, linens and organza for elegant gowns, or simple durable cottons for school uniforms, overalls or bedclothes.

Rosita took her role in the fabrics section quite seriously, sensing she had a gift to share with her customers, whom she guided in the choice of textures and colours and to whom she explained the powers inherent in every colour of the rainbow. She told them of the impact each colour had on the heart, and how a colour would affect the person who wore it.

To get a husband, for example, or to accelerate conception or boost fertility, a woman must wear red, in silk preferably or pure cotton, so that the Earth's fertility could connect with the base of the body. For peace and tranquillity pastel blue would do the job splendidly. For prosperity and to be able to meet all debts, yellow had to be the colour, particularly if the fabric was shiny or stamped with golden flowers or fruit motifs. A nursing mother should always wear green so the milk transferred the love from the Spirit of the Forest. Or failing that, she could wear an orangey-yellow handkerchief, because this reflected the pure energy of the sun. To rise out of hell, or if somebody was in deep trouble, or to improve one's emotional affinity, calypso blue was the favoured colour because the devil can't stand it and his power is muted. Those with money could line their garments with baby-pink silk to bring protection and attract the assistance of the Sachamama, the big snake of the jungle who alerted visitors to impending danger, if she liked you, that is. White was to be worn only at weddings and during any religious affairs of holy honour, for it was the colour of the celestial beings and they could not be messed around with. And if one was going to face an enemy, navy blue had the power to strengthen one's courage and stimulate strategy, especially if inconspicuous pink was added, even if it was only the underwear. Mama said that factory workers wore dark blue to help in their struggle against the machinery that threatened eventually to obliterate them from the market.

In her world of nostalgia and wild imagination she found

enjoyment in assisting other women whose daily drudgery had blurred their own connection with the animated tropical environment, blocked the path of their guiding ghosts and subdued their intuition. Her life had touched the depths of sorrow when she saw how the spirit of her first child, born out of her innocence, glided away like a feather returning to its unconscious thought. But also from it she had derived her colourful insights. Her fashion sense was grounded on her own recipe and style. During the day she preferred to wear beige and pale blue stamped with roses and crosses, which described her condition of transit and transcendence in this world, as she used to put it. Transit because she knew deep at the bottom of her own sea of emotions, where the serpent of wisdom rested, that the wheels of her life would spin again and her true destiny would unfold. And transcendence because she also felt obliged to rise beyond her daily routine as the wife of an authoritarian merchant who believed a woman's source of happiness was to be found exclusively in the service she gave her husband and in the commodities of material life. She did not agree.

Her five years with Don Ramon, provider of goods and father of her two children, was beginning to numb her spirit and passion for life. Her marriage to him was, after all, the result of a desire for protection from public gossip and the need for financial support for the stepmother and her children, and Rosita's father, who, after his release as a prisoner of war, had lost all will to fulfil his family responsibility and dedicated most of his time to composing music. She had felt obliged to protect her father, who was the only member of her family with whom she had shared some of the best moments of her childhood. But duty was beginning to oppress her. The boys were her emotional axis and consolation, but they appeared to be more linked to their father than a product of her own womb. Don Ramon took special care in their upbringing and hired the stepmother as the official nanny and housekeeper. He cunningly persuaded Rosita to spend more time in the shop because he knew she was good for business and had a special flair with customers.

Mama did not mind working there because it helped solidify her creative spirit and initiative. However, it was obvious to her after the first few months of living with Don Ramon that all he ever wanted from her were the children. Her head was still filled with romantic ideas, and the forecast of life with him was a gloomy one. Deep inside she began to long for a daughter. The next link in the chain of her maternal line, and a friend with whom she could savour the taste of vanilla, and share tales of the Blue Cat and the secrets of the Amazons. The scion who would love her unconditionally and who, she wished, would stay with her till the end of time.

One afternoon, as she dusted some rolls of fabric while burning aromatic herbs, the town mayor's wife waltzed in to the shop like the Queen of Sheba, followed by a maid loaded up with parcels. The woman handed Rosita one of the parcels: 'Here you are, my pet, this is a little something in appreciation of your talents.' Rosita looked at the box. They were Swiss chocolates wrapped in yellow cellophane and she grinned. The lady explained that it was only a greeting gesture. Placing her small leather pouch on the glass counter and pulling up a tall stool, she sighed loudly and proceeded to ask Rosita for advice 'on a very serious matter'.

Rosita, who had always considered her colour counselling more a hobby than a profession, greeted the lady with affection, promising to serve her to the limits of her capabilities, knowing full well that whatever she did not know she would pull out of the realm of her imagination anyway.

The mayor's wife was a voluptuous woman in her mid thirties, big breasted, with round hips and a disposition as jolly as Santa Claus. But only when she has happy, otherwise it was better to keep far away from her. Often Rosita had seen the robust woman arguing with street vendors and hawkers parked illegally at the town plaza. The mayor's wife had taken it upon herself to do the rounds on behalf of the municipality. Politics was the woman's passion and instead of 'the mayor's wife' she preferred to be called 'Lady Mayor'. She was famous for her generosity and concern for those in need, a feeling that went beyond her political role.

On that afternoon at the shop Rosita was asked to advise her on what to wear for her next social engagement, a ceremony that reeked of disgrace. She and her husband had been asked to be the godparents of a baby who, she had heard through the local grapevine, was a child seeded by her own husband in the daughter of the Town Hall's chief cook. 'It was obviously a highly clandestine affair. In addition, one yet not proved,' Lady Mayor had stressed. But the problem was that she had agreed to the engagement before she had heard the gossip about the origins of the child. Now all she wanted was to avoid public scandal. Her husband had simply denied any involvement and blamed the 'town's evil tongues' for the spiteful rumour.

'That little scoundrel is going to pay for it,' said Lady Mayor to Rosita, livid with anger. Rosita's eyes were filled with compassion. She placed a hand over Lady Mayor's trembling fingers.

'After all I've done for her,' groaned Lady Mayor, 'I am her own First Communion godmother. And now, she puts horns on me as if I were the devil's wife.'

Rosita knew that the horns turned people into cuckolds and quickly jumped in, 'Oh no, please, you are not the devil's wife.' She tried hard to control a chuckle. Indeed the nature of the affair was hilarious, for Lady Mayor herself had her own secrets, and believed no one knew about them. She could indeed be the devil's wife, Rosita thought. After all, the older woman herself had placed horns on the mayor too. Powerful men had done it for ages, and women too. And she kept silent.

'Just imagine, Rosita, how dare that scoundrel, that purge of nature, do the dirty on me?' yelled Lady Mayor. Rage spiced her groans now. 'That good-for-nothing bitch, daughter of hell!' The more she yelled, the more her initial facade of solidity and strength collapsed, revealing a vulnerable woman, deeply hurt and washing her bitterness away with reverberating sobs.

Rosita gave Lady Mayor a glass of water with a few drops of orange blossom and a nip of brandy to calm her nerves, and promised that she would make a special trip to the river to meditate on the best approach to handle this most sensitive affair, as far as Lady Mayor's garment was concerned.

'You see, Lady Mayor,' said Rosita with refuelled confidence, 'you have everything already within you. All that we need to do is to get the right colour, bring out the best in you, and face the challenge with dignity.' Lady Mayor wiped the tears from her face with a hand-kerchief the maid picked from one of the baskets and handed to her timidly. Rosita patted her on the back and then hugged her with sincere affection. Lady Mayor hugged her back, thanking her from the depth of her heart. For Lady Mayor knew that the young body which she now clasped to her chest had known true sorrow, and that her rites of passage into womanhood had been painful indeed. The older woman had a kind of maternal regard for her. The session came to an end and Lady Mayor bid her farewells.

As she was leaving, a gypsy woman with bangles on her wrists and dancing beads on her chest squeezed her way into the shop. She was carrying a basket of useless knick-knacks and chanted loudly that she was the bearer of precious happiness for humanity. 'Let the Motherrrr of Gawd reveal to you, my child, the blessings of the sky, that I'm here as her humble messengerrrrr,' the gypsy intoned with a rare accent, a mixture of ancient Spanish and an obscure tongue. Mama loved imitating accents and gestures but she did not like gypsies at all, ever since one ominous day in the forest when a gypsy had, in a roundabout way, forecast the death of her first child.

On that particular balmy afternoon, Rosita was running back home after a rendezvous with her first love. Her thin legs wading through the thicket, her hair entangled, cheeks blooming like two hot peaches imbued with the smell of raw passion. Suddenly a gypsy came rushing out of the woods and Rosita ran into the intruder head-on. She stretched her hands to keep the gypsy away. The gypsy, a strong woman of jet black hair and pale skin, stopped Rosita sharp.

'Let me tell your fortune.'

'No thanks, I'm late.' Rosita tried to ignore the woman and moved away, running along the leafy track to make it home before her absence was noticed. She pulled her bag to her chest, just in case, for gypsies were known to be quick with their hands.

'If you accept my request, the blessed sky will always guide you, and your line of children,' squealed the messenger of murky providence, following Mama's steps with insistence. 'The line that you already carry inside you,' added the gypsy.

At hearing the gypsy's words Rosita stopped. Then she turned around to look at the gypsy with curiosity. Nobody knew she was pregnant, not even the father of the child, because she was too scared of the consequences.

'Why do you say I am with child?' confronted Rosita, her face reddening. The gypsy just looked at her with a smirk.

'How do you know?' asked Rosita again, dots of steamy perspiration springing from her cheeks. A touch angry and befuddled by the gypsy's accuracy, she moved closer to the woman, who took a step back.

'I just know because I am a fortune-teller,' she replied.

'If that's the case,' said Rosita, 'then read a bit from my hand and leave me alone.'

The women found a quiet clearing, away from the parakeets' incessant squark, and Rosita stretched her arm towards the gypsy and let her read her hand. She watched how the rugged woman followed the lines with severe concentration, travelling every millimetre of the curvilinear marks on her hand, pointing with her finger at the meaning of Rosita's destiny, and at the magnificent options she was to have in life.

'But for all that to happen, my dear child,' said the gypsy in an almost melodramatic tone, 'you have to sacrifice something in return.'

It was a horrible presage, Rosita thought. As if she had not sacrificed so much already. She pushed the gypsy aside with anger, threw some coins at her feet and ran back home, for the sky was turning dark and it was getting late. Eighteen months later she saw herself in combat against a lethal virus that took her firstborn back to the land of the Blue Cat; it was then that she remembered the gypsy and her bleak omen. Was this the sacrifice?

The day a second gypsy walked into Rosita's life she was determined to nip the blabbermouth in the bud right there with a warning: 'Please leave the premises, or I'll call the police.' She parted her lips but no sound came out. Instead, her eyes glanced towards the effigy of the Holy Mary standing on a small shelf in the corner of the room, surrounded by Chinese silk flowers and two gold candles. It was May the thirteenth, Mary's day. One could never be rude on Mary's day – any other day perhaps, but not on Mary's day. She decided to be compassionate to the woman who, from her gaunt face, appeared to have come out of a concentration camp. She agreed to a reading in exchange for a plate of banana porridge – not a *paco* porridge, but simple mashed banana with cloves and pineapple syrup and enough nourishment to pick up a dead horse.

The gypsy ate with delight and very few manners, slurping the porridge with sound pleasure, wiping her lips with the back of her hand, a gesture that made Rosita wonder whether she was in fact a gypsy or just a beggar. Once the plate was empty the clairvoyant thanked her benefactor profusely, describing the meal as 'Manna from heaven and the most scrumptious meal I have ever tasted in the whole world.'

From the gypsy Rosita learned she was going to have a daughter who would be born near the ocean and who one day would take her own steps further. She also said that, one day, Rosita would fly to a far-away land where she would find a palatial temple by the foot of a mountain. It was in this palace or temple that Mama's 'true fortune' lived. Rosita wondered where on earth this palace would be located. It was obvious that the old mansions of the once-upon-a-time Pearl of the Amazon were now dilapidated residences, bereft of any goodness, let alone fortune. The foretold bonanzas came with a warning about a malicious wind that would furtively roam Rosita's way in the very near future. It would rip through her chest like a hungry vampire . . . but all bad things have another side. This wind, said the gypsy, would also be a catalyst for major changes in Rosita's future. 'Bad wind?' Rosita asked. Must be a warning of a bad cough? She better look after herself. The lifeline on her palm had dictated a medium life span which would take her to her mid-fifties or mid-sixties. The gypsy said fifty-nine, give or take a few. It was all up to her.

Ah! And a daughter! The happy omen drew a smile on Rosita's pallid face. The knots in her heart had already begun to be reflected on the surface of her skin and she was forced to conceal them with extra rouge on her cheeks and a bit more pink on her lips. The doctor had diagnosed her with melancholic anaemia after her last miscarriage. It was a baby girl, the doctor said. Mama had been very depressed. Don Ramon had also been sad on that occasion. The doctor had not been able to explain why she was sick, as there was plenty to eat in the house.

The moment Rosita heard the gypsy forecasting the birth of a second daughter, her smile opened into a warm embrace and she bent over the counter to kiss the gypsy. She brushed the face of her loud messenger with her lips and the woman returned her gesture with appreciation. After the gypsy left, she folded the omen in a piece of golden transparent fabric and concealed it in between her other memories, somewhere deep at the bottom of her heart, away from the malicious wind. That afternoon she would thank the river especially, and would blow a kiss to Bufeo Colorado, who had probably sent the gypsy, she thought. With petals in her heart Rosita picked up the empty porridge bowl and placed it carefully on top of the kitchen bench. She wrapped a soft cotton shawl around her shoulders, closed the shop early for Mary's day was a public holiday, and began to head towards the river to plan the Lady Mayor's attire for the controversial baptism.

The church was being prepared for the big day and the town was buzzing with enthusiasm, eager to participate in the fiesta after the baptism. It was customary to roast a wild pig in the plaza across from the mayor's residence, so that many people could enjoy the event and be merry. White taffeta ribbons adorned the centre aisle of the church and dangling flower bunches were attached to every pew to highlight the significance of the ritual. It had all been planned by the mother of the child and paid for by the 'godfather'. However, it was very odd to place white ribbons along the aisle, as this was only done for weddings.

The church assistants and friends of the child's grandmother had filled all the silver vases with tall white lilies, gardenias and tropical ferns. A chipped alabaster font stood cold and collected at the head of the church as the symbol of sacred cleansing. It was the town's holy font where most locals had been baptised and consecrated as children of Christ. The white basin was rimmed with a crown of gardenias and miniature roses to cover the cracks and splits, and they gave the ceremonial vessel an intoxicating scent.

During her conference with the river, Rosita had been told that the right colour to deal with Lady Mayor's predicament was fuchsia. The mayor's wife had immediately arranged to have a two-piece fuchsia silk suit made with an ivory lace collar and trim. Mama was sure the colour was the perfect one because in her meditations by the river, a flower of that hue had fallen from the sky, or from some nearby tree. The passionate pink was the suitable armour in which to meet a rival. It was a blend of red, which gives strength and magnetism, and a touch of blue, the colour of endurance and strategy. If anything, the very brightness of the colour would blind and outsmart any adversary. A bone-coloured hat of the best Italian raffia and matching leather purse and shoes complemented the godmother's battle gear.

Rosita and her family were going to the celebration, along with the rest of the townspeople who were keen to give it their full attention. Don Ramon was staying home to mind the business, and because he was not a man of parties. Oh no, these things were only for women who did not have better things to do but frolic with abandon, he thought. Besides, he had also heard about the scandal of the child and the alleged fatherhood. He was a man who lived in his own world and observed the passing of time unmoved and indifferent, as if he already knew what was going to happen. Rosita's spontaneity, her love of party-making and celebrating life's special events had never sat too well with him. He had confused her earlier ability to rescue sorrows with a smile as displays of frivolity, and this had often triggered fits of jealousy. So much so that Rosita had opted for storing all aspects of happiness under a serious facade.

She was going to the christening ceremony with the stepmother. Although they had never liked each other, the two women tolerated each other and were often seen walking together on balmy evenings along the main promenade where the river touched the edge of the city and the couples read love poems. The respect Rosita felt for her came from family tradition and because this old and stern woman looked after her father. They had never been affectionate to each other, nor had the stepmother's presence ever replaced the void Rosita's mother had left. No. Of her mother she knitted dreams of hot chocolate and donuts and matinee movies on Sunday afternoons. It was very different with the stepmother.

On the afternoon of the baptism they proudly headed to church together to watch Lady Mayor wear the fuchsia suit with shining dignity. Rosita's children were dressed in little blue sailor suits with white hats and blue-and-white leather shoes, as dictated by the fashion magazines and not by the river. The boys had inherited Rosita's pale skin that sparkled with a few freckles and almond-shaped eyes, slightly slanted. Rosita adored her children and enjoyed dressing them up like dolls whenever possible. Amidst the chronic melancholy of her condition, they were her prime icons of worship and her only source of happiness. Her health had begun to deteriorate rapidly and she was often coughing or succumbing to viral strikes which she soothed with herbal concoctions at first, and medical prescriptions later. Her visits to the doctor had become a regular exercise and little bottles of medicine filled her bedroom and bathroom shelves. The family doctor's recommendation to stay away from the tyranny of the rainy season had not gone unheeded. She always dreamed of leaving, of going abroad. But how could she with the children? Perhaps one day, when they were older.

As a present for the baptised baby she had wrapped a white French cotton suit in yellow paper to augur the child many years of peace and good luck, which, considering the alleged origin, it was something the baby was going to need indeed. Before leaving the house Rosita had given the children a last apparel check and placed a beige linen hat on her head, the colour of her jacket. Underneath, she wore a wine-coloured silk shirt, and had placed a handkerchief of the same colour in the small left breast pocket of her blazer, a colour mix appropriate to engaging good spirits.

The sun was raging outside and Rosita and the stepmother opened their parasols to protect themselves. As the older woman strutted out she began to mumble something about the outrageous significance of this ghastly ritual.

'God is going to punish both people with sacred wrath,' she said, her lips tightening with severe judgment. 'That girl is a scoundrel. To have her baby godfathered by the man who's given it to her and then persuade the wife to be the godmother is outrageous,' she went on. 'How can the priest allow such buffoonery?'

'Perhaps it is not his child,' soothed Rosita. 'You know how people talk in this town. No one is spared of a mud avalanche.' The shadow of her own public trial after her first child died glided into her mind – she was accused of letting the baby die of malnutrition. But the stepmother, who had done little to clear the mud in public, insisted in her judgment.

'Of course it is his. The mayor visited that cheat of a woman weekly and people saw them together. She is only fifteen, you know,' she went on. 'He could be charged for corrupting a minor. But one thing's for sure. She's bitten the hand that fed her and her entire family,' she added, as if she knew some hidden divine plan.

The mother of the child arrived at the church wearing a long white dress that anyone could have confused with a bridal gown. It was not quite to the floor nor did it have a flowing train, but it came down to just above her ankles and that was long by any standard, and enough to spark gossip. She came into the church through the front door and sauntered towards the altar like a grandiose bride, carrying the baby in her arms and accompanied by her elder brother. The locals who had congregated inside the church – mainly town people, for Lady Mayor had refused to invite her own family to avoid scandal – were shocked by the apparition.

'Oh my God! This is outrageous,' muttered the collective tongue. Frenzied whispers fluttered up into the air. But the girl bride did not mind the public scrutiny and continued her staged march all the way to the front of the church.

When the mayor's wife saw the girl in the white dress, ambling like a Bride of Christ, her blood ran wild inside her veins and her face turned livid. The murmur ran uncontrolled. For a second, Lady Mayor doubted the veracity of the gossip. She wanted to. Perhaps it was not the way it appeared? Then who was the father and why this whole theatre? The baby's grandmother, the cook, had argued publicly – and probably following the mayor's instructions – that the pregnancy was the result of a roadside rape. Lady Mayor's intuition refused to believe that, and instead reassured her of a more horrible truth. Suddenly her cheeks blushed the same colour as her suit and she came to understand the significance of the theatrical display. For there is nothing more certain than the intuition of a woman in love, Mama always said. And I believe it to be true.

Lady Mayor kicked her husband's ankle with concealed anger, but offered a tight smile to the priest, who was also surprised to see the girl walking with the baby through the middle of the church. Everyone knew it is customary for the godparents to take the baby into the church as they entered through the side entrance. But the priest also knew about the gossip and preferred not to prolong the ceremony with unnecessary suspicion. He greeted the woman in white without much fuss to avoid kindling the volcano he could see brewing in Lady Mayor's eyes, and proceeded with the ceremony.

As the godmother held the tiny creature in her arm for the priest to pour on the holy water and redeem the child from all sins, a male voice in the middle of the crowd shouted, 'The mayor's wife is a cuckold!' Silence descended and the air in the house of God grew so thick that it could be sliced with a machete. An eerie wind penetrated the temple and time was suspended. Lady Mayor stood frozen for a second or two. Her husband tried to play down the comment, but her contained rage imploded in her head like a tidal wave crashing against her own emotional frustrations. She handed the baby to the priest, turned around towards the guests, and walked over to where she knew the voice had come from. An Amazon in full rage, ready to defend her territory, she walked up and confronted the offender, fully aware she was not making a mistake for her intuition was as ripe as her wound. Lady Mayor stared at the rascal who had yelled the offensive words and, charged with the fire of a thousand volcanoes, and without any hesitation, swung her arm back and discharged a resounding blow on the offender's face, leaving on his skin the mark of her five fingers, nails and all.

She then strutted back to the front, chest up like a peacock, face calm after her emotional purging, and stood in her original position by the side of the font. But her rage had not been discharged fully. Oh no! Immediately after she reached the font she grabbed the young girl by the ruffled collar of her white taffeta dress and dragged her outside the church to give her a taste of the medicine she had given the previous offender. This time the dose would be much stronger. Her opponent, however, did not remain wide-eyed, or in shock. Instead, she struck back at the woman in pink, grabbing her by the hair and shaking her head with all her mighty rage and humiliation.

Angry blows and scratches were swapped; both women fell to the ground knotted and intertwined, struggling against each other, calling each other a string of colourful and obscene names. In her rage, Lady Mayor's hands grabbed the girl's neck and tried to strangle her, but one of the locals screamed and called out for the priest. The man in the white tunic quickly handed the baby to the father – or godfather – and ran out with the intention of quelling the combat of the two Amazons, who by then were in a knot at the front entrance of the church. A circle formed around the wrestlers and people wooed and egged them on, making bets on who would be the winner. The priest went to stop the struggle, which he felt would cast a terrible spell on his church, but when he saw the froth of indignation pouring out of both women, he decided against it, to protect his own skin. Rosita ran away, for she was feeling guilty about the colour recommendation she'd given the Lady Mayor.

'It was not your fault,' assured the stepmother. 'This is the only way the young scoundrel will learn to respect the elders.'

As you can imagine, the Amazon in pink won the battle because the dress had made her feel good and enabled her to focus her energy on one purpose alone, to defend her principles and the integrity of her family. The ceremony ended without a baptism; the battle set a discouraging precedent for young girls daring to outsmart officials' wives; and the mayor, who had run away with the baby through the back door, dropped to his knees before his wife, seeking total forgiveness. The ritual was a public event. The news of the aborted baptism and the Amazon in the pink suit travelled beyond the province, ending up in national newspapers, which satirised the event with comic strips and warnings to all mistresses against such audacious adventures.

'You must always defend what is yours,' said Lady Mayor the day she came with a basket filled with presents to thank Mama for the colour counselling. 'Whether it is a dream, a principle or a basket of fried fish, don't let go if it makes you happy,' advised the triumphant wife who later bought the baby from the girl and raised it as her own child. Rosita noted the advice in her book of memories.

A week later, she had an asthma attack in the middle of the shop. Her cousin Rosa the pianist, eager for details of the baptism scandal, had come to hear the story of how the shade for Lady Mayor's suit had been revealed to Rosita by the river and how the bride had betrayed the Virgin by wearing a snow-white gown, which was only for pure girls. Then suddenly Rosita's face turned from rose to ashen and she began to breathe with extreme difficulty, placing her hand on her chest and gasping for oxygen. A cloud of terror set in her eyes and the sound of asphyxia forced Rosa to fetch a doctor immediately, who with one look diagnosed acute asthma and strongly recommended a trip away.

Don Ramon's jealousy refused to let the boys go anywhere out of his sight. He asked the stepmother to look after them while Rosita, if she so insisted, travelled to the capital to visit her cousin Lisa. It was a very difficult decision for Rosita to make because her intuition had begun to rattle warning signs like the snake that announces doomsday. On the other hand, her chest continued to tighten by the day and she was finding it more and more difficult to breathe. She had no option but to pack her bags and appeal to her partner once more to let her take the children. Her appeal was unsuccessful and, feeling somehow defeated, she purchased the ticket for her first venture outside her home town.

Filled with trepidation and carrying a face moistened by tears, Rosita walked along the tarmac wearing a yellow gown with pale blue flowers for peace and good luck, and a pair of brown snakeskin shoes to anchor her to her land. Seconds before she climbed up the stairs to board the plane, she turned around to wave the children farewell and her eyes drew the faint image of the Blue Cat in the space between the boys and the horizon. 'Is this an omen?' she asked her heart, which in response said no. She clasped this reply tightly against her chest, like a purse with a precious gem concealed in its silky folds, unwilling ever to let go. Soon the image of the cat disintegrated and joined the travelling parade of clouds, and she put the event down to a figment of her own fears and exhaustion. The children, in short pants and sailor's hats, watched their Mama disappear into the plane after their little fingers waved her goodbye.

'Come back soon, Mama,' they called and the wind carried their voices into her heart.

Rosita found a spot in the small plane and fastened herself into the seat. It was an old military machine propelled by a small engine and the courage of those aboard, for it was never a certainty that such old crafts would arrive at the desired destination in one piece. On that occasion it was carrying a few passengers, most of whom were travelling to the capital, Lima, for business or to find schools for their children so they could 'become better citizens'. As they lifted off, Rosita looked through the small window next to her seat and saw her land moving away from her, retaining on its soil what she loved most. The memories of her legendary grandmother cruising along the river on the silver cod vessel appeared in her mind and she wept throughout the whole journey.

On the other side of the mountains her cousin Lisa had come to meet her in the company of her fiancé, a lieutenant in the civil guard. The two women hugged and kissed each other and Rosita poured her feelings of anguish onto her cousin right there. Lisa reminded her that life takes many turns. Perhaps her visit was meant to open up a new path that would allow her to attain whatever she had been searching for.

'To start with,' she ordered with the air of an elder sister, 'your health has to improve. It's better to have a mother away than a sick mother, or a dead one.'

'I don't know,' said Rosita, 'my heart tells me I did wrong in leaving the children.'

'Listen, while you are still alive, you can always recover your children no matter what happens. Remember this.'

The women hugged each other again in a statement of mutual support. Lisa wiped the tears from her cousin's cheeks, trying to brush away her fears, and after a welcoming drink at the new airport and a series of warnings of dos and don'ts, the fiancé drove the ladies home and left them to rest.

Rosita knew that Lima was not used to seeing much rain, in fact hardly any at all, so she trusted that her chest condition would improve. Lisa had an apartment not far from the main square. She had organised an extra bed for her cousin and had written a list of places they could visit together. On sunny afternoons, when Lisa was still at the garment factory where she worked as a supervisor, Rosita would wander off to the closest beach to watch the ocean and be totally mesmerised by its giant waves. Half numbed by the rich smell of salt and fish soup in the air, she stared at the waves, imagining them as waltzing blue hills pumping with the beat of the life force that lived underneath. The swell always brought goose bumps to her skin and made her giggle inside. Sitting on the sand sipping cola to calm the touch of nausea that the fish smell provoked, Rosita watched with awe how the crest of the surf swelled higher and higher in voluptuous ascendance. She marvelled at how the waves crashed against the rocks in furious release, dissolving back into their original source. She watched in total surrender as the next swell appeared with yet another iridescent peak, another mound of silvery blue, ebbing and flowing in a never-ending sway, as in an erotic dream.

After a few visits to Sweet Water Beach, Rosita tried hard to call and connect with the spirits or the nature gods that lived in the ocean. But she could not. Later she discovered that it was impossible because her own story did not live in the waters of the Pacific. It lived in the tempestuous waters of the Amazon River, on the other side of the mountains. In Lima, Rosita learned to step on firm ground and stopped travelling to the In-between for a while, at least while she got better.

'Perhaps all that spirit stuff is making you sick,' said Lisa with a wicked smile.

'Do you think so? How can it be, cousin?' mused Rosita. 'My mother's memories are the only thing that keeps me sane. And the children.'

'Well, you won't be able to do it in Lima. There are no rivers with talking spirits here. It doesn't even rain a decent downpour and there is very little green around here.'

Lisa's practicalities had the best intention. 'If people in the city hear your spirit stories you'll be branded a loony. Remember.' Lisa's warning set in Mama's head, and the spirit world of the In-between remained on hold for a very long time. Rosita reminded Lisa that while it might be difficult to talk to the spirits in there she would never forget about them.

'I will keep my mouth shut if that is necessary,' she promised with genuine certainty.

On weekends the cousins usually strolled downtown, checking clothes and accessories, walking along the boulevards and visiting museums, tearooms and markets. These were different markets from those in Iquitos – crowded mainly with country folk and without the exuberant wildlife. Sometimes the women basked in the elegance of a downtown cafeteria near the city's main plaza, where they sat outside on the verandah sipping vermouth from pretty glasses and watching people meander past.

Across the road stood a bronze monument of the country's independence hero mounted on a horse and waving a flag. It was the main icon of the capital. Against this backdrop a quilt of frenetic life stretched before their eyes and Lisa would patiently explain to her cousin the ins and outs of life in the capital. For example, the man in rags, the one that looked very poor and sold candied peanuts from a basket. Him? Yes, he was probably a millionaire in disguise. And the Indian boy in a starched white uniform pushing a yellow cart and blowing a small cornet to sell ice cream, for sure he was a child of misfortune who preferred to earn a clean living with dignity instead of a life of crime. But that was not the case with the controversial-looking preacher haranguing the crowd in the name of the Lord, calling all to repent before doomsday. He was a charlatan according to Lisa. Why else would he be selling redemption diluted in a potion and bottled in dark little containers? He had to be a quack of the lowest kind. Both women would take the mickey out of most scenes they watched, and enjoyed the rest for what they were: panels of life's queer peculiarities.

Tropical monkeys dressed in tattered tutus sold fortune cookies and self-deprecating clowns beat themselves silly to amuse a reluctant crowd that much preferred to be amazed by hairy freaks kept in iron cages. Union activists paced across the plaza trying to mobilise the people to challenge the authorities against the exploitation of the peasants, but the plaza bystanders, mainly peasants on a day off from domestic service, preferred to amble the square with ears switched off and minds turned blank, or to lick their ice creams with gusto under the statue of the Liberator, oblivious of the activists.

Rosita was particularly bedazzled by the coquettish meandering of young women along the promenade, those of gracious and controlled step who appeared to spice their moves from inside. Together with their chaperones the young ladies made as if they were simply eyeing the lavish goods that lay daintily on silk beds behind shop window glass. With tiny steps they ambled seductively through the historical shopping arcade next to the government palace. But according to Lisa, all they were doing was exploring romantic possibilities of the serious kind.

'These are the real Lima girls,' Lisa said the first time the taunting scene caught their eyes.

'What do you mean, real Lima girls?' asked Rosita.

'Well, I mean the girls fed by the spoon of Spanish history, silly you.'

'What's so special about them?' mused the newcomer.

'They think they are God's gift to earth,' Lisa mocked. 'They still think we live in colonial times when local women believed the whole world was their folly. Look at them, how they flirt.'

'I can't see anything,' Rosita said, studying the young woman's subtle strutting with attention.

'That's it. No one notices but the victim, the one they are hitting with their love poison dart. It is in their eyes,' Lisa pointed out, narrowing her eyes.

As the cousins discussed the secrets of the art of flirting, one such protagonist walked past them swaying her hips with artistic discipline, eyes alert but hidden behind fluttering lashes. The predator also wore a coy pout on her lips. Clad in a close-fitting suit with a frilly blouse that displayed her soft maiden skin, she bounced her body artistically, drawing a figure of eight with her hips, holding her balance on a pair of extra-high heels. An older woman walked by her side, parading her merchandise. Two men in suits crossed their path. One of them took his hat off and said, 'Joyful are the eyes who can perceive such beauty.' Dropping his hat on the ground, he continued, 'Please allow me to place a carpet on which your precious tiny feet can walk so I can keep the memory of this glorious moment.'

Lisa winked at Rosita and smiled, 'Men here are such buffoons.'

'But at least they do it in style,' replied Rosita, savouring another mouthful of vanilla ice cream.

A few days later, as both women enjoyed a glass of after-dinner wine for a 'healthier digestion', Rosita told Lisa the Lady Mayor saga. In colourful detail she etched the events of the baptism in her cousin's imagination, how the brawl was ignited, how the priest ran away from the clash, and how the baby was swapped for a hearty cheque. Rosita had heard that the baby's mother was now forging a better future for herself in Lima.

'Not really,' said Lisa, explaining that she had read the story in the papers and knew the girl's family. The girl was not studying, but working in a nightclub. The money Lady Mayor had given her in exchange for the child had covered her initial settlement expenses but had then run out. The girl began to work as a maid in rich homes. Nothing wrong with that, thought Rosita, who feared the same predicament in the depths of her heart, despite her own determination to succeed. Lisa went on to say that while the girl was ambitious she lacked an understanding of life's strategies and basic education. In the end, she had chosen the easiest option – the life of a bar girl in a nightclub. Rosita bit her lower lip and prayed she would never be faced with such a predicament. Lisa sipped more wine and read her cousin's thoughts.

'If you play your cards right you'll be fine,' she reassured her, 'but you have to be careful. The last thing you want to do is end up in one of those dumps.' Lisa had seen many country girls fall into the net of undesirable circumstances. Women from the Amazon region had a bad reputation; they were seen as an easy catch. Respect was barely extended to them because of their easygoing nature, described by Lima locals as 'open sexuality'.

Unimpressed by the description, Rosita reassured Lisa that she'd let no man break her seal of celibacy until her life was in order: 'I want to start a new life and be able to bring the children up here.' In her heart she knew that Iquitos had completed its role in her life, but she was aware that bringing the children to Lima was going to be a battle against the might of Don Ramon.

Rosita's asthma attacks had decreased to a minimum and her health and complexion had improved immensely. Although Lima was believed to be dry, it was in fact a damp city, often muggy in summer and foggy in winter, but it was not as bad as Iquitos. The weather had not cluttered her chest and she was feeling more energetic and optimistic about her new plans. She planned to look for a job, save money and bring the boys to the city.

Every week she wrote to them describing the novelties that came her way. The colour of the water, the new toys she had seen in the shop windows, the different fur on cute pets of the refined kind, and other curiosities she discovered on her long walks. She described the roar of the ocean, the ships and the sailors she saw in the main port. To the stepmother she described how popular radio soaps were in the capital, and how fans would wait outside the radio station to belt the villain they'd learned to hate on the airwaves. The sheets of rice paper she wrote upon, like the walls of her soul, also recorded what she missed most in the tropical garden of the Amazon and how fearful she was of growing indifferent to the scent of the land. She missed the pungent flavour of river cod, the fullness of the pineapples, the evening melody of the forest and the fish smoked in banana leaves served with corn cakes steamed in herbal wrappings; but above all she missed the rhythmical voices of her children. A few months after her arrival, she had received only one letter in response to her episodic narratives. As she was used to life's hard knocks, this apparent lack of interest did not discourage her from her plans.

The war had ended on the other side of the world and the work in factories and the exportation of cotton for soldiers' uniforms and mineral resources had come to a halt. One day as Rosita was on her way to meet Lisa for the evening movie session, her attention was caught by a rambling swarm of people moving towards the main square. There were thousands carrying placards on which they had written their industrial demands. Rosita had never seen a demonstration before, so the reverberations of the crowd provoked a totally new emotion in her heart. A sense of pride popped up from within. She liked that people were able to air their frustrations. If only she could.

Three men marched at the head of the throng shouting the slogans that the crowd repeated. Behind them, a line of country folk in traditional costumes tapped their feet in small circles and held up banners that bore the colours of the rainbow. The sight made Rosita smile with glee. The rainbow was so very present in her town, always after the rain, always in its almost iridescent tones and giant dimension. Behind the rainbow flags followed a block of men and women chanting for better working conditions and more pay. They were the miners, the sector of the population that bore the biggest brunt of poverty and ill treatment. Standing under the arcade that bordered the plaza, she stared at the men in red and green ponchos, heads covered by multi-coloured woollen caps, as they marched past her.

Half hypnotised by the scene, she hardly noticed the supporters bumping into her until a young man hit her with his camera. He was running to join the throng of people. She started following, magnetised by the crowd, and again he bumped into her, accidentally. Their eyes met and she smiled at him. Her gaze followed the photographer as he clicked away, recording every detail of the demonstration. He wanted to grab every harsh expression, every sign of anger, every message written on the placards, as if to lock the essence of raw emotion inside the square black box. His hopping and skipping made Rosita laugh because his camera was very small and did not look like the professional equipment real newsmen used. At least in the way she'd seen it in the movies. But his manner was intense and she was half convinced that his photos would serve a purpose more useful than wallpapering.

As the young man launched into another of his kangaroo jumps – for he was not too tall – his camera pouch, dangling from his shoulder, hit her bag, which immediately fell to the ground. A swift hand appeared from nowhere, picked the bag up and disappeared into the crowd. It happened in a matter of seconds. Rosita could not believe the scene, but immediately woke up out of her bewilderment; she felt a burst of rage in her stomach, and blood rushed to her cheeks. Heart pumping with fury she dashed after the boy with feline instinct, for Rosita always had honoured her Leo sign. Inside her mind the voice of Lady Mayor pounded: 'Defend! Defend!' She pushed through the crowd, assuring herself she'd get the rascal. Racing like an Amazon across the jungle she pushed and shoved with her elbow. She panted and ran until she finally caught the back of the thief's jacket and with outrageous force pulled the boy to a dead stop.

And then she discharged her full rage upon him. After grabbing him by the shoulders she tried to pull her bag out of his hands, leaving the thief dumbfounded for he never imagined that such a frail-looking woman would turn into a fierce attacker. Rosita shook the boy with ferocious anger, pounced her nails into the side of his face, and pulled his hair until he finally dropped the purse. But that was not enough for her, she continued to hit him with her shoe, reprimanding him for his unlawful behaviour until her aching chest forced her to stop and leave the young scoundrel feeling sorry for himself. The photographer, who had seen it all and had chased both runners, finally caught up with her and helped her pull herself together.

'Please forgive me, it was all my fault,' said the man with a sorry look. 'Would you allow me to buy you a drink?' Rosita did not examine the request with her traditional suspicion, and said yes. She even allowed him to help her dust off the debris she'd picked up in her struggle. She was still angry and her fury had begun to affect her breathing. Urged by the need to sit down and use her asthma nebuliser she let the man lead her into a nearby café where he ordered brandy for them both. His name was Lucio and he was a freelance photographer trying to make it in the news and current affairs scene. But as that was not easy, he did whatever came his way to make a penny and help his family. No, he was not married. He meant he'd do anything to help his seven brothers and his mother, including driving taxis and laying brick after brick under his sweat.

Rosita felt a strange empathy for him. A feeling of connectedness emerged, a rapport of sorrow, a link to the sadness of her growing-up years. He was somebody who, like her, had assumed a responsibility towards the family. She found her sadness in his image, as well as her determination to succeed. After the brandy brought life into her cheeks she checked her watch and realised it was time to meet her cousin. But before she left the young photographer savouring his third glass, they exchanged addresses. She had decided to let him be her first friend in Lima.

When Lisa heard all about the handbag's rescue and the chasing of the thief, she was not too impressed by the fact that it was Rosa, and not Lucio, who had caught up with the robber.

'Umm, and you said that the moment his camera hit your bag, it dropped to the ground?' Lisa took that as an omen. But Rosita dismissed the coincidence.

'They were not in cahoots. I have a feeling Lucio has a good heart.'

'All cities are full of bastards,' Lisa warned, 'some of them with a good heart too. They just can't help it. It's better you don't see that pseudo-photographer.'

They picked a Mexican movie about a peasant girl who had lost her honour to the town chief's son, but after a mountain of struggles the heroine managed to get the villain of her misfortune and love of her life to marry her. Rosita and Lisa wept through the whole film, linking their hearts to the painful predicament of the protagonist. Sobs mixed with nose-blowing and noisy requests for hush. Both women craved this genre of movie; they were addicted to great dramas, as if with every movie they discharged a little of their own grief and their family's collective tribulations. Lisa had her own list of misfortunes, however her fervent pragmatism and versatility had led her to use them to propel her towards greener pastures. She was to become Rosita's source of inspiration for commonsense, initiative and perseverance.

They left the theatre marked by their melodrama: eyes red and puffy, still carrying a heavy gloom in their hearts, never mind that the heroine's honour had been rescued and the marriage consummated on a bed of pink roses. Lisa suggested dinner at a small restaurant where they made great braised beef and the portions were generous; and, better still, the price was right. They walked two blocks clasping their purses against their chests, always looking over their shoulders and avoiding streets with stray cats, because Lisa believed too many cats brought the devil out of his lair. Inside the restaurant, their anguish cleared the instant two succulent dishes of braised steak mounted with fried eggs and boiled rice was placed before them. The dish was called Mounted Loins, and Lisa explained that the meat people ate in the capital was a lot better than anywhere else because the locals refused to buy frozen meat from Argentina, which provided meat for most of the continent. Rosita, who was used to eating fish at home, ate hers with a hearty appetite, agreeing that frozen meat was never as good as fresh and making sure she handled all her cutlery with finesse, as she'd been taught by the Anglicans.

When dinner was over and the vanilla custard had found a cosy place in their stomachs, they decided to catch the bus home. As they were leaving the restaurant, a lean and tall man of elegant disposition walked towards them. His name was Martin Lozano, one of the managers at Lisa's firm. 'A very generous gentleman' Lisa had commented once when she described him to her cousin.

'There is Mr Lozano,' nudged Lisa subtly as soon as she noticed the man heading their way.

'Mr Lozano, how nice to see you around here.'

The elegant man bowed his head to both ladies as Lisa made the formal but cordial introductions. Rosita stretched her right hand out and smiled with dignified shyness. Lisa felt the electric charge in the air as her boss fell immediately under the spell of her cousin.

'It is such a great pleasure to meet you, Miss Rosita. Lima is lucky to have the flower of your beauty amongst us.' Lisa bit the tip of her tongue to avoid a snappy comment, for she had never seen Martin Lozano pay any such compliment before. He stood tall and still against the noise and spice from the restaurant, simply enchanted. He was poised but his eyes flashed sparkles of admiration. It was obvious the quiet magnetism that Rosita had acquired in her cruises through her magical forest had begun to garner credit and recognition. Unfortunately not all it attracted was to be for her benefit or advantage.

A few days later the postman knocked on the door, carrying a small parcel that had to be signed for on delivery. He also handed Rosita a letter. She immediately recognised the writing on the envelope and knew it had come from Iquitos. A slight jolt in her heart told her to open the parcel first. Inside, and wrapped in lavish paper, was a book titled *The Mystery of the Rainbow*, a romantic novel by an English author, and an imported box of chocolates with a card that read 'For the lady whose smile complements the colour of the rainbow, Martin Lozano.' Rosita flashed a smile of feminine satisfaction and placed the parcel on the sideboard. She would be able to express her appreciation next week for he had invited her and Lisa to the theatre. She knew he liked her and if her smile brought out his generosity, she thought, well, she would return the compliment with her company. She then tore open the corner of the letter. As she read it the glow on her skin dissolved.

The small plane landed at Iquitos airport and a woman with an anxious face and dressed in a fuchsia two-piece suit stepped down the stairs and walked firmly along the tarmac. Her head was a whirlwind of confusion mixed with emptiness. Silently, inside her bag, the letter spoke painfully of Don Ramon's threats to take her children away, and of his suggestion that she stay in Lima forever.

Rosita had caught the first plane as soon as she'd recovered from a horrid asthma attack. Lisa had lent her the money for the plane ticket and firmly recommended her to act with guile and commonsense. The rainbow beckoned her in the distance but she did not notice. Holding her hand against her chest she hailed a three-wheeled taxi and asked the driver to take her to Don Ramon's shop, although she did not know whether she could call that place home any more. Behind the counter she found a new shop attendant, who greeted her with a dry smile. Ignoring the gesture, she ran inside, checking every room of the large house, calling out the children's name.

'Where are my children?' she yelled to the attendant. The woman replied that Don Ramon was playing cards at the club. An old servant came out of the kitchen to tell her the children were no longer living at home. They had been sent to boarding school. Rosita froze. The servant could not tell her where exactly the children were, but added that all her belongings had been transferred to the stepmother's house. Rosita tried hard to ignore the feeling that her chest was running out of air and raced to the neighbours to get to the root of the mess. The old couple who lived next door and who knew the whole drama felt sorry for her and told her the boys had been sent to the Christian Brothers College outside of town. Two days by boat. She stayed with the neighbours that night. The wife rubbed alligator oil on her chest and arranged a boat to take her to the school.

At the break of dawn she boarded a rustic craft bound for the Christian Brothers boarding school. She would sleep in a small village that night and continue the day after. Armed with courage and commonsense as Lisa had instilled in her, she did not collapse during the trip. The thought of hugging her children kept her hopes up. To pass the time she visualised Bufeo emerging from the water, soothing her fears, nourishing her confidence. When she finally arrived at the school her resistance collapsed and she dropped to the ground, praying to her mother for help. The principal of the school received her in his office but told her the children were away for a week on an excursion. It was obvious Don Ramon had his influences.

Back in Iquitos, the same man that had bought his way into her family's heart with fruit conserve and imported chocolates refused to see her and used the stepmother again to convey his feelings. The children were to stay with him and he would take care of their education. What she did, he did not care. Don Ramon had realised there was no love in the relationship. They should separate. The last statement was the only bit with which Rosita agreed. The stepmother relayed the message with a touch of remorse. She knew how much anguish had been seeded in her stepdaughter's heart since the covenant with the Chinese merchant, yet she could do nothing now to modify the young woman's fate. The best she could do was assure the daughter of the man she respected, that she would make sure the children remembered and wrote to her. In the same room where the sardine canapés had been served Rosita wept profoundly. To add salt to the wound, the stepmother told her that her father, Desiderio, had recognised that keeping the children in boarding school was the best solution. Rosita's heart was shattered.

That night she had the biggest fit of asthma in her life. The sky seemed to have darkened around her and angry clouds had crept inside her bronchial tubes. She lay in hospital for days, refusing to speak to most people, breathing through a plastic pipe. Her anguish was consuming her. In her heart she prayed to all her gods and spirits to guide her through this darkest tunnel. When Lady Mayor came to visit her she was shocked to find her young friend in such a deplorable state. The town grapevine had spread the news. The local gossip focused on the Chinese man who had stolen Rosita's children. But there was another version. There were those who described Rosita as a 'heartless woman who'd abandoned her little boys to gallivant in the capital'.

Huge rings grew dark around her eyes and a yellow film spread over her skin. Lady Mayor felt pity for her but she could do little to redress the situation. There was only one thing she could do: remind her with the insistence of a loving mother that sometimes battles have to be lost before real victory is attained. She came to visit her at the hospital daily with flowers and fresh fruit, and explained with great tenderness that life always has two sides. She tried to convince her that, for now, Don Ramon had the means to provide for the children, and buy the authorities. It would be a waste of her energy to struggle and get even sicker. One day she could send for the children. One day, after she'd settled in the capital, become successful and had the means to send for them. The words gradually penetrated Rosita's mind and in spite of her pain, and aided by Lisa's recommendation of acting with commonsense, she saw the wisdom in Lady Mayor's words. She decided to get better, arranged some legal papers in regard to the children and implored her father to visit the boys regularly.

Desiderio kissed his daughter on the forehead and gave her his blessings. Locking her pain in the same box where all her other adversities were kept, Rosita packed her bags again and flew back to Lima during a torrential downpour that equalled her tears. She did not farewell the river nor the gardens of her tropical fantasies. With the indomitability that possesses those who refuse to be broken by adversity, she assured the rainbow, for now hidden below the horizon, that one day she would come back to reclaim the treasure that lay at its end. That day she would take the children back.

THE SEEDS OF CLOUDS

THE DAY ROSITA returned to Lima from her failed attempt to rescue her children, Lisa dragged her to the procession of the Virgin of the Clouds to ask for help and protection. She insisted that this Virgin was the true protector of all souls whose lives had sunk in the rapids of pain and misfortune. Rosita was not too willing to go; her heart was filled with grief and her whole body ached, impregnated by the shock of her recent tragedy. But she understood her cousin had the best intentions so she followed without resistance. Perhaps mixing her pain with other people's would be of some assistance, she thought; perhaps the Virgin would be receptive to her sorrows and send her a breath of relief. She had not slept in days and her mind was whirling with a mixture of guilt and fear, and shame. The Virgin of the Clouds was the perfect patron for her – after all, this city was completely enveloped by a thick fog that seemed to place it apart from the rest of the world. Like some kind of purgatory, she had concluded. Coming down in the aircraft had been a weird experience indeed. The first time she had flown in, the phenomenon had not had any effect on her, but this time a cold shiver had penetrated her body and goose bumps had spread along her arms the moment the plane began its descent through the clouds. Have I been sent down as punishment for my sins? she thought.

Silently she followed the throng next to her cousin, her gaze lost in the back of the crowd that moved as a pulsating mob absorbed in its fervour. Waves of trepidation laced with shame hit the walls of her chest every so often. She feared her legs would soon give in; even worse, the ground would open, suck her inside and drag her to the bottom of the earth to burn with the infidels. She fought the feeling and when those thoughts besieged her mind she looked around, searching for a face of hope in the crowd, for an image of absolution, for a feeling that would burst her pain. And she often found it. The locals were fervent followers of one saint or another. They thrived on sin and absolution. They had a strong connection with one Virgin or two, or worshipped several effigies of Jesus, or paid homage to the Holy Spirit, as long as somebody fortified their hearts against calamities of all sorts. To Rosita there was little difference between the spirits of the forest and the statues dressed in gold and glitter that protected the weakness of life. The ceremonies were different but the heart and the pomp were indeed the same. In the city alone lived the Virgin of the Sacred Pain, who protected the martyrs; the Christ of all Calamities, who prevented disasters, or so it was believed; the Lord of Good Weather, often on leave; and the Lady of the Tremors, or the Dame of Divine Succour.

She contemplated her own life as she felt the pressure of the crowd walking behind her, and the pain of those who were in front, and again, her mind would nudge and nag, blaming her for 'abandoning her children'. She could not cry, her tears were frozen. There was no more room in her little box of memories to keep this episode locked. Cold and hot shivers ran through her body as she fought against her prosecutor, herself. The brass band and the wailers in the background blared with tearful melodies. The clouds turned even darker. How could she have done a thing like this? Any other mother would have stayed with the children. Who would read to them in bed now? Who would comb their hair with rosewater and brilliantine to make the strands shiny and soft? What would they think of her, so far away? Would they still remember their trips to the market? Their games with the tigrillos, and the three-legged frogs? A silent lament escaped from her heart and a soft whisper implored the patroness of the clouds to dissolve the haze that had grown around her soul. Amid the chaos of her feelings, Rosita prayed for the courage to go on, to prove to her family that she too could be a good mother, and that very soon she would be able to provide for her children.

Summer had arrived and Lima breathed an air of prosperity, despite the closure of many of the cotton factories. Most of the southern continent had supplied raw materials and uniforms to the Allied forces in Europe but when the war contracts were terminated, and industries began to shut down, the majority of the workers from the country were persuaded to return home. But no government regulation was going to convince the children of the mountains, who had long endured the brunt of scarcity because of centralisation, to return. Instead they decided to fend for themselves and teach 'the snobs' a thing or two. They drew on traditional ways to survive, and invoked their ancient Inca gods for guidance and protection in that very 'cold and hostile town', the bastion of the colonisers' lineage. They stayed on and set up rudimentary businesses in markets and in tents and makeshift kiosks on the outskirts of town; they brought their own live produce and fruit and vegetables, and homemade wares. The sprawling trend persuaded other less skilled workers to follow suit, and soon many began selling flowers from the parks and knick-knacks door to door, trinkets they found or stole from the ports or people's bags, wallets and valises. Others were more responsible, deciding to create small industries such as domestic eateries and laundry houses. Gradually a swarm of street vendors began to march into the city like a giant reptile threatening to take over the parks and boulevards.

The city residents were horrified. They feared that their 'Capital of Dreams', as Lima had been nicknamed during the viceroy era 400 years earlier, was becoming a repugnant hovel. Petty crime was on the rise and the smell of the city changed from lavender, lemon and cinnamon to cheap fuel, frantic sweat and urine.

One day, the wife of an important military officer had her bag snatched. Immediately after this a stout general came out of the ranks, banged his fist, pulled out his gun and brought an end to the mayhem across the city. The classist conservatives cheered and clapped, and peace and quiet reigned for a while. The parks flowered free again and music returned to the streets, for the general had kept his promise to clean up the streets and jail those who disobeyed. Rosita realised that the mood was not too friendly for her to start an enterprise, but she would persevere.

Her journey began in the same arcade where she had sat with Lisa to savour vanilla ice creams and watch beautiful women prance with flair in their flirtatious dance. She walked up and down the streets of the city looking for a job as a sales assistant, trying to convince the proprietors of her special skills, appealing to their good heart. But she was a country girl and her internal grief was so etched in her gaze that no prospective employer was willing to take her in. They said it was her lack of experience in the local trade, and that her provincial accent did not help. Seeing the gloom in her cousin's face, Lisa decided to ask Martin Lozano to accommodate Rosita somewhere in the factory, preferably in sales if he could, for she would do wonders given her experience at Don Ramon's and her magnetism with customers. But it was written that the clouds would not abandon Rosita's life for a while, and, to her bad luck, the last opening in sales had just been filled. Martin said there was only room on the process line, where one hundred other women in blue uniforms folded boxes of different sizes to the marching tick of a giant clock.

It was meant to be like this, thought Rosita, who by then had come to terms with her predicament. It did not matter, she was prepared for anything, she assured Martin. She would sweep floors, launder public linen, or sell pineapple marmalade in the markets – as long as it was a decent job. The admiration of the tall man with the generous disposition towards Rosita was growing; he assured her that her term on the factory floor would not last long.

The evening she got her first pay envelope she lit a candle to the Virgin of the Clouds and bought a cake for her cousin. It was a family tradition, she said. Martin took both cousins to dinner and Rosita gave her first smile in weeks. Soon she would be looking for her own accommodation because the house she shared with Lisa near the city was going to be pulled down to make way for a modern office building. The news had not affected Lisa because it was in her plans to move to a place outside Lima, near where her fiancé was posted.

Life in the factory roared on, and the screeching, clanging and banging of metal and machines in the background began to claw into Rosita's nerves, shaking the glacier of grief that had grown in her heart. A frosty feeling often seized her body and separated her from the others. Amid such industrial cacophony, she strived to do her best.

Her routine began at seven in the morning and ended after sunset. She had to spread a caustic and smelly glue on the edge of cardboard sheets, smoothing the clots carefully and in a straight line, fold the sides neatly, and then straighten the flaps, fold them up, bend down to stack them under the bench and get back up to start again, over and over for twelve hours a day. Her fingers had gone stiff because she had never been used to such a degree of discipline. Her life had been so different, so open-ended and amorphous like the creepers of the Amazon forest, never following a dictated order. She was not used to discriminating boundaries of time or space as defined and measured in the modern capital, pressed by the urgency of revenue and control. In her former world, shapes had been defined by the forces of nature, and even the basketweavers who sat by the river humming to the sun bowed to divine guidance. In the city, life was marked by coercive machines, by fear and detachment. She would mumble to herself as her fingers shook frantically with the flaps and the brush and the glue, her head humming a discordant buzz but dutifully bent, and her long curly hair held by two pins above her ears under a cotton scarf.

Despite her melancholy she had tried to make friends with the rest of the girls, but her co-workers had not welcomed her with the same friendliness they had shown the day she toured the factory in the company of Lisa and Martin. Nowadays, the girls looked at her with unfriendly suspicion. In the ramblings of her mind, she began to see a dark shadow cross the floor and envelop the girls' unhealthy curiosity. Did they know she had left her children back home? Had they heard her old partner had cast her out? Lisa begged her to stop imagining or she would make herself sick.

After a few weeks the smell of the glue was so disturbing that it began to churn her liver. Most evenings when she arrived home from work she went straight to the bathroom to vomit, and then she went to sleep. Her only consolation was the thought of her children, their faces in her photos and her little box of savings. The more cardboard boxes she made the quicker she would achieve her goal. But the truth was that the higher her pile of boxes, the more detached she grew from the rest of the world, and from her own feelings. As the days galloped past, frigid and threatening like the riders of doom, she became more taciturn and gradually lost her appetite. Her face grew gaunt and she became absent-minded, leaving her things here and there, and even when Lisa discussed her engagement plans and her projects to move to the country, her mind was not there. All she talked about was her need to pile up a huge tower of boxes, stack them up and jump through time so she could fly over the mountains to rescue her sons.

One afternoon, as she gingerly carried a stack of boxes, her frail frame collapsed, hitting the floor hard under the crumbling avalanche of cardboard. The girls bent down to help her and noticed her face had turned ashen and that her gaze was blank.

When she opened her eyes, her body lay flat in a faded hospital bed under the image of a wooden cross, and lit by a dangling light above her head which gave off a reluctant glow. The walls around her were a sick yellow and the air smelled of urine and chloroform. She gazed around half dazed, wondering where she was. There was a rambling murmur in the distance, grumbles and groans muffled by the screeching of trolleys and the clanging of bottles along the corridor. Was she dead? She thought it was a bad dream, a figment of her sorrows. She closed her eyes, hugging her arms against her chest under a stained woollen blanket. She was still freezing. A nurse with a starched smile and a blue apron came up to her and gave her a tiny pill and some water in a tin cup. 'Are you alright?' she asked. Rosita wanted to respond but her attempt failed. The force in her was so weak that she simply swallowed her medicine and went back to sleep.

A few days later, almost beyond her control, her legs carried her along a corridor. She walked like a zombie wearing a mournful complexion and loose gown, unable to utter much except to say she was freezing. A trickle of tears would spring from her eyes from time to time and her stare was lost in the labyrinth of her confusion.

The doctor at the sanatorium where she'd been taken as an emergency, and had been allowed to stay at the special request of Martin Lozano, had diagnosed a breakdown. Something like a nervous melancholia. Her life force had receded to a trickle and her heartbeat was sluggish. Her chest had clogged up again and on top of that she was anaemic. It was better for her to be at home, the doctor recommended. Too long in the hospital might convince the young woman that she was incapable of snapping out of it, he said. Wholesome food and bubbly company should help, and a prolonged period in a dry climate too, if possible. Perhaps, Lisa suggested, she could go with her to the country. But Rosita gave no sign of interest in the doctor's recommendations, nor in her cousin's suggestions to go with her to a little ranch for a while. Rosita just stared at the window, unaware of the days of the week or of the light in the sky, as if calling for the Blue Cat to come and take her to the In-between, where her mother and son lived.

For weeks she slept most of the day under heavy blankets and only sipped a little soup when Lisa managed to wake her. The world out-side had lost its appeal. Martin Lozano brought her presents to soothe her grief: flowers and imported chocolates, raisin bread puddings and vanilla custards. Outside, the pallid sun faithfully tapped on her win-dow every afternoon, persevering like the gypsy of her prophecies. One day the morning light had a brighter sheen as the clouds had gently dissolved in the heat, and Rosita sat up in her bed, threw the blankets to the side and walked to the dining room to join her cousin for breakfast.

'Cousin Rosita, you've come back from the dead.'

'The Blue Cat did not want me, cousin,' grinned Rosita, 'so I guess I am here for a long time.' She grabbed a piece of bread from the bas-ket. 'I am so hungry.'

She sat next to her cousin, poured some coffee into a long glass, added boiling milk, and four teaspoons of sugar, and proceeded to slice a fresh hot bread roll and spread a generous amount of pineapple marmalade on it. It was the same preserve she had taught Lisa to make using a recipe from Lady Mayor, who had given her a large pot of *mermelada de piña* as a thank-you gift. It was a special recipe, the politician's wife had whispered as she handed her a basket of delica-cies after the baptism. 'It will definitely bring the soul back when it threatens to slip away. Remember, my child, the soul is fed with prayer and sweet times.' Rosita had not forgotten the advice from the Amazon in pink.

As she soaked the bread in her *café con leche*, Lisa noticed how thin Rosita had become and how her eyes had lost their appealing glow, a feature that until now had always remained with her, even in times of extreme adversity. However, Lisa also realised that her cousin's mood was much calmer and that there was a fresh solidity about her, a kind of fortitude that seemed to come from the edge of life from which she had now returned. *Yerba mala nunca muere* – 'A real weed will never die'. To prove this correct, Rosita's chest got better and her smile returned. The affection she had received, mixed with herbal infusions, doctor's prescriptions, gifts and chicken soup finally worked.

'You must breathe the sun inside yourself,' Lisa would insist. 'Depression is the winter of the heart and you mustn't get too frozen. Your asthma will kill you for sure and you'll never see your children again.' She had spoon-fed herbal medicine to her cousin for weeks and had prepared gallons of chicken and oregano soup laced with orange blossom and ginger. Because Lisa believed that nothing heals an aching heart better than the juices of a seasoned bird.

Responding to the call of her heart's practicalities, Lisa moved to a little ranch not far from the edge of town, very close to her fiancé's new quarters. She would earn a lot more money there because it was hard to convince a Lima local to go to the countryside, 'where Jesus had lost his wits', as they described anywhere past the city boundaries. Rosita combed the streets of Lima, looking for a place she could afford, a little house she could call her own, where she could start weaving the threads of her new life's tapestry. She had never been alone in a strange town, particularly in a town where it was tradition for women to seduce male victims from the corners of their eyes, and where men gambled on cocks that tore each other to death. How abominable! What would Bufeo say?

She had screamed the first time she attended a cockfight with Lisa. Probably they did it in her hometown too, she just had never seen it. There were many things she had not seen because she had spent a great deal of her time 'frolicking with capricious fantasies, floating in the corridors of the In-between,' as her cousin Lisa would say to her when she was angry. There was no way she could float in Lima, it was far too earthy a place, too dusty for the wind to roam in harmony with the spirits, and cluttered with smells of all sorts, but it had some intriguing energy, some special effect that was making her heart more solid and was pulling her feet closer to the ground.

She found a house with high ceilings and a skylight that could be opened with a long stick, a medium-sized room where she placed her table and bed, and a kitchen with a wrought-iron washbowl that served all purposes. It was in a bohemian neighbourhood not far from a leafy park with colonial gates, marble benches and alabaster statues of the Olympian gods and Peruvian heroes. The national sporting ground was a couple of blocks away, and at the height of the soccer season a chain of vendors lined up along the side streets to barbecue *choncholi* and *anticuchos*, grilled tripe and heart on skewers served with chili and garlic sauce and huge pieces of corn on the cob. Most evenings the air was filled with the sweat of frantic crowds and the scent of exotic spices and toasted poppy seeds, so much so that often after midnight Rosita's dreams were infused with cinnamon. She learned to laugh again amongst the constant cries of toddlers and newborns, neighbours brawling, loud whistles and love serenades that pierced the night, when the essence of enamoured hearts poured out with poetic lyrics and two guitars.

'To get the bad spirits out of your house you must clean with kerosene and flaming rum,' insisted Rosita's neighbour Doña Pan-chita, 'and a touch of lavender for good luck, mint for health, and a few teeth of dried garlic on a string to send all vampires away.' Rosita, believer of all things that gave meaning to her life, followed Doña Panchita's rules to a T, driven by her desire to start again, free of the vestiges of ill fortune. She bought the herbs at the markets and scrubbed the floors for days; and when her house was finally clean and the small window polished, she noticed the moon above her house for the first time, a silver balloon that reminded her of a scoop of lemon gelato. The morning after, a line of women and children came to her house, each to bring her a little something they no longer used as a welcoming gift. Outside, two men in blue cotton overalls intoned a creole waltz with a couple of old guitars. A party had begun and in her heart Rosita thanked all the new gods, and returned the hospitality with a plate of salt crackers and pineapple marmalade. 'This joins the essence of all souls into one,' she said as she raised her glass. 'The salt cleanses the soul and the marmalade brings it together.' Everyone clapped and filled their glasses with *chicha morada*, a purple corn brew with added sugar and spices.

The whole gesture had been initiated at Doña Panchita's request. Doña Panchita was a black elder who lived in the tenements a couple of doors away, and she was known to be the voice of wisdom in the neighbourhood. One of her daughters, Lola, was a friend of Lisa and had helped Rosita find her new house. Lola was a full-breasted mulatta with an air of pride and a penchant for seduction. Rosita had met Lola at an afternoon tea party at the home of her friend Renatta. On that day the conversation had centred on what to wear for Mardi Gras. Lola confessed she was entering the pageant for the Queen of the Carnival. Rosita was recovering from her 'journey to the edge of the world' where she nearly stayed with the Blue Cat, and did not have a clue about parties, let alone the Mardi Gras parade. She just gazed absent-mindedly around the room. To get her involved, Lisa told the others that her cousin had a gift.

'What kind of gift?' whispered Lola, as her dainty cup clinked against the china saucers.

Rosita smiled, still in limbo. So Lisa replied that her cousin knew the secret of colours and the powers they bestow on people. She asked Rosita to suggest what a girl should wear on Mardi Gras night to please the gods and secure the title of Queen of the Carnival. Rosita's cheeks blushed red like cherries and she immediately hid her face in her hands, trying hard to ignore the question. She preferred to leave her experiences at Don Ramon's shop untouched, in the distant past. But it was too late. She would not be left alone now that the women knew of her special abilities. She tried to get out of the situation by saying that she needed to speak to the Pink Dolphin from the river, and the dolphin did not appear in Lima. Lola, who had probably inherited her mother's insight, said that if the dolphin indeed talked to her it was because it lived inside her, too.

'Perhaps that is true,' Rosita said, surprising herself. She laughed and decided to join in the mood and once more share her talent. But she promised to all, including herself, that it would be the last time. She closed her eyes for a few seconds, brought her hands together and looked inside herself, feeling the vibrant energy of the jungle in her memory, searching for images of her beloved Pink Dolphin and her ancestors' past. Then she opened her eyes and spoke: 'Because the carnival parade is in honour of Lord Momo, the king of the underworld, Lola should wear the colour of flames with a lipstick to match.' To make sure all the forces were aligned, the contestant should also wear an ivory-coloured flower on her chest, blessed by the Virgin of the Clouds. So that while the ruler of darkness would help her win the title, he could not steal her soul. The girls burst into buoyant chuckles and clanged their cups together in celebration of Rosita's strange abilities and sense of humour, but Lola took notice. A few days later she and her mother were seen scurrying to town to spend the whole of Lola's weekly pay on the right fabric and the perfect lipstick in a new boutique. They did not forget to go to the markets to buy special candles for the church and flowers for the Virgin, never mind that there was still a week to go.

To protect herself, Rosita had asked the girls to shut her secret deep in their souls and never ask her to do such a thing again because 'without her local spirits she felt totally unprotected'. The girls had agreed, mainly because they too feared the unknown. Because 'what a pure heart requests life delivers' – or perhaps because of a happy coincidence – Lola was crowned the local Queen of the Carnival. The whole block bubbled with excitement and the people danced all night in sparkling celebration. During the parade the radiant queen waved at the cheering crowd, proudly wearing her ivory bouquet above her heart. She later gave Rosita the bouquet as a gift.

'Do you really talk to the spirits?' Renatta asked, and Rosita replied that all people could talk to the spirits, as long as they believed in them.

'But remember,' she added, 'not all spirits tell you the truth.'

Nothing more was said on the subject for a long while. Doña Panchita had given Rosita a small bust of the Virgin of the Clouds as a house-warming present. The local carpenter built a little shelf for her and helped her hook it onto the wall. She had her first shrine in the city.

The other side of summer showed its sultry face and winter set in, warning people to wrap themselves in woollens to protect against the damp and the pernicious cold. To combat the chill, Rosita spent her evenings making floral curtains and new covers for the chairs to match her bedspread. She covered up the most stubborn stains on the walls with some paper flowers the local priest had discarded. She dusted the fading petals and arranged the rest of the bundle of flowers gracefully in a cracked vase she had dressed with a ribbon, while her mind explored new ways to make her dreams come true and see the children again.

She planned to seduce her children's curiosity and invite them for a holiday soon. Her letters flew to Iquitos with exuberant details of life in the city. Pages charged with the fortitude of her hopes and the hue of her imagination. She told them of the woman who on Sundays sold breakfast during the day in front of her house wearing a polka dot dress and a scarf around her head, then in the evening became a madam with bulky rings on her fingers and a flowing satin blouse. She had a transparent eye with which she could see into the future aided by a bunch of fascinating cards. And then there was the man with the ears of a cat and the gargling voice, who every morning turned into a clock and woke everyone up with a basketful of fresh bonito and a chime. Oh, and the swarms of men on their way to the soccer matches who, together, looked like wobbling, confused centipedes, and the feverish roars of the goals, and the agitation of the fans.

After her recovery Rosita returned to the factory and at night she took in ironing for Doña Panchita who did laundry for other people. When she had folded the last towel of the pile, and stored her coal iron in the kitchen, she would sit down and write to the children, making sure her sentences were clear and her description bright. Caught by her emotions she would allow her heart to travel to the other side of the mountains, where the breeze carried the scent of ripe bananas, the perfume of voluptuous love, and the turbulence of the mother river. Then she would carefully fold her letters and go to bed embraced by the gentleness of her feelings.

Time, as it always does, gradually melted the frozen armour that had grown around her heart and the sun filtered inside her soul to fertilise the seeds of a new beginning. For a while. Martin Lozano saw her sporadically on Saturday afternoons. They would meet for tea and he would fall victim to her charm and stories about the idiosyncrasies of the people on her block. She knew he was a married man and felt she had no business in his life. Not until he cleared himself of his 'doomed relationship', as he had described it. She would not pursue the mistress alternative, she had not come to Lima for that. For that very same reason she would not allow him to visit her at home, except for one time when he brought her a beautiful decanter of gold- and blue-rimmed crystal that she always kept locked in the glass cabinet where she also kept vermouth for special occasions. One day their meetings ended and she didn't see him again. Not until many years later, when I too met him.

One spring Saturday as she was on her way back from the factory she ran into Lucio, the charming photographer she had met at the miners' demonstrations in town, the one Lisa had forecast as a 'bad omen'. It was a cheerful afternoon, when the sun shone eagerly through the clouds and cast an auspicious spark on the town, and everybody smiled. Lucio was not taking many photographs now, he explained, but was involved in a business with a good friend. They went to the colonial park and sat on a marble bench where they chatted about life and their plans. He had the use of a car and perhaps, if she wished, she could come for a ride. Rosita glanced at him with glee for she felt that this man was the bearer of a new force in her life.

The next Sunday they drove along the coast, checking out the gardens in the rich mansions, the crowded beaches and the stars at night. Later they ate fried fish with onion salsa in a bar, and enjoyed the romantic boleros and practised new mambo steps, and soon his overpowering charm conquered her heart. She confessed to him that she had not been able to bring her children with her to Lima, but she would soon be able to do it, when she managed to save enough money to buy a shop. 'That's a wonderful idea,' he said. Not far from her place there was a little shop that might soon be available, it was just around the block near the markets. She wanted to take it when the old barber moved out. The owner said he was willing to let it be converted into a grocer shop. Perhaps she could start a new business all of her own. Or perhaps with a partner? Lucio was impressed by her ability to articulate her projects and enterprising plans. He had a flair for making her feel good and attractive. His admiration of her convictions, his soft talk and impeccable appearance erased any possibility of doubt. Soon she confided her feelings to Doña Panchita.

'A woman should have a partner, my dear,' said the old lady. 'If you feel you can trust him then why not.'

Lucio declared his love with champagne, two guitars and a love serenade, and asked her to marry him. She was glowing again, with a newly enamoured heart that was aching to be accepted. Besides, living with a partner would help her solidify her plans.

'Two people can build a castle together faster,' she told Lisa.

'And one individual can topple the other's castle,' Lisa replied.

Her warning persuaded Rosita to remember the flower bouquet that Lola had given her after the carnival pageant, which she had dried carefully and kept wrapped in cellophane next to the Virgin.

'It is gift of good faith for you to meet a man,' Lola had said. But Renatta had warned, 'Be careful. A bouquet from Lord Momo might bring a Romeo from hell.'

More than a year had passed and Rosita had stopped seeing Mr Lozano. She had to give herself another chance. Lucio made her laugh, had a way with words and was good at meeting people, features she perceived as good for business. On top of that he was a talented dancer. The day she met his family she became much more confident about her decision. But she was surprised to discover there was no large family to be fed, and they were not as poor as he had described them the first time they met. His mother was a sweet old lady with an affectionate attitude and tender gaze who promised to teach her all the secrets of Lima's cuisine. His sister was a nurse engaged to a doctor, and his brother had a good job with the telephone company. Well, perhaps he was just trying to be poetic, she thought.

Rosita's marriage to Don Ramon had been an agreement between him and her family only, so there was no need to go through a divorce. This meant that Rosita and Lucio could marry immediately. The wedding took place with restrained pomp because Rosita saw no sense in a huge ceremony and expensive celebrations when she had such tight controls on her budget. 'What's the point of showing off? We have to live within our means.' Lucio was not too pleased, but because he did not have much to contribute to the party he agreed reluctantly.

On the day he placed the ring on her finger he whispered a string of eternal promises and Rosita felt drunk with love. That night a new seed was planted in my mother's womb. It was my brother Luis, who nine months later became the embodiment of unrestrained happiness in her life.

Business with Lucio's partner did not last long and soon he began to do small jobs wherever he found them, and whenever he had the disposition to look for them. He complained that 'life was against him'. At first, Rosita tried hard to ignore the emerging character of her new husband: his idle and unconcerned attitude for a solid future, his reliance on friends and associates, and his constant unreliability. He had convinced her that the corner shop would be a failed enterprise because that was a business for Asians. Besides, he preferred his wife to stay at home while he provided for the family, although his ideals dissolved in his unsuccessful attempts to find work. But Rosita managed to keep her job at the factory and saved as much as she could until a few days before the birth of her new son.

Whenever she discussed the weakness of his attitudes Lucio would storm out and slam the door. In turn, he would accuse her about her past, and then she would cloak herself in her armour and recede into her own silence. She began to lose her self-confidence. At night she lit candles on her shrine and invoked the spirit of her mother to help her. A new sense of shame began to form somewhere inside her, a renewed guilt for having been so gullible, so trusting.

After she put the baby to sleep at night and darkness became her only companion, she would break into sobs. She saw how the new ground she had built for herself was beginning to move away from under her. To hide her anguish she always smiled a dry smile in public, keeping her disappointments to herself. However, the neighbours knew, for it was difficult to keep too many secrets between thin walls. Her fate had to change, she kept repeating to herself as she fed baby Luis with milk and barley water from a bottle, for she had little milk herself.

To avoid her silent recriminations Lucio began to stay out most nights, and when he came home he was often drunk, slurring accusations if she dared to look him in the eye. One evening she realised that money from her tin was decreasing and she confronted him. Well, that did it. The glint and glitter of the early days was transformed into aggression. Hidden behind the jolly laughter of their courtship lay a dark monster that appeared in the haze of alcohol. He felt betrayed, he often yelled, because despite his European heritage 'life had not afforded him his rightful place'. He lashed out at the world, attacking those who would not pamper him or soothe his frustrations. The relationship was rapidly disintegrating but Rosita felt powerless, for she was terrified of yet another failure. Amid the looming crisis she had a dream.

She was blindfolded, walking through a lively forest. The trees handed her fruits to eat and parakeets sat on her shoulder. Some of the fruit was exquisite and some made her feel light-headed, but some made her ill. In the distance, a snowy peak stood like a silent sentinel protecting the pastures of all life. Suddenly, a pack of wolves ran towards her. The earth trembled and the trees swayed frenetically, dropping their fruit to the ground. The wolves ran faster and faster, until they passed her. Only one touched her. A red wolf tore the blindfold off her face and stared into her eyes. She stood still, first frozen by fear but then mesmerised by the majestic animal, in whose eyes she saw the depth of her own life. The sky darkened, the birds fluttered away in terror and a bolt of lightning rent the sky. She felt her whole body split open, and, letting out a huge wail, she collapsed in pain.

When she woke up, the Blue Cat was standing by her side. This time its face was not threatening. It had a gold collar around its neck and it looked wise and supportive. The cat signalled her to follow, leading the way in his own feline rhythm, as one who crosses the door of time without fear. It led her all the way up the mountain with the white peak bathed by the light, where a temple stood. She looked at her body and palpated it with her trembling hands, convincing herself she was still in one piece. Her hair was shorter with silver glints, her face bore many creases and her skin felt dry. She was as old as time. A sense of jubilation sat in her heart for she felt that she was being guided. She placed both her arms on the leafy ground to help herself up and followed her spirit guide. And as she did so, she found herself in her room, in the same position, ready to get out of bed. A new feeling of vigour had set inside her. The roar of the wild cat was alive in her heart, and she, with tears in her eyes, bowed to the spirit of her mother. And the Blue Cat. Mama had been given back her memories and had been empowered again.

The next day, when Lucio began to abuse her, threatening her with more violence, she hit him with the string of garlic from behind the door and screamed so loudly that a passerby kicked the door open and pulled him out of the house. The former photographer was so stunned that he attempted to strike back, but when he saw the tall stranger looking down at him, he scurried away like a scared mouse. Soon Rosita filed for divorce and vowed never to trust another man. She decided to go back to her original name, Rosa. She had grown up, and the diminutive did not suit her anymore.

THE ESSENCE OF DREAMS

A STRANGE CLOUD had set firmly above the little adobe house in the bohemian neighbourhood, as if an alien spell had been cast on Rosa. 'I can see a threatening shadow outside the door, my dear cousin,' she wrote to Lisa, also thanking her for a basket of fruit, smoked fish and wild pig she had sent from the country. Besides that one admission of the way she felt and her forlorn anxieties, she spoke to no one of her tragedies. Rosa wanted to cope on her own without spreading her misery around. Despite the neighbours' inquisitiveness and penchant for interfering, the fiasco with Lucio soon receded into oblivion. His name was never mentioned again in conversation and his jokes were never repeated.

She stored all her floral dresses, bright beads, and earrings with dangling parrots and painted daisies that she had worn the previous summer. She packed her autumn hats and silk scarfs in round boxes and placed them under the bed behind her suitcases. Finally, she put all the photographs and mementos of their romantic episodes that she had managed to save from his drunken fits in a shoe box, sealed it with Scotch tape and pushed it under a pile of old linen at the bottom of the wardrobe.

When this chapter of her life was finally closed she soaked herself in a bath of salt and lemon grass to renew her spirit, and burnt a ball of frankincense in every corner of the house to prevent ill omens, just in case Lucio's anger turned into bad luck for his son. From then on she wore plain cotton frocks mainly in beige and cream, and tied her hair up above her crown in a ponytail. Gone also were the tight corsets, red lipstick, the sculpting belts and the high heels with the straps around her ankles. Instead she wore espadrilles or flat rubber shoes and used pastel pink on her lips. The women in the neighbourhood watched her transformation with awe and left her alone for a while, concluding that nothing heals more effectively than time. Weeks and months streamed past her door but Rosa gave no sign of wanting to abandon her monastic life.

Mambo fever had besieged the early fifties and the world bowed to the passion and popularity of Mexican movies, stars of which had made it to Hollywood. Every country had a queen and king of mambo, and people began to sway their hips frenetically, double step and kick their feet. In the block where drums and guitars were always playing, Lola and Renatta tried hard to get Rosa to join the mambo line and represent the locals in a contest. She had always been a good dancer and the locals knew it, for she had taught many of them to bounce their hips and cross their feet in rhythmical animation to dance the Brazilian samba.

When Rosa's twenty-seventh birthday arrived, Lola bought her a session with a coca leaf reader as a present to perk her up. The coca leaf reader was a country woman who had been instructed to sketch a rosy landscape for her. When both women arrived to see Rosa, she pulled out a couple of stools from under the table for her guests, poured two glasses of vermouth from her favourite decanter and played the role of perfect hostess. The coca leaf reader produced a few dry leaves from her pouch, and instead of chewing them, as most peasant women did to get high and wise, she asked for a metal bowl in which to burn them.

'The luck is read in the smoke,' she said. With her eyes fixed on the smouldering leaves, she told Rosa that the fog in her life was due to evaporate and that light was on its way. Well, that was some news, Rosa teased her inner self. 'But for it to enter your life,' continued the reader, 'you have to see it first in your heart.' She added that there was a man waiting for her on the other side of the light who would be 'for life'. Rosa burst out laughing. Lola preferred not to interpret the reaction as a mockery and poured herself another drink. If nothing else, the reader had managed to crack the thick shell she had built around herself.

That night, as Rosa's guests ate the birthday cake and toasted her happiness forever after, Doña Panchita suggested that she tone down her prayers to the Virgin of the Clouds, 'Perhaps all that fog is doing you harm, my child.' Rosa told her she had not prayed for a while, although she still lit candles for her children. 'What if we get you another saint to soothe your heart?' the black elder said, promising she would look into it.

The sun appeared once more to cast its pastel glow on the city, then the leaves fell again and new buds flourished – and all this time Rosa Lujan zipped her life up. She had left the box factory because the fumes made her ill and had started to work in a winery. After hours she helped the seamstress from across the road to cut and draw frock patterns, while at night she continued her casual ironing for Doña Panchita. She was forever looking for people to mind her toddler. He was a hyperactive child who got into trouble more often than not, and refused to eat. Once a week she took him to his grandmother, who often helped because she was familiar with the behaviour patterns Luis had inherited from his father and because she had a great deal of affection for Rosa. Sometimes Doña Panchita let Luis sit in a large wooden box under the washing table while she worked, and even the corner grocer helped to take care of him, letting him spread glue and marmalade over his face and crawl behind the counter.

Meanwhile, the pages of the calendar on Rosa's wall were torn off one by one as the seasons waltzed past her life without asking her for a dance. Until one day, the glossy poster with the numbered sheets fell off the wall with a thud. So did the vase with paper flowers on the dresser and the photographs of the children and of her father. The effigies on her shrine, which had been left abandoned for a while, tumbled down and the pots and pans in the kitchen rattled. She had never been shaken by an earthquake. She had experienced torrential storms, and witnessed floods and animal stampedes, but she had never seen the earth shake under her feet and the walls wave. The blow jolted even the marrow of her bones, forcing her to reflect on the direction of her life.

All the people on the block stood under their door frames, barefoot, crying madly and praying, surrendering totally to the moods of Nature. And then the trembling stopped. The elders quickly checked if anyone had been injured and brought out bottles of orange blossom water, tins of bicarbonate of soda and brandy to help people grieve freely. Doña Panchita realised that it had been Rosa's first major experience with this earthly phenomenon, so she asked Lola to keep her company that night. 'We are all here to help,' Lola had said as Rosa wept deeply, Luis clasped against her hip.

Tucked up in bed under flannel sheets and woollen shawls, hands across their chests, they whispered to each other soothing words and things that mattered to them in life. The tremor had unleashed a torrent of pain and anxiety in both women that they had carried for years. It had revived old memories that hurt. Lola told Rosa that her life had not been easy, that her father had abused all her sisters, and that her mother had not had the courage to ask him to leave because she had fallen under his spell. But on a day when there was an earthquake, Doña Panchita had mustered the courage to whack the man out of the house with a broom, and sweep him away forever. 'Did you know that earth tremors announce big changes?' Lola asked. Rosa shook her head.

The men in Lola's life had victimised her, assaulted her and given her only children and tribulations. It was not that she did not love her children, but it would be nice if she received some financial support too. And her beauty title, well, that had not opened any respectable doors, only of vehicles in which salivating men tried to grope her in the darkness. It was a woman's lot to endure adversity, Lola grunted, and one had to learn to handle it. Rosa listened with tears in her eyes. The young mulatta propped herself up, poured herself a drink and suggested that Rosa face life always with a smile. 'You see, my friend,' Lola said, 'misfortune leaves your home soon if you serve it with a happy face.'

Later that night, as Rosa fell asleep on a pillow soaked with her tears, her dreams took hold and the pillow expanded into a cloud of feathers on which she rode back to the Amazon forest, to her rainbow and the ascending sun.

Not far from Rosa's house lived a handsome elderly man with a heavy Italian accent, deep blue eyes and a few silver wisps on his head. Every time he met Rosa at the corner bakery, the Italian never failed to greet her with a courteous bow and a chivalrous smile. Rosa liked him and was pleased by the elegance of his manner, and had gone so far as to notice an attractive dimple on his chin that reminded her of Kirk Douglas. Despite the vigour in his voice when he placed his 'Four-hot-rolls-make-sure-they-are-fresh' order with the baker, the spark of his laughter spread gentleness. His house was close to the colonial park where Rosa took Luis most afternoons. Standing outside his door there was always a group of handsome young men chatting and laughing, and whistling at pretty girls as they walked past, stirring all eyes with their hips. Sometimes the young men argued politics loudly, and soccer even more loudly; sometimes a couple of them stood quietly after sunset, one leg against the wall, holding a cigarette in one hand and a drink in the other.

One stood out. His name was Alberto Bresciani Jnr, although some knew him as Pepin. He was tall, subdued and always well groomed, with an air of uncomplicated maturity that often saw him mediating disputes amongst his brothers. People liked him because he was always in a good mood, despite the occasional grunt or growl when his brothers teased him about his private affairs. A thin moustache, which he combed carefully every morning, was his mark of elegance. A birthmark on his face reminded him he was not perfect. To all women he was truly handsome and people who knew his family claimed he was the spitting image of his father, the man of the hot bread rolls and the dimpled chin, except that he was darker and his eyes were chestnut brown.

The locals called Alberto's family the 'cinnamon and *caffè latte*' family because of their varying perceptions of the skin tone of their mother, Mrs Bresciani, a mulatta of German extraction who had died long ago. While some of her children alluded to the fairness of her skin, others liked to link her more closely to the heavily scented cinnamon stick.

There were twelve Bresciani children still alive, at least of the official family, for it was known in discreet circles that Alberto Bresciani Snr had a large family spread across the city. Most of his children were already married with several children of their own, while others had only children, no husbands, and two or three lived in concubine arrangements, which were considered as valid as marriages when there was a pending divorce. Out of all of them, two were single and very eligible. One was the youngest and most animated. He was also the tallest, at over 190 centimetres. That was tall in a mestizo country, but he was still young and people believed he would keep growing.

The other was Alberto Jnr, the most reserved and cool-headed one when it came to flirting games. His sisters worried about him, for it was unusual to see a vigorous and virile man in his early thirties without a steady girlfriend. The women preferred not to assume anything, for fear that any assumption could become real. His brothers thought he had been born 'without a screw in the brain'.

But Alberto did not care what they thought. He felt that women were a hassle if you went out with them only to prove your masculinity. He was waiting for the right moment and for the right woman. Somehow he felt the keeper of his heart's treasure had already appeared, although she was not an easy catch.

He had noticed her over a year ago, strolling across the park with friends. One day he caught her with her gaze fixed on the lake and he thought she was having a chat with some ghost in the water, because there was nothing on the lake except a few ducklings. When she lifted her head their eyes met and he became embarrassed; he bowed his head and smiled politely. She picked herself up, turned around and left the spot, somehow mortified. From then on he began to visit his father more often, always looking for the woman with her hair in a ponytail, who despite her serious disposition had a magnetic appeal for him.

One day as Alberto headed home with his younger brother, she appeared from around the corner. His brother greeted her politely; she smiled back curtly and walked faster. He searched his mind, remembering an episode his brother had shared with him.

'You have no idea, man! I plucked a pushy little bastard out of this poor, gorgeous woman's house,' the younger brother had boasted.

'Why do you have to meddle in married people's affairs?' Alberto asked.

'But you have no idea. He was torturing her,' his brother argued.

'So what are you going to do now?'

'Well, what do you think? I am not going to introduce her to *you*!'

Alberto knew immediately that the woman with the ponytail was the same woman with the 'pushy little bastard' of a husband, or a lover. He also knew that his brother had tried unsuccessfully to befriend the woman. Apart from a half smile of appreciation she had not let him past her door. 'She is such an ingrate!' his brother had grumbled. Rosa's image slowly disappeared in the distance and the younger brother brought up the episode: 'Do you remember the woman who –'

'Yes, I can imagine,' growled Alberto, 'you don't have to give me the details.'

Rosa also remembered the scene by the lake and had noticed Alberto Jnr every time she walked past his father's house. From Lola, who had often spoken of the eligible Bresciani bachelors, she knew that the boys did not live with Don Alberto but only came to visit and do business with him. The old man had a distribution and transport business which he ran from home. Some of his sons shared the business with him and Alberto Jnr was one of them. Rosa had noticed how Alberto stood still every time she walked past the house. She recognised him from a distance, the way he held his poise and blew smoke rings in the air. With Lola she had joked once, 'He thinks he is Clark Gable.' 'But he is also polite,' she had added. She had noticed the dimple on his chin, the way he filed his nails, and the way he glanced at her from the corner of his eye, with reserve. In the back of her mind she knew he liked her, but in a society where it was tradition to flirt, to court, seduce and compliment women, even if only to reinforce their femininity and make them feel desirable, his attentions were natural.

Rosa was terrified of the feelings sprouting in her heart, like tiny buds that grew bigger every time she looked into his eyes. She was falling victim to her emotions again. One day she caught herself staring at Don Alberto in the bakery, comparing his features with his son's, searching inside the creases around his eyes. Unwilling to betray herself, she stopped walking past the old man's house, and even changed bakeries. Fortunately, wisdom had its ways, and the feelings in her heart burst forth and followed their own course. One day as she was on her way to the shop she met Alberto Jnr standing at the corner and found that her smile had warmed up as she recognised the dimple on his chin.

The night of the earth tremor she had promised Lola to join the girls at a bullfight during the ensuing October festival. Rosa could not refuse the invitation after the moving sermon Lola had offered her about suffering and being part of it and enduring. Although the idea of animals being killed in public made her feel uneasy. 'It is such cruelty,' she said, and Lola thought her friend was a bit goofy because at the time it was the courage of the matador that mattered, not the rights of the animals. Pinched by her curiosity for the bizarre, and because bullfights were part of the city's tradition, Rosa decided to go and see for herself.

October was Lima's favourite month. It was the time when the capital celebrated its traditions and people truly bared their inner selves. Apart from the matador's fiesta, the main feature was a religious festival. The whole city dressed in purple, the colour of sin and absolution; the air was congested with the scent of frankincense; and city shoppers stuffed themselves with shortbread iced with honey, and yam donuts swimming in molasses. Everyone went to see the matadors, although the women wept if they became attached to the bull because of a famous Spanish movie, *The Boy and the Bull*, which revealed that bulls had feelings too. But never mind the tears, they also cheered '*Ole!*' as the little man in the fitted suit and glimmering tights chased the bull dizzy, pulled the dagger and plunged it into the animal.

Renatta, who was flirting with another of the Bresciani boys in a roundabout way, organised tickets to the premier bullfight session. All the women brought their best dresses out of the wardrobe. It was customary to show off at the Plaza de Toros, where all misses and mistresses, spinsters, matrons and widows became ladies of glamour and strutted about with grace on stiletto heels and in cocktail frocks, regardless of the mayhem, the animal stench and the dust.

At home, Alberto Bresciani Jnr brushed his suit with care and made sure no stubborn fluff stayed on the wide lapels. He polished his belt and filed his nails smoothly before he shined his hair with brilliantine, pushing it back in slick fashion. He looked at himself in the mirror, fixed the knot of his tie and concluded that he was pleased. The next thing to do was be a true gentleman, he said to himself. His mother had always said that good relationships follow good manners, and he had great respect for the wisdom of his mama.

She had been gone now for so many years, more than he wanted to remember. And since she had gone he had longed for the love of a woman, but not just any woman, he once said to me. It had to be the right one.

On this October Sunday it would be the first time Alberto would call on Cupid in an affair of the heart. He wished he could awaken the god of love in his heart and let it prick Rosa with the arrow of his own passion. He was nervous as he placed his felt hat on his head and fixed a silk scarf in the breast pocket of his jacket. All he had to do was light a cigarette, blow rings in the air and look at the smouldering ashes, that would give him support. He hoped the lady of his heart would give him a hint of some sort, a leading clue, an indication that she was not uncomfortable with him. That was all he needed to know. The rest would come later. He buttoned his double-breasted jacket, jiggled the knot of his tie again, and left. '*Que será, será,*' he said. Whatever will be, will be.

At the plaza, Renatta introduced the couple with a conspiratorial smile. In the sky the love gods debated with each other about Alberto's suitability. Under the glow of a reluctant sun, my parents' eyes met and their souls recognised each other, never mind the gods above. Soon, a raging bull appeared in the ring, snorting and pawing, and the public roared '*Olé!*' The small man dressed in glittery tights stared at the powerful black beast carrying a death sentence in his eyes, and the beast returned the stare with pride, pawing the sand with its hooves again, assessing the intention and the strategy of his rival.

Rosa sat next to Alberto, her heart locked in a strange feeling, and her eyes glued to the spectacle. She watched, half horrified and half mesmerised by her own curiosity, making sure she had a handkerchief close to hand in case her guts betrayed her and she had to run to the toilet. It was an unfair match, she told Alberto later. The matador stood in the middle of the ring and opened his chest to the crowd's cheers. With glamour and glitter he boasted his courage in his bright attire and offered his prey to a beautiful woman, as in

Roman times. Alberto was far more interested in watching Rosa, relishing with his eyes the softness of the back of her neck and the few strands of hair that rebelliously escaped the band intended to hold it in place.

The crowd continued to egg on the matador and he prepared himself for the kill. '*Olé!*' and a wave of dust arose from the ring; Rosa covered her eyes. In a few minutes the jet black animal was losing his wits, bedazzled by the flowing and entwining cape, entranced by the colour red and mortally wounded by a dagger. Slowly he wobbled his way around, as if begging for compassion, and the matador puffed out his chest again. '*Olé!*' The animal hit the ground and his life escaped forever, painting the dust on the ground scarlet. '*Olé!*' cheered the crowd.

Unable to swallow the scene Rosa ran past Alberto and left the ring to get some fresh air and dab the tears from her eyes. Alberto watched her, pleased. He liked a woman who did not approve of this 'circus' and he followed her outside. As he offered her a drink to soothe her nerves he told her that he had never enjoyed bullfights either, not so much because of his solidarity with bulls, but because he did not like Spaniards anyway. Rosa was impressed with his honesty. Not many men would say that they objected of the most macho of all games, unless they wanted to have their testosterone levels checked. It was obvious Alberto did not live off people's approval.

From that day on a genuine friendship sprouted; Rosa felt safe and secure, protected by the pillar of his kindness and the quality of his earthiness. Time allowed their hearts to be soothed by strolls across the park, movie matinees, Italian ice creams and Rosa's tales of dancing piranhas, which made Alberto chuckle but which he never believed. My father always said that these stories were the essence of my mother's dreams and without them she could not exist, so he celebrated them when he could and was in the mood. After months of strolls along every promenade and boulevard in town, and when the gods in the firmament finally agreed, Rosa Lujan unlocked the door of her heart and let a new man into her life. When it happened,

Alberto Bresciani Jnr became the happiest man on earth, and loaded with the best of intentions and a suitcase, he moved in, reconstructed her palace, and never left.

Rosa had made it categorically clear that she would not let anybody scoop her out of her little house until she had the means to buy a new one. Only its destruction by an earthquake would force her out, and that was a rare possibility because, despite their frail appearance, most houses in the area had been built on solid foundations and with reinforced frames. Rather than arguing, Alberto began, with her assistance, to think of ways to stretch the house a bit. A new roof went up, a bigger skylight was installed, and several coats of paint gave Alberto the chance to get rid of old posters and calendars, and dusty paper flowers.

Living close to his father was convenient for Alberto because of his involvement in the old man's business. The company transported luxury items, such as white goods and top-of-the-range foodstuffs from large warehouses to the wealthy and to department stores. Alberto did not drive the trucks but travelled on board to make sure all the goods reached the right destinations and did not end up in some illegal market or in his workers' homes.

Rosa said goodbye to the winery and took up dressmaking with the seamstress across the road. When she was not tightening up buttons, sewing hems and finishing frocks, she was selling duty-free goods that she got from Iquitos, or running raffles. In the afternoon, as she swapped one task for another, she would hear Don Alberto in the distance, dragging his heavy feet along the kerb, carrying his paper bag of hot rolls and a smile filled with good intentions. Then she would quickly put the kettle on the stove, and set the table with fresh pineapple marmalade and vanilla cake, which she had learned to make from Lucio's mother, to whom she took Luis to visit every week.

Her father-in-law was always happy to see her, always keen for a mug of black coffee and a bit of chitchat; he particularly liked to hear her tales about flying frogs and ghost ships. Unlike his son, he was happy to believe her, for in his past he had seen a lot of strange things in Lima.

Rosa enjoyed the company of the old Italian immigrant, always asking details about his beginnings, boosting his pride in his achievements, and making sure he was well fed. 'Would you like some more, Don Alberto? Otherwise your beautiful eyes will lose their glow and turn dull. And we don't want that, do we?' she'd say as she placed on his plate one more roll spread thickly with layers of marmalade or fried sweet potatoes, made to the recipe of Dorita, Alberto Jnr's youngest and favourite sister.

Dorita was the only sister-in-law who had welcomed Rosa into the family. She was not legally her sister-in-law, for Alberto and Rosa were not married but were living together on a trial basis. Just in case. The other sisters kept their distance, wondering what savage bug had pricked Alberto's reason to make him fall in love with a woman with a mysterious past, Renatta had told Lola that the sisters were sure Rosa had given Alberto a dose of *chamico*, a herbal potion known for its seductive qualities and not sold in the markets. 'Why should I care?' Rosa told Renatta when she next saw her, 'they certainly don't pay my bills.' But she had developed a genuine affection for Dorita and admired her spontaneity and generosity. The young woman lived up the road from her, in an old *quinta*, a row of workers' houses where several families shared the toilet and shower. Sometimes one could hear their yelling and swearing for miles, when a mischievous brat cut the water off from the outside, forcing an unsuspecting bather to come out soaped up and in the raw.

Dorita, who later became my most beloved aunt, was a charmer of grand style. An individual who walked the path of her fate with one hand pointing to the ground and the other to the sky, like a magician. She was forever creating miracles to make ends meet and had an incredible ability to sweet-talk most debt collectors. Her vivacious character and oozing optimism always got her out of trouble. She preferred to keep her sorrows to herself, and of these she had many, for she had a child and no partner.

When her mother died she was still very young so she had brought herself up the best way she could. As a child she was often found on the roof gazing across the haze of the city and meowing with stray cats. Sometimes she would disappear for hours, only to be found in her sisters' wardrobe hidden under their clothes, all made up but with nowhere to go. She became used to brushing a more colourful world across the canvas of her life and learned to relish the few crumbs that the world had to offer.

It was in her humble kitchen of adobe bricks covered with a rough coat of lime, bathed by a tenuous light filtering from the roof, and with the Great Caruso singing in the background, that Dorita told us the story of our Bresciani roots. Like my mother, I fell entranced with the passion in her voice as I helped her peel sweet potatoes, watching the sinuous sway of her hips as she imitated the people of the golden era. Her husky voice transformed the dim room into the narrow cobblestone streets of the past, her feelings saturated in colonial traditions, echoing the poise and pomp of the legendary dames. She mimicked the ladies with their elaborate hairdos and their black maids, strolling around the ports, scrutinising eligible suitors arriving from distant territories.

It had all begun in the early years of the twentieth century in Latin America. An air of mystery still reigned in the fertile and exotic land, alluring foreigners with bountiful opportunities. People from Europe had heard all kind of stories about rivers that spoke in ambiguous tongues, large blue cats that possessed maidens, virgins who flew up into the sky, unexplored golden cities, and, most importantly, about the naive nature of local communities that welcomed foreigners with open arms. Large ships crammed with adventurers docked at ports all around the continent, carrying the cravings of young and old willing to seed their dreams in the wombs of exuberant and receptive lands. My grandfather, Alberto Bresciani Snr, was on board of one of those ships, a carrier from Genoa loaded with hopes and eager aspirations of the romantic kind. At that time, Lima was still very much a Spanish colony, despite its eighty years of independence. The Spanish conquistadors had established the city 400 years earlier as a trading port from where they shipped precious jewels and gold artifacts they had usurped from the Incas in order to subsidise European wars. The city was irrigated by two rivers, making the spot a prosperous valley nestled between the Pacific and the Andean mountain range.

In North America, colonisation had produced its own social and political hybrid without much racial integration, but in the south, evolution had followed another loop and acquired a different colour. The Spanish and Portuguese had fathered a new creole race called the mestizo: a blend of indigenous and Hispanic, with many variations including African, Asian and other European mixes. Illegitimate children proliferated in every corner where new settlers released their passions, harvesting new breeds and seeding the fruits of confused identities. The spell foreigners held over the psyche of the local population was said to correspond to an ancient Inca story told by the mighty Pachacutec, the most famous Inca of the empire. He had forecast that one day Wiracocha, the creator god, would return to bring with him the elixir of eternity. When the ruffed conquistadors made their sudden entrance into Inca territory, dressed in shining armour, indigenous priests became the victims of their own expectations and made the biggest mistake of all time. They trusted them.

The conquistadors had followed a path to the Americas that had been traced by an earlier Genoese, Christopher Columbus. They would be followed by later generations in search for the same magic which, they hoped, would make their hearts glow and their coffers swell. The explorers who made it to South America were the most adventurous and macho at heart, we were told, but I guess this is a matter of opinion. If one thing is true, it is that these men had been seduced by the scent of jungle aphrodisiacs, and were driven by lust for power and thirst for adventure. Only a few had worthy ideals and good intentions.

As a young man, Alberto Bresciani Snr had heard the call from the other side of the seas, a haunting melody like the hum of a marine maiden. There, watching from the shores of his home town, Genoa, dangling his legs above the same water that had seen great explorers depart, Alberto pondered his future. He sniffed the scent of maiden fertility on the wind and sensed the vibrations of his wild desires. He had to make a move, leave the old rules behind, the stiff orders and the limitations of a continent in trouble. He would not have to miss his homeland, he thought, for he could always take a handful of soil with him and read in it the memories of what had been. After he had wrestled with the guilt of leaving his mother, a large ship bound for South America stopped briefly on his shores. Loaded with enterprising schemes and a hole in his pocket, he boarded the vessel that was to take him across the Atlantic, to the land that basked in the golden glow that made most foreigners happy, or so he had heard. For weeks, he and a bunch of other defiant boys travelled across a restless sea towards the place where the sun ruled strong, the winds spoke in roaring echoes, and the women smelled of ripe bananas and fresh oysters.

Lima was waiting for him on the other side, dressed in its colonial attire of baroque architecture and distinguished flavour. Its soul sheltered in a veil of elegance and intrigue, calmly watching the afternoon sunset. It was a place that spoke of forbidden love and hidden pleasures. With its coquettish promenades and accentuated scents it was famous for providing foreigners with genuine opportunities for love. Legend has it that the beauty of the city was a gift from one of the viceroys to his forever-beloved mistress *La Perricholi*. She was a famous and accomplished singer, a lady of legendary beauty whom he truly worshipped but could never marry because she was of a different social caste, and he was already married anyway. It was rumoured that the viceroy had made his wife sick on the pretext of taking her back to Spain and leaving her there for an unlimited time while he enjoyed the affections of his mistress. As an expression of his flaming infatuation, which the population thanked forever, he embellished the parks and promenades with such romantic extravagance that for a while the city became the setting for the one thousand and one nights of passion in Peru.

Balconies of the finest timbers, handcrafted by the best tradesmen in Europe, adorned the city's main streets. Lavish sculptures in marble and alabaster adorned the broad avenues, lit at night by handsome lantern posts. Ornate portals, parks with wrought-iron gates, Venuses and Dianas, bridges and rivulets, and bronze statues of the nature gods and winged cherubs complemented the lovers' nest. Residents were proud of the city and artists were inspired to write poetry of love and splendour. In the afternoons, just before sunset, enamoured couples could be seen strolling along the boulevards, seduced by the melodies of string quartets and the aroma of fresh jasmine, frangipani and cinnamon.

One Friday afternoon a crowded ship loaded with young Italians and repressed hormonal anxieties docked in Callao, the port at the edge of the city. The area was swamped by entrepreneurs, busy bees and a row of persuasive vendors who sold everything from women's favours to aphrodisiacs and potions to heal any condition, including nostalgia. Alberto Bresciani Snr pinched his arm to confirm he was not dreaming and, carrying a small suitcase that contained his whole life, he stepped onto his new country, half excited and half sick. All the toing-and-froing in his berth had rattled his insides. Once on land he invoked the name of his God and made the sign of the cross, thanking Him for the opportunity to be in a new land. Only God knows what is to become of me, he thought, and moved on. He had promised himself he would never regret the trip for it had been the answer to the deep restlessness he had always felt in his heart, a craving for the unknown and the uncertain.

He looked around, sighed with relief and breathed in the damp air. Callao was covered in afternoon fog and Alberto's senses were immediately hit by poignant smells and a deep feeling of melancholy. The mood was grey and the looks on the people's faces sorrowful and deeply sanctimonious. He learned that the city had just recovered from a killer bug which had wiped out nearly a third of the population. 'It was the wrath of God,' people said, explaining that the Almighty needed to be appeased. The mysterious bug was finally stopped with a humble leaf in the shape of a scythe which a poor boy had discovered by the side of a tomb in the town's cemetery. The leaf contained an antidote to kill the virus, and one simple infusion did what ordinary medicine had failed to do. The herb became known as *La Redentora*, or The Redeemer.

'Fancy finding one's medicine in the house of the dead,' mused Alberto after he listened to the story, sipping his first drink, a shot of the local white brandy known as *pisco*. Wanting to reassure himself he had not made a mistake by coming to this place, Alberto headed down into the city with the same determination he had used to pack his bags, knowing full well that he could not turn back even if he wanted to. Soon he found himself alone on the cobbled streets, watching the sun being swallowed by the evening shadows as they marched across the sky. He bent down, picked up a small pebble and put it in his pocket. It was the first stone in the cairn of the Brescianis' Lima story.

The port had a seductive appeal for Alberto so he worked in the area for a while, getting to know the real city, the coquettish soul that moved with audacity and guile. His first job was as a carrier boy, moving bundles on his bare back. He managed to save enough to buy himself a cart pulled by a donkey. That's how he started his own business of transporting goods from the docks to their destinations in town. Later, his carts multiplied and he was able to provide work for the locals, who learned to trust him. In time, he rented an old shed near the barracks as a warehouse, where he sometimes slept. Eventually, mares replaced the donkeys, until engines came to boost and modernise his business.

Although the country had already become a republic with democratic elections, the system was still very much feudal. The people had no option but to elect members of the same conservative force which chronically ousted each other to give the country an apparent feeling of change, though the result was always the same. Sometimes, when corruption mixed with scandal and disgrace, a military leader would play the role of the masses' vindicator and like a true macho he would ride in mounted on a wild horse and storm the palace. Once there he would kick the rulers out, harangue the population with promises of peace and prosperity, and rule in the name of God for a while. Soon power would poison his head, and when the coffers were empty he handed the country to the next anxious politician, in the name of democracy. When new elections were called, the same old candidates would campaign in the name of freedom, and the oligarchy would win again. The wheel of fortune hardly turned, although people continued to spin their complaints round and round.

In such an atmosphere there was a certain class of affluent people seeking the luxury goods that Alberto transported. In particular, those who loved indulgence and feathers of charm: women. My grandfather had no problems providing the goods they desired with slick dexterity and business sensitivity. As the clock ticked on, and the days sauntered past the weeks and danced around the months, a new identity began to grow roots in the heart of young Alberto. Despite the risks of uncertainty he had become comfortable living in a city built on a foundation of deep contrasts. In the silence of his reflections he realised that greed and generosity were twins, for one could not exist without the other, like the two faces of a coin. Every day as he went to work he gave money to a beggar who sat outside his house, and he thanked the universe for sending the man to soften his heart.

In those days, the Catholic Church had a firm grip on the spiritual identity of the population, although Peruvians have always found great pleasure in indulging in the forbidden and the bizarre, giving the Christian rituals a flavour of their own. Alberto loved the madness and mayhem of his new home, the smell of spice in the women's breath and the scent of sanctimonious piety in church. It was a city of entwined emotions, which after dark smouldered in its own lust and at dawn woke up to the prayers of remorseful hearts. Alberto's reputation as a charmer grew, spreading across the after-hours circles like a vigorous grapevine, and his name was heard in the whispers of the night, fused with cries of passion and carnal satisfaction.

One afternoon my father read in the paper a warning against a murderous gang called the Pishtacoes. Three people had been found dead in one week, their bodies sprawled by the edge of the river, their entrails gone and their tongues chopped out. Lima was horrified; police brought out dogs and went for the chase. Luis got sick with *el mal del susto* or the 'evil eye', and Rosa, following Dorita's advice, brought a local shaman to pass an egg around him, as is tradition, to get rid of all negativity. Alberto Jnr was sure the whole thing was a scandal and chased the shaman away, warning Rosa: 'All *brujos* are frauds and need to be cleansed and purified.'

The women packed their fears of the murderers into bundles of lemon grass tied with red ribbons, and placed them under their pillows at night to bless their dreams.

'What does the carnage mean?' asked the press, and the archbishop replied that 'The world is on the threshold of its dark stage, where it will stay for forty years, before we move into the next millennium.' Newspapers multiplied their sales, religious devotion was boosted and Sunday services were packed. The murders had rekindled the city's memory of a series of killings long ago, said to have been perpetrated by the legendary red-headed killer maniac. Rosa wanted to make sense of it all so she went to Dorita's house filled with urgent curiosity. She found Dorita humming a waltz about a doomed love while carefully placing five slices of sweet potatoes in the frying pan, patting them with a long fork and the best of her affections to make them taste better. 'It is all in the feeling,' Dorita often said when people asked her what she did to make her meals taste so good. Rosa unwrapped a tin plate with a cake on it for afternoon tea and quickly pulled up a chair by the kitchen bench.

'Alberto is minding Luis. Please tell me all you can now,' she said with eagerness in her heart.

'It was the era of the blue devil, you know,' explained Dorita, pacing the kitchen floor and fixing her kinky hair under a floral scarf. 'It was the time when the air stunk of putrefying wounds and evil rats roamed freely in town.' Her tone swung between eeriness and theatrical sarcasm.

She explained that it was some time early in the century and a mysterious killer had terrified the population with a string of bizarre murders. He slayed each victim with a careful incision in the shape of the cross, scooped out their heart, chopped it and left the pieces in a tightly wrapped bundle by the side of the cadaver. He would also pluck out the eyes of his prey, as if to protect his own identity. Panic swept the streets. The cardinal was short of words to explain the meaning of the evil deeds and placed a blessed cross in the main square. Suspicion grew that the murders had been conducted by religious fanatics, 'probably acting on behalf of an all-judgmental God'. Indigenous people thought the killer was the ghost of the Inca Atahualpa getting back at the Spanish rulers for having betrayed and killed him despite the astronomical ransom he had paid for his freedom. People in the black quarter held animistic rituals in bombastic fashion, the Catholics prayed, the Indians fed the land with brews and herbs, and the police were at a loss.

It was then that my grandfather, Alberto Snr, had his first brush with the workings of the mystical underworld.

At the insistence of a friend, Alberto Snr had gone to see *La Bruja*, a black sorceress who gave him clues about the murders. She described the killer as a man who had 'fire on his head and was the product of a ghost ship'. Alberto Snr could not help but let out a few guffaws. *La Bruja* was not impressed but did not hold it against him because she realised he was just a foreigner without a clue of the world in which he now lived.

The killer was still on the loose and soon the victims' blood had stained many dark alleys. Tired of scratching their heads and chasing their tails, the police hid their pride in their back pocket and finally approached the *brujas* to ask for help. Within a week the head of a red-haired man was found inside a hessian bag on the steps of the cathedral, and a few days later the eyes of the victims turned up in a similar bundle. The killings stopped from then on, but the rest of the man's body was never found. Subsequent inquiries determined that the head belonged to a mentally disturbed man who had jump overboard from a condemned ship. My grandfather never again mocked the powers he did not understand.

The Pishtacoes disappeared and no one was ever convicted. A rumour spread that the murders were not due to the Pishtacoes at all, but were carried out by a headless ghost who had turned up fifty years later to complete some unfinished business.

Alberto Jnr finished the repairs of the house, installed a wider skylight, and added more shelves to the kitchen, and they held their first party, with live music and traditional dishes, which carefully excluded hearts on skewers and grilled tripe.

THE COLOUR OF SIN

I WAS BORN on the day my country purged its sins in delirious repentance and for the grace of God's miracles. It was the eighteenth of October, the day of the Purple Christ, the Lord of Miracles. On that day, people genuflected on broken glass and dragged bleeding knees along the floor to exorcise evil from their souls, praying with overt remorse. My mother said it was the day of forgiveness and of festive celebrations because it was the only occasion when sin and mercy danced together in sacred alignment. The day she told me of my birth, she also taught me how to polish the glass cabinet and all the precious trinkets from our past. The cabinet was a beautiful piece of furniture made of walnut and stained glass, which always remained locked and protected from our mischievous attacks.

On its polished shelves, amid glasses and punch bowls and colourful knick-knacks, sat the gold-and-blue decanter from Mr Lozano, and behind it, a little glass box that held a tiny piece of leather. It was my dried-up umbilical cord, which Mama kept as a treasured memento. She said I was born under the spell of a purple sin but not far from the route of salvation. Keeping my dried-up umbilical cord would remind me of this story and keep me in balance.

Mama taught me to see the world with the eyes of my soul

because '*El alma*, the soul,' she said, 'sees into the core of people's intentions.' She recounted the day of my birth with much love in her heart; she always made sure each of us children believed we were 'the apple of her eye', although at times she had some weird ways of showing it.

'On the day of your birth,' she began, 'a few stars were sleeping discreetly, their glow tucked behind silky pillows, wicked dreams unfolding beneath the clouds. The night was thoughtful and melancholic, like the minds of people when they feel remorse. Suddenly, a mischievous spark bounced out of the emptiness. It flashed through the clouds, searching for a being to enter. The little spark darted in and out of the evening shadows, jumping here and there, leaving a glittering trail across the firmament, until it found a place to lie. In a corner of an adobe house a pink droplet burst out of the sea inside my belly and your tiny soul woke to the smell of eucalyptus, vanilla and cinnamon tea, and the reverberations of spirited women.'

As I polished a brass goblet, I pictured the scene on the shiny metal chalice. We were sitting at the table, the same spot where I had been born. My ears were entranced by the rhythm of Mama's voice and my soul drew the shapes of Lola, Renatta, the corner grocer's wife and the midwife standing around the bed in a suburb called La Victoria. They called on Mama to have courage, to hold on a tiny bit longer, patting her forehead with damp towels, pacing across the floor with a touch of uncertainty but proud in the spirit of sisterhood. They huffed and puffed and prayed, and finally they held hands and rattled blessings around the bed. I have them etched on my memory, ponderous women with generous hearts, rubicund smiles and passionate secrets.

My life began in a dimly lit room, in a country about which tales of all sorts are told. Tales of magic and mystery relating to kingdoms believed to have existed long ago, in another space and time, when gods came down from the sun to teach the children to be wise. Kingdoms that Mama said still exist in not too distant universes. As she told the details of my story I saw in the image in the brass goblet that the air in the room turned stuffy, the light became shrouded by darkness and the mood became mysterious. My infant heart shivered in its new surroundings. Shadows moved in slow motion, gradually taking human form. The scent was strange. I smelled anxiety and tenderness in the folds of skin of the large women in the room. Soon I touched the women's fear, it melted into my skin, behind my neck. Then I felt as if my soul wanted to turn around. This world scared me. 'Could I have gone back, Mama?' I asked. And she said, 'No.' She insisted we each came here for one reason. And our task, she stressed, pointing her finger at me, was to find this very reason in our life. 'I am looking for my temple,' she clarified, 'that's why I am here.' So on that October day, my soul entered a new space and my body nearly succumbed to asphyxia.

Wrapped in Alberto's love, Rosa had grown into a more beautiful woman, her gaze was deeper and she bubbled with good spirits. Her soft brown eyes and the dimples on her cheeks had acquired a more profound dimension, which she said was the mark of life's hard knocks. 'As long as they make you beautiful, sweetheart,' Lola enthused, 'never mind the bumps.'

A few hours before my birth, Mama ambled all the way to the corner shop to buy a packet of biscuits and have a glass of Inca Cola, a local drink named in honour of the ancient empire. Smiling a candid smile she dragged her swollen feet into the Takanakas' shop, providers of exotic ointments, flavours, sex potions and cures to relieve ulcers, improve your enchantment abilities and kill cockroaches. This was the same shop Mama had wanted to lease in the past. Now it had become an exotic chamber of curiosities and artifacts, each to satisfy the most demanding cravings of the soul or the flesh, and beyond. Whatever pleased your fancy the new owners sold. The neighbours thought the Takanakas were smart, cunning and subdued. I liked them because they stocked everything we needed and had done extremely well in the time they had been in the country. They had three children and a peculiar accent that gave Spanish a singular reverberation. They were good cooks, and had titillated the tongue of the neighbourhood by introducing an extraordinary taste via a white seasoning powder they sold in small sachets, and which had the rare power of changing the flavours of food.

On this particular day, Mama also needed a packet of special candles for the big purple parade, the procession of the Lord of Miracles, the biggest show of faith in the country, which was attended by at least a million devotees. She had promised to accompany Doña Panchita to the procession. The old black matron had become her guiding light and had instilled in her a new devotion to Christ.

Mama wanted her new baby to be a girl in order to continue her maternal line. After a tribe of boys, she was ready to try anything, even asking for miracles from a new purple god. Never mind the colour as long as he delivered, she thought. We must remember, as Aunt Lisa would point out, 'Christianity has many faces, even in a very Christian world like Peru.'

In the corner shop, Don Takanaka lifted his gaze and stood up from behind the counter, on which he'd been resting his elbows lazily, his mind immersed in his Japanese crossword. Pushing his glasses up from the tip of his nose, he folded away the paper and greeted Mama, 'How is the baby coming?'

'So far so good,' she replied, walking with such difficulty that it was as if she were carrying a baby elephant in her belly; her hand supported her kidneys. She pulled up a stool next to the counter and sprawled her heavy hips on it, and then sighed, 'Oh my God! This one is heavy. May I have the usual please, Don Takanaka?' The Japanese man quickly turned to scan the shelves and served her with his traditional diligence, but his eyes stopped on the calendar.

'Hope this month we have no earthquakes,' he grunted. They looked at each other with an air of incertitude. October was renowned for earthquakes and other periodical disasters designed by life to shake complacency out of the population. Takanaka pulled a bottle out from under the counter, for Mama did not like her cola cold, but lukewarm. He poured the contents into a glass and handed it to her solicitously. 'Here you are!'

It was always the same: a packet of vanilla biscuits and a medium-sized bottle of cola, the colour of urine and the flavour of lollipop. 'And some special candles for the Purple Christ,' she ordered. He headed towards a crowded showcase in the corner of the room, a feature that gave the shop an aura of prosperity and an air of frivolity. Down came sacks of sugar, birdcages, crocodile creams for arthritis, syrups to repair broken hearts, and coloured bottles to change the texture of your emotions. Amid the mayhem, Don Takanaka found a box of purple candles which he claimed had been soaked in a unique aromatic infusion of purple paraffin and sacred herbs, and embellished with golden glitter to make them truly worthy of the day of the Lord of Miracles. The Japanese migrant had already acquired the Peruvian flair for colloquial hyperbole.

Mama had spent nine months under her new rule of yellow cola and vanilla biscuits because Doña Panchita, who never doubted the power of the miraculous Christ, had whispered that lots of sugar kept the spirit of women strong. 'Much better for the making of girls during pregnancy and good for the brain too,' she had advised. Mama had a great deal of affection for the wholesome woman, on whom nature had graciously carved a large mouth that spread widely when she greeted people and even more widely when she was angry. Her eyes were round and kind and always spoke of surrender to one's lot in life. Doña Panchita's advice was respected in the community for she spoke with the voice of popular wisdom and pure connection with the forces of the unseen. Her wisdom flowed from the strength of her African ancestry and from the sum total of her experiences. The neighbours never questioned her sources and her advice was carried by the wind on the back of transparent butterflies to the four corners of town.

Doña Panchita had advised Mama to rub her belly with sugar seven times clockwise in the morning and seven times anticlockwise in the evening. It would be much better if she performed this ritual in front of her shrine where the effigy of Mary still stood. 'The Holy Mary will pay you back if your prayers are sincere,' she had said in all solemnity. And Mama, a true believer in anything divine, powerful and female, followed the matron's suggestion to the letter, adding her own formula of yellow cola and vanilla biscuits.

Mama was sipping her cola quietly and recounting past disasters and earthquakes with Don Takanaka when I tapped from inside her belly, stretching in boredom, and anticipation. Her waters exploded and trickled down her legs; she screamed, sure she would soon flood the grocer's floor. 'Oh my God! The baby is here.' She folded her arms around the base of her big belly and Don Takanaka, rather embarrassed at the scene, for he knew that this was not men's business, sent his wife to get help. Doña Takanaka rushed along the streets in panic, panting and puffing, murmuring some secret chant of forgiveness, as if running away from the rumblings of an earthquake.

Every year, just before the major procession, people remembered the killer earthquake that had terrified the city long ago. It had occurred one eighteenth of October in the mid-seventeenth century. The sinister blow shocked Lima, tearing the earth wide open as if the universe had cast its wrath and sent demons from the underworld to swallow homes, government buildings, schools and churches. Terror had spread wide, for people truly believed the devil had been unleashed. 'Satan is here,' ghostly voices had murmured in ancient catacombs, the secret passages of the city's subterrain, as the doors that had locked in the heathens and the infidels in the name of the Inquisition burst open. Hundreds of thousands died, palaces tumbled and towers crumbled, crushing those below into tiny pieces. The waters of the ocean roared ferociously, enfolding the shores with torrential tides, traumatising the population so much that they truly believed the end of the world had arrived. The earthquake was the worst disaster in the known history of Peru.

The day the killer quake struck and almost transformed the whole city into pulp, something strange happened. On the outskirts of Lima, a black man had seeded a miracle: an African slave had painted a crucified Christ on a large adobe wall, in the colour purple, and the wall remained intact after the catastrophe. It was the one thing in town left upright. It had remained oblivious to the screams of horror, indifferent to the decapitated bodies, avalanches of mud, and the bloodstained hopes of the perishing population. This visual expression of faith by a black slave had remained erect, poised with pride and dignity, much to the astonishment of the town. The local population, originally terrified by the mysterious occurrence, was later moved to passionate devotion. Fresh believers flocked to the site to pay homage to the miraculous image, to ask the Christ for forgiveness. And the wall, charged with luminous magnetism, answered their requests, and even granted them their most desired wishes.

This miraculous painting, whispered Doña Panchita, who knew the story of African Peruvians by heart and was ready to retell it any time, had been done at the time when Lima was still the famous 'Capital of Dreams', populated by a haughty and condescending local aristocracy and filled with pretentious officers who felt they could redeem their sins by flagellating others. It was purgatory for the lower castes and hell for the slaves. The Spanish lords had brought a contingent of slaves, mainly from Angola, to this new land to help them mine gold. A clan of these slaves lived on the outskirts of the city in an area called Pachacamilla, a sacred site used by the ancient tribe of the Pachacamac Indians to appease both heavenly deities and underworld spirits alike. 'For this tribe knew very well that all gods would repay the offering made by a heart that did not discriminate,' said Doña Panchita when she told the story.

The famous painting had been created on top of this sacred site. It was not a coincidence, but an omen. Despite his sad predicament, in sublime devotion, the slave of our story had painted the image of Jesus looking down from a pool of purple gloom, exceptionally sombre and pitiful. 'But behind this heart-wrenching sadness the black artist also added a symbol of hope,' Doña Panchita said, 'a glimmer of light that could only be perceived by those who looked deep into the eyes of Christ to find relief in the depths of his despair.' And people did. The black artist, who never had any art training, had completed the work with astonishing skill. A Christ imbued with complete sorrow yet emanating the light of hope.

But in creating the miracle, the black painter had broken the law. Instead of canvas, the slave had chosen to splatter his divine passion on private property. Not just any private property, but the house of a certain government official, an opulent man of cruel reputation and obsessive anxieties. The discovery made the official squeal with such rage that even now, on foggy nights, the echoes of his anger are still heard in the barracks of Pachacamilla. The angry officer wanted nothing less than for the slave to be given a thousand lashes, in front of his family if possible, 'so these blacks will learn once and for all to respect their superiors'. But the Church took the painter under its wing, arguing that the purpose of the painting was to lead the slaves onto the path of the Christian God. In the archbishop's opinion, it was 'time to discard old African deities'. The Church said the Africans needed their own image of Christ. A Christian vision to understand the concept of suffering. This would 'help them accept their sad predicament in life without much complaint'. The slaves had lived in subhuman conditions for a hundred years, metamorphosing the cruelty of their new world into anger and resentment. Such was the strength with which they endured subjugation that the painting on the wall would never fall.

The Spanish authorities were struck by fear. A gnawing anxiety set in their hearts as they came to believe that the painting was a sign of dark forces that had penetrated the slave to discredit the work of the Catholics. Such power would only bring troubles and, who knows, break the slaves' chains. They were terrified also of the exotic rituals slaves performed when they offered prayers to their gods, rites impregnated with heavy drumming, pungent potions and delirium. The Africans needed to invoke their nature spirits to connect with home, and to request all sort of favours and retributions. The Church and the Crown began to look at each other with suspicion, and at the painting with dreadful disbelief. Now that the blacks had their own mystic wall, one that granted favours, even miracles, what would happen next? A rebellion? Something had to be done. They had to get the slave on side. So the lords came to pray and celebrate the work of God.

Crammed like sardines into the small shack that served as a provisional chapel, the stuffy castes sat next to their servants to supplicate themselves for miracles, smouldering in the heat of fervour, dazed by the scent of flesh and fermenting resentments. Enthralled by the proximity of agitated souls, they invoked the presence of God, breathing the power of sacred passion and forbidden lust. The odour of frivolity, eau de Cologne and rose fragrances on pink taffeta mingled with the scent of faith in the black servants' hearts. Blue eyes peered out from under black lace, blending their gazes with dark skins and sandalwood, igniting prayers with remorse. Feverish and forbidden sentiments stained the atmosphere and, as the prayers soared in fatigued devotion, sweet cinnamon smells and vanilla cleared the path to sacred surrender. Reigning supreme was the most pungent of all smells: the smell of guilt, which slithered its way out of remorseful hearts, rising to the surface of the skin, moist and salty. Guilt was the traditional heirloom of all who lived in the world in which I was born.

As the authorities calmed down and realised that the power of the image was a dictate from the heavens and not from the incomprehensible incantations of the slaves, they accepted the Purple Christ as a miracle maker. A decent chapel was built around the wall. Later, it became the Nazarene church, my favourite sanctuary for many years. Soon the fame and reputation of the sacred painting travelled beyond the seas and across the oceans, and Lima was filled with visitors from abroad wishing to be anointed with the divine compassion that came from the painting.

Three centuries and countless miracles later, the grocer's wife was running anxiously along the streets calling for help, for Mama was about to have her baby at the shop. 'Where is Don Bresciani?' she cried out, but Papa was nowhere to be found. She strode through the streets faster and yelled even louder, 'Please help. Baby coming out, water out, all out, please help!' Some neighbours poked their heads out of their mudbrick houses in morbid curiosity, wondering what malevolent curse had befallen the grocer's wife, or whether Japan had gone back to war. But it was the eve of absolution so they made the sign of the cross and stopped their gossiping. Mystical fervour was brewing inside every small dwelling perched along the narrow streets. It was late, and children were already in bed, bound for the land of dreams. The elders, on the other hand, sipped cinnamon tea and purified their houses with frankincense, and quietly mopped the floors with kerosene, and the windows with rum and a drop of lime, to keep ghosts away.

It was the tradition in my neighbourhood to embellish the family shrine with special purple-and-gold candles and flower offerings of the best kind, to keep the blessings in the house and the miracles at hand. The effigies had to be dusted and the clothes on the religious busts washed with holy water and ironed with corn starch 'as God instructs, for no favours from heaven will enter a dusty house'. In October the altar was dressed in purple with the image of the Purple Christ, surrounded by small figurines of other holy assistants, and illuminated by purple lights. On it were placed small photos of relatives for whom miracles were being sought. Smiling and frowning faces – ambassadors of their souls who looked out, sometimes with curiosity and sometimes with total disregard.

In the pleasure department there was succulent *Turrón de Doña Pepa*, a traditional sweet, carefully arranged on top of a lace serviette on a round tray. It is made weeks in advance in a sort of ritual, as though the women poured secret ingredients of the sacred type in with fennel seeds and sugar syrup. The recipe came from a black Angolan matron who kept the secret in her own quarters to be passed only to those of her lineage. In October, any variation of black was significant because of its links with the slave who painted the Purple Christ. Be it coffee, chocolate, honey or cinnamon it certainly made people feel special.

In response to the yells of Doña Takanaka, Lola came out, leaving her tea on the table and her mop behind the door. Lola's hips had grown rounder and her honey colour had lost some of its glow, although her generous contours still swayed invitingly as she walked past any possibility. She loved being admired, recognised for her attributes and praised for her existence, if only with a couple of spicy remarks, which sometimes bordered on obscenity. Her face was more jovial and trustworthy now, inviting genuine affection with its plump lips and an imperial set of black eyes which would annihilate any crooked intention if she was angry.

With a shawl wrapped around her to block the evening dampness, she strode up to the shop, muttering a Hail Mary and sighing at Doña Takanaka's cries of distress. It was cold outside. Despite the spring season, the firmament was shrouded by a dull mist. Lola found Mama now resting on a rattan chair at the back of the shop, legs sprawled wide, and sipping cola to calm her anxieties.

'Oh Lola, you are here!' she sighed.

'This will be a miracle of a baby girl,' the woman forecast with a mischievous grin as she examined Mama's afflicted face. 'Keep sipping cola,' she ordered with a medical tone. Sheltering Mama with her shawl, Lola helped her up and walked her carefully along the kerb towards the house, whispering laments because Mama would miss out on all the October festivities, including street fairs and, what a pity, no more bullfights. 'Oh no! I don't want to watch that butchery!' cried out Mama. And now there was no need for religious processions either. 'I want her to have my mother's name,' Mama muttered as she ambled with difficulty into the house. She walked towards the wardrobe and pulled out some sheets. 'But I also think she should have her other grandmother's name. Don't you think?' she asked. Her certainty in the vanilla miracle had left its mark on Mama's heart. She had traditions to consider.

Lola went to get the midwife and returned with her and Renatta who had become the 'other' wife of Uncle Arnaldo, my father's elder brother. When they arrived Mama confided her anxieties: 'She must carry the names of both grandmothers, so she'll always be protected.'

'Let's see how she looks first,' grunted Lola. 'She just might be a Loretta or a Madeleine. You never know.' I could never imagine myself as a Madeleine but perhaps there is a bit of a Loretta in me.

The house where I was born had grown from the one room that saw Mama's tears a few years earlier into a tropical chamber. The ceilings had stretched even more – a second level had been introduced – and more shelves had gone on the walls. To invoke the magic of her forest of rich luminosity Mama had dressed the house with bright colours and added flamboyant ornaments wherever she could, although the timber furniture had been left untouched. A couple of cages of red and green parakeets hung in the corners. The little Amazon birds chattered and sang all day, and were allowed to fly indoors as long as they went back to their cages for their basic necessities. Crepe-paper flowers, and multisized bottles containing remedies and aromatic potions that made life vibrate with uninhibited zest, complemented the jungle cornucopia at home.

On top of the large wardrobe, stuffed animals peered down with menace in their eyes, terrifying some visitors, who swore that the teeth-baring creatures were alive. Mama would mock them for their fear, saying that it was not the animal but some hidden guilt that made people terrified of the innocent straw-filled alligator or of the red piranha showing its piercing fangs. But Papa was never amused for he was not too sure that these animals could not be resuscitated by some jungle incantation. Mama believed that although animals' souls went back to their collective source, their spirits always cast a spell of protection and wandered in silence around those who loved them. Papa did not like that and gazed at the glistening piranha with distrust. By

then the neighbours knew that Mama was a bit 'special' and celebrated all her presents from the Amazon, particularly the jars of jungle
potion that cured all sorts of shocks and arthritis, or the slices of dried
fish for Easter. Mama was famous for the special bark brews that she
served her visitors. Tonics that revitalised their hormones and probably altered the colour of their minds, for after taking them they
always found everything exciting at home.

Mama had made new chair covers with cotton prints of giant
bananas and placed fragrant bowls of forest fruit and smoked fish on
the dining table. On the new mezzanine, in between the ceiling and
the floor, Papa had installed beds, wardrobes, an ironing table and
dressers, which he, with the help of his young brother, had assembled
out of large wooden crates. Above the kitchen, there was another
room where my brothers played, slept and climbed out onto the roof
chasing cats, peering into other people's houses, and clashing as cow-
boys and villains. When we grew up a bit, we often dangled from
there like monkeys or Tarzan, plunging to the floor every so often,
when the spirits were not aligned, and we dropped unconscious and
unprotected. Our heads bled often, and then healed and hardened,
and our spirits grew stronger I guess, fuelled by the constant dives and
subsequent resurrections that kept Mama's nerves on edge.

A week before my birth, Papa decided to assemble the main bed in
the room downstairs where Mama had insisted she was going to have
her baby, refusing to go to the maternity hospital where previous
pregnancies had left her with a sour taste, a chronic backache and
cramped muscles. 'No more hospitals for me, thank you very much.
They're all butchers!' she had complained on her return from the
local maternity hospital, a raw slit in her belly. No women's circle had
been around her to sing and soothe her when my brother was born,
as was the tradition in the Amazon. Instead of the singing birds and
the smell of fresh fruit and boiled banana, she was shocked by the

noise of trolleys screeching along the bleak corridors, and the sight of soiled linen piled in dirty corners. She could not bear the despair of women with contorted faces, drenched legs and aching bodies, who had to line up waiting for tickets and beds to have babies.

Mama was not aware that in the very corner of the house where she lay panting and palpitating, legs trembling and back aching, Uncle Pietro, one of Papa's brothers, had been found dead of unknown causes some time before she moved in. I do not know for sure how my uncle died because details about this death were never discussed in the family. I have often wondered what on earth he was doing in that place, away from his family. My father was not a man for remembering indiscretions, so he refused to give me details. But as I grew up I often stared deeply at the haunting corner, peering into the unseen, eager for a clue and longing to see a minute sign that could reveal a connection of a ghostly kind with Uncle Pietro. But he never appeared, leaving me in suspense.

Still on the eve of the day of the Purple Christ, Mama sweated the sweat of childbirth at the same spot where the ghost of Uncle Pietro floated. My father was at the Nazarene church finetuning the arrangements for the parade of the Purple Christ. The miracle-making art piece on the famous wall had been replicated and turned into a glittery float which meandered through the streets of the city accompanied by a million remorseful devotees. It is the tradition in my birth town that all Christians accompany the float every eighteenth of October, whining and howling in feverish trance and delirious lament, fusing with the spirit of divine forgiveness. Women would greet the procession as an opportunity to claim their rewards for virtuous behaviour and pious sacrifices.

At the church Papa was busy discussing with his purple-robed peers how best to tackle the huge palanquin edged in gold and silver that would carry the sacred image through the city streets. He had no idea that Mama was already in labour. He was one of the seven hundred men who would carry the float on their shoulders in groups of thirty-five. Our family was proud of his position in the fraternity because it was a privilege not often conferred. To us it was like a sort of aristocracy of the spirit. Despite his father's connection with the Church – for it had been a priest who had introduced the Italian dandy to my grandmother – Papa had never enjoyed religious affairs much. This procession was different. While secretly believing that all priests were frauds, he was sure his contribution to the procession would lead him to the portals of St Peter when the day came. Mama was not convinced but she went along with it, following her new formula for good relations. 'Never contradict in public a man who believes he is right, unless he asks for your opinion, for a content man is a useful man,' she would often remind me as she lit a candle to the Virgin of the Clouds on his behalf.

As Papa was fixing the silver vases to the top of the float his sister Dorita came screeching through the church towards him. The priests were not amused by the sight of her, because the preparations for the procession did not involve women. But she had pushed her way in, claiming she was a 'special messenger' with very important news. 'Your daughter is about to be born,' she yelled at my father, who immediately dropped his screwdriver, packed his sister into the car and drove like a maniac through the city.

There were no doubts amongst the women that the baby was going to be a girl. And it would be a baby with a sweet tooth. So sure were they that the sugar rites would work that a pink frock and woollen booties were laid on the bed before I was even born. When Papa arrived, he was sent to buy a bottle of champagne to celebrate. At exactly one-forty in the morning of the purple day in Lima I came to see the light of this world, in a dimly lit room with restless shadows in the distance. I was born four-and-a-half kilos with a head of black fluff and my umbilical cord around my neck. My skin was purple like the night and I gasped for breath. The midwife, a fat woman of resolute disposition, grabbed me from Mama's insides, dangled me in the air as if to rid me of any disillusions, and proceeded to slap my bottom with a bang that grounded me on this planet for ever. My skin turned pink and my pipes unblocked to let the scent of new life filter through my lungs. I smelled a sweet scent and I broke into a loud and terrified scream. The sugar rites had worked and I began my life inhaling the raw scent of vanilla in Mama's breath as she cried tears of joy.

DELICACIES OF SEDUCTION

FROM THE DAY I was born my eyes sketched adventures in my mind, images accentuated by the colours in Mama's heart. I grew up in a large room with music and parakeets, in the house that had witnessed Mama's many tribulations but had also celebrated every chord of her laughter. In that room I learned to smell the scent of her fear and her melancholy, and the early breaths of her jubilation. I also learned to make cakes with a wooden spoon, and wash the floor with kerosene and the windows with flaming rum. The once melancholic room had grown by the day, expanding with every visit of a family member or heart-torn refugee. Mama was always willing to create extra space when her friends from the jungle arrived, or when a marriage broke up.

I often wondered where she hid the magic wand that made our house grow to accommodate so many people, sometimes under the table, sometimes behind the wardrobe. At school, I told my friends that my mother had the power to make things grow and expand like a magician, and my friends' interest in our family intensified. But when the inquisitive little girls came home to ask her for proof, Mama recommended I keep such details to myself because, 'Women are not magicians, darling. Women with magic powers are called *brujas*, and they get burnt!' So I shut up, for a while.

In my reveries, Pancho the cat developed the enigmatic fur of the Blue Cat and the roof became the terrace on which the jungle spirits landed from the far away forest. Perhaps one day I would be able to catch a glimpse of the long-lost island that had been swallowed by the In-between, I told myself. Mama's flamboyant spirituality gave our lives an added dimension, as did her ability to pull stories out of cups of tea, and her penchant for predicting events, although sometimes she saw more gloom than glow. As she talked of the Blue Cat and the Pink Dolphin, a sombre cloud crept into her soul, threatening to cast darkness for years to come. It was a sense of responsibility that rose from within her, tainting the glow of her character – an urge to get things right. In the capital she was under the protection of different gods, those who lived in different temples, dressed in pastel satins and white tulle, with anatomies of white clay and alabaster. I always asked Mama where exactly God lived. Was He a strange force living in the little shrine at the centre of the altar from where the priest brought out the chalice of wine? Or did He live in the heart of the cold statues to whom people, including ourselves, prayed? Or was He transparent fluff that lived in the pores of a leaf and could dance on a drop of dew, gliding away with the breath of a butterfly? 'Yes, there too,' Mama would snap, 'God lives everywhere, my dear, and in the gutters, and in the bones of the poor and the emaciated.'

'Really?' I marvelled. She added, with a touch of irritation, that God talked to everyone who made the time to pray, but heavy meals at night did not make communication easy. So she taught our family that it was better to have a hearty lunch and a light meal at night, although Papa was not at all interested in establishing links with the cosmos if such connections were going to affect his meals. My Papa was a pragmatic man.

'How come saints can make miracles and ordinary people can't, Mama? The priest has not made one, has he?'

'Not that I know of,' said Mama. But we all knew of the famous priest who had actually walked through a wall when the devil persecuted him. He had been beatified and later sanctified, but there were not many like him, not anymore.

Mama dutifully took my brothers and me to church once a week, as the rules of the city dictated. Perhaps one day we too could make miracles, she said. Inside the Catholic temple she taught us to pray with deep devotion and high expectations. 'God delivers all things we ask of him, if we pray with a genuine heart,' she would say. And I obeyed. She prayed for her children in Lima, for my brothers in boarding school, and that they would never forget her. She prayed for her health, for her skills to be sharpened, for ideas to blossom and, more importantly, she prayed to find a hand of guidance that would lead her in the right direction. With her knees on the weathered pew, her permed curls under a black mantilla, and wearing a long-sleeved dress, each Sunday morning she repeated the chants of mercy and the prayers to Mary. She always felt good afterwards. I suppose I did too.

I also breathed the jungle air that oozed out of Mama's good moods, tasted the smoked fish that we received as gifts, and absorbed the harrowing stories of her adolescence, the sudden death of Hernancito, her market rounds, the border wars and her father's breakdown. I grew up with the shadow of the stepmother behind my back, the jealous fits of Don Ramon in my ears, and her guilt for her lost children at the base of my heart. 'Poor Mama!' I often lamented, her pain aching inside me as I dragged my feet upstairs at night. Lying in the bed that Papa had made, tucked under two layers of woollen blankets to protect myself from dampness and asthma I would relive Mama's dramas and turn myself into the protagonist of her past miseries, as well as the muse of her dreams. It was my way of suffering with her. However, whenever I stood next to her I always sensed the pillar of strength that held her up from inside. There was a strange force that lived in her heart. It was as if some unearthly engine endowed her with a driving force that did not discriminate, no matter how many clashes she had with destiny.

'I still have to find the temple where my fortune lies,' she would often mutter, remembering the dream she had the day before she left Lucio, in which the Blue Cat had signalled the way to the white peak. There she had seen a glowing palace, bathed in the light of recognition. It was an image she always enjoyed remembering and that perhaps was the hidden engine in her cells. Where would this temple be? My brother said it was probably in Disneyland or Holly-wood, but Mama was serious. 'What about the Vatican?' guessed Aunt Dorita. 'Or somewhere in the East,' suggested Aunt Lisa. No, it could not be in the East. She was a dedicated Catholic now. Although she also followed the advice of Doña Panchita, who felt all gods must be made happy, no matter where they come from. 'For the days are yet to come when all souls will rise out of their graves,' she would whis-per ominously in Mama's ears, reminding her that the end of the world was near. But there would also be a new beginning, she claimed, a dawn signalling a roaring tide of transformation.

The black elder came to our home most afternoons, either to have her arthritic wrist rubbed with alligator oil or to check on us when Mama was out working. Every time Doña Panchita's apocalyptic statements fell on our table Papa would roll his eyes, but he kept his mouth shut out of respect, only snorting a subdued chuckle or two. 'That lady is off the planet,' he would sneer quietly after she was gone, with a mocking grin on his face. Mama did not like his scoffing and would stare at him, pour a glass of homemade lemonade and hand it to him, reminding him that Doña Panchita carried the same wisdom as his own mother – the African heritage that was so controversial in some veins of Papa's family. Aunt Dorita did not have a problem with openly admitting that the family had a line of African ancestry, and Aunt Renatta had become a bit of a raconteur and would tell Bres-ciani tales, having a crack at the pretentiousness of some of the family. She was always ready to reveal the secrets of our concealed past, par-ticularly after the midnight dance of the *Humiteros*.

The *Humiteros* were a group of black vendors with drumming boys who marched along our streets once a month in the hour before midnight. They used to come down from the black quarter at the edge of town, singing and dancing in a parade along the pavement. They sold *humitas*, a kind of corn cake wrapped in banana leaves, specially recommended for changing the colour of dreams. We knew them as the 'Children of the moon', visitors of midnight and messengers of Venus. Their earthy rhythms pricked our dreams and their drums stirred us from quietude. When I heard them I would sneak out of bed in my pyjamas and join the rest of the children in a circle under the moon. My brothers Luis and Roy, who was born one year after me, would stand by my side and peer at the black boys who twisted and gyrated their elongated bodies, leaping into the air, as if trying to scribble musical poetry in the space between the asphalt and the sky.

I would always practise their steps the morning after. Dancing was my passion and I never missed an opportunity to let the 'dancing goblins', as Papa called them, escape from under my skin. Aunt Renatta said that my addiction to music came from my African heritage: 'African music runs in your blood, my child.' However, this heritage had not shown up much in my looks, for my hair was as straight as steel blades, and my eyes the shape of sad almonds. But Aunt Renatta was one of those women who never fell victim to appearances and was convinced that we were closely linked to the Angolan slaves of our unmerciful past.

Aunt Renatta was a beautiful woman and people often compared her to a movie star. She was tall and curvaceous with eyes that were green like the sea, and an abundant cascade of hair the hue of ancient gold. Papa often joked that 'Aunt Renatta made the effort to get up early when God distributed good looks . . . and that was probably the only time', because her house was always in a state of mayhem. A museum in disarray, with pieces of furniture chaotically spread around the room, shawls and colourful scarves entwined around boxes, parcels and dolls. Her delicate china would often sit on tin saucers. Never mind the mess, for she always served delicious food. I liked going to see her because her house was in direct contrast to our home – Mama had managed to convince us that magic could not happen in a house that was untidy. We often visited Aunt Renatta for tea after our customary strolls in the colonial park where we fed hungry ducklings and where the youngest of my brothers nearly drowned once when nobody was looking. According to Papa, the ghosts of the big lake had been well acquainted with Mama, so they had pushed him back, out of courtesy. We agreed. In the room with the hanging shawls and the crawling toddlers, I would stuff myself with iced biscuits, chocolate cakes, bonbons with caramel, cheese bread rolls with purple corn custard, and cinnamon tea.

Aunt Renatta would sit in the middle of the room like a goddess of the ancient oracles and tell stories that respected no boundaries of space or time. My soul was impregnated with the seeds of my family history, starting with the story of the romance between my father's parents. Through Aunt Renatta's voice I discovered how a chocolate-coloured girl and her sisters had cast a love spell on my grandfather, in the way women knew how to do at the time.

It took place long ago, Aunt Renatta said. My *nono*, my grandfather, had gone to see the black she-shaman *La Bruja* to get some good luck herbs. Not that he 'believed in all that mumbo jumbo,' he claimed, but his friend had convinced him. *La Bruja* gave him a bottle of syrup that was to make him successful for seven years, as long as he played his cards right and did not exploit his workers too much. The tonic must have worked, for business did extremely well. For forty nights and forty days Nono Alberto celebrated the success of his enterprise and, in true family tradition, spread his generosity to all who came along and toasted with him. Nono Alberto was a man of moderate ambition who had not sold his spirit to the lord of darkness, nor had he ever tainted his objectives with the exploitation of those beneath him. For him, having a content worker and enough money to meet his needs was a formula that created less trouble.

One afternoon, Nono Alberto's best friend came to tell him that *La Bruja* wanted to see him.

'I wonder what the old lady has for me this time,' growled my grandfather, knowing full well that *La Bruja* only called when something was important. And he could not refuse.

'I think it has to do with a romantic introduction,' volunteered his friend, smiling a cocky smile.

'Romantic introduction? Bloody hell! I am not going to let any old she-shaman tell me what is good for me.'

Alberto had been living in Lima for nearly a decade, and had flirted with just about every woman he had come across. He was a man who liked to play the game of love in all its variations, totally absorbed in the uncertainty and excitement. He was the sort of man who knows that tragedy and delight are sisters in the night and he had learned to accept them too. He avoided commitment at all costs with the excuse of 'not being ready for it'. Everyone knew that he had several lovers, one of whom was a young widow with three children, to whom he brought flowers every week, and confided his deepest secrets. But to whom he would never commit. His heart had been speared badly once in his home town and the episode had left a scar. His Italian friends wondered why Alberto had not already chosen a wife or gone home to bring one back with him. 'Oh the lovely Genoese. Too hard to get,' they chanted mockingly. In response, Nono Alberto roared, 'Who should care? I marry whom I want, when I want.' He assured his friends he was truly happy the way he was, moving on impulse, exploring new cracks in life, dancing and drinking till late.

Not far from his house, three sisters, ripe and ready for marriage, lived with an old aunt. Rumour had it that the aunt was a distant acquaintance of the black priestess, but this has never been confirmed. These girls were the Eckart sisters. Only a year apart from each other, it was difficult to tell who was the older or the younger when the three of them walked together on the streets. Despite their German surname their complexions spoke more of their Angolan ancestry. Their skins had a velvety texture with chocolate shades and coffee scents.

Dressed in starched organza and satin tight around their waists, and ribbons in their hair, they strutted like peacocks along the narrow streets of the colonial town, glancing demurely at the gracefully carved balconies when a romantic whistle caught their attention. Prim and proper, they braced their chests and tightened their hips, feet marching graciously in laced-up boots, sprinkling the scent of fresh lavender behind them as they headed to church.

On close inspection, one noticed that the eldest was the most serious and guarded of the lot. No one would joke with the older Eckart girl, because she knew just about everything there was to know for a girl her age, and that put others at a disadvantage. Her wit was renowned in the neighbourhood, and her chili tongue too. The priest had been working on her quick-snappy ways, telling her that God did not like his food too spicy. She had agreed to tone it down, but she excused her quick tongue as a way of protecting her sisters from the savage avalanche of gossip about their private lives. Yet behind her sharp tongue, she was always ready to give a helping hand to whoever was in need, never mind the gossip. The youngest, on the other hand, was the flavour of fun and the spark of life. She was the chattiest of the group, and the most playful and sweet of the lot, with a string of pearls for a smile and the air of a young princess.

The middle Eckart was the personification of duty and responsibility. Not too chatty or smart-witted, but decidedly industrious, resourceful and genteel. Impregnated with a sense of tolerance for the wicked tongues and a tender docility in the face of the stubborn, she was always helpful, but these attributes often misled people into thinking she was submissive. God, no! On the contrary. She was known to possess subtle powers beneath her quietude, which raised her sisters' hackles with jealousy when, for instance, she transformed an ordinary rag into a chic gown good enough for Mardi Gras. She worked as if to prove to God that she existed because she'd been told that God rewarded hard workers. Perhaps that was the reason for her boundless energy that made some people joke she had been seeded by a bull. The other side to their good attributes was that the eldest was extremely catty, the youngest a trickle too vain, and the middle one would drive anyone to despair with her hard-working obligations. Their skills were fortified by the herbal brews given to them by their aunt. And when they were in balance, the sisters were able to operate in perfect unison.

Their mother had been dead for a long time; their father, holder of the family name, was never discussed. Whispers were heard in the underground chambers of town that the girls were indeed the daughters of the mysterious aunt. Wicked tongues had it that she had been forced into being the mistress of her German master. The woman had taught the girls to call her aunt, and despite the 'stain on her soul' she had managed to convince the father to give the girls his name. Neither the girls, nor the aunt, had ever confirmed such murmuring, instead they concentrated on attracting the Church's blessing and good fortune to their home.

One evening, the aunt came home and told them that she had been informed by 'a wise friend' that there was a healthy bachelor in the area, a man of the Old World, who was worth casting their eyes on. A possibility indeed! The next day, the sky boasted an eloquent blue, the sun shone more happily than ever before, and the grudging clouds parted to let Eros dance above the Eckart sisters' home. Immediately, the eldest girl began to study Alberto's every move and came to discover the young man's marital status, his taste for women and good food, his gregarious inclinations, including his evening outings, his friends, and his connection to the widow. She understood that men were free to do things that women were not, and she also knew that women could do some things men had no idea of. As long as nobody found out.

The Eckart sisters had decided that one of them was to marry Alberto Bresciani, and they each began to work on their own love spell. The girls were determined to catch the elusive man and keep him in the family no matter what it took, in addition to prayers. The eldest, who was known as the organiser, decided to enlist the help of the local priest, but the youngest protested, saying that a man like Alberto would not be likely to have an inclination towards religious affairs. In the meantime the old aunt kept quiet in the back of the large kitchen cooking herbal brews, wiping benches and carefully carrying pans from the pot belly stove onto the oak table at the centre of the room. All in ritualistic quietness.

'It doesn't matter if Alberto is not religious,' retorted the oldest Eckart in the lounge room whilst puffing up the sofa cushions carefully and spraying lavender dew on the seat covers. 'The priest will not ask him to come and *pray* to God. Instead, he'll ask him to come and *help* God. That'll please him.'

'Umm,' said the middle one, as if setting her own plan in motion, 'A man who thinks he can help God likes to be pleased by him as well.' The sisters agreed to leave the eldest to plan the seduction, for they knew she was the strategist of the three. Meanwhile, the middle one began to plan the party menu and the youngest prepared the invitations and thought about how best to embellish their house for the occasion.

A few days went by and Nono Alberto arrived at the local tavern, fuming from his visit to *La Bruja*. He ordered a shot of *pisco* and told his close friend that he was feeling confused. The black priestess had told him that the time had come for him to make a commitment and to find a wife. She explained that the 'protector gods' had discovered that there was a woman in town with skin the colour of cinnamon and a heart of gold. She was to make him happy and give him a set of healthy descendants in the new land he was beginning to call home. 'It's about time,' she had said. 'You must plant seeds in a place if you are going to stay. The protector gods do not help men who are not prepared to seed fruits of gratitude.' The chosen woman lived in his own vicinity and he would meet her soon, in very special circumstances. Alberto felt too embarrassed to ask how he would identify the woman chosen by the protector gods if he kept meeting women in the extravagant corridors of his own mixed circumstances. *La Bruja* said that when the time came he would know. 'The chosen woman will be like a spark that will ignite the flame of your heart,' she said, 'something like a prick on your skin, a hunch behind the belly and a sweet taste in your mouth.' But Nono Alberto was befuddled and understood nothing of the message. He did not like the bit about the protector gods asking for compensation. He did not believe in them anyhow. But on second thoughts, he decided it would be better if he did not upset them. He would look out for the chosen woman, for any new woman was an exciting woman.

My Nono Alberto was not surprised when the local priest approached him on the street to invite him to support a local charity function. The priest had always tried to gain his assistance in the affairs of the church but the young Italian had always refused, limiting his help to nominal donations. A luncheon was to be held at the Eckart sisters' home and the proceeds would contribute to the building of a new orphanage. My grandfather had never been a man of Church affairs but his business had done so well that he wanted to financially show his appreciation to the country which he felt had welcomed him so warmly and voluptuously. He thought the Church was as good a vehicle as any other, as long as the priest did not get too involved in his life, because for him, priests were all pests. But perhaps not all of them were, he thought on that day. Perhaps they also brought good luck. Thinking of the protector gods softened his heart a little bit. Or perhaps he was just feeling guilty because he had stopped seeing the widow. So, he agreed to support the Church event and come to the luncheon at the Eckart sisters' home, because a meal made by women was always a delicious meal. And he decided to bring his close friend, just in case.

The young and excited Eckart sisters managed to spread news of the luncheon across the neighbourhood. So much so that hot expectancy hung in the air and the luncheon tickets sold out. In a series of domestic councils, the three sisters analysed minute details of the menu and the ingredients. Each of them agreed to have a go at cooking special dishes, but of course they would follow the lead of the middle Eckart girl, for she was the most creative of the lot.

The day arrived with exotic flowers, frantic excitement and a sparkling radiance at the table. Laid exquisitely on a white lace tablecloth was a string of spicy dishes. Hors d'oeuvres of green beans and carrot with cheese and dill sauce, garnished with lime; baked fish with onion, coriander, chili and shallots; fresh prawns stuffed into cucumber boats with turtle egg mayonnaise; and potatoes with feta, banana chili and milk sauce. Tripe casserole with carrots, peas and saffron sauce would also be served, with garlic risotto, roasted suckling pig and poultry in a tomato sauce with baked potatoes, yams and pumpkin in honey, with toasted sesame seeds spread on top. These were crowned by trays of assorted sweets, all soaked in the scent of cinnamon, cloves and nutmeg – flamboyant desserts dipped in syrups of brown sugar and carob purée, vanilla and sugar cane leaves soaked in a chocolate rain, luscious rum balls, rice puddings, bean custards, and aromatic ice creams and fruit tarts. Carafes of wine – red to ignite passion, pink to tickle romance and clear caramel to subdue arousal – were paraded elegantly next to crystal glasses, and there were large bowls of fruit punch for the young ladies who did not drink, or not in public.

The guests arrived, sporting their best Sunday clothes, grinning at each other with well-rehearsed cordiality. They were all willing to contribute to the orphanage in the best way they could, and the depth of their contributions matched the density of their curiosity, for they were indeed keen to discover the real reason behind the function. The men herded themselves into one corner, boasting long cigars and polished hairstyles, and the women mingled around the table rattling their bracelets and nibbling canapés while sharing giggles, toasting to life and a good cause. Alberto stood in the corner with his friend, his thoughts still caught in *La Bruja's* prediction of the bride-to-be who lived in the vicinity. Perhaps she would be here? He looked around, scrutinising most of the guests, sipping wine and behaving as jovially as he could. But after a few glasses of alcohol, still no girl had caused any of the predicted reactions. Neither his heart had sparked, nor his skin pricked. So he just kept sipping more wine and nibbling the roasted almonds and stuffed olives with feta cheese from the sideboard, unwilling to approach the table and talk to the women. But disobeying his head, his feet glided to the table and he picked up a potato ball in cheese sauce. Suddenly, as he bit into it, his tongue melted in the smooth creamy dressing, his mouth kissed the tinge of saffron, and his whole consciousness shifted to the realms of heightened pleasures. As he swallowed the melted cheese, he saw a white veil float past his eyes and the silhouette of an exquisite figure sparked a light in his mind. His entire body shivered in ecstasy. And he sunk into an ambrosial dream.

His friend nudged him to indicate that the three hostesses were heading towards them, accompanied by the priest. Alberto came out of his trance and, still dazed by the food, greeted the hostesses with a huge smile and an elegant bow of the head. The three sisters smiled at him with identical kindness and a tinge of flirtatiousness. Alberto drank more wine and entertained the three impeccably dressed ladies in the tradition of a gentleman. He tried hard to ascertain who had prepared which dish, but it was in vain. The girls had worked as a team. Finally, he gave up, admitting that it was impossible to singularly identify the entanglement of flavours that had planted the seeds of paradise in his stomach. The rest of the afternoon he charmed the sisters, commending them on the decoration of the house and their interest in charity. Offering a generous contribution to the Church, which shocked him the morning after, he recovered from the food spell and invited himself for a second meal. The girls gave a smile of conspiracy and accepted gladly.

Forward in time, I found myself chewing every word that Aunt Renatta uttered as we nibbled cake. I watched her theatrical moves as she pranced around the table imitating the way my grandmother and her sisters had waltzed with Eros in their hearts on that portentous night after the guests had left.

'His heart had definitely been kidnapped by his stomach,' Aunt Renatta declared as she cut one more piece of Black Forest cake.

Fresh in my head was the lace tablecloth and the smell of potato balls with cheese and dill sauce.

'I'll make sure I learn how to cook when I grow up,' I replied.

'Your Nono knew that whatever produced such pleasure had to be a good sign,' my aunt said, reiterating that the flavour of the food cooked by the hand of a lady was a very important criterion when men chose a wife.

Nono Alberto did not waste much time, and a week later he found himself drinking aperitifs at the Eckarts' home in the company of his best friend and the priest, and anticipating the same culinary delights that had provoked an array of sensations on the previous occasion. He was not mistaken about the quality of food and variety of flavours he would experience at the second dinner. But he was unable to determine the source of his pleasure, so he decided to give the girls a subtle quiz and examine their inner qualities.

He asked them to be spontaneous in their replies, and put to them the following hypothetical situation: if they were to suddenly receive a prize of a trip to Europe, what would they bring home to share with their families? 'Umm,' said each of them, looking up and around, imagining themselves packing their chests and hatboxes for their journey back from the other side of the world. The Old World. The eldest Eckart, famous for being quick at everything, gave the first answer. As she had a keen interest in the ancient philosophies, mysteries and traditions of the old continent, she would definitely like to bring back books and mementoes for the benefit of her sisters and the orphanage. The middle Eckart said she would like to explore the ways of village people, learn their cultural codes, collect their seeds and discover recipes and ingredients. 'Well, I would do something wild,' erupted the third sister. 'I'd definitely have plenty of fun, dance all night, indulge in chocolates, and bring loads of glittery presents back home.' After a few slices of Madeira cake and several glasses of port with the priest, Alberto's stubborn heart allowed Eros to lodge.

On his way back home he told his best friend, 'Any woman who can produce such pleasure in food has to be a good woman.'

Both men chuckled and headed down the cobbled road and into the local tavern where they drank until the sun reminded them of another day.

'It must have been *chamico*,' his friend said slowly, thinking of the herbal aphrodisiac.

'It was all in the seeds, my friend. In the seeds she wanted to bring from Europe,' said Nono Alberto.

'Well, there is no need now. For you have the seeds with you,' laughed his friend.

'You are so right,' Nono said, pulling his long legs out from under the table.

'Alberto and Emilia, hmm,' both men muttered.

Soon Alberto Bresciani became convinced that love tastes better when it comes spiced with cheese sauce and toasted poppy seeds. He married the middle sister, Emilia Eckart, with whom he was to have eighteen children, twelve of whom would survive. The wedding was celebrated with a great fanfare and tables of food stretching all the way along the street. Guests danced for a whole week, and each received a gift of one golden coin, a bar of chocolate and a few sesame seeds, to harvest good fortune and relish the sweetness of life.

Nona Emilia spend her entire married life with a child inside her, and possessed the mature intuition that many pregnant women have despite her protected lifestyle. As a consequence my grandfather's business flourished even more.

Sadly, Nona Emilia died during the birth of her last child, leaving my grandfather lost in grief. With the passing of his true partner, who had become his backbone for nearly twenty years, Nono's entrepreneurial spirit faded. He released his responsibility to his family, dumping the burden of the business on his grown-up children. From time to time he was submerged in prolonged states of gloom and isolation. He would snarl and growl at people when his agony became too hard to bear, a feature that my father somehow inherited and that became the secret link to his father's pain. But the spirit of Nona Emilia was forever present in the house and business picked up a bit in the following years, enjoying the protection of the Conservatives in government. However, on the occasions when the military rose to power and the rich fell out of grace, the creativity of Nona Emilia was not able to balance things out and interpret the market and political moods. Soon a war raged on the other side of the Atlantic, and factories began manufacturing wartime goods. The Bresciani family had to tighten their belts and sit around the fire reminiscing about the flavours of Nona Emilia's cheese and saffron sauce over baked potato balls.

My father's heart had shattered when his mama died. Still in his early teens, his pubescent dreams froze in the tears he could not shed, for he, like all of his brothers, had been taught that men should not cry. Still, he had done so on his mother's lap many times when she was alive – he had been her errand boy and her helper in the many charitable deeds she was involved in. He soothed the pain of her absence by placing himself at the service of his sisters, assisting them in the running of the large household. He was a timid boy, highly impressionable and prone to believing what others said about him. He left school before his time and followed the example of his elder brothers with a season at his father's trucking business. But he was not very keen on driving trucks, the city's noise and heavy duty affairs. Instead he much preferred to use his time by doing tasks that did not get his clothes dirty.

Thanks to a recommendation from a friend of Nono Alberto, he managed to get a job in the national library, a favour that pleased him very much because in between shuffling papers and serving borrowers, he had the chance to flick through the pages of pictorial books, particularly those about ancient history. He would travel in his own imaginary chariot, watching from the clouds the magnificent events that had changed the course of life. He would spend hours studying old maps and visualising the journeys of ancient heroes such as

Alexander the Great and Mark Antony. He had been born during a voyage by his parents to Italy and because all the movement on the journey had made him very sick he much preferred to be on steady ground; travelling through books and old encyclopaedias was much more enjoyable than the real thing. Reminiscing about his library days, Papa would often say to us, 'by natural law all empires have to fall because life is like a pendulum that moves from one extreme to the next'. So Mama made sure we ate lots of spinach so our own pillars would never crumble. His job at the library did not last long, because, following the natural law of the political pendulum, it was pulled away from him when the Conservatives lost government. He tried his hand at odd jobs until he finally agreed to again work in his father's business. Later, he inherited his own truck, the contract and the workers that came with it. In time he learned to handle the traffic, and the fuss and flurry of the roads.

Papa always remained a conservative in politics, believing that one half of the world had been born with the best ideas to rule and protect the weaker. The other 'less apt half' was better off protected, guided and governed, he said. He felt that it was those with European blood who had the knack and know-how for leading the herd. But Mama did not enjoy listening to his naive observations for it had been her own ideas that always set plans in motion, although it was Papa's who brought them to fruition. From her imagination had flowed most of the home improvements, which she coordinated with militaristic precision and unremitting perseverance. Her idea of building hanging mezzanines to stretch the house became popular in the block and soon people were buying one-room houses and turning them into four-room residences with attics and all.

She ran our home as if she was running an army, with tasks assigned to each of us, and rosters pinned on the wall for the washing of the floors, dishes, and windows, and assistance with the shopping and cooking. In a way she very much acted out what Papa believed in. But she did not vote Conservative. She always voted on the side of the labourers. Her relations with blue-collar workers and her own experiences at the factories persuaded her to support any party that defended the poor, the handicapped and the underdog, and any party that opposed the oligarchy. Never mind her own authoritarian approach to running our home. Of course, her political inclinations collided often with those of my father, who did not look upon the descendants of the ancient Incas with high admiration. Except of course for Mama, who by virtue of coming from the 'enchanted forest', and not looking Amazonian Indian, had a uniqueness about her.

'You see,' he'd say, 'with the Incas gone, these Cholos don't know the difference between black and white.' My mind began recording these observations of humanity, registering people according to their colour and features, wondering why an Indian or a Cholo – who was part Indian – got the worst of the lot. After all, I was one of them and Mama too, though her features were more European than mine. It was very difficult to reconcile.

I realise now that Papa's paternalistic views of the world were a product of his own insecurities. He always had to justify that his observations came from a credible and respected source. After his mother had gone, he became imprisoned in the belief that he was not good. His brothers often made fun of his quiet ways and of the birthmark he had on the side of his nose, convincing him, foolishly, that it impaired his sight. For many years he preferred not to drive a car. The day he inherited the trucks he hired a driver and an assistant. He was a tall man in a country of small mestizos; he was never a forceful person and never used violence to defend his views, instead he would just chuckle, mock or grunt when he was annoyed.

His heart always missed the intimate rapport he had with his mother. His grief filled him with a sad sense of acceptance, a melancholic mood, and a sluggishness of the soul that often made him growl when life got too much for him. As a young girl, when I tried to hug Papa, I felt I could not penetrate the shell that had grown around him. It was like an intangible shield that only Mama could remove in the privacy of their hearts. We knew that he kept a lot of

pain inside, but what secret was in his heart I never exactly discovered. That it had been there for a long time, I knew.

At night, when Papa slept soundly and his breath made a whistle
that pierced through the calico curtains separating our quarters, I lay
on my bed imagining his pain like a restless beast locked in a vault at
the bottom of the sea, roaring every so often when life's injustices
stirred him. Many years later, Life would send one of its unexpected
envoys to break the lock on the vault and let the beast loose.

My parents lived together out of matrimony for many years. And
when they finally decided to tie the knot, I proudly led the
entourage, with my brothers by my side. Mama's divorce papers from
Lucio had finally come through, and no Catholic school would
accept my brother Roy and me if we were not legitimised by proper
marriage documents. We spent the night before the wedding arrang-
ing baby's breath and other tiny flowers the neighbours had helped
pick from the colonial gardens. Inside a small basket, a little satin
cushion held two rings that were supposed to entrap Eros forever in
the small house in the bohemian neighbourhood. Nono Alberto was
the first one to congratulate my parents, and brought as a gift a porce-
lain angel, which Mama immediately locked in the glass cabinet next
to the decanter and the crystal box containing my umbilical cord.

She looked radiant in her pale yellow tailored suit with navy blue
trimmings, a matching hat and high-heeled suede shoes. It would be
her third marriage. A wisp of anxiety hid somewhere in her heart.
'Will it work?' it asked. It had worked so far. Next to her, my father
looked proud and handsome in his new brown suit with wide lapels
and beige stripes, soft cream shirt and a newly grown moustache,
which made him look like Clark Gable. In the sky, Eros celebrated
and the stars held a huge party, for Mama had finally found her soul
mate. I vividly remember how I sauntered into the local town hall in
my yellow organza dress with a huge bow on my head, carrying the

treasured rings in the flower basket. Under the rose petals and dried rice that Aunt Dorita, Lola and Renatta gaily sprinkled over Mama and Papa's crowns, they signed their promise of love forever until death were to bring them apart.

WHERE THE GODS LIVE

MAMA NEVER FORGOT the promise she had made to the rainbow: to come back for her children. Every day, come rain, hail or shine, she worked incessantly to save enough money to take my brothers out of boarding school and bring them to 'have a better life' in the city. She had fallen in love with Lima, and her often ebullient personality had allowed her to make good friends and develop her knack for business.

Mama was always searching for ways to reduce expenses, do without luxuries and make a small profit, even out of the food purse, so that she could put money aside. She instituted the purchasing of wholesale food such as grains and rice, flour and sugar on the weekends, and reduced most buying from the corner store. This did not please Don Takanaka, although he understood because he did the same. Out of every three pennies that she earned she would spend two and save one. Papa's earnings from the trucks covered the house expenses, the movie matinees and ice creams, while Mama's earnings paid for our education and savings. Her most important goal was to buy a house near Aunt Lisa, who was now married to the police lieutenant. They had settled in a new garden suburb boasting tall pines along the main avenue, a huge round park in the centre which reminded me of a wheel of fortune because of its layout, a Catholic school and a modern church.

Our house was always filled with visitors, popping in and complimenting Mama on her organised ways. So much so that she decided to offer lunch menus to workers from around the corner, who swapped Don Takanaka's braised food with MSG for Mama's lentils and sautéed green beans. She also sold some of the healing ointments, herbal tonics and curious knick-knacks she was sent from the jungle. Mama was now addressed as Doña Rosa because she had become a respectable lady with three children – starched clean and well behaved, at least most of the time – and a husband who valued her and did not hit her. But they mainly admired her because of her ability to be independent and have no debts.

Her lunch customers, who bought her alligator balms and piranha teeth necklaces for their girlfriends, became the vehicle for her savings operation. They began to buy bigger items, such as silk fabric for a dress or a suit, a special perfume, or a piece of costume jewellery, all on credit. One day, a customer suggested that instead of buying a brooch, he could buy a sum of money on credit, to be paid with added interest at the end of the week. When the neighbours heard of this favour they too approached Mama with similar requests and swore on their mothers' graves, invoking God and all the saints, and calling on the firmament to fall on their heads if they did not pay.

Papa did not like Mama lending money one bit, and warned her to be very careful because not only did people often forget their debts, but the courts did not protect anyone who ventured into such a business. Mama thought about it for a while and asked her own guides to give her a clear direction. One day Doña Panchita came to ask for an advance. One of her grandchildren was in hospital fighting meningitis. Mama could not say no. Then came Aunt Dorita with another sorrowful story, and Aunt Renatta behind her, and finally Lola. 'How could I say no to the people who have helped me settle here?' she said to Papa, who observed her deeds with disapproval. Soon, Doña Panchita brought along a cousin who was a doctor but needed an advance to pay the private school fees of his son. He paid on time at the end of two weeks. And then came Aunt Renatta's friend, the seamstress, who also paid on the due date.

Mama soon realised that this business needed a structured program. She thought long and hard, and finally she decided to create a series of saving programs called *panderos*. These were based on numbers from zero to ten, which people selected according to their own needs and paid weekly or monthly. Number zero was the house earnings but it always served as guarantee money in case others did not pay in time. In fact, that happened quite often as people got used to the routine.

In little time Mama became the informal local bank where customers could borrow in an emergency, and in the name of trust. She made advances to members of her investment programs, and lit many candles to Mary hoping that all would go well.

It was with these *panderos* that Mama planned for our future. I would see her light up with satisfaction every time she gazed at her savings books. Sometimes, after breakfast, she would dress me in thick socks and woollen sweaters and we would march out on a debt-collection journey, knocking on doors and trying to persuade debtors with the utmost courtesy to be honourable and pay. Sometimes it worked. It was my first insight into how other people looked in the morning, which was very different from the show they put on in the evenings, with lipstick, perfume and a self-confident attitude. Quite often I saw people pouring out the most intimate details of their convoluted lives on Mama's shoulder. Sometimes her eyes would moisten in solidarity, but she never failed to remind them of their debt at the end, even though she understood why they could not pay. She could not do anything else, for the law was not on her side – and even if it were, it would cost a hundred times more to take somebody to court for bad debts. She asked me never to comment on what I saw in some of these houses, not even to my father.

At some houses I was offered a piece of cake and told to play with the cat in the corner while Mama did business with her client. But in other houses the scene was a lot more dramatic. We found women with eyes swollen like figs, covered with scratches, their children crying in the background. The whining women told Mama things I did not understand and always sighed with relief when she gave them a hug and agreed to wait for their payment. It was then I decided that Mama was a noble woman, always keen to help younger souls in their journey through the maze of life, despite Aunt Lisa's warnings: 'Remember, Rosa, beware of the ravens you breed, for they might end up picking out your eyes.' She would often remind Mama of this when she saw her extending loans and selling *panderos* to people she felt were trouble. Ironically, sometimes Aunt Lisa would visit with a big ice-cream cake for afternoon tea and borrow money from Mama.

Once all of our collection errands had been done, Mama would take me to a cafeteria and order *café con leche* and vanilla cake for two. Under the table, she would remove her shoes and rub her toes against each other. Her feet were small, her toenails always neatly cut but never coloured, the skin on her soles pale and still soft despite the thorns upon which she had stepped along the path of life. She always had a handkerchief handy in her bag to wipe the dust from our faces, which slid off easily due to the humidity. We would go to the bathroom to fix our hair, and she would put some lipstick on her lips and a touch of Angel Face powder on my cheeks so we looked presentable for our succulent *lonche*, the Peruvian name for afternoon tea. Her favourite place was a little joint next to the markets with colourful trinkets hanging on the wall and a man who always made sure he warmed the milk the way she wanted – boiling hot. Otherwise she would drop the following line: 'This drink is frozen. The temperature has not tickled my throat; it has to tickle my throat.' I inherited her bad habit of drinking everything boiling hot, never mind the ulcers it caused in my digestive system.

During these café sessions she would tell me of her plans to buy a house with three bedrooms, preferably with two storeys and a garden. The house was meant to be for us children because we could not grow up for much longer in such a small house, which had been dubbed by my aunts *El Cuchitril de Pepin*, or 'The Hovel'. It was no place to invite my school friends, Mama claimed, although to me the house was big enough and the roof the perfect place for the spirits of the forest to land. Perhaps I saw more than she did; perhaps I preferred to enhance my boundaries with the tool she passed so successfully on to me – the imagination. How could I not, as she had filled my head with stories that defied ordinary perception, such as the one about the girl who lost her soul behind a mirror for being too vain. One day, she said, when this girl decided she could no longer live without her soul, a little frog came to help. He told her that to rescue her soul she had to sit by the mirror for one whole week and watch every shape, distorted or not, that appeared before her, and greet each with humility and acceptance. If the girl avoided the sight her soul would definitely die. That's why Mama did not spend time in front of the mirror, or let me do it. At least not when I was with her.

Sometimes we went out on Saturday afternoons to check department stores, examining the quality of electrical appliances, curtain fabrics and house accessories that would probably be obsolete by the time we bought a new house, but Mama was always planning and visualising ornaments and flowers to go with the intended furniture. Her determination to buy a new house knew no bounds even if at times the pursuit seemed illusory. With both of my parents working for themselves, their incomes were not always guaranteed.

The loan profits helped Mama pay for our school fees. Aunt Lisa had convinced her that the gods lived more comfortably in private schools. There, she assured Mama, I would learn the art of refinement, 'essential for a young girl with a wild nature'.

I still remember my first year at the nuns' school, particularly the day we rehearsed a play for Corpus Christi.

'No! No! No! That's not where God lives. He lives here . . . here, you understand? Do you?' It was the grumpy voice of a robust nun as she stamped her feet on the floor and dragged me, frowning, across the school courtyard. She was the Mother Superior, a large woman with a roaring voice, who scared the wits out of most of the girls who attended the school.

'But Your Reverence, you said yourself God lives everywhere, and now you have changed your mind,' I argued. It was all I could say before I felt her divine rage on my earlobe as she pulled hard, intoxicated with exasperation. She pressed so viciously that I believed she was about to extract the essence of my stubbornness right out of the tiny hole in my earlobe, where Mama hooked my earrings on Sundays before we went to Mass.

'Bresciani, you are incorrigible, just like the devil's daughter,' the old nun said and I grew embarrassed. I was in awe of her long black robe and of the headpiece that framed a face shaped like an avocado with a pair of protruding eyes which I always saw staring at me when I ate Spanish olives. I knew that deep inside she cared for us. Everything she did was to curb our rebelliousness, she claimed, and we had no other option but to believe her. On the day of the Corpus Christi rehearsal Mother Superior had pulled me by my angel wings from the middle of the courtyard and dragged me across to another spot, where she seemed to be certain God had set his headquarters. We were preparing for the *Journey of the Angels*, a play for our Year One presentation for the festival of the Holy Spirit, which was held every June with religious pomp. It fell around the same time as *Inti Raimy*, the Inca ritual that celebrates the Kingdom of the Sun, which we also acknowledged but never celebrated in the city. In the play I was meant to be a holy messenger who announced the arrival of a celestial delegation just before the end of the millennium. The role had filled my heart with a sense of purpose, and every night after dinner I rehearsed my lines and movements, despite the sniggers of my brothers who mocked my eagerness.

The instant I noticed that Mother Superior had pinched the delicate new wings I was wearing, I got so angry that I stomped on her toes, making her yell with anger and pain. I had even tried to shoot flames with my gaze, like a dragon. The wings were special. Doña Panchita had kindly donated the special feathers for them, a deed which had made Mama very happy. The black matron had laboriously plucked the plumes from the ducks she kept in a cage on the roof for eating on special occasions. The moment she heard I needed some wings, which happened to be a few days before her loan repayments were due, she decided to turn her ducks into a succulent casserole with coriander and chili, half of which she gave Mama as part-repayment, a barter that my Papa had totally approved of. It had taken my whole family a week to stick the dainty feathers on the white taffeta-and-cardboard wings that Papa had made. On that disastrous day, the eve of Corpus Christi, a limping Mother Superior sent me home to write one hundred times that I was the devil's daughter and I should be purified in holy water.

Mama was used to my fits of rebelliousness and had her own ways of dealing with them. With the whip. But I never understood all the fuss. I often rebelled when people's behaviour did not match their words. After all, it was my mother who taught me to see with the eyes of the soul, to look for the meaning in people's actions, for these, she claimed, reveal their true personality. But Mama was the first one to point out my rebelliousness as a 'terrible flaw'. 'Don't be so rude,' she scolded. 'Little girls should just listen and shut up.' I did try, but I found it very difficult to control my outbursts when my reason and my feelings did not hang in equilibrium. When Mama deeply apologised to Mother Superior for me turning her toes black, the nun calmed her down, assuring her that it was all a matter of time: 'She will see the right way soon because she has the skill to learn quickly.'

My mother always wanted to be a teacher, but fortune did not lead her onto the academic path. Instead, she played school mistress at home. From the age of four, before we started school, we began studying with her. She initiated us on the path of learning with her tales of the jungle, then with the adventures of Gulliver in the land of Lilliput, and then with arithmetic. No adding machines were seen on our table; instead, we had a handful of beans spread on the plastic tablecloth, with chopped carrots on the side. For fear that we would become restless and stray from our lessons, Mama bought a blackboard with Disney animals painted on the sides. She collected reference books, maths charts and stationery to create our own classroom. We accommodated our stuffed animals on small stools that Papa had built for them, so we felt that we were attending a real school in the middle of the jungle. Even the stuffed alligator and the piranha were part of the class. Mama would stand in front of the blackboard and, charged with passion and discipline, would speak with certainty about the need to be a righteous, cultivated and knowledgeable citizen. Sitting at a small blue desk built onto the side of the wardrobe, I learned to spell, read and write, as well as arithmetic. Because of our still-soft brains, we didn't find it too difficult to learn. In fact we saw it as a game.

Mama would prepare our lessons in the morning before she went to the market to buy fresh meat and vegetables for the *sancochado* soup. 'I am going to buy a quarter of a kilo of rump, which is twenty soles a kilo; how much money should I take, children?' she would ask. I would pull the rules out of my memory and, competing with my brothers for her affections, quickly jump up with the answer: 'You must take five soles, Mama. You must take five soles, Mama, five soles!' She would then bow her head with pleasure and bestow on us the most beautiful of all mothers' smiles, 'Very good, very good.' Then she would open the wardrobe, pull out her beige cardigan, change her blouse, add a touch of rouge to her cheeks, fix her curls with a pin behind her ear, and lock the door behind her, in case 'the monsters' came to bother us. Once she was gone, we made the sign of the cross, hoping here would be no earth tremors for we no longer feared the monsters.

With Mama gone, we would put the breakfast dishes aside and take our seats at our small desks. After I'd finished my lesson, I would peel the carrots, shell the peas and clean the rice, picking the little black bits out, washing it two or three times until the water ran clear, and then I would soak it so it would be ready for cooking, as Mama had instructed. Rice was a staple food of the country and people would die if they did not have it on their plate for lunch or dinner. It was the ways of the Chinese that we had already integrated, we loved eating braised food with soy sauce too. Sometimes my two brothers helped with picking the bad bits out of the rice, but sometimes they got playfully nasty and bathed me in homemade lemonade and sprinkled me with breadcrumbs to turn me into an *apanada* – a flattened schnitzel – in revenge for seeking Mama's attention. Defending myself against physical aggression had never been my forte. 'Hitting is for brutes,' my dad had once said. So I would protect my head with my arms and wear the rage of others with tears and resignation.

At eleven o'clock Mama would return home with a happy or a long face, depending on how her debt collection had gone. We would dutifully help her unload the basket and place the goods on the bench. Then I would tell her whatever I remembered of the ten o'clock radio soap, and together we would listen to the eleven o'clock drama while she chopped onions and crushed garlic. I would hand her a tea towel to wipe away the tears she shed in solidarity with the radio characters – a collection of villains, and a peasant girl whose true origins were more distinguished and for whom all the women in the capital cried every day, keen to discover who she really was. I imagined that there must have been a whole universe of heroes and villains living tiny dramas inside our radio set. Together we would weep as we sliced the meat and washed the dirt off the potatoes, our hearts drenched with the pain of the victims of social discrimination exposed to the immoral vices of the higher castes.

Papa would come home for lunch about noon and the workers would soon follow. The table was always ready, with the menu scribbled on a little board above the table. *Sancochado* soup, a blend of fresh vegetables, beef chunks and herbs with large macaroni noodles; lentils with braised beef and rice; and Russian salad on the side. For dessert, *mazamorra morada*, our purple maize custard. To drink, we offered homemade lemonade *chicha* or apple juice. When the dishes had been set aside, Mama would test my homework, and I was always ready to regurgitate the material I had learned. Learning how to read did not take long and soon I began to memorise the lessons. First, one paragraph, then two, and then the whole lesson.

Because Mama was such a good teacher, by the time I got to primary school I knew a lot more than what was prescribed, so one day Mother Superior told Mama that I could be transferred to a higher class. She was shocked. 'Oh no,' she cried. 'She is too young and must learn to play with girls her age.' The nun agreed and nothing else was said of the matter. But I was so disappointed that I wept for days – convinced that Mama wanted to stop my development. I didn't eat and vomited as often as possible. But Mama, who had learned from Doña Panchita the best way to handle this sort of 'odd' behaviour, gave me an enema of lemon verbena 'to release all demons', and scrubbed my skin with soda soap in a tin bath, under her mournful and stern gaze. If that did not work, then an egg would have to be passed around my body to clean me of all naughtiness. It never got to that stage. Soon after the enema, I hid my resentment deep in my heart, in the same way that Mama had. 'It is much better to bury it away than to keep it with you, in your head,' Mama said, and I always thought she was right. Until later on in life when the corpses of the past were resurrected.

Several weeks after my disappointment had healed, the dance teacher asked me to rehearse for a ballet, in which I would play the role of one of the Columbines dancing with a Pierrot. My heart glowed because dancing was my passion. It was the heritage of my ancestors, who swayed, shook and thrust their bodies in every direction; a much better way to 'release any demons' than lemon verbena. Mama had taught me to move rhythmically before I could walk; most babies in Peru are taught to dance while in their mother's arms. I felt that the universe had determined my path in life the day the dance teacher called me. I would be a dancer, just like *La Tongolele*, the famous Mexican dancer of the big screen, who had been inspired by Carmen Miranda. She often came to Lima on tour and the whole city would be electrified by her sizzling personality, primeval moves and frenetic steps, particularly when she did the mambo in her shimmering outfits of silk and feathers. Mama was happy to see me involved in something I truly liked, but all the rehearsing after school hours left less time for household chores.

When the day of selection for the show came I turned up to school earlier than anybody else, and when I found my name on the selection list, I was thrilled. Mama had always said, 'Those who get up early enlist the grace of God.' But when I informed her of the news that night, Mama told me to wait a few days, until she had discussed it with my father. I withdrew to my bedroom, expecting the worst. And it did come. Mama said the family simply could not afford to subsidise my dance inclinations. She told the teacher of her decision, and nothing more was ever said about it. My heart was further eclipsed. All I wanted to do was disappear, join the wandering gypsies and jump into the river of sorrows, like my mythical grandmother. I was so enraged that I felt my anger could have pulverised my bones. I knew that my father had nothing to do with the decision, for it was Mama who made the rules at home, and Papa always said that my affairs were women's business.

I began to look at Mama with the eyes of my soul. Through them I could see that sometimes she wore the stepmother's mantle of severity. She would suddenly become strict and puritanical, particularly when the mood had been good and smooth for a while. None of us knew what triggered her sudden changes. I began to diet in silent protest, for I knew that loud tantrums would only lead to another enema. One day, seeing the desolation in my face, Mama tried to explain that dancing was beyond the family's means, that the pink tutu was very expensive, and so were the shoes and the socks, and the crown with pink pearls, and the extra lessons from the ballet teacher. With tenderness she revealed that the family was finding it hard to pay all the private school tuition, and that she was not feeling too well in her belly, or in her chest. I accepted her excuses with resignation, because we all knew her program of financial austerity. She was, after all, saving to bring her children to Lima, and for the big house, the house that she said would bring us all together. A big house for friends to visit and for tea and ice cream to be served in style, like on American television and the rich houses on our own TV soaps. I did not want a bigger house, all I wanted was to dance.

'Dancing may be your passion but you must also study to be a prosperous person,' Mama said, giving me a little pat on the shoulder. 'Art will never lead you anywhere.' Deep inside, Mama resented her father's artistic inclinations. She felt that it was his love for music that had taken his support away from her at the time when she most needed it – when he did not support her refusal to Don Ramon. I also knew that Mama did not want me to suffer her disgraces and humiliations. Instead, she wanted to create a successful person out of me. She wanted to have the means to grant me prestige and happiness in life. It was the best she could offer, she believed. As the days went by my stomach stopped churning. Eventually, I swallowed my tears and hugged Mama with the love of a daughter who knows no other goddess beyond her – except for the Virgin Mary, who, back then, I thought was Mama's best friend. After a glass of hot milky coffee and a piece of cake, I promised her I would always do my best. And I kept my promise. For she was the best role model I ever had, even if I eventually had to move away from her and live on the other side of the world. My life developed its own strength through following the motto she always taught me: that dreams do come true, despite the obstacles we find along the way.

With my ballet aspirations thwarted by circumstances and the sad forecast that art would never make me an important person, my wish to pursue artistic expression evaporated. This is how sadness settled into my soul, gradually blurring my perception. I spent weeks in

subdued gloom, wandering from place to place like a ghost, searching for the Blue Cat to take me with him. I went to school and
learned new lessons with complete indifference, as if the turbine that
generated happiness in my heart had irretrievably broken down. One
afternoon after class I went to see Mother Superior, who was con-
cerned about my depression. I confided my disappointments and told
her I wanted to become a nun. I explained that my heart was broken,
that frustration was taking the best part of me, and there was nothing
else for me to pursue in the world. My face was deeply etched with
sorrow. I had become the best student in Mama's school of
melodrama.

Mother Superior listened quietly and attentively, as if she could
read what was going on in my head and in my heart. Sensing that I
had a shattered ego, she gave me a pat on the back, extolled my 'amazing abilities to deliver drama' and advised me to come back when I
turned sixteen. 'You could pursue drama if you don't make it anywhere else,' she called out as I dragged my feet out of her room in
deep disillusionment. She added: 'Jesus does not want brides who are
frustrated young ladies who feel there is nothing else for them to do
in the outside world.' I retreated, grumbling, my head down in apparent humility.

I then found a more serene environment. Alone in the school
chapel, I prayed to Mary, asking her to give me clues about my future.
I always felt good when I cast my eyes on the statue with the look of
tenderness. A few minutes later, one of the other sisters walked up
behind me and put her arm around my shoulder. She was my religion
teacher, the holder of a gentle disposition and a soft gaze, who had
always attracted me to the path of service. If the love of God can
make a person so beautiful, I often thought, then I want to be a nun.
But when I looked at the other nuns, I had my doubts. My teacher
quietly led me to the head of the chapel and guided me to kneel on
one of the leather cushions next to her. We recited a couple of prayers
together, and I felt the immense kindness and compassion coming
from her. I told her of my conversation with the principal and she

replied, 'God will always shine a torch along your path as long as the heart is sincere.' I noticed that her eyes radiated tiny sparks as she went on to say that it was up to each of us to see as much we wanted to see. I decided then to look at her heart. I visualised it pulsating with the fluid of life, a soft radiance spreading around it. My teacher said that this torch exists in all our hearts 'Will God light his torch for me tonight?' I asked, and she said He would. I gave her a kiss and walked slowly out of the chapel. 'Although this torch is in your heart, try always to imagine it above your head.'

'Yes, Sister, I always will,' I replied. And I still do. Although the holder of the torch has changed image and name, the light has always shone. There have been times when I did not see it at all. But that was because my eyes were shut with fear.

Not far from our house there lived a saint. A lady of sacred abilities. Her name was Doña Santitos, and her heart was made of love and rose petals. My mother met her at the local church fête and had felt an immediate affection towards her, as if her memories had been touched by the light of recognition. Doña Santitos marvelled at the cake Mama had brought for the fête, and described it as having been prepared with the very essence of love. Mama said that she used vanilla essence, and Doña Santitos replied that in her opinion both were one and the same. How she came to live on the block we never knew, but the petite lady soon became the soul of the neighbourhood, bringing out the good in people and the hope in all of us. The children began to call her 'Pie from Heaven', a favourite term of endearment in Peru. She was tiny as a gnome, with hair that reminded us of corn silk, pale skin and compassionate eyes that were the colour of fresh chestnuts. She had a small, triangular face and thin lips, which she used mainly to pray. She walked so quickly that people thought she was always running away from death or rushing towards the kingdom of Heaven.

Doña Santitos knew how to look through people's inhibitions, and past the layers of their miseries and afflictions. She had seen Mama's true essence, which it would take my mother years to find. We all loved her, although when Doña Panchita had met her she had felt the hairs on her back rise, and told us that the little woman was a bit too strange. 'One has always to be careful of rare things. The devil comes in all disguises,' Doña Panchita said. But even the black matron fell under Doña Santitos' blessed charm eventually. She often visited her to seek advice when her own guides from the underworld, or from the sky, did not answer her prayers. Mama never knew whether Doña Santitos was a mystical apparition or a real person, for her appearance was changeless; she ate very little; and there was a glow around her, a radiance whose source no one could determine. She would share the occasional cup of tea or glass of vermouth with Mama for she loved a bit of alcohol every so often, explaining that a touch of fun goes a long way towards dissolving minor sins. No one knew where she was born, but one thing we did know: she was not a local, for while she spoke Spanish, there was something unique about her pronunciation. She offered very little about her past, in fact she offered nothing but a smile and the reply: 'A woman must keep her mysteries.'

Her actions spoke more than her words. She didn't waste energy preaching or lecturing people; instead, she listened to what they had to say. Generosity was the principle she lived by; she would always have a plate of food ready when the needy knocked on her door, and she would pluck a coat or a jumper out of nowhere for a child from a family who could not afford winter clothes. When people asked her who she was, she would reply that she was 'just one of the messengers of the light'. She preferred to use such a description rather than mention God, explaining that some people do not identify with Christianity, and that in the end, all deities are of the same family. People did not understand her mystical rhetoric most of the time, but they liked her all the same. We'd never seen any of her relatives visit her home; at least no one had seen a stranger in the neighbourhood asking for her whereabouts. Nor did she have any family photos on her dresser.

One All Saints' Day a group of neighbours – the more devoted ones – tried to convince the block that she was an angel incarnate, sent by Heaven to teach us to be nice to each other. They lit a large torch to make the announcement. Doña Santitos was very moved, but not at all happy with the publicity.

Others in the neighbourhood were sure she was an alien who had lost her way back home, and was roaming around our world doing good deeds, waiting to be spotted by her cosmic family. Others were sure she was a reborn saint, though no one knew how old. A few even believed that, like the soul, she would be eternal. Some neighbours consulted with her before buying a lottery ticket, and some preferred to confess their sins to her instead of going to see the priest at the local church, whom many distrusted because it was believed he had fathered a son in our neighbourhood. When one of the neighbours won a small prize in the lottery, the rest of the neighbourhood forced him to give Doña Santitos a healthy donation for the poor.

On the other side of the road lived Loretta, a mambo dancer with a highly seductive swing of the hips and a most enchanting face. Her expression emitted such an angelic air of seduction that it often strangled women with their own insecurities and left men's tongues hanging. When she laughed, her chuckles were filled with earthiness, and the rings in her ears would bounce. Loretta's home was often filled with friends from work, bohemians who celebrated life with guitars and castanets and who danced all night, stomping on the floorboards and waking the whole neighbourhood. They were always partying, sometimes to celebrate a triumph or to commiserate with each other over a defeat. The men drank until they were stupefied by alcohol and inebriated with indulgence, while the women shook their beads and their bangles in an entanglement of basic instincts and primal desires. Often the parties ended in rowdy brawls that would become either public entertainment or dangerous disputes, depending on the level of aggression and the quantity of alcohol. The police would appear in a paddy wagon from around the corner, and would stack the ruffled boys and girls one by one inside. My brothers and I would watch through the bars of our windows, giggling; keen to watch the next episode. The wind always brought the news that Loretta would be having a party, even though she would surreptitiously carry boxes and bottles from the corner grocer to her house. It was then we warned Mama to fill our ears with cotton wool before we went to bed, and she would make a valerian and chamomile infusion for herself. Some of the women on the block looked at Loretta with animosity and even disdain, and many of them would have preferred that she moved out. Although she often provided a reason for good gossip, which kept everyone in a frenetic buzz.

Aunt Dorita did not like Loretta much because she believed that a woman with the quality of fire such as Loretta had to be linked in some way to hell. She told Mama to watch over her shoulder just in case. The truth was that although Loretta was a stripper in a club of not very good reputation, she was a decent woman, who sent most of her money home to pay for her sisters' education and the care of her brother, who was not too well in the head. Somehow, Doña Panchita discovered that Loretta's father was a member of a shaman clan known for its dark powers, which operated in the northern regions where the mountains married the ancient desert. The clan, she said, practised all types of 'works' to alter the direction of innocent souls, but also to straighten the crooked ones. The clan practised in caves where people from the capital flocked when nothing else would heal their anguish. Apparently, Loretta's mother had been kidnapped by the shaman when she was a teenager. He had made her pregnant and intended to keep her there as an assistant, but the woman finally escaped, half mad. 'You see,' Aunt Dorita barked, 'Loretta has to be carrying some curse.' Doña Panchita heard further rumours that Loretta's young brother had gone mad after claiming to have seen God in a cave. The mambo dancer hardly spoke about her family, only to say that her sisters were doing well.

Doña Santitos defended Loretta when the gossip became too destructive, always stressing that beneath murky circumstances there often lies an innocent soul. She saw something in Loretta that had remained untouched, kept safe inside her heart despite constant violations. The mambo dancer always wore a little charm on a gold chain around her neck, which she said was a gift from the nuns of her town. She had held on to that gift tightly, trusting the amulet's power of protection. She was like a flower that refuses to perish despite stormy weather.

Mama became friends with Loretta one afternoon when Loretta had pulled me out of battle with some kids at church and brought me home. Time presented both women with a platter of healthy jokes and a variety of mambo steps, and soon Mama and Loretta became close. The young woman would keep an eye on our house when Mama went out, but most importantly, she always paid her loans on time. Mama believed that people who paid their debts had little to worry about when their turn came to face the grim reaper. I guess she also liked Loretta because she was always in a good mood. Sometimes she came to our house in the afternoon to learn how to bake cakes and to have private talks, and Mama would send me to have tea with Aunt Dorita.

I discovered much later that Loretta had been repeatedly abused since childhood, and that her father had cast a curse on her whole family. But despite all the tragedy and exploitation, Loretta had survived, and had maintained a love for life and a vibrant talent for dancing. Although she had won a series of competitions in the capital, to earn a living she danced in a seedy nightclub somewhere on the dusky side of life. It was a place of dim lights and curtains of heavy smoke, where she undulated her hips and stripped to the bare minimum, teasing the restless spirit of her male audience. 'What else could a dancer of no means do?' she asked. Mama would just listen and pour a tiny bit more vermouth in her glass, knowing too well that in a world with daughters and sisters, women should always help each other.

One day Loretta brought Mama a bottle of Greek aniseed liqueur to put in a cake for Aunt Dorita's birthday. After a feast of cake and when all the women were drunk, Loretta told them that when she was a child her grandmother had given her a little doll blessed with holy water by the convent nuns. The doll was meant to dilute the curse of the shaman and always remind her of the scent of innocence. She said that dolls were good vehicles to carry blessings, or curses. Mama was to remember this story.

One hot afternoon in the neighbourhood, when sweat trickled down the necks of the men at the repair shop and the wind had come to a halt, I saw Doña Santitos returning home at her customary swift pace. Then I saw her stop suddenly. A couple of metres away, on the other side of the road, Loretta was struggling on the ground, trying hard to defend herself against some hairy creep. The men in the repair shop were too tired even to react. But Doña Santitos' chestnut eyes turned into fire bolts. The assailant was one of Loretta's stoned boyfriends, one of those who had made terrible noises at night. A gambler and a drunk who believed she was his 'fountain of resources'. He had dragged Loretta out of the house by the hair and was trying to force her to let go of her purse. Loretta clasped it firmly against her breasts, trying to save the last of her weekly earnings, and probably Mama's money for the saving program. Doña Santitos was incensed by the sight of the victim and the predator. She leapt across the road, threw herself onto the man's back and, with amazing strength, gripped her tiny hands around his neck. The assailant, who was roaring like a raging lunatic, noticed the petite lady on his back, and, as a lion annoyed by a fly, turned around to grab Doña Santitos and turn her into a soft pulp. But as he did so, he lost his balance and released his grip on Loretta. Instantly, a kick between the legs from Loretta forced him to drop to the ground semi-conscious. Exhausted, Doña Santitos bent down, grabbed him by the head, and, peering into his eyes, called on the Holy Spirit to exorcise the devil from him. Finally the police came and dragged the hairy boyfriend away. Loretta fell on her knees to thank Doña Santitos, kissing her hands and promising to do penance to clean herself of the bad spirits she felt had begun to besiege her. All Doña Santitos asked for in return was a cup of tea with a nip of cognac to pull herself together.

My seventh birthday was looming, so Mama prepared my purple tunic for me to wear during the sacred festival of the Purple Christ; it was a promise she had made to the Lord of Miracles. I never looked forward to October because the purple tunic meant service and penance, and no parties. While it made me feel special and worthy of God's love, it also meant a month of contrition. It was never in October that I wanted to be a nun. Mama claimed I had received my life back thanks to the Purple Christ after a serious illness had threatened to take it away. She said I was a product of a miracle, 'never to be forgotten'. I grew up believing in miracles, always trying to discover how they were made. Every time I threw a tantrum and rebelled against my mother, calling for justice, she reminded me of the sacred covenant. 'You are lucky to be alive, you know,' she would say, pointing her finger at my heart and moving it immediately towards the small picture of the Purple Christ stuck on the wall above the dining table.

The story was that I had fallen seriously ill with some sickness, the details of which I never found out exactly, but which I gathered later was rheumatic fever. I was still a baby and so ill that the doctors gave Mama no hope. Papa's eyes always saddened when Mama told the story. It had been the first trauma in their relationship. But Mama decided to fight, and while I was in a coma, she prayed without interruption, as Doña Panchita recommended. It seemed, in Mama's words, that my soul had been lured by the Blue Cat, which for all intents and purposes was the Angel of Death. My mother was not going to let the Blue Cat take me away, not without a fight. Doña Panchita counselled her to quickly acknowledge the power of the Purple Christ, famous for making the impossible manifest. Mama, who had learned from Aunt Lisa to be truly practical, put this faith to

the test and prayed night and day, promising her new god of suffering my life of service in exchange for the Blue Cat to be given
another date to claim me. Her faith was rewarded, and the Blue Cat
has not come to bother me again . . . not yet. In return, I sacrificed
my birthday parties.

Together, Mama and I dusted the altar, polished the frames around
the pictures of the Purple Christ, and took note of how many candles we needed and discussed whether this year I would get a new
purple robe because I had grown so much. We listened to the latest
'Miracles Melodrama' on the airwaves, in which actors wept and gave
testimony for the most incomprehensible sacred phenomena in our
history. As I helped polish the candlesticks, Mama asked me what I
wanted for my birthday, although she had never asked before. I
thought that perhaps the dancing affair had softened her heart. Following Mama's teachings and my spiritual mood I said that 'whatever
God offered would be nice' but soon added that I really wanted a
party. 'Umm,' Mama murmured, rubbing her chin with her soft fingers, 'we'll see.' I said no more, lowering my head and working even
harder on the candlesticks.

She unlocked the special glass cabinet, took out a packet of cookies, and arranged some on a plate. She then handed the plate to me
and suggested I take it to Doña Santitos. 'Perhaps she has a surprise
for you,' she said with a tone of secrecy. I took off with a smile from
ear to ear, happily carrying some of the imported cookies that Papa
often brought from work. 'Never visit anybody without taking an
offering,' Mama always insisted, particularly when it was a person
whom you wanted to ask for guidance. I was excited because I had
never been inside the little lady's house, and I enjoyed checking out
people's homes. Inside, I would silently observe the things that hung
on the walls, the texture of the furniture, the scent of the food, and
sometimes even the shadows that hovered around their emotions.

Doña Santitos asked me in and I was immediately filled with glee.
It was like stepping into another world. I felt that if the Virgin lived
in Peru, she would live in Doña Santitos' house. One could not hear

the noise of the street, and it seemed we were in a distant galaxy. The light was so warm; it appeared to be filtered from some celestial spot above her roof, which was quite unusual because her house hardly had any windows, except for a small opening above the door. I smelled sweet fragrances emanating from the bed, the table, the chest of drawers, the apron hanging from the wall and the pots on the stove. The whole house was inundated with aromatic freshness, as if she had sprayed soft perfume on every speck of air that we breathed. Mesmerised by the religious knick-knacks, I felt light, as if my body had melted in her presence. The petite lady realised my state of ecstasy and softly explained that her house was showered by the light of the Queen of the Universe. She said that good deeds attract this quality of light. After I finished scrutinising every little trinket and figurine, she asked me to sit down and listen to a poem from an Arab poet who she called The Prophet. It spoke about accepting one's predicament in life. Doña Santitos counselled me, saying that although I had not become a dancer this year I might be able to become one later on if I really wanted it that much. 'Before we enter the door of our true happiness we have to push other tiny doors that at times seem extremely heavy. But if we really want to get inside the main door we just have to push hard and persevere,' she said. And I listened, hypno-tised by the sound of her voice, the resonance of her verse and the glow of her aura. I spoke to her about what was important for me. I told her about my doll Mercedes and of my wishes to have her 'do the right things' as Mama wanted me to do.

'What should I do to guide her?' I asked.

'Well, if she is going to follow your steps, you can start with bap-tising her,' she replied with a smile, handing me a piece of nougat, which she knew was my favourite sweet.

'Really? Will that clean her of all sins? Will she really be protected?'

'I am sure,' she grinned. 'All you have to do is soak her in a bit of water and have a party,' she added.

I skipped home with a piece of nougat still stuck in my teeth, the pleats of the tartan skirt Mama made me wear on Saturdays bouncing against my legs. I was rapt in Doña Santitos' suggestion, and touched by her genteel aura. Getting my doll baptised would be such a good idea, I thought, if only Mama would say yes. Perhaps we could have that party after all. Suddenly a new light had switched on inside me. Little did I know at the time that it had been Mama's idea to have the doll blessed.

THE MARK OF LIFE

NEWS OF MY doll's baptism travelled around the block with the speed of lightning. The neighbours rattled and tattled about the reasons behind this 'most unusual celebration'. 'Have you ever heard such idiocy? A doll being christened! It is a sacrilege!' Those who knew Mama well were not surprised for they were familiar with her peculiar ways. But those who resented her compared this latest move to the work of the black sorcerers, a rumour that nearly gave Doña Panchita a heart attack. The leader of the gossip was the Catwoman, famous for her long, painted nails and for being the priest's lover. People swore that she had borne a child to him. The poor woman had been the victim of many ill rumours, some of which had solid bases, some of which did not. In the end, she transformed herself into the very essence of gripe and gossip, always ready to find faults and imperfections, examine scars, and search for disabilities in the people who crossed her path. In my mother's opinion, the Catwoman was just looking into her own mirror.

Not far from our neighbourhood lived two of my father's sisters, who often strutted past our house, heads held high, without calling to say hello, even when Papa was home. They were still giving Mama the cold shoulder. Nono Alberto said that they were 'not too well in the head', but I was convinced that they resented my mother because she did not kowtow to their caprices, as other women who entered the family had done in the past. I had trained myself to hide my resentment when I saw them, but it was always there, well camou-flaged under a courteous smile, when they patted my head. I guess Mama's planned revenge was to buy a house bigger than they ever had, although that was going to be difficult for the Bresciani children had lived in large quarters when Nona Emilia was still alive.

Aunt Dorita knew her sisters well and often described them as 'pompous birds of paradise'. 'Just because their skin is bleached and they have gringo eyes, they think they are God's angels,' she sneered. But the truth was that only one of them had inherited Nono's blue eyes, the other just basked in the reflection, always feeling superior to black-eyed people. Mama promised herself never to speak a word of criticism against them, for she considered them, to be 'weak souls'. At least that's what she said when Papa was around – the truth was that she knew they were a pair of snobs. To show them that she was 'beyond their reach' she had sent invitations to my doll's baptism party to my cousins. My aunts were horrified – not surprisingly, as one of them was a friend of the Catwoman. My cousins were keen to come to the party, and pleaded to be allowed to attend. But the aunts had not been invited to the party for adults that would be held afterwards. They were even more shocked when they discovered that my doll's godfather was going to be Angel, the son of Aunt Dorita. 'They belong to each other those two. A couple of nuts, I'd say,' one of the aunts told Nono, who replied that he preferred them that way because their 'uniqueness makes them good cooks'.

Despite the Catwoman's clawing on his conscience, the local priest agreed that the ceremony was a good idea, for anything that kept people close to the spirit of God was good. But he decided to send one of the altar boys to represent him in the ceremony, as the affair con-cerned a younger generation. He wanted his acolyte to be empowered by exercising the holy sacrament. By the grace of God and Aunt Renatta, the altar boy happened to be another cousin, Tato. This boy was an emissary of goodness, whose journey had been filled with more crosses than roses. I had always been fond of him because he was endowed with a cheerful disposition that was often contagious, though his legs were getting more feeble by the day. A virus had lodged in his nervous system and was gradually eating away the strength of his limbs.

A couple of weeks before the party, Mama sprang up on her bed in her sleep to forecast the arrival of her sister. 'Techa is coming soon,' she said. Papa was fast sleep, so the eerie announcement was met by a ghostly silence, interrupted only by creaking mattress springs and a sleeping whistle from Papa. The next day, as she hummed her morning song while pouring hot milk into the breakfast mugs, I asked Mama when Techa would arrive. My question seemed to assault Papa's serenity for he frowned and his eyes turned darker. 'I did not know your sister was coming,' he grumbled. Mama placed the jug on the table and looked at me inquisitively, as if the news had been carried to me by a butterfly. That was because she had not yet received a letter. When I told her about the announcement I had heard her make before dawn, Papa froze. He knew Mama had a knack for forecasting events, and he did not want any more visitors from the jungle. Certainly not Mama's sister, who spoke like a parakeet.

'You are always right and that is dangerous,' he grunted as he left the table.

Later, Mama pulled a candle out of a box she kept in the wardrobe and lit it in front of the Virgin, to whom she offered a smile from her heart. Now that Techa was about to come she would definitely have fresh news from her sons in the jungle. She then checked whether there were enough sheets in the drawer, as she had loaned her spare set to Doña Panchita, and whether the foldable bed had been returned by Aunt Dorita.

The next Saturday, we found downtown Lima pulsating with madness. The riot police, who were in force at a miners' demonstration, had 'accidentally' dropped a tear gas bomb in the middle of the plaza. Frantic pedestrians ran amok, forcing Mama to drag me away from the scene. As we pushed our way through the mayhem of vendors and the protesting mob, a large gypsy woman in a scruffy shawl began to follow us, asking Mama to let her read my fortune. Mama walked faster, holding her head up and pursing her lips in defiance. Perhaps the gypsies stirred the side of her that she preferred not to have, the side that could see beyond the boundaries of tomorrow.

Mama had disowned her intuitive inheritance. But more often than not, she could not help it – the warnings would just slip from her tongue. She predicted the pregnancy of one of her clients, who was believed to be sterile. 'I am sure you are going to have a baby,' she said. 'In fact, you might be having it soon!' By the grace of the universe, it happened. More dramatic was her forecast that Pepito, the son of a neighbour, would have an accident. The child had been pestering me, and my mother had warned him, 'Stop being nasty to little girls or else the sky will drop you.' Sadly, Pepito fell from a tree the following day. After that Papa begged Mama to avoid trouble with the neigh-bours by shutting up. 'Just don't play with the occult,' he appealed to her. Doña Santitos, on the other hand, encouraged Mama to nurture her skills, reassuring her that she was just 'well connected'. But Mama recoiled at any suggestion that she had mysterious powers. 'Call me anything, but not a witch.' Mama always wanted to be a lady. She had come to live in the capital to forget the market girl, the rainbow and the Pink Dolphin. But I knew Mama's heart always rejoiced when the Green Spirits came to visit, riding on the banana leaf wrappings and in the rice cakes from Iquitos.

We walked past the tallest building in the capital, the Ministry of Education. It was the first time I had seen such a huge structure. Curiosity made me turn my head upwards. I could see up to the top of the building to the symbols on the coat of arms on the waving flag at the top. I saw the llama, the quinoa tree and the cornucopia over-flowing with gold, symbols of the country's former wealth, which I had just learned about at school. On the steps outside, cigarette and peanut vendors squatted behind their baskets of loose tobacco and candied fruit and nuts. A man with plumes on his head sold small green lizards as talismans to bring good luck. I tugged Mama along, eager to explore more of this fascinating bazaar. The gypsy still followed us, chanting in a strange language. Finally, she tapped Mama on the arm. Well, Mama did not like that at all. In response, she elbowed the gypsy, flaring a fierce look at her. 'Go away or I'll call the police,' she snarled. But the gypsy would not yield.

'I have a message for you,' she shrilled ominously.

Mama believed that all gypsies had disordered minds. 'What they see is not exactly what civilised people see,' she whispered 'and that can be extremely dangerous, because insanity is contagious.'

'You have to hear me, dear one. It is all written here,' the gypsy screeched, grabbing my hand. 'You have the mark of life.'

I turned my gaze to her face, and felt scared. Mama turned around and stopped, holding firm against the tide of smelly pedestrian traffic, red anger drawn on her face. 'Listen, you dirty old woman, if you don't go away I will whack you with my bag.' But the gypsy stood her ground and would not go, looking at Mama with defiance. Fully aware of the persevering nature of gypsies, Mama's anger transformed into practical pity. Sighing with impatience, she opened her bag, pulled out a coin and handed it to the woman. 'Here you are. You may go now.'

The woman grabbed the coin and patted me on the head. 'You have the mark of life,' she said, then winked and moved away, comically prancing.

I looked at Mama and asked what she had meant by the 'mark of life' and Mama said, 'Nonsense, darling, pure twaddle.'

The gypsy's statement echoed in my brain. The air was impregnated with pungent aromas of food, incense, sweat and Chanel No 5. The sky had turned a mournful grey. Pedestrians pushed and shoved, as if chased by their own shadows, mixing intolerance with resignation. On the road, a procession of scruffy vehicles intoned a cacophony of mixed toots and honks that blended with drivers' outcries and toxic fumes.

Mama and I shopped for the material for my doll's baptism dress, which Mama had convinced me would have to be white organza with silk ribbons, and a white satin petticoat. We moved quickly in and out of fabric shops, haggling and bargaining, bumping against hawkers who claimed to sell the key to happiness and the meaning of life in a bottle. Perhaps some did, I wanted to believe. We checked baptism accessories – white gloves and new shoes for me – and selected the party menu from a scrumptious display at an Italian cake shop. I was on cloud nine. Suddenly, I felt Mama's hand tightening on my wrists; her cheeks had turned crimson. 'Let's go inside that shop,' she said, pulling my hand hard and heading towards a cafeteria packed with people, smoke and cakes. We made it to the door after shoving through the crowd, but before we could disappear inside, an older gentleman came up to us.

'Rosita Lujan, happy are the eyes that see you,' he said.

'Mr Lozano, how are you?' Mama forced a smile and bowed her head in politeness. Her cheeks were red as fire. The man looked at me and patted me on the head with gentleness. His hands felt warm. The three of us stood outside the cafeteria, interrupting the pedestrian traffic.

'Your daughter?' asked the man with an agreeable smile. He looked distinguished, with a confident poise and a clear face. Tall, slim and elegant, wearing a tweed jacket and a cashmere sweater. Probably in his mid-fifties. A businessman by his appearance.

Mama and the stranger exchanged polite words, and talked a bit about the morning's earth tremor and how much Lima had changed. After these controlled courtesies, Mama excused herself, saying she had to attend to some of my urgent needs. The man was not fooled at all, but accepted Mama's excuse. His elegant frame bent down and he smiled a warm farewell to me. 'You are certainly as pretty as your Mama,' he said, and I liked him immediately. Nodding politely, he disappeared into the crowd. Who was this stranger? Mama looked a bit shaken, as if a piece of her past had come back to greet her. I was eager to know the full story, for I had never seen or heard of such a gentleman in my whole life, not from Mama's tales or from my relatives. But she was not willing to say much at the time, except that he was an old friend. Many years later she told me who he really was.

Mama's romantic revelation came one evening after an earth tremor, as we sat at the table by candlelight, waiting for Papa to come back and fix the electrical fuses that had blown. Then she opened this new window on her life. The man's name was Martin Lozano, and he had offered Mama the world, together with the sun, moon and starry galaxy in exchange for her love – but marriage had not been part of this heavenly basket. He was married to a woman whom he felt he could not divorce. She had been ill for a long time, although Martin Lozano believed she did not want to get well. Rosita was not willing to become his mistress. 'I had not come to Lima for that,' she impressed upon me. That was the fate of so many country girls whose first mistake was to fall in love with, and then to fall pregnant to, a man who they later discovered was married. Martin wanted to set Mama up in an apartment with all the comforts of life, to treat her like a queen, to make up for what he could not give her: the title of wife. A very important title in the country where I was born. Despite Mama's polite refusal, they kept their friendship alive. Martin became her permanent escort to the movies, the friend with whom to stroll along the beach, and her confidant. Poor Martin Lozano, his heart grew very confused. One day, when he could no longer bear the call of his emotions, he discussed the possibility of a divorce, never mind his wife's illness. 'What if she kills herself?' asked Mama, thinking of the radio soaps.

Martin's story was an entanglement of rejection and revenge. He had married a woman of higher station, and they had two children. But their passionate love was short-lived. Once the romance wore out, the sparkling new wife rejected his affections and constantly reminded him of his less privileged background. One day while he was at work and his wife was out partying, their first son fell into the pool and drowned. The nanny, who could not swim anyway, was blabbering on the phone at the time. Martin never forgave his wife for the loss but stayed in the relationship for the sake of their second child. The wife gradually succumbed to a guilt-ridden illness. Her skin lost its lustre and she spent most of her days indoors, weeping and pounding on her chest.

As they sipped vermouth on ice with a slice of lemon, Martin would pour out his sorrows and Mama would listen with undiluted attention, her eyes travelling from his lips to his clear eyes, admiring the premature silver wisps on his temples, unconsciously fertilising her own affections for him, and further igniting his. The day Martin spoke of divorce, Mama gave the affair some thought, for her feelings were entangled. Yet she felt an uneasiness in her stomach. Martin's wife was sick, and she believed that no woman deserved to be emotionally abandoned. She always hammered on my ears that no woman can build happiness on the sorrows of another woman.

The unconsummated romance between Mama and her benefactor came to a turning point the day Mama received an unexpected visit. The previous night the earth had shaken even though it was not October, the usual month for tremors. It was a hot afternoon. Mama dusted and disinfected the small house into which she had just moved. There was a nervous knock on the door. She placed the broom behind the kitchen door – to deter any guest from staying too long – untied her apron and fixed her hair. Who would it be? Hardly anybody knew where she lived.

'Are you Miss Rosa Lujan?' asked an elegantly dressed young woman. Mama did not recognise her, but her heart assured her that the holder of such a pretentious pose had to mean serious business.

'Yes I am,' she replied with her chest puffed up and her head held high. 'Can I help you?'

'I am Pepa Lozano, daughter of Martin Lozano. Do you recognise the name?' said the woman with an imperious tone.

'Yes, I do,' replied Mama, on alert but truly wondering about the purpose of this visit. Was Martin sick? Local snoopers walked past and looked at the young woman with curiosity. Mama asked her to come in to avoid unnecessary attention. The discomfort was obvious in the girl's face; she was probably a couple of years younger than my mother. It must have taken courage to come and see me, thought Mama. Inside the humble room with a bed, table and two chairs, the women stood face-to-face, engulfed in a silence that spoke more than words. Mama pulled up a chair and offered the girl a seat, then went to the kitchen to make some tea. Pepa looked around, wondering what on earth this girl had that had brought such chaos to her family. Mama came out with two cups of chamomile tea, and ears ready to listen. The exchange did not take long. First from Pepa came the cries of recrimination and the terrible fear of abandonment. Mama listened while she sipped her tea, to which she had also added some extra calming herbs, just in case. Pepa began to weep, the thick shell around her disintegrating.

Sobbing profoundly, she begged Mama not to take her father away.

How could she take a father away when she knew what such a loss meant? Suddenly Mama realised that life had placed this woman in front of her for a reason. To look at her own pain. After handing Pepa a serviette to wipe her eyes, she assured Pepa of her understanding.

'Your father is a wonderful person and I don't believe him capable of ever abandoning you. I am only grateful for all he has done for me, but I am not his lover nor will I ever be his mistress.' Her words flowed with certainty, as if pushed by the force of her soul. The lump that had risen in her throat when she saw Pepa at the door dissolved. She had never been more convinced of a decision. On that Saturday afternoon, within twenty-four hours of the earth tremor, Mama sealed her destiny. It was up to her to move on in life. She would have to rely on her own resources to fight her battles, to forge her own future. Never mind the falls, never mind the failures, she would not hurt people on the way. 'You and your mother can rest, for I am not going to take your father away.'

Mama erased Martin Lozano from her memory for good, refused to receive him at home, and sent back all his letters and presents via Lisa. Until that muggy afternoon when I was about to turn seven, and he told Mama that his wife had died a year after she had severed contact, but by then she had already married Lucio.

With Martin Lozano gone, Mama and I hurried along the wide avenue in front of the Nazarene church to a stall where we bought *Turrón de Doña Pepa* for Papa and the boys; they had made us promise to buy some in exchange for them bathing the dog, painting the kitchen cupboards and feeding the parakeets. Perhaps, Mama wondered, Techa would already be at home by the time we got back. She had received a letter from Techa two days after her own announcement, and she was expected any day now. Mama had devised a program for introducing her half-sister to the ways of the city. After buying a kilo of *Turron* from the Sisters of the Good Succour, we scuttled quickly into a shop to buy embroidery cotton for the new set of damask sheets Mama had just bought for Techa's bed. The young woman had to be initiated into a lady's rites of passage. Mama knew that to tame Techa, to really transform her, was not going to be an easy task. 'She eats like a lizard and runs like a monkey,' Mama would say, 'just like the stepmother.'

But although the girl with the swarthy skin and thick long hair had not been brought up by Anglican missionaries, or exposed to the ways of the city, she had her own natural charm. She did not like to have much to do with frilly home affairs, or taffeta dresses. Instead, she preferred to read the signs on the moon and the writings on banana leaves. It was better to spend the afternoon throwing pebbles into the river, listening to tales about legendary turtles, or teasing the small alligators that chased the glittery fish in her tropical garden. In the city, such games were only for savages, the uncivilised Indians who dwelled within the boundaries of magic and superstition. In the city, anybody who spoke with an Amazon accent was believed to be a Shipibo who could shrink your head. Mama did not want to remember the realm she had once shared with her sister at the Bethlehem markets. This was Lima and here there were no alligators in the river. The moon hardly shone above the streets because more often than not heavy clouds swallowed the houses and deposited seeds of depression in people's hearts. Having been born in the city, I had no choice but to learn to embroider a better life in my mind and to imagine the moon shining like a giant scoop of vanilla ice cream in the sky.

When we returned home, we found Aunt Dorita making banana patties, and frantically looking for cinnamon sticks to make tea. 'You have so many herbs here,' she said, peering into the old jars of dried herbs and fungi. 'Are you a real enchantress?' she joked. Mama ignored her. Papa had just finished painting and was getting ready for his piece of *Turrón*. Plates, pots and pans were scattered over the kitchen bench on which Dorita, filled with God-given patience, shaped banana patties with her fingers and placed them into the pan. Mocho the dog was clean, wiggling his tail at the sight of the parcel wrapped in white paper, assuming that a piece of *Turrón* was going to be allotted to him too.

Papa had painted the kitchen, and he would soon start on the lounge room and the ceilings, so the house would be ready for the party. Mama inspected his painting job, brushing the kitchen walls with her finger, checking how smooth they were after all the holes had been filled, and she was pleased and proud of her handyman husband.

We ate and blabbered about the earthquake, the party invitations and what dresses to wear, and about the miners' demonstration and the tear gas let off by the riot police. 'That was no accident,' said Papa. 'That was a sign of another military coup coming.' Dorita grunted and said that no matter who was in government, the workers always got ripped off. Papa spurned her comment, believing that women were better off doing the things they knew best, but as his eyes met

Mama's gaze he stopped mid-sentence. Feeling aptly recompensed with tea and *Turrón*, Papa took the boys to the park on his way to Nono Alberto's to borrow some tools.

Left on their own, the women scuttled into the kitchen to discuss something 'only fit for grown-ups'. I could tell that it was about the fate of my godmother's stepchildren who lived on our block. My godmother's husband had fathered two daughters with my god-mother's sister, and all of them lived under the one roof. I could barely hear; although my ears were glued to the wall, the parakeet chirped loudly. All I could hear were whispers tinged with conster-nation. Dorita hissed rumours whilst Mama seasoned the meat with salt, pepper, cumin and crushed garlic, kneading her fingers through it. She massaged the chunks intently to make sure the juices pene-trated right through, all the while becoming more and more horrified by my aunt's accounts. Dorita was seeking refuge for the girls, whose mother was being repeatedly raped by her brother-in-law. Everyone on the block knew about the situation and gossiped about it quietly. The poor woman had six of her own children to look after and worked as a seamstress day and night, making everything from table-cloths to evening gowns. Lately, the situation had deteriorated – despite my godmother's pleas her husband kept sexually harassing her sister. In the end, my godmother was forced to ask her sister to leave the house, an option that broke her heart.

Aunt Dorita was concerned for the girls. 'Who knows, the man is so deranged that he could turn against his own daughters,' she said. My godmother was tortured by the guilt of her own inertia. 'Shame and disgrace weigh heavily on me,' she once told Mama, explaining that her destiny had been designed in the underworld and not in Heaven. She had accepted her sad predicament, believing she could do nothing to remedy the situation, as if there were no other option for her in life. Not even her children gave her the strength to fight, to break away from the morbid entanglement. To make matters worse, her sister was following in her footsteps – she had developed the inability to escape her daily violations. The truth was that my godmother's biggest fear was that her secret would come out, for she was incapable of imagining that the neighbours already knew. Mama agreed to take in the youngest girl, Clarita, for a while. That was all I managed to hear.

Aunt Techa arrived in Lima carrying two parakeets in a cage, a parcel of smoked wild pig, and her skin soaked in the scent of fresh pineapple. Papa looked at her with a speck of mistrust for she reminded him of a 'young sorcerer'. My aunt, who indeed had an aura of wildness about her, had come to Lima to ask the Lord of Miracles for a husband. Iquitos was losing its appeal; the town had succumbed to the indifference of the central government. The once lively capital of the tropical forest was now shrouded by a veil of grim abandonment and degeneration. Techa brought news and photos from the boys in boarding school, regards from the stepmother, and a letter from grandfather Desiderio that Mama read with avid attention.

During lunch, Mama carefully instructed her sister on the rules of the house and the manners to follow at the table. 'Make sure you don't slurp your soup or touch the food with your hands. That's not proper,' she said. Theatrically, Techa made sure she took every bite of food with extreme care, hiding her giggles under her tongue. We watched the scene with controlled amusement and pursed lips. Once lunch was finished, the table cleared and the dishes done, Mama washed Techa's hair, energetically rubbing her scalp with a mixture of insecticide and disinfectant to kill lice, and rinsing her thick mane with soda soap and a few drops of glycerine for a lustrous shine. Then she dragged her sister to the hairdresser, who transformed her long, straight hair into short and acceptable curls, to soften her looks and give her a streak of urban chic.

Papa approved of the changes, because he was sure that Techa's original look would scare any possible suitors. It was odd enough that the brown girl spoke with a 'strange accent', and possessed an intense

gaze and a penchant to attract trouble. Techa was an archetype of primal intuition and immaturity who more often than not transgressed
the boundaries of social acceptability. A tendency which I had also
inherited. I liked her very much because she was always looking for
mystical meanings in whatever she saw, as if she was able to read signs
in the water or in the stillness of the air.

On the day of my seventh birthday, I woke up to a serenade of chirp-
ing parakeets, which Papa would have preferred to see in a stew with
carrots and potatoes. Mama had been keeping them as a prize for a raf-
fle. I woke up curious to know how much I had grown. Down below,
the clattering of the breakfast crockery and my brothers' blabbering was
in full swing, as they were getting ready for the procession of the Purple Christ. 'Happy birthday to you, happy birthday to you,' the family
cheered as I climbed down the ladder in my pyjamas. I felt taller already
and quickly ran to the large mirror to measure how many more centimetres I had grown, making sure not to spend too long in front of it
for I did not want my soul to be kidnapped. Suddenly I noticed something on my chest. Wow! This is new, I thought. It was a three-spot
moon mark above my right breast. Three dots in the shape of a triangle.
   'Look!' I yelled. 'A gift from the stars.'
   'Let me see, let me see,' cried Techa. 'Oh, I see!' she said, her voice
soaked in prophetic tones.
   'What do you see? Tell me, tell me please.'
   'Well, let me see . . . three spots in perfect distance from each other,
umm.' Her gaze turned upwards. She took a deep breath and hid her
eyes behind her red, polished nails. 'A voice from the far distant forest tells me that your destiny is to find your true spirit.' Her gaze
changed to tenderness and she broke into warm laughter, giving me
a soft-hearted hug.
   'Oh wow, that's really nice,' I said, hugging her back.
   'But . . . there is a but,' she added as she looked into the emptiness

again, 'I must warn you that those chosen to follow their destiny will meet terrifying monsters.' My cheeks changed from red to ashen. 'But remember,' she continued, 'in the end, those who search for their true spirit will win,' she grinned with big white teeth, and bubbled with more ominous laughter.

I felt cold, my smile disintegrated, and covered in goose bumps I ran to the toilet. Mama was not at all amused by the spooky premonition and scolded Techa, severely reminding her I was far too young and impressionable for such jokes, which after all were not appropriate on a birthday, let alone on the Day of the Purple Christ.

'How do you intend to ask for miracles if you scare young children?' she blasted her sister.

'That's right,' echoed my father, 'you will never find a husband because you are a witch.' Techa zipped her lips up, while I climbed upstairs to get dressed in my purple tunic.

My discovery of the three dots married with the statement from the gypsy and began to resonate in my head. 'I will see my true spirit, Mama. I promise you. I just hope the blows are not too hard,' I said.

Mama reminded me of my promise many years later as I departed, bound for Australia. But on that birthday, she hugged me and assured me that Techa was only joking. 'It's not Techa, Mama. I just know it,' I said, with a newly discovered certainty that surprised me. The voice in my mind seemed to come from unfathomable depths and incomprehensible sources. Mama looked deeply into my eyes and, with the rigidity of those who fear insanity in the family, shook my frame and said, 'Promise you are going to forget all this silliness.' I promised, because I didn't want to end up in one of those big horror houses where they gave people electric shocks without killing them, and also because I did not want to upset her on my birthday. But how could I ever forget such a prediction? It was she who had taught me that memories are never forgotten. Instead they are stored in secret places.

The date of the party arrived, a couple of days after the procession, so as not to offend the Purple Christ. My doll was ready on the main chair, dressed in a glorious organza dress that made her look like a little princess. The minuscule gown had been made by the shaking hands of my poor godmother who was still suffering the aftermath of her drama, with her sister now gone and a husband angry. She had managed to create an angelical garment with puffy sleeves, satin petticoat, frills and tiny flowers. Cinnamon and vanilla iced cakes were laid on the table next to bowls overflowing with chocolates and jelly beans, jam rolls, potatoes stuffed with raisins and sultanas, purple *chicha* with pineapple chunks, multicoloured jellies and a giant pineapple filled to the top with lollies. The centrepiece was a huge birthday cake with a tiny doll dressed in white on the top. The adults would have their own party too that night. For them, the women in the kitchen added the final touches to the rice with duck and coriander, potatoes with feta cheese and green chili sauce, and fresh white-corn *chicha*, fermented in an earthenware jug on top of ashes in the corner of the room. The *chicha* had to be fermented in a corner because tradition said it would get the spirit from the four directions and people would not get drunk, just tipsy. When it came to cooking, tradition always dictated the technique.

Aunt Renatta was the first to arrive, with her children all dressed up and pretty, except for Tato who had gone to the church to pick up his surplice and the holy water. My father, who thought the whole affair was a bit strange, but went along in the name of matrimonial solidarity, had prepared a makeshift font in the middle of the lounge room using a ceramic bowl on top of two wooden boxes that he had wrapped in white, shiny paper. Tato had been instructed by the priest to sprinkle holy water on the doll to clean her of any sinful toxins, and to do the same to the guests.

The children, on their best behaviour, all gathered in a circle around the font, the girls holding their dolls, the boys keeping a sense of solemnity, more out of novelty than religious reverence. Renatta moved around the room with a plastic camera, clicking away at every smile, whilst Aunt Dorita made sure everyone showed their teeth – if they were not missing.

Once the ceremony was finished and little charms were pinned on the chests of all the guests, music burst from the four walls and the children began to shake their bodies in a fervent rhythm. They tapped heartily to the Colombian *cumbias*, rock songs and *merengues*, for they knew that the more they danced the bigger the piece of birthday cake they would get. I sat next to Tato in the corner. Despite the celebration, I still had to obey the vows imposed during October, which prevented me from dancing.

Soon the party raged. Aunt Dorita shifted around encouraging everybody to join in the festive mood. 'Hey you, Chee Chee, why don't you dance with Nee Nee, huh? And you, Anastasia, dance with Peter and smile please, let go of that long face. And you, hey you in the white coat, I don't know your name but it doesn't matter, come here and dance with Clarita.' Everyone had to dance. Mama said that to dance was to transcend into the realm of life's ecstasy.

The kids eventually began to drop one by one onto their seats, inebriated by the birthday cake and purple *chicha*. Suddenly, Pepito, the son of a neighbour, went up to Clarita and pulled her skirt down. Clarita, who by then was a guest in our home and knew how to defend her space, turned to him and slapped him on the cheek without hesitation. She then continued to dance with another boy. Enraged by what he thought was an unfair strike, Pepito struck back, pulling her by the ear and whispering something that made Clarita's cheeks red with fury. Enough fury to make her claw her tiny nail down Pepito's face. Aunt Dorita pulled the fighters apart, took Clarita into the kitchen and without giving her the chance to explain, called her insolent. Weeping, the girl whispered into Aunt Dorita's ear what Pepito had told her. Dorita was shocked. She walked up to the young brat, grabbed him by the back of his collar, dragged him outside and shook his ear furiously. She then wrapped a piece of cake in a serviette, picked his hat off the hook, and with no more explanation than that he was a bad boy, sent him home and ordered him to wash his mouth out with holy water. To calm everything, Renatta began taking photos again. Although I had discovered that her camera did not have film inside, the other children did not know this detail and kept smiling and waving. In the kitchen Mama filled jugs with more *chicha* and tasted the texture of the chili chicken with cream and saffron.

Techa suggested that Pepito should have his tongue cut off by the priest. 'They should hang it on the wall for all children to see,' she said. Papa sneered, saying she was a wild creature with cannibal manners, unable to understand the civilised ways of the city.

'God protect me from your shrinking head inclinations,' he snarled. Techa replied with the hiss of a snake and said that the city was a place where people killed each other out of insanity, a hell of a lot less civilised than her home town. And she quickly shut up. A few seconds rolled by, then the front door was shaken by a series of loud bangs. Outside, under the darkening clouds, stood a bellicose woman next to Pepito. She was ranting and raving, and waving a wooden spoon with one hand. Possessed by anger, she protested that her son had been brutally abused by the 'mad cow', Aunt Dorita. Who did we think we were? she yelled in the middle of the street. Papa opened the door and told the woman to go home. Then he shut it in frustration. But the woman would not go and continued to bang with the spoon, yelling a litany of filthy accusations. Egged on by Renatta, Dorita decided to come out with the punch ladle in her hand, and in an identical ferocious tone, she threatened to knock the woman down if she did not leave. Papa moved in quickly to stop the whole scandal whilst, in the kitchen, Mama wondered whether the idea of the doll baptism had been a good one after all. Doña Panchita had told her that rituals and dolls can also bring the sleeping demons out of their hellish chambers.

Her reflection on this was interrupted as she heard Papa screaming, 'If you don't disappear within five minutes the sky will fall on you.' The door slammed again. Papa had never said anything like that before. Dorita and Renatta looked at him with surprise for he was not a man of warnings or premonitions. Let alone holy forecasting.

Suddenly, there was a resounding splash, followed by a horrified scream. Our hearts were paralysed by the sound. We ran to the door. Papa opened it, and we saw, with stupefied surprise, a dripping woman running away, swearing at life. The punishment had not been from the sky, however, but from the top of the roof, where an amateur team was in charge of karmic retribution. It had been Techa's idea. A solution that she said had been sent to her by her gods to punish those who spoil children's parties. Aided by some of the more daring boys, she had surreptitiously carried the bowl of holy water onto the roof. 'It was the only way to cool this woman and drench her toxins,' said Techa. For the first time, my father approved of my aunt's weird ways. 'Miracle! Miracle!' the children screamed when they saw the wet woman, in line with Papa's prediction. But Techa had not even heard the prediction. She had already been on the roof and keen to turn the basin over the screaming woman. It was one of those moments of perfect synchronicity, when two souls act in unison. Techa suggested in a humorous tone that Papa had become a full *Brujo* with shamanic powers, which brought goose bumps to the back of his neck and made him shiver with horror. Renatta attributed the coincidence to my father's membership of the bearers of the Purple Christ, whilst Dorita said it came from the hand of divine providence. Mama came out of the kitchen and brought everyone down to earth by instructing them to help her prepare more salads for the evening party. Soon the dancing kids were exorcised of all sins by the beats of the rumbas. Slowly they pulled their jumpers off the hangers and marched home happily to let the next round of guests in to dance a bit and chuckle about the 'splashing scandal', news of which had travelled across the neighbourhood with the pieces of birthday cake the children had taken home.

When Mama asked Clarita what the quarrel had been about, she replied that Pepito had called her mother a whore. All the grown-ups were shocked, and Mama ordered Clarita to forget such a word immediately. As I already knew that things could never be forgotten, just hidden, I promised Clarita that in the summer I would help her throw the word into the ocean. Until then, we would just keep it in a little bag under the bed where no one could ever find it.

THE GHOST FAREWELL

SPRING NEVER FAILED to remind the population that souls, like bedspreads, needed to be aired in the sun, cleansed and purified before the holiday season. However, one spring day, instead of the sun, a sinister cloud appeared in the sky. Darkness gradually enfolded our street. And the bohemian tunes vanished, as if the chords in our hearts had snapped violently, all at once. Doña Santitos had disappeared from the face of the earth. She had not been seen since her last prayer session, in which some of the women had joked about reported sightings of flickering lights above the mountains. 'They are probably coming for you,' the women had teased. Doña Santitos had smiled and said, 'I am a lot more human than you can ever imagine.'

No one had seen her in more than a week. Heading the search team, Loretta banged on her door for hours. There was no response. Frustrated, she finally asked a friend to kick the door open in case Doña Santitos lay on the bed unconscious, although she could not believe that a woman like her would encounter such a fate. Sadly there was nobody inside. Not a soul, just the echo of emptiness and the smell of dried flowers. No more glow in her room, no more vibrations or tingles in the knees. 'Hope is gone forever,' cried out the woman at the corner shop who made takeaway breakfast on Sundays and read tarot cards by night, her shawl covering her distraught face. We all cried deeply, searching for a clue. In the cellars of our mind we fought to keep a glimmer of hope, wishing that wherever she had gone she was well. 'Too nice to last for long,' said Mr Takanaka who, despite his pragmatic nature, had fallen in love with the small woman who always blessed his shop whenever she bought candles. We wiped our tears and went about our business in the hope that soon the earth would return her to us. Our hearts sank because we believed that her warmth, tenderness and compassion would never come back. The men on the block, led by one of the mechanics who saw it as an opportunity to pursue Loretta romantically, did not waste time in moaning about her disappearance. Instead they began to investigate it. They spoke to friends of friends connected with people they knew who worked in hospitals, in police stations and in municipalities – in case new records had been made. The key was to discover the identity of Doña Santitos. A police investigating team was set up to appease the block.

Local children went so far as to write school assignments about the fate of Doña Santitos. 'Where has the angel gone?' was one of the titles. A few of the young ones, including my brother Luis, were sure she had been kidnapped by the same UFO that had threatened to land on earth and consume all earthlings. Some wrote that she had ascended to the heavens because she had been a saint in disguise. I asked my mother whether Doña Santitos had returned to the In-between and Mama agreed that it was a good possibility. But Papa was set in his idea that she had been kidnapped by the Catholic Church. 'She definitely put up a good fight against the priests. I will miss that,' Papa said when the disappearance was announced. In a customary extravaganza, Aunt Dorita suggested that perhaps there had never been a Doña Santitos and we had imagined her. Perhaps the lady was somebody else whose personality we had not liked at all and had decided to change it. As one massive hallucination. Papa felt his sister was losing her wits and needed to get married soon. But Aunt Renatta, who was an eager fan of the television program 'The Twilight Zone', found a degree of reason in Dorita's theory.

Even the fish vendor missed Doña Santitos, because at the end of the day he had always kept the loose scraps for her stray cats, whom she affirmed had a mission on this planet. She once told us that cats were here to teach people to live and love without attachment and without conditions. We did not know what she meant, but what we did remember was that cats certainly got rid of all the rodents on the block, which were hairy, large and fat. I remember the day when our cat, Pancho, got run over by a car driven by one of Loretta's friends. My heart broke because Pancho and I were like twins, for Mama fed both of us with fresh fish cooked in the same pot. Mama said that I had probably been a cat in a previous life because I would salivate whenever I sniffed the scent of raw fish and lemon salsa. We took Pancho to be healed by Doña Santitos' prayers because his broken body was as limp as jelly, yet his life force was still present. Consumed by guilt, Loretta lost her smile and broke with her friend for being so inconsiderate. The friend promised to buy us a new cat but we bluntly refused because Pancho was a hero with a special brand of courage. Doña Santitos placed Pancho on her dining table, chanted some prayers in a mysterious language, smoked some herbs around him and asked us to light two candles to the Virgin. One to forgive the driver, and the other to connect with the divine cat force that would help Pancho's recovery. Once the rituals were completed, we carried our limp cat home, with instructions to bind him from the hips down to a piece of timber as a splint. We were to keep him in a wooden box under the table for as long as it took him to recover. Doña Santitos stressed that if we truly wanted the cat to recover, he would. We fed and pampered him for weeks, attentive to his every whim, analysing his movements and meows, and finally watching how he dragged his body across the lounge room floor as we trained him to walk again. In the end, Pancho came back to life, resuming his rat patrol on the roof and still able to dive onto the road whenever he saw a rat crawling out of the gutter.

A week after Doña Santitos' departure, as the fish vendor wrapped two fresh fish for Mama, she overheard a conversation. 'God knows, she could have been murdered and her body chopped into bite-size pieces to feed the lions at the zoo.' It was one of the neighbours remembering an old and highly peculiar case.

It involved a country maid and her boss. Forced by humble circumstances, the girl had found employment in the house of a well-known family, famous for their high morals and generosity – at least on the outside. Her duties included cleaning, shopping and serving the master, even when he slept in on weekends. The girl was pretty and meaty around the bones, and enjoyed a healthy constitution, an indispensable requirement for she needed a certificate of good health before she could be employed. It was a new regulation following a strange murder case where a nanny had baked her employers' baby with herbs and garlic because she could not find the suckling pig in the cold room for dinner. When the parents came home they found the baby on a platter on the table, garnished with lettuce and tomatoes. The case stunned the nation, sent the parents to hospital, and alerted the well-to-do circles to the 'dubious intentions of any servant'. The nanny was put in an institution for the not-too-well-in-the-head, for life. But the country girl did not have that problem. She was as lucid as a morning bird, smart and energetic, and the possessor of an enigmatic allure that provoked her master's desire. Every time she walked past him he would try to brush his privates against her hips. The country girl ignored the gesture, convinced that such were the ways of the city. In her town, boys let girls know of their amorous intentions during dance rituals, body bumping against body, hip against hip.

The master's pursuit of the country girl went on and on. Often he would return home early, looking for chances to touch her breasts and tickle her nipples. She always pushed him back bashfully, which the master interpreted as a sign of consent. Convinced the girl was only playing hard to get, one day he opted for exposing himself to her, an act that filled the country girl with horror, for she claimed she had never seen such an evil contraption. The master asked her to help him shower, and to soap his well-endowed constitution. The country girl obeyed with the submissiveness of those who conceal their disapproval in the depths of their resentment. She began to hate her job, but convinced herself that perhaps the master would get tired of her as the novelty of her innocence wore off. Lying in the darkness of her room, she dreaded the master's entrance, the sound of his footsteps and the lusty smell of his breath and his skin, which reeked of cologne. Until one day, engorged by his sense of ownership, and charged with a voracious appetite, the master burst into her room and forced himself upon her. He imposed on her the darkest side of his desire, revealing a window of his soul that not even his wife knew. Night after night he forced her to satisfy his cravings, to help him dress in bizarre outfits, and to quench his thirst for the perverse. Her patience came to breaking point the day he asked her to perform the role of a bed pan. Inside the country girl's wounded adolescence, her resentment was growing to monstrous proportions. One evening, after excusing herself from the master, saying she had a belly ache, the country girl began to plan the unimaginable. The seeds of cruelty were germinating in her heart.

The following weekend, she went to the zoo because she had never seen wild animals from the forest. The country girl quivered at the sight of the huge reptiles grinning their rotten teeth at her, hinting at the misery of their own imprisoned conditions. The wide-eyed girl moved from cage to cage, enjoying every minute of it, buying candied peanuts for the monkeys and bananas for the gorillas, meandering along the corridors in between birds and felines, inhaling the scent of the animals and checking out the zoo attendants, one of whom she befriended.

The next day, the girl managed to seduce and excite her master to such a magnified degree that he lost control and allowed her to lead him into total surrender. She convinced him of new ways to intensify his pleasure. Blindfolded, he let her tickle him with adoration, brushing him erotically with a feather first, then with a plastic fork, a spiky brush, a metal comb, and a small rake, tools that made the master shiver with delight. Such were his erotic urges that at the height of his excitement he did not feel the sharp rake tearing his throat. The country girl had stood over him on the bed and, with the same resigned look with which she had accepted his warped inclinations, shoved the rake into his neck, without any remorse. Later, aided by the zoo attendant, the girl took the corpse to the slaughterhouse at the zoo, where the wicked master of the mansion was transformed into chunks of meat to satiate the ravenous appetites of the lions. No one discovered the crime, for the wife thought her husband had eloped with a secretary. Until the day the young girl and the zoo attendant who had turned vegetarian after their deed, persuaded by their conscience, poured out in full detail the sad predicament of the 'lustful master'. In her defence, the country girl said that the master had seeded worms of venom inside her heart. The nation, especially its women, felt sorry for the young girl but the law, unwilling to believe the girl's story about the master's perverted disposition, convicted the girl and her partner of murder.

Strange men dressed in dark suits began to investigate Doña Santitos' disappearance. That she had gone on holidays was ruled out, for she had taken nothing. Her rosary beads were still there, which made the whole affair reek of kidnapping as she was never separated from her beads. Her religious books, mainly prayers to the Virgin, lay on top of the unruffled white lace bedspread, which we all adored and always wondered about its origins. The lace was so brilliantly white and silky that at times it appeared iridescent. She said it came from overseas, from the land where women mixed good intentions with the sparkles that came from the stars. If it belonged to Doña Santitos it had to be from very far away, where iridescent people lived, we believed.

Interestingly, Doña Santitos' disappearance coincided with the news that the world was about to end. The newspapers splashed huge headlines across their front pages announcing apocalyptic times, warning people to perform generous parting deeds. A sense of panic had struck at the people's hearts. The world was being invaded by hungry Martians eager to colonise new lands because they were on the verge of destroying theirs. The initial reports were humorous commentaries by comedians, but later they were followed by fear-ridden articles that told of impending menace. I heard the original reports a few days before Doña Santitos' disappearance and ran to see her. I felt I was suffocating. Perhaps the Blue Cat, upset that he could not take me, was now keen to take everybody else. Doña Santitos said it was very unlikely, and Papa asked Mama to retract the story of the Blue Cat and my near-death experience. But she could not for it was true, however, she never spoke of the Blue Cat again. I imagined we would die like worms floating in the bellies of unscrupulous aliens. But what if we were able to talk to the extraterrestrials? I believed that if Doña Santitos interceded they would spare us. At first, my parents believed I was just exaggerating in the tradition of the family, but later they realised the fear was truly choking me. Terrifying headlines continued to assault the population each day. Interviews and commentaries on how people were preparing for the huge catastrophe abounded. It was all the result of the strange experience of a farmer on the outskirts of town who claimed that one morning, as he tended his crops and fed his cattle, he had seen a dazzling light in the sky. This unidentified thing, which emitted a brilliant glow, hovered above the middle of his field before eventually settling on the ground. It was a craft he had never seen before, not even in movies. An alien emerged from the round ship, but to his surprise, the farmer had felt no fear. Instead, he had been receptive to a message the alien relayed telepathically. The farmer insisted that the alien had taken him to visit his world, to show him how life would be in the future.

This sort of story had been the order of the day in my home town since time immemorial. The city of Cusco, capital of the former Inca empire, even boasts a sign on the road to the main temple that reads, 'UFO Airport'. The farmer was told by the alien that for ages, starry beings had landed in Peru because the area has a certain magnetism, like a global chakra that attracts supernatural activity. That is why many ancient cultures had flourished in that very spot. The Incas had been the last.

Throughout the sixties we were told that as the planet moved towards the end of the millennium, life as we knew it would change, priorities would shift, and new values would emerge. The final stage would bring about a new beginning. Of course the tabloids were not going to wait until the end of the millennium to stir people's fears, so they decided to pick a date: October. It was the month of disasters, the season for the city to be cleansed of all impurities. It would beat any tremor, or justify the same. In their frenzied attempt to whip up interest, the newspapers concocted the lowest and most sensationalist of anguish-ridden headlines: 'TIME TO CONFESS' and 'SHAKE IT BEFORE YOU LOSE IT'. Articles and humorous columns encouraged people to indulge in pleasure before letting go of their carnal costumes. The naive believed the story, and the sceptics revelled in their scorn. Shaken by the news, some prepared their wills; husbands confessed their cheating; the wealthy, ridden with guilt, gave generous dona-tions to convents and orphanages; and the poor just wept. The population hated the media for its crude approach, but bought all the papers. As they had done always. I was too young to know better, and was perhaps one of the few who truly believed the story.

I stopped eating and lost several kilos. At last, in sheer fear, I decided to stop growing. The shock of the end of the world accelerated my development and ended my childhood abruptly. One morning I woke up on a pool of red fluid. Mama explained the meaning of my discovery and took me to the movies to see *Mother India*, a harrow-ing drama about a poor family in the subcontinent, which melted my heart in anguish and brought a million tears to my eyes. We wept together and hugged in a silent contract that we would always look after each other, no matter where life took us. As I continued to lose weight, Mama eventually took me to the doctor to be pumped up with extra nutrition pills.

The investigations had led nowhere. Loretta and Mama had asked the neighbourhood to hold an evening of prayer in the name of Doña Santitos, who had taught Mama that all spirits benefit from prayer, particularly when they are in trouble. 'Wherever she is, she will connect with our prayers,' Mama said and the rest of the women agreed. In Doña Santitos' tiny room, the neighbours dressed the table with a tablecloth, fresh flowers, candles and her belongings in a box. Deep in their hearts, no one wanted to believe the ceremony was a wake. Better to think of it as a ritual of gratitude. Wherever she had gone, we wanted her to know how much she had touched our hearts, and the impact she had had on our small community. Loretta wept into the hot chocolate that the Catwoman had brought to the ceremony. Despite her initial impressions of the little saint, the Catwoman had come to like her, and on that evening she even made up with Loretta. No one missed the little saint as much as the mambo dancer. After Loretta's street fight with her boyfriend, the small woman had become Loretta's true guide, a compass that helped her sail through the rapids of life. Drenched in tears, Loretta told Mama that Doña Santitos had taught her to accept herself as a good woman, to keep good thoughts about herself, to treat herself with respect. In the process, she had been able to reconstruct her faith in life and let her innocence re-emerge.

Mama and Loretta became close friends, for they were a reminder to each other of the options that life had to offer. Mama was a very good dancer and more than once had been invited to dance in public as a job when her work in the factories got too depressing, but she always refused out of embarrassment. 'I could not bear my body to be on stage,' she cringed. Yet there was nothing I wanted to do more than dance. Mama felt guilty if she enjoyed life a bit too much, if she chuckled for too long, if she faced life with open abandon. On the other hand, I began to imagine myself dancing on high heels, balancing fruit on my head and shaking my hips in shining outfits.

Drinking vermouth, Mama and Loretta explored each other's emotional landscapes and poured out their innermost beliefs and anxieties.

Loretta mourned Doña Santitos because she had never judged her, neither for her loud behaviour nor her dancing naked in public. Loretta's working life had never been easy. She liked dancing, but on stage, she had to bare her flesh and contort her hips provocatively, undulating them to the beat of the mambo, no matter what sort of men drooled all over the tables. She would pull her garments off seductively one by one until she was left with only a tiny sparkling patch covering her most treasured possessions. But Doña Santitos had never judged her. Not even when she told the tiny woman about her secret, that sometimes men asked her to have a drink with them and bought her affections for a few extra coins so she could help out her family, especially her sister, who was studying. With Doña Santitos gone, perhaps Loretta would now follow her suggestion to start a course in dressmaking. She could start designing gowns for her fellow dancers – after all, she had the knack. It was a safe trade and she would no longer have to expose herself to the voracious appetites of her audience.

The warnings about the end of the world faded, as did the investigation of Doña Santitos' disappearance. Eventually life went back to normal, but from the girl of robust appearance I was transformed into a long stick with narrow hips and languid face. Mama's serene appearance slowly filtered away as she got more and more stressed by the day. The skin on her face tightened and her weight increased considerably.

Techa had been praying for years before the image of the Lord of the Miracles, asking for the miracle of love. But Doña Panchita assured Techa that finding a husband did not require a miracle. What required a miracle was keeping the husband at home. 'It is indeed a lottery to keep a good man,' the old matron preached, 'it is not the person you should ask to keep, but love. So pray for the right method to make him feel loved.' Techa changed her tune and began to concentrate more on her looks and learning to cook and keeping the house tidy; however, she did not stop praying in her own individual way.

One day Papa brought one of his assistants home to lunch, hoping that Techa would find him attractive. The boy was from the highlands, the son of a decent family, and he had serious intentions and a sincere heart. In addition, he was completing his technical studies at night and was planning a comfortable life. But Techa did not like him and found him too boring, too predictable, and too difficult to connect with. She felt uncomfortable with his seriousness about life, with his plans for a perfect future. Mama, on the contrary, thought that the boy was the perfect match for her sister, somebody to keep her in line, somebody to adjust her loose screws. In vain, Mama tried to persuade Techa to give the country boy a chance. To avoid Mama's disapproval, Techa found herself a job at a factory and soon moved out of home, 'to start her own life'. Mama felt betrayed because she had invested so much in her sister, but Papa reminded her that no one owned anybody. Mama had to get accustomed to letting people go.

Three months later, Techa came to visit Mama and, after a few tears that Mama branded as 'crocodile crying', she announced she was to marry her new boyfriend, whose baby she was carrying. When the boy came to visit, Mama could hardly hide her bewilderment for she met a handsome and tall African Peruvian, keen to sing and dance, and therefore a bit 'suspicious' when it came to family stability. Papa remained silent and all Mama could do was to bite her lip. However, she was relieved that Techa would in fact get married. 'Well, each to their own,' said Papa. Mama was simply annoyed at the circumstances.

Techa's pregnancy made her glow with a special iridescence and the wedding preparations were hurried so as not to arouse suspicion. When we asked her why she had chosen her fiancé she said it was because he could read her heart, and Papa warned her that a lot more than heart reading was necessary to sustain a family. Techa brushed aside his comments with raised eyebrows and a sneer. As Loretta was already experimenting with making gowns, Mama asked her to help create Techa's wedding dress. My godmother was no longer the dressmaker of the block. Her husband had beaten her up for asking her sister to move out. So big had been the scandal that the neighbours had no option but to call the police and have them take him away. The poor woman had gone to work at a garment factory, and her sister had finally returned to the house. In solidarity, both women worked from dawn to dusk to help feed their eight children. Mama heard the eldest daughter was also pregnant and did not dare ask with whose baby.

Techa's baby, Pelusa, was born a gorgeous little girl, a magnificent example of the double-A formula – Africa and the Amazon. The two appeared to have mixed well and the baby stirred the first grand matriarchal sentiments in Mama. The feeling was contagious because the baby also gave me my first taste of the chores of motherhood. I learned to change nappies, bottle-feed her, put her to sleep and pace her around when she cried. Techa stayed at home while her husband, having realised that heart readings did not feed babies, drove an interstate truck carrying bananas from the jungle.

Babysitting was such a physical experience that it grounded me in the real world, stopping all my peering and squinting in the corners of the house to check for Uncle Pietro's ghost or to chase the Blue Cat. But when Mama went out on her debt collection errands, I would enter into a secret dialogue with Pelusa because Doña Santitos had told me that children were closer to the universe and therefore knew the truth more clearly. She had said that babies' souls were purer, and because their brains were still forming they were more celestial than terrestrial. As we grow up, she would whisper, most babies disconnect from the heavenly source and follow the rules of the material world. If we are conscious of this, and behave with an open heart, the connection will always be kept; then we can make miracles happen. It was a nice story and I chose to believe it, for it was much richer and more fanciful than the alternatives. So when Pelusa and I were on our own, I would ask her whether she had seen Doña Santitos in the world where she came from. But it appeared that Pelusa had not seen her anywhere in her previous galaxy, for she never made a sign, nor did she communicate with me telepathically.

Instead, she would burp, pass wind or yell for more food, and I would pick her up from the cradle, hold her to my chest and dance a bit of *merengues* with her until she stopped. We had great dancing sessions, Pelusa and I.

In return for the babysitting, Techa would teach me all sorts of things, one of which was how to walk as a 'seductive woman'. She said that the key to sensual magnetism was the way a woman carries her body. She had learned such details from Loretta and her friends, and was very keen to pass them on to whomever was interested in listening. And I was. So she would prance around the lounge room with high heels on, showing me how to carry my hips under a flowing dress or a fitted suit, to half hide or half reveal the body's contours. To rehearse the art of seduction, I would put on one of Mama's dresses, step into her shoes, which were already tight on me, and imitate Techa's sway of the hips. Her formula was to place one foot in front of the other in a direct line, the hips remaining loose and relaxed. The movement had to be fluid so all the joints could bounce in a natural rhythm. 'Let one hip play ping-pong against the other,' she would say. Lacking round hips, I found it difficult to play ping-pong. Techa had learned to keep her back straight under the weight of many baskets during her rounds at the Bethlehem markets. To achieve the same effect with me she would place books on my head and make me walk across the room. I relished Techa's grand tuition because I found her fascinating. She had interpreted Loretta's visions of Doña Santitos. When Loretta confessed that she kept seeing Doña Santitos everywhere, Techa diagnosed her with nostalgia ardorosa, a condition of fervent longing for something that we believe is lost. She then recommended her to move into Doña Santitos' house.

Techa's lessons didn't last long because every time Mama caught us she would scold Techa for 'teaching me things fit for older girls'. And Techa would always reply, 'But, sister, your daughter was born an adult. You know it.'

One day when Mama was at home on her own, a man in an old and dark suit knocked on the door and told her that Doña Santitos had died in an asylum. He went on to say that she had been found wandering by the lake and had been taken there. When Mama asked him what lake, the man did not answer and simply stared at her. She shivered. Seeing that she did not take to him too well, the man took his hat off, bowed courteously and left without giving any more details, except that somebody would come back to pick up Doña Santitos' belongings. Days passed and nobody came. Mama was never sure whether the mysterious man had been an apparition, whether he had come in her dreams during a nap, or whether he was as real as she was. Papa wanted to believe her but added his own theory that the mysterious man was probably a messenger from the Vatican, trying to convince us that all that we had learned from the old woman was 'insane'.

Soon after that incident, Mama's pain began to leak from the cellars of her heart, filtering through the premature creases on her face. The tragedies of her childhood and adolescence, originally soothed by her Amazon tales, seemed to fester inside her, causing pain and discomfort. To make her feel better, we insisted she tell us stories. Sometimes she did, and her face shone, her laughter was heard again and Papa chuckled with genuine happiness; but such episodes grew more scarce by the day. While her business had expanded, it had also brought her more tension. There was never any certainty that her clients would pay her back. Many did pay and many did not, slamming the door in her face when she called to collect the payments. Sometimes I would go with her, and my heart boiled in frustration whenever I had to watch people being rude to her.

One day I looked on with pain as one of her clients blatantly refused to acknowledge that he had received money from her, never mind his signature on the contract. He impudently reneged on his debt, threatening to call the police and have her taken away for being 'a bloody usurer'. But Mama did not go away. She stood outside his door, challenging his gutlessness, tearing him apart with her gaze. She had an invisible armour to cope with his vulgarities and absorb his verbal injuries without bleeding inside. I stood next to her, shaking in anger, holding my feet back from kicking him in between the legs. He was not tall but his anger made him look big. Like Mama, I directed my anger at him like bullets from my eyes, in silence. Oh how I wished that evening that I were a man! If only to crush his balls flat, to show him that the meaning of manhood was courage. I had heard that from my father. I know that the bastard would never have behaved the way he did had I been a man. Mama forbade me to tell my father about the wounding episode and I promised I would not. Papa was already upset. It was bad enough having a wife who worked. Worse to have one with a risky business.

'Why are you so obsessed with buying a house?' he would snarl, slamming his fists on the table. 'Why humiliate yourself with those bastards? We could just rent a bigger house and live off my earnings.' His amber eyes seethed with fury and his back arched like a cat, as he placed his strong hands on the table. Mama always came back with the same line: 'Our children deserve a new house. Their own house. They must move on and move up. That's just the law of life.' Papa would light cigarette after cigarette to quash his anger, puffing with frustration and cursing under his tongue. I hated seeing them argue over Mama's visions and obsessions. To show us how hurt she was, Mama would lock herself into a sour and silent mood for hours and Papa would leave the house, slamming the door to cool his mood down. Sometimes he went to have a cup of coffee with Don Takanaka and talk politics or soccer, or sometimes he visited his father or sister. Once, he did not come back until past midnight, and we never found out where he had been because Mama did not ask.

But he never stored resentments, never was upset for long, and never sought revenge. He could see through the veneer of Mama's anger when she ached badly. He knew she wanted the best for all of us, although the way she went about it lacked flexibility. When his frustration had eased, he would come home with a bottle of Inca cola and a packet of vanilla biscuits and would place them on the table where

Mama could see them. It was his form of truce. There was no need for apologies between them, at least not verbally. Once the altercations fizzled out and the soap on the radio detoured her attention to other people's tragedies, Mama would go into the kitchen to prepare the evening meal. Vegetable fritters, or beans creamed with milk and hot spices, or braised beef with onion and garlic, all served on a bed of steamed rice. Then father would come down and indulge in the pleasure of his food, like a contented cat. Food and dance were the best medicines at home, although Mama liked her doctor's pills too.

Not long after Doña Santitos' disappearance, a wicked wind flew past our house and blew an evil omen. Mama was on the way to the markets to pick up some new fabric for a dress she intended to have made for me, when suddenly she felt that her life force was about to leave her. Without much warning she collapsed on the ground and lost consciousness.

Papa went straight to the hospital and when he returned home alone his face was the colour of ash. Mama had a terrible tumour in her belly, which had kept growing and growing despite her pills. Now she had to have everything inside removed. She was to have a hysterectomy. The operation was going to be dangerous for her because of her history of bronchial problems.

I ran to the neighbours to ask them to pray for Mama, and we all lit the candles on the altar of Mary at home. That night I lay in bed and wept deeply, feeling guilty. Her words echoed in my mind: 'One of these days your stubbornness is going to send me to hospital.' The morning, while kneeling beside my bed, I promised that if she was saved I would not make her spend one more cent on me. I also pledged all of my energy to help her buy a house, and I swore I would never owe money, nor would I ever extend loans unless I was prepared to forget about them. Every day that passed, a fresh candle would be lit on the altar, with a new promise from all the family. A week went by, with me and my brothers taking turns to help in the kitchen. Papa carried special food to the hospital daily. Loretta came to see us in the afternoons to help with the food preparation, always under the guidance of Dorita, who had not yet learned to trust her completely.

'Why don't you like Loretta?' I asked.

'I do like her, but Loretta reminds me of your Mama when she was younger. I am only protecting your Papa.'

The doctors did their best on the operating table and Mama came out of the hospital renewed and relieved, for they had removed all the bad bits that would have given her cancer. It was good to watch how gradually happiness returned to her heart. It was such a relief to have her in bed, free of worries and concerns about new houses and the future. We sang with joy, and when she came out of hospital we offered her a special cake we had baked. When she had finally recovered, we visited the Nazarene church to offer our prayers of gratitude. We lit a large candle in front of the statue of Christ, promising that we would never get cancer.

After Mama's operation, peace reigned at home for a period. She began to bake cakes again and send pieces to friends and neighbours, as she wanted to share her best wishes around. When her energy fully returned, she began to organise bingo games on Sunday afternoons, allotting special prizes which we helped wrap up in cellophane the night before, but only if she traded our help with jungle tales. Loretta invited many of her new friends to the event and the house was filled with laughter and the scent of joy for a while. Amid number calling, teasing, chuckling and cheers with Inca cola, one of Loretta's friends became Aunt Dorita's suitor.

Encouraged by Aunt Techa, Loretta had moved into Doña Santitos' room and had embellished the place the best she could. The former chamber with lights dangling in the air and mystical scents had now become a charming dressmaker's den with posters from *Vogue*

hanging on the walls, and lace curtains over the tiny top window; and of course the shiny bedspread lay proudly on her bed. Her presence in the house made the stray cats happy; they returned to the roof, meowing in glory, once again members of the domestic feline patrol, free from wild brawls. The glow inside the house reappeared. Every day a new client would visit and ask her to make a special new gown that she had seen in some boutique window. Loretta was never short of ideas and the pizzazz to create styles that suited people's personalities. Mama had passed on to her some of her formulas for colour and emotion coordinating, and Loretta had added her own interpretations of cuts, patterns and lines, fabrics and lengths, and the effects of these on the wellbeing of the wearer. Loretta's clients asked for her advice before buying a piece of fabric. And she advised them on the best choice depending on the occasion and the impression to be made. It was all in the mixing of colours with perfumes, the mix of metals, and the wearing of gold, silver, plastic or pearly accessories to attract certain vibrations.

Loretta had joined the Hermetic Society, a group that studied the ancient science of alchemy, while Doña Santitos was still alive. The holy lady had encouraged her to learn about mysticism and non-traditional Christianity, because the more people know, the more power they have. In her meetings at the society she learned things to do with stars, metals and alchemy. She learned of the Pleiades and of the link between the ancient Peruvians and that constellation. But this sort of knowledge was beyond Mama and the neighbours. None of them was able to make any sense of Loretta's new inclinations, so she preferred not to talk about it.

She came to find satisfaction in her dress designing. Gradually she withdrew from her dancing engagements, becoming instead the dancing girls' wardrobe adviser. With my godmother out of the business, most basic frocks, uniforms and cocktail gowns in the neighbourhood now came from Loretta's sewing machine, because the local women could not afford to buy ready-made clothes.

In the four years she had lived in the neighbourhood, Loretta had conquered the hearts of most people, and pricked the interest of just about every man in the block. Her heart, however, was always imprisoned in some impossible romance. It was as if deep inside she believed that no one could really love her. I had seen a young man, with the appearance of an existential poet, visit her at night, but she would not talk about him, not even to Mama.

One afternoon when the air was quiet and the clouds had parted to let the sun greet us, I went to see her to try on a new school shirt for summer, but most importantly to clarify a few questions of a sensitive nature to do with conception and love. Despite my inquisitive nature, Mama and I had never spoken about sex.

I arrived at Loretta's door with a plate of cakes and my heart full of expectations. It was unusually quiet for I normally heard the sound of the sewing machine or the echoes of Loretta's laughter. I approached the door quietly and heard her whispering, as if she was talking to herself, or to somebody who was mute. Doña Panchita approached from Don Takanaka's shop and found me with my ear to the door. Making a sign of disapproval she moved away, and so did I. There must be somebody in the room, I told myself. I decided to sit on the footpath and watch my brothers playing soccer with other kids, kicking their soccer ball and tackling around their ankles as if dancing, learning how to play the most exciting game in the whole world, I was told.

I crossed my arms against my chest and my gaze rested on the spot above my nose, where Loretta had once said the boundaries of time meet. I enjoyed the weird nature of my block and its people. I would certainly miss it when we left. It would not take long now because Mama had already saved for a deposit and was busy looking around for a house. But there was a dark side to the neighbourhood too, which I longed to see come to an end. There was the constant harassment from the men around the corner, the lewd gazes from the workers in the repair shop, and their heated comments about how they wanted to use their tongues to make me happy. But that was not all – I had an uncle, a relative of Mama who sometimes stayed at our house, who would not stop rubbing the front of his pants every time he and I were in the house alone. It was indeed a weird situation because at the time I was not sure what he was doing. But by the look on his face I knew it must not have been too good. His gestures embarrassed me but I felt as if there was something inside my throat stopping me from telling Mama. Papa would have killed him perhaps. I guess I was a coward, but I did not want any scandal. The rude uncle was a paragon of saintly behaviour when people were around. Was my mind playing tricks on me? A terrible sense of insecurity overtook my early adolescence. I had been removed from the safe cocoon of my imagination. As I grew up, I became scared of my own reactions, of having to make my own decisions. Mama had always wanted life to be so perfect, like on the radio soaps, where good always triumphed over evil, no matter what the cost. Sometimes I thought that the perfect solution would just be to go away, to love Mama from a distance.

The sound of a car engine snapped me out of my reflections. It was a police car. All the kids disappeared through cavities in the walls, because it was illegal to play on the road. The car stopped outside Loretta's house and two men in green uniforms and polished boots stepped out and headed to her door. Politely, for police demand respect in my home town, I told them that Loretta was busy doing some fittings for her clients. I explained she was a dressmaker and that I too was waiting for her and showed them my vanilla cake on the plate. The men in uniform nodded and grunted, and turned towards the Takanakas' shop to have a drink before returning. 'Tell Miss Loretta we have answered her call,' one of them said, and they walked away.

A few minutes later I knocked on the door, and Loretta opened it. 'Hello.' She looked relaxed, her smile chirpy as usual. She wore a scarf around her neck and her hair pulled up with a couple of loose curls falling over her ears. She had put on some kilos but her curves were still pronounced and regal.

'I heard you talking to somebody,' I whispered. 'Did he go out through the roof?' I looked around inside, placing the plate on the table, but all I noticed was that she had rosary beads in her fingers.

'Yes, I was talking to somebody, but not just anybody.'

'Umm?'

'I cannot tell you because it is a secret,' she said softly.

I guessed that she wanted me to plead, to beg to know her secrets in the tradition of the women of my town. I insisted, 'Please tell me.' Loretta had always been like a little girl, playfully engaging people in her reveries. She was an amiable person, always empathetic with those of lesser luck, always ready to offer a favour. I wanted to dance like her, seduce like her. Mama once said that it was a pity that with Loretta's personality she had missed so many opportunities. I knew I would never have her luxurious curves or her cascading hair, but she said we could all make the best of what we had.

'Can you keep a secret?' she asked.

'Of course. You can count on me. I have so many secrets that I have created a special crystal box in which to put them. Moreover, I have also built a little propelling machine to shuttle this crystal box to the stars when it gets too full,' I replied, finding a comfortable spot on the bed.

'Well, do you remember my dreams of Doña Santitos?' she said, looking around as though the secret police might be in the room.

'Yeah,' I whispered, biting my lower lip.

'Now, I don't dream about her. I actually see her and she talks to me.'

'What?' I yelled, unable to contain my surprise.

Immediately a red blush of embarrassment lit up Loretta's cheeks. She told me that she had asked Doña Santitos to come to her not just in her dreams but whenever she needed her. Now this wish had come true.

I chewed a piece of the nougat that Loretta always kept in a jar. Perhaps the sugar would help make some sense of what she was saying. My father's observations about her came to my mind: 'That girl is going to go down. Her grief over the little lady might bring up the insanity in the family.' Mama asked him to be fair. Loretta was not crazy, just 'original'. Sitting by my side, Loretta looked very serious, so serious that I could not doubt she had in fact seen the face of the little saint. Doña Santitos herself had said that people never die if somebody keeps their memory alive. The first time she had appeared to Loretta was at the sewing machine at night. Doña Santitos stared at her in silence, beaming a peaceful smile, floating in midair. Later, the apparition became more three-dimensional and delivered information telepathically. I was not sure whether to let Loretta keep talking, or go home and cry deeply because she was going bananas. I found the courage to ask for some details, trying to appear blasé.

'Really? And what does she tell you?' I asked, taking another bite of nougat. 'Has she told you where she's gone?'

'She's gone to the same place where she came from. A place far away but also close enough if you want to touch it.'

'Oh I see, and how do we get there?'

'To do that you have to believe in it.' That is all she said, or all I have ever remembered.

In time, I accepted that such a place existed, and later I would even get visitors from there myself. But on that day, I did not want to think about where the spirits lived. I did not want to imagine the space that allowed souls to rest before they returned to earth or went on to cosmic pastures. I had forgotten about it because Mama had asked me to do so. She did not want me to talk about the In-between unless I wanted people to think I was crazy. We could not allow that, could we? I had a big future ahead. Mama had imprinted this message in my mind the day the spirit of my grandfather Desiderio came to say goodbye, as his body was dying in Iquitos.

Desiderio came to bid his farewells one spring afternoon when Mama and I were busy with our household chores. The boys had gone to play soccer and Papa was at work. The house was quiet, lit by a pale glow which filtered through the small window above the door.

The lunch dishes had already been washed and put away, and Mama had asked me to come upstairs with her to help her fold the ironing and do some mending. She pulled out the sewing basket and handed me a needle and a light bulb, which I had learned to use to mend socks. Our bedroom was filled with shelves and containers, like a giant storage unit – double-decker beds, bottom drawers, shelves and foldable desks on the walls, false ceilings for extra storage, homemade wardrobes and the sacred sewing-machine table, which served as my desk or a shrine, depending on the occasion. Now the sewing machine was serving as the base for the long Oregon board that we used to iron all our clothes on. Sitting on Mama's bed, I dressed the light bulb with one of Papa's brown socks that had a hole in the toe, threaded the needle and prepared myself for the mending operation, like a domestic surgeon. Mama placed a white sheet on top of a thick blanket over the board, and began to iron, while humming one of her father's clarinet tunes.

'Tell me some jungle stories,' I asked, noticing she was in a good mood.

'Okay, I'll tell you the story of El Mayantu,' she said. 'El Mayantu is an elf with a frog face who lives in a cave of giant pineapple trees. His most important mission is to help people search for their lost souls. Although his ways are not always very noble. One day, a lost girl . . .'

My hands followed the rhythm of her voice, my soul commencing a journey to the world beyond. Suddenly, I heard the sound of a distant clarinet. It was as if an icy blast of air engulfed Mama. She shivered and turned pale, like a candle.

'Oh my God, it's your grandfather,' she cried, covering her face. I ran to hug her.

'*Mamita*, please, what's happening?' I pleaded. She sobbed and sobbed.

'Mama, what's happening? Please, what's the matter?' I hugged her more tightly, pleading for an explanation.

'It's your Abuelo Desiderio, sweetheart. He's come to tell me he has died,' she said, her voice shocked with grief and resignation.

'It might just be a false alarm,' I dared to suggest.

I was wrong. A letter arrived a few days later. It was from the step-mother, and confirmed that my grandfather had died on the day of Mama's presentiment. I closed my eyes and journeyed back in my imagination to the afternoon of the ironing and the mending. I replayed the clarinet tune in my mind. Then I saw Abuelo Desiderio float into the room. I saw him, round and jolly, dressed in his army band uniform, holding a clarinet in one hand, and touching Mama's shoulder with the other. I saw him kiss her goodbye. Then he turned around and walked away, accompanied by the Blue Cat. It was my first introduction to the spirit world. And it was a vision that I would never forget.

I was less willing to believe in Loretta's visions because I hoped that Doña Santitos might still be alive. Perhaps she was projecting herself for Loretta, like the old saints had done. We knew that our local saint, Saint Martin, whilst he was still alive and working in Lima, projected his image to Angola to help the Portuguese soldiers in hospital. Loretta assured me her vision was as true as our friendship.

'Doña Santitos' presence is like a guide. I even get ideas for my dress designing,' she alleged.

'And what was she telling you when I came to see you this after-noon?' I asked.

Loretta remained silent for a while, then uttered in a soft voice that the apparition had told her that her boyfriend had been killed in an accident.

'Killed? And why aren't you sad?'

'I am sad, but not devastated. Doña Santitos said he'd chosen his death.'

What Loretta did not want to say was that the man she was obses-sively attracted to had killed people. He was a member of the rebellion that nurtured hopes of social transformation, dreaming of going back to Inca times. It was obvious she had not met him in the nightclub. He had come to one of the meetings of the Hermetic Society with his mother, although he was not much of a believer. He preferred to live in darkness, and went out only at night. During the day, he read books and communiqués from the guerrilla movement's leader, who had modelled himself on the late revolutionary hero, Che Guevara.

'How do you know he chose his death?' I asked.

'Well, he killed a man one evening as we were driving home. It was a hit and run.' Loretta sobbed as she covered her eyes, feeling a sense of shame. I understood why she was so willing to believe in Doña Santitos. Perhaps Doña Santitos was nothing more than her own sense of guilt. I shivered, and remembered the police car out the front.

'I promise I won't tell this to anybody,' I said.

The police knocked on the door while we were talking and confirmed that her boyfriend was dead. She had called them because she had not been able to find him for days. His mother had had no news from him either. It turned out that he had been caught and shot by paramilitary forces. No one knew who had killed him, and no one would be arrested. Tears welled up in her eyes and she grimaced bitterly. She had loved the guy – it showed. She picked up her bag and a cardigan, and silently accompanied the uniformed men to the morgue to identify the body. I did not doubt Loretta any more. I never revealed her secret to anyone, not even to my mother.

WHERE GOOD AND EVIL MEET

MAMA'S DREAMS HAD come true. My brothers from the Amazon, the seeds of her perpetual anxiety, were on their way to join us in the city. It was a glorious time for the family. We busied ourselves like dutiful bees striving to make our queen happy.

My father was the most excited because he was sure Mama's emotional injuries would be healed once and for all. Mama had placed most of the fun things of life on hold, had never taken holidays, and was always careful with her expenses. Even laughter was rationed if my mother was feeling anxious, a condition that had worsened since her operation. But now life was going to be different, we hoped. Hidden in her heart had been a deep sense of shame for not having fought harder to take her children back.

The night before their arrival, Mama dreamed of Bufeo Colorado, who, aware of Mama's renewed happiness, had given her a number of clues as to how best to handle the new adolescents in her life. 'Remember, they have not grown up with you,' the dolphin said in her dream. Papa echoed the advice of the wise one, trying to make sure Mama did not get over-excited. We knew her imposing ways, her outbursts, and her anxiety-ridden methods, and we knew such methods achieved order at home – but the new boys did not have access to such privileged information. They had grown up in a boarding school, which perhaps could have been authoritarian for it was a Christian school, except that it was set in the middle of the jungle, where people were very independent. Well, Mama listened to Papa with eyes half meandering in the In-between, half focused on his face. She assured him that she would do her best.

Papa had built new bunks for the boys. He also repainted the house and even built a new ladder to the second floor because the old one was becoming loose due to Mama's extra weight. The boys' room was repainted green for gratitude, our bedroom blue for inspiration and the main room yellow for prosperity, while the kitchen was washed with pink lime for creativity – and because it camouflaged the cracks and rough surfaces. The boys' pillowcases had been embroidered with their names, which had taken Mama and me several weeks to do. The kitchen was packed with extra supplies from a dozen bottles of champagne, beer and vermouth through to imported jams and canned fruit, special biscuits and *panettone* that Mama had hidden since last Christmas. Loretta had made her own version of pineapple jam and bottled it in a pretty little jar with a huge bow around the neck that she had made to honour Mama's special day, while Doña Panchita had given Mama a picture of the Heart of Jesus for the boys' room.

'They might not take to Jesus,' teased Papa. 'Remember, they come from the jungle.' Mama frowned, reminding Papa that her children were coming from a reputable Christian Brothers boarding school fit for refined boys, and Papa chuckled, reassuring her that his blabber was only meant to soften the mood. Hugging her, he promised he would do his best to make them feel at ease. A party was to take place the following weekend, and Doña Panchita had been informed that all the furniture would have to be moved to her place as usual when we had parties, so there would be enough space to dance and be merry.

A few days before the boys' arrival Aunt Dorita confided in my mother that Aunt Renatta was very worried because my cousin Tato was now in bed unable to move. She might not be able to make the party. Tato was the eldest of the seven children Aunt Renatta had with Uncle Arnaldo, whom I had just found out also had another seven with his official wife.

We visited Tato, took him gifts, and told him stories about angels and green frogs. His face had become gaunt; his life force dripped quickly out of his body now, although his gaze was always peaceful. My heart was clasped by a terrible feeling of despair. In his face, I saw innocent, angelic resignation. I wanted to protest, to scream loudly, to beg all the gods I had ever known to let him live or take him away immediately. When we left, we promised to bring him a little lizard from the jungle.

Some people in the neighbourhood had been murmuring that the soul of my cousin Tato had been tampered with by wicked spirits. In other words he had 'been done' by somebody, an evil *Brujo* who did not like Aunt Renatta. Mama forbade me to digest such barbarous rumours. But she did make me spray blessed water all over the house. Every corner of every room was sprayed with lavender and mint to greet the souls of the newcomers; all windows and mirrors were polished, sparkling like radiant stars. The floorboards were also treated with a special mixture of kerosene and holy water to kill any bugs and prevent wickedness from entering our living space.

As the day approached, the spirit of jubilation moved into our house and sat perched on the parakeet's cage, chatting to the bird about tropical affairs all day long. The heat of summer reached its peak on the special day. We jumped out of bed at the first ring of the old alarm clock, which frightened Mocho, who barked at Pancho, sure that the cat was the source of the aggressive ring. Both pets had been washed, perfumed, and treated with anti-flea lotion and talcum powder. We got dressed in our best clothes and sprinkled on a touch of French lavender to attract angels and tease mischievous spirits. Mama's heart was beating like a mixed-up drum machine but she did not show it as she set the table for breakfast and thoroughly prepared us to be on our best behaviour.

'Make sure you don't say the wrong thing or pick your nose,' she warned me. 'And you, Luis, watch where you go and don't get into any mess.' We were all as excited as she was.

Dolled up, we boarded Papa's old Chevrolet bound for the airport, humming a Beatles song in the back, while in the front seat Mama battled against stubborn fluff on her lapel. Fear was gnawing at her heart. Would they reject her? Once the fluff of her lapel was gone, she began to pat nervously at the dew of perspiration on her neck; when that was done, she fought to fix a rebellious curl on her forehead, in order to 'look presentable'. The old Chevrolet drove into the airport two hours before they were due to arrive; then their flight was delayed. We had not been to the airport, so we were treated to a light breakfast, and stood at the window counting the planes that took off and landed. It was then that I secretly promised myself I would be on one such plane before the end of my second decade. Finally, the boys' plane arrived and they stepped out.

I recognised them from the balcony, for we had watched them growing up through photographs. They walked along the tarmac with a mixture of adolescent self-assurance and apprehension. They turned their heads, searching for the family they had not yet met. I was also nervous. They were my brothers, but they were also two strangers who had indirectly been the cause of Mama's anxieties. I was a bundle of curiosity, with a tinge of resentment tucked neatly inside. In addition, I felt a touch of fear because two grown-up boys were coming to live in my house. As if we did not have enough men at home. The house that had once belonged to a woman with hopes and a table and two chairs was now going to be the home of seven people, a dog, a cat, two parakeets, and probably a monkey and a turtle, for we knew my brothers were bringing their pets too. Could we all get along? For the first time, I was glad that Mama ran the show in the way she did, with the 'either follow the rules or be punished' attitude.

The boys walked through the door, approaching Mama politely and reservedly. How well did they remember her? It was hard to know. They hugged Mama, amid passengers running to leave, or farewelling friends. They looked tall to me, and had tanned skins and a fresh cadence to their voices. I smelled their intentions, scrutinised their movements, inhaled their initial apprehension, and finally accepted them with a big hug and a welcoming kiss. They shook Papa's hand, but Papa gave them a paternal embrace. Mama was so proud of how good they looked. The elder, Alfonso, was a slender boy with exotic eyes and a serious disposition. As we drove back in the car, packed in like sardines, we discovered that, like Mama, Alfonso was prone to mythical descriptions of life in the forest. His boarding school had been 'perched in between giant trees, wild rivers and alligators that consorted with sirens'. The younger one, Leo, was taller, fairer, and more vivacious in character, always ready to play a joke. 'Where have all the trees gone? Do they have to work in the city too?' he asked, peering at the desert that bordered the road.

'It doesn't rain here,' I replied. 'We have a submarine current that modifies our tropical weather and prevents the rain from falling.' It was the El Niño current which, on the positive side, did help our fishing industry. I was keen to show off, eager to let them know I, too, was an important member of the family. It was true about the rain. The wicked El Niño current had destroyed the prosperous valley of the viceroys, transforming it into a sad desert. Radical voices claimed it was due to the Curse of Atahualpa, the Inca betrayed by the Spaniards.

Alfonso gazed at the clouds with a look of resignation and said, 'If is to be the will of the gods, then so be it.' We were all shocked, for none of us had been told that the eldest had developed such a spiritual connection. Well, it was better to have a religious boy than a rebellious one, Papa thought. The rest of the trip we remained silent, allowing the boys to check out their new city while I spied from the back seat how straight their hair was, how Leo's laughter reverberated with good spirits, and how sweet their accents sounded as they talked to Papa, their words like musical notes swaying in a hammock.

After a sumptuous breakfast of grilled pork chops, feta, smoked ham, fried yam and blood sausages, the boys laid their presents from the jungle on the table. Out of baskets lined with calico came jars of conserves, fruits, smoked game, tiger balm, silks, the most beautiful tortoiseshell comb for my hair, and a beautiful piece of hot pink silk. It was fuchsia to be more exact, a present sent by the Lady Mayor, who reminded Mama that many battles had to be lost before victory was achieved. Mama could not contain her tears, which honoured the advice of the wise woman of her youth. Many leaves had fallen since the Lady Mayor's notorious clash in front of the church, where Mama had learned to 'defend one's own self-respect, even if the battle has to be fought against invisible enemies'. We opened our presents around the table, giggling and yelling, amazed at the outlandish display of jungle paraphernalia.

A three-day celebration followed, with a three-piece band, festival costumes and colourful streamers dangling from the ceiling. To offer them a genuine taste of the ocean flavour and the large variety of food on the coast, Mama had hired a cook to prepare some special dishes. My elder cousins and daughters of Mama's friends wore their most stylish gowns to make a good impression on the boys. The glamour of the party was further accentuated by the fact that it coincided with national carnival celebrations, the period when people frolic and let go of grief and stress. It was always an occasion to celebrate the harvest of life, to honour Lord Momo and Lady Nature, to give thanks for the rapture of the senses and the passion of life. As it was a ritual to honour the pagan gods, churches kept their doors closed and the nocturnal enchantresses opened theirs. My brothers joined the celebrations with enthusiasm.

We taught them to make harmless powder bombs and hurl them against innocent bystanders. It was a wicked trick, but carnival was also known as retribution time, when no guilt would dare assault a person's heart. Alfonso had found it difficult to applaud our mischievous behaviour; in contrast, Leo was always ready to prepare more ammunition, filling small balloons with coloured water and talcum powder. He eventually managed to convince Alfonso that water had a good effect on people. 'It will attune their emotions,' he said.

Filled with music, beer and duck with coriander, my brothers finally succumbed to the spell of maternal love, the girls in the city, and the call of their hormones. At carnival time, it was a sin not to indulge. We swore that on carnival night we were able to see flying goblins riding on silver-rimmed clouds, announcing times of plenty. On the last evening of carnival, we took the boys to the Mardi Gras parade, for we wanted them to be hypnotised by the sight of the lavish floats with dancing queens and radiant goddesses wearing enchanting costumes over golden-painted skin. Dressed in our fantasy costumes, we cheered as the ladies stretched their ear-to-ear smiles, waving their delicate wands at us, bestowing magic on our lives.

It had been an unforgettable party. A week later, all the Mardi Gras masks had been put away for the next year, the unopened champagne bottles went back to the bottom of the glass cabinet, and the furniture was brought back from Doña Panchita's. The four boys managed to sleep in the room above the kitchen, which now looked bigger with the attachments Papa had installed for hanging clothes, and writing boards, which folded down off the wall. I had explained to the boys that life in big cities forced people to live in constrained spaces, just like in the pictures of New York we saw on television. Leo said the squeezed space did not matter because soon he would be going to New York, so it was good practice. Alfonso, on the other hand, had plans to join the air force. I felt sorry for Mama, with her plans to buy a new house to bring the family together in comfort, and I did not tell her anything. Mama was determined to get them enrolled in a reputable school, a task that was going to prove difficult for the school did not look upon boys from the country with fond appreciation. But challenges had never deterred Mama, and she was prepared to use magician's spells if necessary to secure them both a place.

Through a friend of Loretta, she had discovered that a certain

Social Sciences teacher at the school favoured wild animals from the jungle. The school museum had not been able to display any in its gallery, simply because it had been too difficult to procure genuine specimens from the Amazon. Nothing would be difficult for my mother if she decided to do it, so, dressed in a gorgeous fuchsia suit with her curls set in place, she fronted up to the office of the head Social Sciences teacher with a colourful parakeet in a cage as a greeting card. She wanted to tell the man that there were many more where the bird had come from, but the next ones could be filled with special stuffing, if the teacher so desired it. Moreover, the animals she could obtain, she assured the wide-eyed teacher, were prepared by a tribe that had special taxidermy skills, and always made sure that the soul of the animal was protected. Highly amused by Mama's persuasive appeal, the teacher promised nothing more than to take a good look into the matter. Immediately after the meeting, Mama took pen and paper and wrote to her relatives asking them to obtain the most rare and precious animals for the school. 'The Amazon wildlife would have a rightful place in our city schools,' she had written, 'but make sure the shamans don't make a fool out of you.' Many con men deceived their clients by selling them animals with plastic limbs and artificial fur.

Papa was not impressed, and scolded Mama for not respecting the rules of the city schools. Aunt Lisa supported her, reassuring her that all problems can be solved with gifts of a special kind. 'What else can we do, Rosita? One has to survive.' However, there was no need for Mama's relatives to chase animals or shamans, because, aware of her intentions, Don Ramon, who was still powerful in town, found the most fascinating wild animals ever seen. Time on his own had softened his heart. He had persuaded the boys to finish their schooling in the city, allowing them to reconcile with their mother and pursue their dreams. When a large parcel arrived, we threw ourselves at it, filled with curiosity. We unwrapped the box with pounding hearts. Then we saw them: they were real animals! So real that we were sure some magic spell had frozen them in suspended animation. A small alligator stared at us with sharp teeth, and we were horrified; a small tiger looked out with an ingenuous expression and we fell in love with it; and a flamboyant parrot with silky rainbow feathers gave us such a wide-eyed look that Aunt Techa assured us its soul flew back at night. The principal of the school was so captivated by the quality of the taxidermic work on the wild specimens that the school rules were easily bent, my brothers were enrolled, and the stuffed animals found a privileged spot on a glass shelf at the school gallery, from where they haunted the janitor. He swore the animals' souls glided through the air when it was dark. He was not wrong.

Alfonso arrived home pale as a fading ghost; his legs were shaking and his hair was straighter than usual. We were waiting for lunch to be served when he walked in, and the moment he saw us he ran to the bathroom to release his nauseous condition into the bowl. I stared at him for I had never seen our well-composed brother in such a condition before.

'I have seen a black rabbit,' he said, as he joined us at the table.

'A black rabbit?' Luis yelled. 'There are no black rabbits, brother. What you have seen is a captain rat.'

'I am sure it was a black rabbit, and black rabbits are ill omens,' he said.

Papa took little notice, and smiled with his resigned smile. Not long ago, a troop of black rats had terrorised the city, but Alfonso was sure he had seen a black rabbit as he stepped out of the school bus. Papa explained that perhaps Alfonso had seen a guinea pig that had escaped from a neighbour's kitchen, dreading his fate in a casserole. To prove our point, we switched on the news to find out whether there was a rat plague, but instead we heard another dire warning. The El Niño current had reversed, and the fish that fed all the sea birds, which produced guano fertiliser, were on the verge of extermination. 'Days of plenty have gone,' grunted Papa. The next day, we saw thousands of pelicans perched on the city's roofs and gathered at all the markets, desperately searching for food. The cats disappeared, for the large birds nested in their habitats. The whole town soon stank as heaps of the birds' droppings plastered the streets. The tabloid media had a feast, telling citizens that it was all the politicians' fault. These corrupt men, the media said, had squandered our valuable resources. They blamed the Department of Fisheries for transforming the number one producer of fish into a dung-filled town. The military came out onto the streets to handle the smelly situation, but could do little about the birds that had invaded the city. The opposition claimed that El Niño had nothing to do with the fish disappearance. The fault lay with the fishing lords, whose limited vision had made them fish indiscriminately, leaving most sea beds nearly empty.

Whether the black rabbit had been real or not, Alfonso had been right and the times of plenty did come to an end. An avalanche of adversity fell upon our people, ironically coinciding with the visit of a group of foreign astrologers to the city of Cusco to examine a strange phenomenon. International students of the occult, and a few Hollywood stars, had flocked to the ancient capital of the Incas, for well-known astrologers were interpreting a predicted planetary align-ment as the gateway to a new era. Deep in the country, the military had launched an offensive against a student rebellion which had called for a return to Inca times, encouraged by student protests in France. Even our own neighbourhood had its share of horror stories – not far from our block the police had used tear gas against clashing soccer fans, killing hundreds of them. The collective social climate had turned sour. And Loretta, who claimed she had spoken to Doña Santitos over the happenings, stated that we were entering the era when good would meet evil. She had learned at the Hermetic Soci-ety that 'three decades before the new millennium, a confrontation would occur'.

'How can you be so sure?' I asked.

'These things are written in ancient scriptures. We are entering the Dawn of Aquarius.'

She was seeing one of the more advanced students, who was a so-called 'alchemist'. He recommended that she acquire jewellery to attract light, fortune and divinity. He explained that alchemists are *not* people who try to blend metals to make gold, but people who mould the spirit in order to reach the golden light of spiritual growth. It sounded suspicious. Anything that had to do with gold, the spirit, and the mixing of metals, had to be looked upon with a careful eye, I thought.

The time came for us all to go back to school, exams began, and the boys struggled to adjust to Mama's rigorous ways of running the house. More often than not, these ways defied all methods known to them, including those austere and strict methods of the Christian Brothers. Initially, they played deaf and ignored Mama's brooding or her severe demands for order, particularly when she became agitated because the boys did not make their beds properly or did not help her when she came home loaded with shopping bags. First, they laughed, then they asked her to mind her own business, until one day the volcano erupted. It was early one morning when Alfonso tiptoed his way into the house after a late-night party. Mama was already up. 'This is not the time to come into a decent home,' she scolded. Well, that did it. Who did she think she was? Why did she care so much now, when in the past she had not given a damn? All hell broke loose. Leo awoke and joined in the argument. After years of having their feelings pent up in boarding school, the chance came for them to expose the shadows of their loneliness.

Their accusations, filled with rage and recriminations, hit Mama unexpectedly. She had no idea her ways were so strict. How could she? We had no chance to tell her, to make her realise she was some-times over the borderline. The boys' reaction pierced her heart like a needle filled with poison. She struck back, defending her right to seek her wellbeing, to forge herself a future. It was not because she did not love them; it was for her survival. The atmosphere reeked of festering emotional sores, comparable only to the foul smell of the bird manure on the streets. The boys had grown up with the version of the story that Mama had abandoned them to pursue flippant endeavours. They heard that she had left them behind to chase selfish interests; that she had *never* loved them.

Papa applied the art of diplomacy he had learned as a member of a large family. With subtlety, discretion and best wishes, he managed to pacify the boys, explaining the quality of Mama's affection, the fabric of her dreams and the strength of her sacrifices to bring them to Lima. He explained that, sometimes, stories are misinterpreted as they are passed from one person to another. Perhaps the story they heard was not the real one? Perhaps their perception had been clouded by the storyteller? Without judging them, he helped the boys adjust to their new world, applying commonsense and fatherly affection. The boys slowly accepted that Mama had acted in the best way she knew at the time. The heated episode allowed them to develop respect and admiration for my father, and they became long-term friends with him.

As for me, the shadow of these struggles was deeply engraved in my heart, and it took a long time for it to be erased. I hated my brothers and wished they had never come. I did not understand most of what they were arguing about. I did not know whether to blame the stepmother, the boys, or their father. I had to put the blame on somebody. I had listened to their confrontation from my bed, racked with hostility and indignation. Resentment crawled into the folds of my memories, making me distrust the quality of love I came to encounter. Now, I am able to cast a new light on these episodes, and I understand. Who was I to cast blame? So what if Mama had indeed been selfish? So what if the stepmother had spoken out of naked ignorance? I have learned that circumstances persuade people to behave in the most peculiar ways. I now know that the boys had simply obeyed their feelings, and that they needed to let them out. Years later, after a series of my own disappointments and betrayals, we began to see the best in each other.

Doña Panchita was very influential in helping Mama understand the boys. She would sit at the table, stirring her cup of lemon grass and valerian tea, her eyes filled with tenderness, silver wisps of her hair around her face, listening as Mama poured out the fears and pain in the depths of her troubled heart. 'Cry, my child, for tears are a shower for a distraught heart,' she would say.

Finally, the dust settled at home, and the time came for us to grow and fill each other with laughter and affection.

My school year came to an end, with a collection of 'Well done' report cards, a mixed attitude to Christianity, and poor marks in the area of good behaviour. Obedience, compliance and submissiveness were assessed by our teachers and recorded on cards that our parents had to sign, acknowledge and act on if we registered the lowest mark – which was often the case with me. School was the only place in which I was able to release my pent-up frustration, lose control and obey my overflowing hormones before going insane with the rules at home. I admit, however, that I was born with a strong insubordinate streak, a penchant for questioning everything and highlighting imper-fections. My father said it was no wonder I was born in Peru, a country of contrasts and eccentricity. My mother felt that a public school would put the brakes on my 'unbridled' behaviour, but to make up for the 'refinement' I would lose in a non-private school, she also enrolled me in English classes, which she believed would double my chances for the future. 'It's not what you possess, my dear, but what you learn that will give you the opportunities.' Life has proved to me that she was not at all wrong.

My heart, however, had never abandoned its aspirations for danc-ing professionally. I spent endless evenings dreaming of myself in a pink tutu leaping from one side to the other, flying through space. The next best thing for me to do was to join the Afro-Peruvian dance group at my new high school, which to my good fortune was attended by a lot of black girls who were sports-minded and dance-crazy. For performances, I had to have my hips padded with moulded cushions in order to play the part of a black dancer, and make the movements more pronounced, more provocative and rhythmical, as tradition required. Before a performance, I would cover my face with burnt cork, tie my hair in a polka-dotted scarf, insert myself into layers and layers of starched petticoats and skirts festooned with multicoloured ribbons, and then look at myself in the mirror and smile – my teeth were the only feature I could recognise. On stage, which was always in the courtyard, I would carry burning candles in my hands and flaming passion in my heart, imagining I was one of the *Humiteros* performing their splendid leaps on moonlit nights an hour before midnight. Those were the happiest days of my life, and even now, when I bring the memory of my dancing days up from the cellars of my mind, a childlike smile settles on my lips.

Lola – who Mama said was my milk mother, for she had also suckled me due to my insatiable appetite – gave me a few tips, for she knew how to contort her hips like no other. 'Your mind has to be fixed on your belly button, my dear, forget about anything else.' But when that diva of African dance was not available, Loretta came to the rescue.

One day as I headed towards Loretta's house carrying a few cookies on a plate and my polka-dotted dress for rehearsal, I noticed a sour-looking man leaving her house. The mood surrounding him smacked of tragedy; I could read anguish in his eyes as he bid his farewell. I pushed the door open carefully. Inside the dimly lit room, I found Loretta distraught, crying and choking with despair. Her face was crimson, her eyes swollen like two ripe tomatoes. The man was from the Hermetic Society, and a bearer of terrible news judging by the landscape before me. Her voice cracking with pain and an unwillingness to believe her predicament, Loretta revealed that her boyfriend, the one who had taught her the secrets of alchemy and the pursuit of the golden light, had blatantly and shamelessly robbed her of her jewels. Lying on Doña Santitos' bedspread, her face distorted with pain, Loretta kept calling herself names – not very nice names –

and lashing out at herself. 'I am a child of hell, stupid, ignorant . . .' she went on and on, until I gave her a glass of water with citron blossom to calm her. She explained that the scoundrel had asked her for all the pieces of jewellery she had collected over the years including all the precious rings and gold chains she had bought for her younger sisters. Weeping again, she exclaimed, 'He promised he would turn them into an even more precious metal.' I didn't want to believe that Loretta could have been so gullible. 'What can be more precious than gold?' I asked. Sobbing, she replied that much of what she had given him had been silver, but he had also taken the gold jewellery 'to match the frequency' of the metal and blend all of the pieces into one single golden bar of light.

The man had disappeared from the face of the earth; and Loretta was filled with a sense of alienation and was scared ever to trust again. 'It is not that bad,' I reassured her. 'He could have robbed you of your life.' I left her house promising that we would find the man or the jewels, one way or another. There was no dancing practice for me that night.

My soul walked home downhearted, unable to see the bright side. Doña Panchita had been wise in her assessment that the world is constantly pulled by two conflicting forces. She taught me that we are each born with two angels on either side of us and we can never get rid of them even if we want to. We are a reflection of both of them. The best thing is to befriend them both and show them utter respect.

Why did Loretta attract so many rascals? Was she really cursed? Doña Panchita and my parents wanted her to go to the police and press charges. But Loretta refused, for it would mean admitting to herself once more that her life was surrounded by some form of malediction. 'You must not let people do this to you,' Mama protested, handing her the leftover fuchsia silk from the Lady Mayor. 'Make yourself a blouse or something that gives you power, and I will go to the police with you.' But Loretta would not do it; she preferred to swallow her tears.

Spring came and many changes were taking place in our home. My father's driver asked for prolonged holidays so he could look after his dying mother. 'It will not be too long, Don Bresciani. She is already talking to Saint Peter,' he said when he left. My Mama, with her judicious approach to economics, persuaded my father to drive the vehicle himself and save on salaries. Papa was reluctant at first. He did not want to drive the heavy truck in the fume-filled haze of the day, with all the noise, the crush of the traffic, the ditches and the bumps, and the important merchandise in the back. Nevertheless, he agreed to do it.

Alfonso had become an air force cadet, and looked great in his blue uniform and gold-rimmed cap. Leo was busy preparing to travel to the United States. The plans excited my mother, for she had the travel bug. Perhaps if I went overseas, I might be able to take her with me. My father didn't share this dream. He did not like all the turbulence or the sea sickness, or the buses driving on the edge of canyons.

. The biggest shadow on the family's soul was my cousin Tato, who lay in bed with his back covered in sores. He could not move at all. The gods of indifference had kept him alive, dozing in chronic pain. He was unable to do anything for himself, only flicker his eyelashes once in a while, roll his eyes, and mumble a bit. But he never lost his angelic disposition. Aunt Renatta visited us often to get support and consolation from Mama. Tato's disease kept her eyes perpetually swollen, robbing them of their natural beauty and fading her looks. 'Aye, Rosita, if only God would send an angel for him!' she wailed, and I would beg all the gods, including Lord Momo, to grant her request.

The news of Loretta's lost jewels had reached every corner of town. The alchemist was being tracked down using the Hermetic and obscure methods her friends from the society knew. Doña Panchita suggested that Loretta needed a bit of help from a *Hechicera*, a woman who uses special herbs to purify the soul. 'There was a very good white *Hechicera* in town', said Doña Panchita. And so it was that the cleansing ritual was held on All Souls' Day, in early November.

Accompanied by Doña Panchita, Loretta, Renatta and Mama went to see the white *Hechicera* – Renatta to help her sick child, Tato, Loretta to recover her jewels, and Mama to improve her business and find a house. Loretta was the first one to lie down on a table covered with white linen, while the rest waited in the next room, drank a herbal brew, and chanted the rosary. The statue of Saint Rosa de Lima, who represented the purity of all things in life, stood in one corner of the room lit by a dozen candles and adorned with flowers. The *Hechicera* was a bony, silver-haired, but tender-looking, woman from the highlands who drank coca tea and wore a loose caftan and a multicoloured shawl. After calling out a few prayers in Quechua, the ancient Inca language, she proceeded to brush Loretta with a bundle of white condor feathers to open the doors of freedom, intoning chants and tapping her foot on the floor. Then she brought out a rattle stick to scare evil spirits away. Foam started to bubble out of Loretta's mouth, the remnants of a herbal concoction she had drunk earlier. Once the evil spirits were gone, *La Hechicera* burnt a sprig of coca leaves and other herbs while walking around the table, still chanting with her rattle stick. To end the session, Loretta was asked to get into a tin bath filled with fragrant water and rose petals.

Mama underwent the cleansing rites next, but did away with the smoke because of her asthma. Instead, the healer brushed her firmly with a specially treated porcupine brush to strip away all the jealousy and hostility she claimed Mama had around her. Her skin turned burning red and Mama was terrified it would peel off. Her main fear was what Papa would say. But some lanolin and a soothing massage returned her to normal, and then she too had a rose bath. When Aunt Renatta's turn came to be brushed and cleansed, she vomited so much toxin that she became weak. When the whole ceremony was finished, the three women swore that no one was ever to know about it, except for Doña Panchita, who had watched it all from the corner of the room where she sat on a rocking chair, knitting a woollen scarf.

La Hechicera said that the ritual would only work if the clients followed her post-ceremonial recommendations. She told Loretta to go back to her home town, seek out her long-lost father, face him and forgive him. To release the curse once and for all, she was to find an injured dove and nurse it until it was well. It had to be a dove – not a parakeet or a pelican. The recovery of the dove would signal that Loretta's soul was mended. My mother's task was to forgive the stepmother. An affectionate letter would suffice, recommended *La Hechicera*, before moving on to the issue of my father's sisters, the snobbish aunts. They would be coming to visit soon, *La Hechicera* told Mama, and when this happened, Mama ought to be kind and understanding. Not just polite, but generous with her heart. Aunt Renatta's mission was to forgive Arnaldo's official wife, let go of her struggle for priority, and accept the ways things were. The women still dizzy with all the scented rites and bitter beverages listened to *La Hechicera's* recommendations silently, an expression of disbelief grew on their faces. They were almost certain what they had heard was a product of the herbs, a mental hallucination.

Loretta appeared at our front door with a packed suitcase to say goodbye. I admired her for taking on the challenge to go and see her father, the Shaman of the Huaringas, the City of *Brujos*. Mama was glad to see her wearing an elegant short-sleeved jacket made with the fuchsia silk. The two women toasted to good fortune. 'To the fuchsia power!' they sang. Suddenly there was an ominous-sounding knock on the door, the type one prefers never to hear. Mama opened the door and two serious-looking men asked whether she was Mrs Rosa de Bresciani. 'Yes, I am,' she said. 'What's happened?' Her voice quivered.

'It's your husband, Madam, he is in hospital,' one of the men replied. 'He's been in an accident with the truck.' My heart froze.

Mama ran to get her bag. Loretta said she would go with us to the hospital, but Mama refused for Loretta's bus was due soon. It was her mission to catch it and follow her road. Mama would have to walk her own, with us by her side. They wished each other well, and parted.

We found Papa lying in a hospital bed. We immediately gave our thanks to the sky gods and promised to take more flowers to Nona Emilia at the cemetery, for surely she had protected him. Papa's truck had run into another and tipped over on its side, hurling him out. Papa had damaged his back and shoulders so they wrapped half of his body in plaster, and ordered him to stop work and stop smoking tobacco for several weeks.

Mama was devastated. Her best friend was injured, and she was lost without his strength. She put her business on hold to spend time tending to Papa. The accident had not only broken his shoulder bones and a few ribs, and damaged his muscles; it had gone deeper into his mind. Something that had been hiding in his heart had been disturbed, something he had numbed with nicotine. It ached and ached, disabling him for a long while. We did not understand what was happening. Papa, the strong and charismatic man, was now crying like a little boy with an open wound. His pain came from beyond the agony of the flesh, it was rising up from within, from a realisation of the incomprehensible nature of life. It was the first time he had cried since his mother died. The older boys rubbed his back with tiger balm and lizard oil, and the younger ones smuggled cigarettes into his room when Mama was not looking.

It was a tough time we endured, a lot tougher than when Mama was sick, because she was used to enduring pain. Feeling confused, we filled Papa with strong analgesics to calm him. The result was that he became a bit of a zombie for a while. I wanted my dad to be strong and able to endure his pain, but he could not. Whenever we saw him in pain we would immediately hand him a painkiller.

As predicted by *La Hechicera*, Papa's sisters came to see us when they heard their brother was crying and moaning. Mama was polite, offering them a civilised smile that I knew came from the heart. She had forgiven them. It showed on her forehead, for her forgiveness had ironed out a few worry lines. At first, the aunts were rather reserved, and perhaps a touch uncomfortable with my mother's approachable disposition, for they had a different image of the Amazon woman with the jungle potions and mysteries. It had fallen upon me to mediate, to play the balancing role and wipe away all misunderstanding, and I was happy to do it. I offered them tea and cake, and did most of the talking. 'Your Mama sure knows how to make cake,' said one. They looked around in wonder, for they had never seen the inside of our house, the one room turned into four, with the parakeets, wall shrines and the brightly painted mezzanine floors and bunks.

They left in peace, shaking Mama's hand as they bid her goodbye.

'Perhaps you might like to come when we celebrate Alberto's recovery?' asked Mama. After fifteen years, the ice had been broken. I saw how Mama hugged the visitors with her heart, though in reality she simply stretched one hand out in accordance with protocol. The rift that had haunted us for years had finally been healed, and Papa was able to breathe more easily. After six months he finally recovered.

At the same time as Papa began to feel well again a letter arrived from Iquitos announcing that the stepmother would be coming to Lima to visit Techa. The visit gave Mama the opportunity to begin to dissolve some of the resentment she had stored up for years. However, I found it harder. Mama's stories about her life under the stepmother's control had filtered into every nook and cranny of my memory. She was persona non grata in my world. I would never call her *Abuela*, or Grandmother, that was for sure. But I would be polite.

She arrived from Iquitos by bus, as she was terrified of anything that made her lose touch with the ground. She was not aware, however, that her coach would take a highly dangerous route along a road that clings to the sharp edge of the mountains. One always prayed the driver was well-rested and sober. She survived the cliffhanger and told us of the beautiful Sleeping Beauty range in the Andes, where the mountains form the profile of a sleeping queen. Once again, we were exposed to the smell of wild fruit and smoked cod, which we ate fried, with chili salsa. There were few traces of the wicked stepmother of Mama's tales, but then a long time had passed. Her main concern was the happiness of her grandchildren, including me. I think Mama found some peace after her visit.

All the weeping had transformed my father into a softer man. It had refined his ability to approach life with temperance and justice, and had toned down his paternalistic ways. The other transformation was the end of his trucking business and of the era of fine biscuits and cornflakes. Mama stopped looking for a house. The deposit had shrunk considerably, and the main priority was to search for a new business for my father.

Loretta wrote, telling us she had found a shimmering white dove with a broken leg, which she was now nursing back to health. Aunt Renatta's catharsis had also begun. We never knew whether she forgave the wife and stopped vying for preferences over Uncle Arnaldo but Tato's suffering came to an end. His blistering sores erupted with a clear fluid, and soon he lost focus on the physical world. His spirit chose to let go, releasing his body from the pain of living. He died never having uttered a word of reproach or complaint.

I grieved inside more than I could ever express for I loved my cousin with a purity of affection that I never experienced towards any other member of my extended family. Perhaps because Tato never gave us the chance to see his dark side. Or perhaps because he was born without a dark side, thus making him vulnerable to the cruel virus. Maybe he knew his time here would only be of short duration, and his mission was to touch our family so we would all realise that angels did exist in the people we met. The last time I saw him, he was snuggled in a white coffin lined with pastel blue satin. He wore a serene expression, as if he were enjoying the journey back to the source. In the background, I heard the sound of mandolins and I perceived the Blue Cat by his side, escorting him in his final sleep.

A few days after Tato's death, the clouds amassed like never before. They were etched clearly against the sky, then they grew darker, more dense, more furious. The neighbours came out to watch them march across the firmament, defying all weather forecasts and rules of meteorology. Doña Panchita made the sign of the cross and muttered a prayer. Soon the thunder hit our ears. A storm was moving in over the mountains with unprecedented fury. Within a few minutes, the city was drenched – a new experience for the population, which had never seen rain like it. At first we all panicked, but soon realised that rain is a sign of fruitful times to come. The downpour washed away all memory of the pelican manure. The fish returned to the ocean, and flowers blossomed in the parks.

THE SOUNDS OF LIFE

'ARE YOU SURE this is the house you want?' I asked Mama as we stood in front of a yellow townhouse in the middle of a row of five.

'Yes, darling, I like it, don't you? Yellow is the colour of prosperity.'

After years of chronic fatigue, breathing difficulties and palpitations, Mama's cheeks had regained their rosy glow. Her health had returned following a second operation, which cleaned up what the first one had left inside.

'Yellow is the colour of jealousy too,' I replied, remembering Mama's teachings about the dark side of colours. I felt a strange apprehension. There was an invisible weight hanging over the house, waiting for the right time to drop and shatter our exhilaration. Despite the scent of fresh timber, which swept my imagination to the enchanted forest, the aura of the new house did not fill my heart with happiness. But how could I say that to Mama? It was the fruit of many sacrifices and years of saving. My premonition was fleeting and I let it pass, infected by Mama's overwhelming enthusiasm. The house really was nice, and we all grew to like it. It was three floors high and had many rooms.

Papa had taken a while to recover from his accident. To make matters worse, his brand new minibus, which he had bought to join a private transport business, had arrived from the factory with oodles of mechanical flaws, so it broke down more often than not. There were other problems with it too, like the radiator was out of balance, the new seats had to be screwed properly, and the roof was too low. Poor Papa, there was a lot that had to be repaired.

The house preparations brought Mama and me closer. She did not complain any more, and seemed to believe that the purchase was about to change our lives. We worked like bees, in unison. I helped her choose the new curtains, sofa covers and blinds. Gone were the giant pineapple and banana floral spreads, now we felt big and rich and important. We placed the blue sofa here and the new dining table and chairs there, and moved the glass cabinet around. It looked extremely neat. The lounge suite was covered in thick plastic so dust would never impregnate the fine fabric. It was all shining and divine. 'You will have to leave the jungle one day,' Papa had often teased. Now we had.

Together, we swept through most of the shops in the dusty streets behind the markets. Streets where women ran from lewd men, where fruit carts pushed past your legs, and stray dogs picked up the scraps from the muddy ground. 'Let me be your son-in-law,' men would call out and Mama's lips would pout in disapproval. It was exciting to be noticed, to be admired as special. The streets had acquired a new scent for me, a smell that went beyond toasted poppy seeds and cinnamon. It was the smell of masculine sweat and musky aftershave. But my mother would not hear of that. At thirteen, I was still a child to her. We chased bargains: lace and cotton fabrics, Murano vases and Italian trinkets. We bought ornaments, china dolls, landscape pictures and new frames for the family photographs. We also ended up with a new tea set, a coffee jug for Papa, salad servers and plastic flowers that would last forever. 'These flowers are far more cost effective, darling,' said Mama. The afternoons of romantic tales over coffee and cake returned, as we huddled under striped café umbrellas in the scorching heat of an invisible sun.

According to Mama, everything would be better now that we were in the garden suburb. Far away from bad people, some of whom even molested their daughters and cheated on their partners. I felt I was the most privileged daughter in the whole world. I no longer thought of the beatings and the slaps I received whenever my ways challenged hers. There in the new house it was all forgotten, for a while.

One day, a portrait painter knocked on the door offering his skills to Mama. He showed her portraits he had done based on photos of Hollywood stars. Mama was very keen, and gave the artist photographs of my father and herself in their prime years. The artist smoked a few cigarettes with Papa and had tea with Mama. Several days went by and he returned with the finished portraits. Papa's image was irrefutably handsome, but Mama's face appeared more matronly than she cared to imagine. 'This is definitely not me,' she said. It took us a while to convince her that it was her face, with the soft dimples on her cheeks, the gold chain and Virgin Mary medallion on her chest, and the curls on her forehead. It was her soul he had painted, the strength of her character. Grudgingly, she agreed to pay the artist. Never mind strength of character, she would have preferred to be immortalised looking a bit more like Rita Hayworth.

It was as if Mama wanted to relive her youth. Now that she had created a new world for herself, she wanted to be given another chance. Our new neighbourhood was much more elegant than the old bohemian block with its smells of fried sweet potatoes and early morning sex on the dressing gowns of the women who lined up outside the communal shower next door. In our new neighbourhood, all the houses had lavish bathrooms with bathtubs and lavatories. There was no need for our tin bath or plastic buckets. The new chalets, as they were called, had pretty porches, ornate windows and curved wrought-iron gates. Maids in starched white uniforms took small children to the school in the park and flirted with the gardener on their way back. Many families who lived around the park owned more than one car, which the men proudly polished on Saturday mornings dressed in floral shirts and sunglasses. Even the sky looked a deeper blue in the new suburb. I daydreamed all I wanted, staring at the sky through my bedroom window. In the clouds, I tried to decipher messages from nature, as Mama had done in the Amazon.

Deep inside, though, I missed the spiciness of the old block, the familiar grunts of Nono Alberto as he walked in every afternoon at four o'clock with hot rolls in hand, and a heart keen for affection. I missed Doña Panchita's visits to have her wrists rubbed with lizard oil, or to bring us duck and coriander and share her wisdom. She had been left behind in the old neighbourhood, washing and ironing and swapping domestic gossip with the rest of the neighbours, who would probably stay there forever.

But elegance had its price. It was hard work keeping the house free of dust, the wide windows clean and the laundry and patio tidy. The tiles in the kitchen had to be polished, as did Mama's new set of electrical appliances, for which she had saved throughout my childhood. We no longer needed to apply kerosene to the floor to kill the bugs, but red wax to make it shine.

My room had a view of a large vacant lot in which children played during the day and lovers kissed passionately at night, hugging and fondling each other in heated embraces, camouflaged by the shadows of a jacaranda tree. Sometimes a man came there on his own, a man with swarthy skin and strong hands. He appeared in the twilight and stood against a wall, placed his bag on the ground, and carefully inspected the landscape to make sure there was no one around. He would fiddle with his belt, looking up and around every so often. Then he would find what he wanted, enfold his big hand around that forbidden spot, and shake it. From behind the blinds, I watched the man, feeling his sin in my own body. As he frantically stroked his object of pride, I savoured newly discovered sensations. My heart throbbed, my legs shook and my soul hid in shame. I stood with my eyes fixed on the sight until he became inebriated in the fluids of his male fantasy. Then I shut the blinds tight, made the sign of the cross to erase the vision from my mind, and ran downstairs to dust the house. I suspected that whatever he was doing with himself was not good, so I never revealed the secret to anyone.

Our new local church was a modernist monument that had been built in a bid to halt the flight of those who were becoming devotees of the psychedelic era. The house of God, which was in the park, was a smooth triangle with a myriad of miniature mosaic tiles covering the roof. Out the front was a steel sculpture of Madonna that I did not like at all, for it gave her an extremely frosty look. All ceremonies were now conducted in Spanish, which we did not mind, but did not enjoy that much either, for it was nice to hear the voice from beyond speak in Latin. It was indeed a great departure from the grand three-priest ceremonies, Gregorian chanting and children's choirs we were used to, and which we sometimes likened to a grand musical in Latin. Papa was sure that no matter how much cosmetic surgery the church did to itself, it would never attract more people unless it cleared its heart. With the informality of the rituals, and the relaxed approach of the priests with their songs and guitars, this new temple was not the place in which I could speak to the Virgin and the saints. The church in our old neighbourhood had its own ghosts and wandering spirits hidden in the cracks in the walls and, in the past they had revealed secrets to me. In the old church, I had received messages from the Holy Mother, which I often wrote down on holy cards and would sell for a few coins the day before exams. One afternoon while I was praying, a little voice in my head told me what sections to study for an exam. The voice proved to be right. I chose to believe that the message had been relayed from a cosmic source, so from then on I often went into extended silent prayers before testing time. The idea to trade such sacred information came to me when a friend asked me to pray for her and ask the Virgin for advice. It was no different from what the priests did during Mass, I thought. So I went for it and found advice for my friend after kneeling and saying a few Hail Marys. I did this for other students after that, but kept it secret because I knew it would get me into trouble should the teacher ever hear about it.

This worked for a few seasons, until the priest found out. A girl from school anxiously asked me to find out whether her boyfriend would ever leave her. I knew that the boy was not good – and perhaps the Virgin knew it too – so after I prayed I replied: 'Yes he will leave.' Well, the sky fell on her. She took her complaint to the principal, accusing me of fraud because she was sure 'the Virgin would never say a thing like that'. How would I have known that my school mate – who was only fourteen – was pregnant? When the truth came out, she was expelled from school, and I was suspended for 'playing with fire'. When Mama found out, she was furious. 'Where do you get such grand fantasies?' she said after hitting me with the broom. I felt betrayed, for Mama had taught me that God spoke to us through prayer. She chased me with the broom up to my bedroom, stressing the fact that only 'special people or saints' could speak to God. I was not special, let alone a saint. After that episode, we began to drift apart. I would spend hours on my own, knitting the strands of my fantasies, perhaps hoping for the romance of Sarinha and the feather prince to once again crystallise. I would gaze at the horizon, searching for the canvas on which to draw my own perfect world. I even had an imaginary friend, Walter, who had lived in the backdrop of my mind ever since after Abuelo Desiderio died. I hid my melancholy, trying hard to disguise it with iridescent eye shadow.

Loretta's fate had changed since she followed *La Hechicera's* advice to return to her home town, where she had nursed an injured dove back to health. Meanwhile, in Lima, the fake alchemist had suffered a more sour destiny. After he had taken the jewels from Loretta, he fronted up to a police station to declare he had been mugged. The mugging, he claimed, occurred on the day he was taking a set of jewels from his girlfriend to be valued. The police did not know what to make of the story, as the guy looked a bit suspicious. They locked him up until they could find Loretta. But Loretta was in her village, burning aromatic herbs and dried petals, invoking prayers and calling on the spirits of her ancestors. She released the dove after tenderly dabbing holy water on the soft crown of its head. It flew happily over the sand dunes and Loretta experienced a sense of reconnection. She would now have to meet her father and release the curse, a task she did not look upon with exhilaration. Immersed in thoughts of her father, she crossed the sand dunes barefoot and headed back home. Her hair flowed in the wind, her soft cotton dress caressed her skin, which had been toasted by the northern sun. A man watched her from a distance. He was mesmerised by the apparition that smoothly floated along the sandy beach like the luminous maiden in a mythical tale. He pinched his arm to make sure he was not hallucinating, that the powder he had snorted the night before to keep him up all night was no longer affecting him. He was a constable from Lima bringing Loretta news about the alchemist and the jewels. A romance soon developed between Loretta and the young policeman. The jewels were never recovered, but a new light came into her life.

The last time I saw her, on my thirteenth birthday, she looked radiant. Perhaps the soul of the dove had flown into her heart, bringing serenity and equilibrium. She was going to have a baby, and she was leaving the old neighbourhood. I looked around her tiny house with melancholy as she peeled the cards and posters off the wall. I bid my farewells to these memories, silent witnesses to a special time in my life. The aura of Doña Santitos appeared suddenly and a sweet smell of rose and lavender pierced the air. We both smiled and silently made the sign of the cross. I snapped loose a gold charm from a bracelet Mama had given me, and handed it to her, 'This is for your new child.' Her bags were neatly packed by the side of the bed and all of her mystical trinkets were in a box for the Hermetic Society, which was one of her priorities.

I confessed to Loretta my anxieties about boys, my lack of

self-confidence, my love for the mysterious, and my concerns about Mama. In her opinion, Mama and I were part of the same tree. Whatever happened to us – either together or separately – had a meaning that would reveal my mission. One day I would learn to read those meanings. These words engraved themselves in my memory, never to be forgotten.

The garden suburb revealed its ugly side one terrible evening. Mama was returning home from one of her debt collection errands when a young bandit tried to mug her. Papa usually picked her up, or waited for her at the bus stop, but that night he had gone to a work meeting. There was no one to walk with her through the evening streets, made darker by the trees that dulled the light from the lampposts. She had a habit of walking fast, as Doña Santitos had recommended to avoid running into evil, yet on that night nothing would have been quick enough to deter the demon that possessed the mugger. Her attacker jumped out of the shadows and glared at her with the eyes of a starving wolf. It startled Mama to the core. Who would have thought, to be robbed in such a 'decent neighbourhood' just a few steps from her own house? The mugger demanded her bag, her rings and all her other valuables. 'I'll force you to undress if necessary,' he threatened. How dare he, thought Mama. She would never surrender the money, she had just collected to pay the mortgage. Never! She held her breath for a few seconds and gathered her thoughts, invoking all the gods and spirits to protect her. Inside her bra, against her left breast, she had hidden a roll of money.

'Listen, Mister, I have no money. If you take my bag all you'll get are my documents,' she argued but the mugger scowled angrily.

'C'mon lady, drop it.' He flashed a knife under her nose. His breath reeked of alcohol. Mama froze, numb. She would never let her wedding ring go. She would prefer to die if necessary. Suddenly a loud scream escaped her lips. The mugger grabbed her head, holding his knife to her cheek, threatening to cut her pretty face if she did not let go of her bag. He pushed her up against a wall, forcing his weight against her.

Well, somewhere in the In-between a spirit must have heard her pleas, for a child came out of a house and called out, 'A man is killing a woman out here!' Mama screamed even louder and kneed the robber where it really hurt. The man buckled over, then ran away, with the empty purse which he quickly pulled out of the bag, disappearing into the shadows. Mama collapsed on the ground. Fear had planted its ghastly seeds in her heart. By the time people came to her rescue she was in a state of deep shock. Several glasses of orange blossom water eventually calmed her down. We were proud of her courage, but from that moment on she did not see herself as invincible anymore, nor did she trust anyone.

Mama began to withdraw from us, giving herself even more severe financial deadlines. She felt that the quicker we paid off the house, the sooner all our problems would come to an end. There was no rush whatsoever, after all no one was going to take the house away. But she wanted to do it her way, demanding that my father bring home a set income from the minibus business. Their relationship began to deteriorate, although Papa did his best to keep the peace. All laughter ceased for months; even the parakeets hardly sang, intimidated by Mama's growls.

I spent more time at the park to keep my sanity, staring at the bark of the trees, hoping to extract revelations from nature. In front of a small mirror I often inspected the triangular mark on my chest, hoping it was a sign of something unimaginably wonderful still to happen in my life. I had become a true romantic, addicted to love ballads and boleros, movie dramas and romance novels. In real life, I was shy with boys, camouflaging my shyness under a veneer of aloofness, or that of the nonstop joker. I found it hard to connect the two worlds in which I lived. There was the one in my imagination where things worked perfectly well, where Mama was sweet, Papa was the breadwinner, and I was special. The other world was less perfect, where Mama whinged and Papa just put up with her. It was a world riddled with flaws, which I did not know how to repair. I suffered with chronic migraines and began to wear glasses for eye strain.

Time passed and the park lost its iridescence, the grass had turned yellow and dried up. Mama became really sick and we feared that she would not last much longer. Her nerves were in a constant state of uneasiness and her outbursts became a menace to us. She tried hard to silence her pain with pills, and developed a total dependence on doctors and prescriptions. She could not hold a conversation without referring to a new little bug or bacteria that was annoying her, a sore spot here, an inflammation there, or a feeling of discomfort in her heart or liver. Papa sometimes joked that all her little gods were out of control. The doctors said she was having a breakdown.

'It's just that today I have some palpitations, probably brought on by the new pills for my liver,' she would sigh in resignation to her cousin Lisa.

'Pull yourself together, Rosa. And prepare yourself a good chicken soup,' Aunt Lisa would reply, watching Mama take all sorts of little pills – white, red and yellow, antibiotics and anti-inflammatories. Little pills that held the fabric of her daily life together.

I assured Mama that as soon as I finished school, I would get a job and help her pay off the house. She touched my cheek and gave me a hopeful look. 'Ah, my darling, I really wanted you to study overseas,' she said. A week later, I woke up to a new feeling in the house. Mama was cheerful, humming a lullaby and dusting the furniture. How strange, I thought. Mama had always stayed away from dust on the grounds that it could give her asthma, and none of us wanted that. Why was she so happy today? She put down the feather duster, patted my head and sat down next to me. She whispered to me that she had had an amazing dream. I ran to the shop in a celebratory mood, got a large packet of vanilla biscuits to feed her storytelling spirit, and sat by her side. It was Sunday morning and Papa was out fixing the car. I took out the best cups and saucers and pulled two chairs up to the laminex table so my Mama could tell her story in comfort. Her eyes shone, the scent of cinnamon tea brushed the air and her voice took me into the chamber of her dreams.

Before the break of dawn, in the gap between her dreams and reality, Mama saw herself chased by a roaring brigade of half-naked riders on dark horses. Behind them marched a battalion of women in red cloaks; each had curled around her neck a serpent with a flickering tongue and sparkling eyes. The women were followed by a band of feathered people, like tall birds with human heads. They carried a child's coffin. The sky was dark red with only one tiny star shining faintly. Filled with fear, Mama crawled inside a cave in the side of a hill, hoping these beings would never catch up with her. The group came to a halt near the cave and placed the coffin on a fire. The serpent women formed a ring around the fire, and the black riders circled them. A tall bird walked up to the fire and opened the coffin. It released a stench of putrefied, maggot-ridden flesh. Inside the cave, Mama closed her eyes and pinched her nose. One of the bird people scooped up some of the stinking pulp and headed into the cave. The presence of the stranger was very powerful, but not at all intimidating. She could not run away, so she was forced to look at the stinking pulp. As she walked closer to it, she experienced a familiar feeling. Pain. She was looking at her own wounds. Something burst inside her, causing a flood of tears. She cried and cried, and as her tears fell on the rotting pulp it changed into shiny little fragments, like gleaming rubies. The bird offered them to Mama, encouraging her to touch them, to pick up some of the newly transformed glittering seeds. Her fear had gone. The stench was transformed into a scent so sweet and inebriating that she put the crystals in her mouth and ate them. She awoke in a preciously happy mood.

'Mama, you ate the jewels!' I said, and she burst into a childish giggle.

'Yes, my darling, and I hope they won't upset my stomach.'

Three days later, my father was having coffee with another driver at the depot cafeteria. He was a new friend, a man who was popular because of his happy disposition and ability to remain calm in the face of adversity. His name was Antonio, and he had a reassuring word for anyone who was down in the dumps. Papa vented his frustration and confessed his worries about Mama's irritable moods, so Antonio asked whether Mama was sick. My father said her sickness came from her soul – or something else he did not understand very well – for the doctors said that her organs were fine.

'Who is to know, my friend?' sighed Papa. 'People who come from the Amazon are indeed a little bit weird.'

'Perhaps I can help,' said his mate, with the humble certainty of a man who has descended into the pit of his own darkness and has successfully crawled his way out to recover.

'How can you? You aren't a doctor, are you?' asked Papa, ready to refuse any folk cures or suggestions to visit yet another specialist.

'Well, no, I am not a doctor, but I have a prescription,' said Antonio.

'Then let me have it, and please don't feel offended if I laugh,' said Papa lighting a cigarette.

'I have joined a group where I am taught how to change my destiny,' he replied.

At dinner that night, when Mama asked for her red pills, Papa said, 'Do you remember my friend Antonio, dear?'

'Antonio, the black man with the gracious manners?' asked Mama.

'Yes, the same. He has told me an amazing story.'

'Oh yes?' Mama's eyes sparkled.

Papa listed Antonio's good qualities – how kind and generous he was, what a good worker he was. Mama's frown deepened and she got fidgety as Papa went on and on with the embroidered details of his friends' valiant deeds.

'So what happened to Antonio?' Mama lost her patience, stretching her hand out to take another pill. 'Is he dead?'

But before she could swallow her nerve relaxant capsule with lemonade, Papa replied, 'Oh no, Antonio is not dead. On the contrary, he has brought himself back from the dead.'

'Oh yes? How?' Mama challenged.

'He has been going to a place where they teach you to do just that,' said Papa.

'What are you trying to tell me?' Mama said, giving Papa a fierce look.

Papa put down his cup of coffee with a thump. He had said enough for one day. No longer was he the growling bear we were used to, and somehow I missed that in him. All the crying and suffering during his accident had turned him into a softer man. We were grateful for that, because Mama's constant outbursts were enough to keep us on edge, but at the time I would have preferred him not to be so accommodating. In Mama's view we had become her persecutors, the seeds of her unhappiness. In fact, she had accused my father of being one of the riders of the dark horses in her dreams. Papa had not liked the comparison one bit.

'It's not me you are seeing in your dreams but the labyrinth of your own nerves,' he yelled, and he recommended that she check out Antonio's group before she ended up in some very ugly clinic. Mama burst into tears, which immediately made Papa change his tune. Soft again he suggested that as Mama was partial to ceremonies and magic rituals, perhaps she might find the group interesting.

'They are nice people,' he said. 'Antonio tells me he is a Buddhist, and they ring bells and burn incense,' Papa explained. 'You might just like that.'

'Buddhists? What are Buddhists?' demanded Mama, staring right between Papa's eyes.

Papa searched for an explanation, but could not find one. In his eagerness, he had not asked Antonio this most important question.

'All I know is that you chant a mantra or something and then you feel happy.'

'Happy, just like that? Like a drug, happy?'

'No, my dear. Happy like in paradise.' Papa's eyes pleaded. 'Antonio looks like a good man to me.' He pushed his chair away from the table and headed towards the door.

'Buddhists, huh? That's all I need. Do you expect me to cross my legs grow a belly and rest on my laurels?' Mama demanded.

Smiling, Papa said, 'You know what's good for you, dear. It's only a suggestion.' And then he left.

The seed had been planted, and my mother spent the next few days in a thoughtful mood. Aunt Lisa came and brought her a bright little parakeet to replace the old one, which had died of melancholy. Perhaps the new parrot was a good omen, she thought. She remembered Doña Santitos' words; there is one God with many faces. Why not check out the Buddhists? She had nothing to lose. Probably nudged by her friend Bufeo Colorado, she agreed. 'Okay, I'll go. I'll try anything that promises to make me feel better.'

The special evening came and Mama made sure we were all well fed, the parakeets put to sleep for the night, and the doors locked. Papa fetched a taxi to take them to the place, a shantytown on the outskirts of the city. The driver insisted he would have to charge extra for reasons of personal safety. Papa argued but eventually the men agreed to a suitable sum, which made no man richer or poorer, and Mama got in. The weathered taxi burped and rattled as it went along the dusty streets, limping over potholes and leaving a veil of smoke and fumes in its wake. They headed towards a silent mountain shrouded in hazy clouds, but as the car approached its destination, the foot of the slope became clearer. It was dotted with makeshift housing, lights flickering through tiny windows. The car slowed down, coughing, and painting the air black before coming to its final stop by the side of a gloomy street. Mama glanced ahead. She tensed as she noticed the maze of alleyways that seemed to lead to the end of the world. Nothing bad would happen, she told herself, but she clutched her purse just in case and said a prayer under her breath. Papa paid the driver and led the way through the shacks perched haphazardly on the side of the hill, guarded by a few underfed dogs that barked at every pedestrian, out of starvation more than vigilance. Papa held Mama close, placing his arm around her shoulders, shielding her against any possible attack, praying it would not happen.

Only a few years earlier, the hill had been uninhabited, with development applications for modern and profitable projects under consideration. But a troop of indigenous highlanders eager to find jobs in the city had invaded the site. Invasion of vacant lands was the done thing amongst highlanders, who marched down en masse, charged with determination and sacks of potatoes, keen to reclaim their rights. Once the correct spot was found, and in the tradition of the first Inca, Manco Capac, who had founded the empire in Cusco by sinking his golden staff into the ground, the leader of the invading brigade would sink his wooden staff to claim the new settlement. In a few hours, used boards were turned into house walls, damp earth into hardened floors and planks into furniture. A council would be democratically elected, a source of water would be found, and the new inhabitants would use their creativity to pull electricity from the main power grid. In a blink, before the central government had heard about it, or had time to ask them to fill in a myriad of forms requesting permission, a new suburb had burgeoned. It was a regular phenomenon on the outskirts of the capital. According to local rumours, the invasions were the result of the Curse of Atahualpa's prophecy coming to pass; descendants of the ancient Peruvians would gradually take over the city. The same curse had sent the earthquakes, the maniac killers, the rats and the pelicans.

Now, the hill was the site for another type of revolution, one of the spiritual kind. Mama and Papa walked down a dark, winding lane that

led them into an even darker alley. The darker it got, the more determined Mama became not to let her fear take over. Finally, they
reached an entrance to a patio, above which hung an old kerosene
lamp. A few metres ahead was a blue door bearing the number nine.
They hurried towards it. A strange humming noise spilled through
the crack under the door.

'Are you sure you're fine with this?' asked my father, sniffing the
aroma of incense. A different kind of incense, not like the one he
knew from the procession of the Purple Christ. This was another
world.

'I am fine,' Mama said. 'As we have come all this way, we might as
well go in.' She knocked on the door with her right hand, for Doña
Panchita had recommended that all forward movements be started
with a right limb. A short woman with swarthy skin opened it, and
wearing a humble smile, she ushered them inside. She pulled out two
stools and my parents moved them to a corner and sat quietly. The
woman went back to her spot on the floor and rejoined the chanting.
Mama and Papa looked around with subdued curiosity. Antonio was
not there. The people sitting on the floor looked poor on the outside
but displayed a sense of inner dignity that Papa had not observed
before. It was as if they had stopped searching for an avenging hero, as
if they had already found one under the surface of their own skin.

They kneeled before a small shrine containing a scroll bearing an
ancient scripture. A small bowl of water, a plate with a piece of fruit,
incense and two candlesticks engraved with the image of a bird stood
at the foot of the shrine, signalling the balance of the elements. The
scroll was a copy of one that had been inscribed by a Japanese priest
called Nichiren, who, in the fourteenth century, had rebelled against
the religion of the day, claiming that ordinary people could find the
way to enlightenment in this life. His rebellion led to his persecution
and exile. However, his compassionate deed conceded him enlightenment. The scroll had a simple message: no matter how low or desperate
any individual gets, there is always a way out. The mantra they chanted
was *Nam Miojo Renge Kio*: 'I am at one with the universe.'

After the ceremony, the group introduced themselves to Mama and Papa. They were mainly locals, children of the ancient Incas who felt that their protector gods had led them to this new practice called the Buddhism of the Sun. They were not praying to any gods, but were training themselves to live in a state of equilibrium, in line with the Universal Law. They believed that their practice would revive their spirit and return the true life force to every cell.

Mama had been to a great many religious meetings, but something snapped in her heart after this particular one. She went home that evening with her head full of thoughts about the power of prayer and meditation, the causes of her predicament, and these very strange Buddhist teachings. What she found most fascinating about the new practice was that it involved connecting with her 'Buddha self'. Mama liked this, as the meeting with her soul had been long overdue. Despite the difference in prayers, and the new terminology, she recognised that it had much in common with the practice of kneeling in front of her shrine to the Virgin Mary, accessing a divine aspect of herself. Deep inside, she had never forgotten the enchanted island, the maiden of her legend, and her hope that one day the lost girl who had swallowed far more vanilla syrup than was recommended would eventually find the boy with the feathers, her guiding spirit who would teach her how to live life in the right measure. Her spirit had already come to see her in the dreams, had given her a taste of the sweetness beneath the stench. All she had to do now was respect the order of things, and honour all aspects of life.

Like a newly ordained nun, Mama got up even earlier and chanted in the morning, then chanted with the other Buddhists in the afternoon, and with Papa before dinner. She was convinced that she could change her destiny, and was determined to do it. Gradually, the invisible rope that had been strangling Mama's serenity dissolved. We were all happy that she was on her way to recovery, no matter in what language she prayed and how much incense she burnt at home.

However, her new faith removed her from us. She had no time to spend with the family in the evenings, as she was always on her way to a meeting or to the home of somebody who needed assistance. For a while I was jealous, then I got angry, but nothing would stop her. In the end I could only admire her total surrender to the process of change. But when my friends came to visit I had to swallow my embarrassment when they asked what on earth was happening at home. I told them that Mama had become a messenger of a new faith that turned people into Buddhas. 'Oh sure,' one of them replied, 'I suppose you'll be selling the new messages at school next.'

The big, heavy weight that I had sensed invisibly hanging above our house when we first moved in finally dropped, and nearly crushed my parents' hopes. The builder from whom we had bought the house was jailed for fraud because while he had sold the house to us, he had also used it as collateral for a loan. This meant that once my parents had paid off their own mortgage, they would then have to settle the builder's debt. The house turned into a cage, a prison from which my parents would never be released. Fortunately, Mama's nerves had been a lot calmer since she'd been meditating, so she was able to wear the news with resignation.

Mama had converted most of her family and friends to her new faith. The first one to follow her example was Aunt Techa, who had already had a few children and was barely making ends meet. Her husband, who had been out of work for a long time, was also persuaded to change his karma, although I do not remember for how long. Soon the house was filled with the chants of Mama's new disciples, including my nasty uncle and Mama's cousins, nephews and the friends of her friends.

With Papa by her side, Mama became a spiritual worker. She talked about the awakening of the spirit with market sellers, truck drivers, distant friends, and even those who owed her money, as she believed that fortune came from seizing the 'gem within'. She spoke about our internal power and the ability to make all efforts produce something of value. There was much more to her faith than the act of praying – there was decent behaviour, a sense of appreciation, courage to act despite fear and inertia, and strength in times of despair. Gone were the tales of the Pink Dolphin, and in their place came a Buddhist image of all humanity sitting on a special cloud at the beginning of time, listening to the words of wisdom that permeate our universe. She never imposed her faith on us but I listened to her, learning that karma is not fate but action, and can be changed. 'We are the only ones responsible for what happens to us,' she would say, 'Nobody is to be blamed.' I liked this aspect of the teachings, because it stopped her blaming us for her own misfortunes. Her most famous act of attrition was her confession to me that in her 'former dark period, whilst ignoring her Buddha self' she had often made her family unhappy.

As we watched her tears flow and her new strength develop, we wondered what life had in store for us as we commenced our own rites of passage.

THE DRIVER'S DAUGHTER

WITHIN FIVE YEARS, my family's financial obligations towards the house had grown to massive proportions. My parents regularly visited our solicitor, but his only advice was to finish paying the mortgage, and wait. If we were lucky, the titles to the house would be handed to us. If not, we would have to fight for them in court – or pay all the builder's debts. Mama felt it was all her fault for having been in such a hurry to buy, for not having checked the legal documents properly, for missing the fine print. No matter how much I tried to console her, she still felt responsible. Papa felt that he too was to blame. He believed he could have prevented this drama by going with Mama to all the meetings with the builder during the purchase of the house. But his car kept breaking down. I know now that it could never have been prevented. The system in which we lived allowed for such scams to occur against the uninformed. All my parents were told was to sign here and there, pay this duty and that fee. It was all going to be fine, the builder had said. I began to have dreams that a sandstorm was suffocating me.

My parents would never be able to pay back the loan within the time they had planned, let alone help me pay for a trip overseas, or full-time studies at university. I did not have to look up at the overcast

Lima sky any more to feel that a shroud of grey misery had enfolded my life. No matter how bright and psychedelic my clothes were, my heart felt wrung out. I had been numbed by my family's legal dilemma. No one cared any more. There were enough problems on the streets – unemployment, riots and rebellions. The city's population was about to explode as people moved in from the country, and there were people starving, homeless, begging and dying around me. 'Why did I think I was so important?' I heard a voice say from within me.

The prevailing mood was very anti-American. The nationalist government, led by an Indian General, hated the gringos from the north and blamed white people for sucking our natural resources dry, exploiting our workers, and hunting our rare animals. Never mind the greed of the local authorities who had let them in. Planning to study overseas would have been seen as an act of treason by the community. My brother Leo had managed to go to New York to work, but had to return home sooner than he had expected. 'They work you like a slave, sister,' he complained after having washed a million dishes and inhaled fumes from gallons of industrial cleaning fluids. Leo had described in detail the shadowy side of the North American life we watched on television. He had seen the resentment of the less privileged and the callousness of the ones on top. 'The streets are filthy and the air stinks,' he scorned, pulling a face. Although he had hated living there he was hurt for having been asked to leave by the US immigration officers. Leo had also told us about the girls who sold their souls, and everything else, to buy a visa, a husband, or both. 'If you go,' he said to me, 'you'll probably marry a blue-eyed devil who will clip your wings.' He warned me that gringos made their women lick the floor for the right to live in their country. 'If they do not do it, the gringos lash them with specially made whips.'

In my dreams I saw these girls wearing dog collars and walking on all fours. I woke up bathed in sweat. I would never go to the north as an illegal. I would never submit to such contempt, if I could help it. Papa would not hear of it either. If I was to go overseas, it would have to be with a legal visa. Ironically, given his political views, Papa supported the General's claim that the US had always seen the southern continent as 'the backyard on which to feed its dogs'.

'I wish the English and not the Spanish had come to colonise these lands,' Papa grunted, 'then we would not be a country of lazy bums.' But Mama quickly pointed out that he probably wouldn't be here had the English been the colonisers.

'They are not into mixing blood,' she said.

Marrying for a visa had never been in my plans. In my book, one married for love and for love alone. 'Where would we be without romance?' I asked in my first speech in English. 'Nowhere,' was the answer from my school audience. We wanted to feel we had been the product of love. Papa mocked our romantic illusions and said it had made our society the way it was: dependent and poor. Nevertheless, I daydreamed incessantly, floating each afternoon in the company of my transparent soul mate, Walter. I had chosen this companion because he was ethereal, and hence he was no danger to me. Walter appeared from my own In-between whenever I called him. He was my secret.

Mama said that 'the best asset a woman has is her innocence'. She was referring to the thin membrane that lived a guarded existence somewhere between my legs. I would not even have known how to find it, as I had hardly ever touched myself, except to wash and dry. I was not the sort of person who explored her body. Real adventure for me lived in the depths of my imagination. Feeling one's own private zones simply did not exist in my world, and I'd never spoken about it with anyone, not even with Loretta. She was the one who taught me about sensuality, and the one I went to after seeing erotic pictures for the first time, at the age of twelve.

I had been sneakily looking in the suitcase of one of Mama's relatives who was visiting. The visitor had caught me, but instead of being angry, he offered to elucidate the meaning of such strange displays. He had emphasised that the tuition had to be a secret. I nodded. After a few such sessions, he disappeared from the house and we never saw him again. From then on I knew that men could do anything they wanted with themselves, and did. But not women. Oh no! It was not the thing for us to do. Mama taught me a very important skill. How to defend myself against the cavalcade of sexual advances from men, particularly older men. I was to fight the overt advances. The subtle ones I was to ignore, disintegrate with my indifference. She told me to use my knee or my foot at the first sign that a man was getting too close. In Peru, this was difficult, private space might as well be inside your own skin. Men always imposed a tight physical proximity upon women, particularly on public transport. The buses were swollen with people. Mama was adamant: 'The instant you feel something hard against you, kick, and aim right at the shin. That will keep them quiet for a while.'

What Mama did not know was that I had already let a man get too close, during my last year at high school. And of all people, he was a European priest who had been posted to our school. I was smitten by Father Raymundo's air of sacred innocence, but I was also magnetised by the little devil I sensed lurking over his shoulder. One side of me wanted to believe he was a messenger from the heavens, the other side knew he was a man with earthly weaknesses. I had never studied religion as rigorously as I did then, forever competing for his attentions with the rest of the girls. He was like a celestial pop star to us, for he liked to sing and play praises to God on his guitar. We discovered that he was a man of secular desire when we saw his voracious appetite for the cakes and chocolates we brought him, which had not spoken too highly of the Christian virtue of Temperance. He must have been aware that we thought of him day and night, as he was the only male teacher at the school. He never missed an opportunity to place his arm around our shoulders, squeeze our bodies against his chest, or hug us with 'divine love'. He was a priest and he was a man, and I guess we liked him because of that.

As he was to stay with us only for a brief period we took him every-where we could. We invited him to picnics, the circus, and parades.

One afternoon I requested a private audience with him and he suggested I come to see him the following Sunday afternoon. I put on a miniskirt, polka-dot stockings and long boots, and decided to let my hair hang loose, bouncing like in the ads Mama and I saw on tel-evision. I left home without telling Mama where I was going. Since becoming a Buddhist she, like Papa, had become suspicious of priests. 'Watch that priest, for he seems like an octopus in a robe,' she had warned.

He greeted me with the same affection he showed all the girls, though in my naivety, I wanted to believe I was his favourite. We strolled around under the arches of the silent convent, the buzz of the city far in the distance. We sat on a lonely bench to discuss the work of God, under the branch of a jacaranda tree which gave the patio the appearance of a Renoir painting. My heart started pounding faster. In my anxiety, I tried to pull my skirt down. Realising my apprehension, Father Raymundo made a few jokes. Feigning self-assurance, I told him about Walter and about my wish to travel and follow the steps of Nono Alberto. I spoke of my thwarted wishes to be a dancer and a nun, and of my mother's amazing talents. Then he placed his hands on my knees, as he always did during open confession, only this time he gazed into my eyes flirtatiously. 'How can a gorgeous girl be so sad?' he said. I blushed with confusion. I knew he was crossing the boundary when his fingers began to slither slowly above my knee, towards the hem of my skirt. I did not care. His gesture made me feel special, as though I was cradled in the intimacy of pure love, right-fully selected by a representative of God. The blush on my cheeks fanned out over my whole body, like flames. I remained silent. He looked at me expectantly, as, after all, it was I who had requested this private audience. There was very little he did not already know about me, for I had confessed all of my petty wrongdoings. His gestures had given me the green light to confess something beyond the rules so I decided to tell him about the man in the vacant lot.

The opening words of my confession seemed to bewilder him, for he removed his hands from my thighs and his eyes opened wide. I spoke with all the confidence of a fifteen year old sure of the world around her. I told him that this man was doing things I knew were not right, and while I did not understand what he was doing, as I could not see very clearly from my window, I always searched for him. I explained that my body longed for the strange sensations it felt whenever I saw this wicked man on the vacant lot. Father Raymundo's gaze did not stray from my lips. He looked puzzled. I, on the other hand was experiencing a feeling of redemption. A bell rang and he got up. He suddenly appeared much bigger, and a lot more powerful. Gently, he took me by the hands and helped me rise to my feet. We took a few steps and stood under the jacaranda tree in the shadows of an early evening. He wrapped his arms around me in a friendly hug. A godly hug, I thought.

'How are you feeling now?' he said.

'Much better,' I whispered against his chest. His hand glided along my shoulders, caressing my hair. His gaze, moistened by intrigue, penetrated my soul provoking a turbulence in my senses. He pulled me closer and his lips touched my forehead. I stood motionless, my heart beating faster and faster. Then he kissed my temples and the space between my eyes. I felt a tingling on the tip of my nose as he blew his warm breath across my face; it felt like petals falling from the sky. He said that God loved me. His body pressed against mine a bit harder, and I dissolved, ashamed and deliriously receptive.

'How do you feel?' he asked again.

'I don't know. Is this good?' I asked hesitantly.

'It's innocent,' he replied. And I chose to believe it was. Then innocence gave way to passion as he held me even tighter, his lips brushing against my ears exhaling incomparable affections, romantically fertilising the woman in bloom that lived under the surface of my skin. Silence embraced us for a moment and our eyes met again. He clasped my face in his hands and riveted his eyes on my trembling lips before pulling me to him. His lips touched mine; he moistened them with the tip of his blissful tongue, the same he used so skilfully to preach the word of God. My senses were like a raft on stormy waters. As my lips fused with his, melting in confused passion, I felt that this was a sacred moment, and that I had entered the chambers of the forbidden and the occult. I thought that this was divine love. But then I did not know any better. To him, it was probably just a release of his erotic passion, stimulated by his contact with my teenage anxieties. To me, it was a celestial visitation that made my heart pound faster for the love of God, who, I felt, lived in the image of Father Raymundo.

Now, as I re-examine this episode, I cringe with embarrassment. In my early days as a journalist I judged and condemned those who abused their power over the weak, but I had chosen to wrap this episode in the silkiness of pure love. Father Raymundo had taken advantage of his power over me, and indeed crossed the line. But I was young and dizzy with the power of flirtation. His vows and responsibility could have persuaded him to control himself, as men in his position should in the full understanding of the natural exuberance of youth. But I must admit I had innocently seduced him, like a young temptress, certain of the power of my adolescence. In confessing to Father Raymundo the story of the man outside my window I knew I was exciting him. And it was wickedly nice to enjoy my budding power of seduction over a man in robes. Perhaps a side of me needed to prove that we could all be prey of our own foibles, that we could all be tempted. And how boring would life be without temptation? How could we measure our strength if we had no failings?

But since then, I spent many afternoons kicking guys on the bus on my way to university where I was studying accountancy. I had never enjoyed the art of counting other people's money. In my teens, it was far more important to me to explore the ghosts and demons that inhabited people's minds. I wanted to discover the source of the voices that some people heard in their despair. What I really wanted to study was psychology, because I felt there was a link between madness and spirituality gone wrong, and because I wanted to explore my own psyche. I had devoted many weekends to visiting our local asylum, where a friend's father was a psychiatrist. I would buy a few apples and oranges and head to the asylum on a Sunday afternoon. I leaned up against a big fig tree in the grounds of the hospital and read. I would nibble my fruit quietly, waiting for a resident to sit by my side and talk to me. It was usually patients whose relatives had forgotten them, or vanished from their lives, who would approach my spot. Sometimes, they would just stare or mock me, but sometimes they would tell me about their lives. The women often saw themselves as Cleopatra, the men as Napoleon. The more often I visited, the more my interest grew in the grey areas of human existence, and my heart filled with compassion for those lonely souls. Something inside me had always longed to discover where in the mind the In-between was located. It had to exist somewhere, for Mama could not have plucked all of her stories out of nowhere. I came to the conclusion that the imagination was a different form of reality, one that we chose to penetrate at will. Perhaps some people's souls got caught halfway on their journey and they never returned.

Unfortunately, studying psychology was out of my boundaries, because the course had to be taken full-time during the day, and my family could not afford that. Instead, I studied accountancy and got a job as a clerk in a tailor's shop on the outskirts of town. I shuffled receipts and invoices, and dusted old pages before I carefully did the accounts. My desk was an old table, which at night served as a cutting board, dining table and perhaps even a bed when the boss stayed overnight. Inside a tiny alcove lit by a squalid light, I spent eight hours a day sitting on a wooden box with a plank for back support. I had been recommended for the job by a friend of my mother so I felt I could not complain, despite the creepy crawlies that scuttled past my feet as I laboured with the handle of the antique adding machine.

'It belonged to my father,' the old man said, gazing at the top button of my blouse, straightening the little round glasses on the tip of his nose.

'Perhaps it should be in a museum, sir,' I suggested, getting up and 'accidentally' knocking his glasses off with my shoulder.

The old fox never missed a chance to boast about his appeal with the female sex and of his well-maintained constitution. One day, when he came a bit too close for comfort, I told him I had something to confide in him, something I had never said to anyone. His eyes moistened in anticipation and he rubbed his sweaty hands with glee. He sat down next to me, eager to listen. I whispered to him very softly that a ghastly Amazon shaman had cursed my Mama many years ago because she had left to come to the city, though he was in love with her. The curse, I told him, was designed to fall on her first daughter. The terrible malediction had traversed the Andes on the wings of a bat that had landed above my roof on the day of my birth, resulting in a chronic and, probably, very contagious skin condition. A rash, I insisted, appeared every time people came too close. 'In elderly gentlemen,' I warned, 'the condition could affect very "sensitive" areas of the body.' The old man immediately understood the message. The bit about the rash was true, although I didn't know whether it came from a shaman or was just hormonal. All I knew was that when somebody I didn't know too well gave me a kiss, I broke out in a rash. I did not care whether the old man thought I had the plague, as long as I didn't have to breathe his rancid perspiration every afternoon before banking time.

A week later, I overheard him telling a customer that his assistant had a great ability to put men off with incredibly horrid stories. From then on he did not bother me at all and, instead, he brought me *empanadas* for my lunch to avoid 'my parading on the streets in such suggestive miniskirts'. I left the tailor when I was able to obtain a good reference.

My next jobs were not much better in the groping sense, but in time I learned a different art of defence and dissuasiveness: extreme indifference. I called on the power of aloofness, which sometimes bordered on scorn. In Peru, there was almost a rule: if a woman walked past a man, the man had to react. A whistle, or words of flattery were fine; I could handle that. Unfortunately, this tradition sometimes turned into the most gross of verbal affronts, aptly described as verbal rape. Sad to say, in the seventies when many women were burning their underwear in the north, in the south, our men's improper ways were often seen as cavaliers' graces. When I complained, I was accused of being too much of a utopian. 'You think you come from planet Crystal,' one of my male friends said. 'A pinch on the bottom makes you feel alive,' an uncle joked. I accepted that we were humans with flaws and faults, some with massive earthly urges. But there were limits. I much preferred a single flower than a line from some moron on the street about his need to lick me you know where.

Time came for me to have my romantic idealism shattered. The first boy for whom my heart throbbed swapped me for my best friend Linda, who was a lot more meaty around the bones, and had a more flexible attitude and a glittering smile. I was numbed when I saw them arm-in-arm from a window in my house. My feelings were trampled. And I did the same with the flowers he had sent me on an earlier date. One side of me did not want to believe it was true. His hugs and kisses had been real – a huge departure from the imaginary interludes I used to have with my soul pal, Walter. This real boy, Alberto, was an elegant lad from a well-to-do family, and he and I had long and complicated raves on the meaning of life and the freedom of love. 'Feelings can act as a propeller for a more dynamic sex life,' I would argue, without having much of a clue about the practical side of the act. Alberto, on the other hand, would argue that feelings repressed men and stopped them from having a genuinely good time. 'Why do you think men do it with their maids?' he said.

I was meant to go with him to the circus, but he took Linda instead. I cried till I had no more tears. I refused to see Linda that night because I suspected she was carrying a lot of guilt. Her parents had sent her to an expensive school so she could meet the right people and marry well. My mother had never approved of our friendship because she did not trust Linda's sweet smile, which she labelled 'the grin of the alligator'. 'May the universe protect you from calm waters, for treacherous reptiles do not live in wild streams,' Mama said.

I swore I never would cry for a boy again. My innocence had been snapped in two. Life would never be the same again, I thought, feeling a whirlwind within my heart. Mama came into my room and found me in despair; she gently dried my tears with a lavender-scented handkerchief. 'The world will not end,' she said. When my puffy eyes were about to burst with tears again, she ran her fingers through my hair and patted my head tenderly. 'In the future, my dear,' she said, 'it will be much better if the boys are the ones who do the crying over you.' I pressed my cheek against her bosom to listen to the voice of her heart, and promised that I would follow her advice to the letter.

A few days later, Linda came to see me with a new set of smiles, a bunch of excuses, and a box of truffles. She said there had been a ghastly mix-up. 'You can't take life too seriously, sweetie,' she recommended, pouting her lips in response to my frozen gaze. I wanted to punch her face but I controlled myself, for I also wanted to hug her and forget. I wanted to convince myself that what I had seen was not true, that she was right, that it had all been a mix-up. I fought to hold back my tears when she hugged me. A very strange feeling seized my heart, a sense of understanding about the emotional space she was coming from. I did not know what drew me to this friendship. Perhaps it was because I had always longed for a sister.

Outside in our garden she lit a cigarette and offered me one. With an innocent expression on her face, she said in an almost conspiratorial tone, 'Listen, sweetie, all I wanted to do was help you.' She puffed on her cigarette and cleared her throat: 'You must understand that Alberto's parents would never allow their eldest son to be serious about a driver's daughter.' Her words pierced the night and cut through me like a burning dagger. My fingers let the cigarette drop, and my foot felt too heavy to put it out. The cigarette burnt slowly on a newly planted patch of turf. It burnt into the grass in the same way her words burnt into my feelings. But my pride won over my anger, and I took the blow without flinching. I stared at her with ice in my eyes, and my tears dried instantly.

Her words echoed in my mind, for years gnawing at my self-confidence, driving me towards achievement, and urging me to seek people's approval. That night, after her visit, as I tossed in my bed, a little voice inside me said that no revenge would be sweeter than to climb to the top of a mountain. With my blood still boiling, I swore to the universe that no matter how long it took, I would manage to reach the top. I would show Linda, and everyone else, what the driver's daughter could do.

And that's how I began to travel. I decided to see the mountains of my own land, and set out on a train journey along the Cordillera de los Andes, a long range that traverses Peru all the way from Chile in the south to the northern tip, at the border with Ecuador and Colombia. I was mesmerised by the colours of the highlands, the ragged cliffs and the plush foothills. I was so proud of my territory, which spread out before my eyes like a picture book of endearing valleys and sparkling cascades. It was easy to take my mind back five hundred years, when a great empire had flourished here. There had been no unemployment or homelessness. A parcel of land was allotted to every person, which they could work, and revere, for the land was very much a symbol of worship. They called it *La Pacha Mama*, the 'Big Mother'. She was the goddess who gave birth to food after being impregnated by Father Inti, the Sun. I imagined the bountiful terraces stepped into the mountains, bearing every variety of crop. In my days, there was no land for the Indians. There was little food for them, and hardly any respect for the earth, let alone reverence. They lived on memories alone.

The train journey gave me a taste for travel, and I began going on hitchhiking adventures during the holidays, and whenever I was between jobs. Armed with a penknife to peel my fruit, a rope, a blanket, and an evening dress and a bright lipstick in case I ran into Prince Charming, I hit the road. It was undoubtedly a huge risk, but I did not have any trouble. I grew accustomed to getting on the back of trucks, squeezing into a corner in a fruit van, or climbing on top of a four-wheel drive. It nurtured my blossoming spirit, and was a genuine way to discover my country and the soul of its people. I was enchanted by the tenderness of the highland women with their multicoloured weaving and chants to the river, and I learned the local way to strengthen the spirit – with highly alcoholic *pisco*.

I travelled with friends from university, and on occasions with Linda. We went to country towns, mainly during festivals when the locals spread their wares on the streets, danced all day and night, and put on pageants, parties and processions. We had a bet as to who could travel on the smallest budget. We would sleep in the open air, behind a church, or in a no-star hostel with a bedpan for a toilet. If we wanted a proper shower, we went to a posh hotel after befriending a tourist to whom we would tell stories of extraordinary fantasy or healing wisdom. Sometimes I would put on an accent and convince them that we too were foreigners. We met hippies, Mormons, monks, hawkers, preachers and Bible-bashers, but our preferred companions were travelling salesmen. They had expense accounts and would often buy us a meal for the price of a spooky story or a dance in a local nightclub. If we really liked them, we'd let them kiss us, but that was an individual choice. Apart from blisters on our feet or bruises here and there we never faced real danger.

My main expense was buying presents to take home: trinkets for the glass cabinet and delicacies to eat. My parents had never known the meaning of a holiday. 'Here is a piece of cheese, Papa, so your tongue can taste the northern grass and read the soul of the contented cow that chewed it,' I would say. He loved getting coffee from the 'jungle eyebrows' – the place where the jungle meets the mountains – a region that produced the best quality beans. Like my father, I loved the ritual of a coffee, a cigarette and a heart-to-heart chat. I convinced Mama to ask the Pink Dolphin 'why the aromatic brew makes people so intimate.' Making me promise never to tell her Buddhist congregation, she returned to the magic space where her river friend lived, and asked the question. In response, Bufeo Colorado told her the story of a prince named Caffiro, who had fallen in love with a beautiful girl. But to the maiden's misfortune, a demon that lived under the treacherous rapids of the river was also entranced by her beauty. Unable to cool his lust, this demon snatched the maiden and swallowed her mid-river. Caffiro threatened to end his life, but out of compassion the wise soul of the jungle turned the prince into a highly attractive bean which could melt the feelings of his beloved. He would come to life when mixed with a cup of water from the river, once this was purified by sacred fire. The memory of this romance is said to live in every bean, so when people take a sip, their hearts are moved by the love of Caffiro.

My eighteenth birthday found me on top of a pile of straw four thousand feet above sea level. The air was crisp and I had a feeling that it would be my last birthday in Peru, at least for a while. I had spent the previous day bouncing on the back of a wobbly truck, strapped to the side to avoid rolling out, but happy. It was the only time I travelled alone; I was catching up with my friend, who had already reached our destination. I nibbled an apple next to a couple of gloomy looking sheep and observed how the Indian driver negotiated a winding road on the edge of dangerous precipices with incredible ease. I wished I had been able to sit up the front and chat to him a little bit, but he was not interested. With an air of arctic detachment, he had signalled me to climb on top if I wanted a lift, and I had accepted. After a few hours, a small mudslide forced him to stop. The local rangers would have it cleared in a few hours, we were told. By that time, it would be late evening, and knowing our rangers the task would extend until early morning. I pulled out a little card Mama had given me to take on my trips; it bore the words of her mantra. I decided to remain calm. The driver appeared to be a family man, over twice my age, and he inspired my trust, and my fascination. There was a convent nearby, in which he suggested I could get shelter. I hopped in the front seat and we drove to the door of the stone fortress. When we got there, though, we discovered it was a monastery. I would not stay in a monastery – Papa had told us some creepy stories about ghosts in monasteries. The only other place was a grocery store manned by a strange-looking character. I took the plunge and spread my blanket over the pile of hay on the back of the truck. The driver parked it by the side of the road in a place he said would be safe. I kept my eyes wide open. It was a gift, I thought, to be there staring at the brilliant sky, counting the stars a few hours before my birthday. It would be the day of the Lord of Miracles in a few hours, so nothing bad could happen. After counting nine hundred stars I fell asleep. The driver checked every so often that I was still in one piece. By morning, he had earned my greatest admiration. I came to the conclusion that his truck was a chariot of the ancient land which he rode calmly up the mountain, waiting patiently for the mudslide to be cleared, and protecting his passengers. That episode showed me that despite a few twisted branches, the tree of my culture was still rooted in solid ground. Dawn broke and the sky seemed to be humming a birthday lullaby. I told the driver it was my birthday and he curtly offered me a piece of his cheese roll and a cup of coffee from his thermos. I savoured it with real gratitude and when the moment came to say goodbye, my eyes were moist with tears. I gave him a hearty hug and a little charm that I had snapped from my bracelet for his daughter. He smiled a sad smile, picked me a wildflower from the ground, and drove away.

I stored the episode in my box of secrets for a couple of days, inventing an excuse to tell my friends to justify my late arrival. But that was until we drove past the spot where I had slept. 'Are you sure you did not want to seduce the brother of Tupac Amaru,' mocked my friend when she heard my story. She was referring to the Inca hero who had fought the Spaniards in the eighteenth century.

'No,' I quickly retorted. 'All I wanted was to trust again.'

When I arrived home from the mountains, Mama sang 'Happy Birthday' and handed me a letter from the Australian Embassy. My application for a two-year working visa had been accepted. I would be heading west, across the Pacific to a land offering new opportunities. I would be able to help my parents pay off their loan; perhaps I could also study psychology. I ran to Linda's house to tell her the news. She was not very happy, because her boyfriend had just left her. I hid a wicked grin.

I visualised the flaming torch that had once illuminated my grandfather's path as he left Genoa. It would now point the way for me to cross the seas, to soothe my restlessness, and test my courage. Nono had died in his sleep one day, after a hearty meal. I will always remember his words on the day I last saw him: 'Life is a journey that each generation takes a step further.'

CROSSING OVER

KNOWING THAT I would soon be departing, I began to visit pockets of the city that held warm childhood memories. I went to my old neighbourhood and saw the churches and the market stalls; and toasted with a glass of Inca cola at Don Takanaka's shop. The Japanese grocer enjoyed my descriptions of the kangaroos and the old Australian inhabitants, and on my last day he volunteered his secret for good fortune: 'As long as you keep a coin in your pocket, you will never go hungry.' It was advice I would never forget. I stood in front of the corner shop and imagined the old street parties and my mother's women's circle. At the park, I sat on a bench next to an alabaster Venus and admired the fig tree's blossoms. Then I went to the Nazarene church, lit a big candle, and prayed to the Purple Christ to guide my trip and make it worthwhile.

The scent of the incense, and the paintings on the wall, stirred my emotions. It carried my thoughts to before I was born, when Mama had rubbed sugar on her belly, hoping for a miracle. I was overtaken by a mixture of feelings, ranging from fear to exhilaration. I would soon fly to distant lands, far away to the Antipodes, where Doña Santitos had told me black angels once lived. Part of me jumped for joy, while another part of me was pensive and doubtful. I had never been so far away from my family and I was not sure that I was ready. I had lived all my life connected to Mama. She had been my compass and the rudder of my life's vessel. Now I had to learn to steer my life along the path of my own destiny, alone. I walked the crowded streets of Lima trying to capture the sounds and smells in a little corner of my heart. I bought some *Turrón de Doña Pepa* to help sweeten the sadness that had entered our home.

On the evening of my departure I carried a lump in my throat, the farewell of my friends in my heart, and a scarlet bag containing my most treasured mementoes in my hand. Mama had packed in my suitcase little bags of dried herbs and curative salts, and a pot of red Chinese balm that would soothe any pain, or warm my heart if it ever froze from loneliness. I had put a lock of her hair in a silver locket and tucked it inside my wallet for protection. And she had given me, carefully wrapped inside a tiny red flannel pouch, a piece of my umbilical cord. 'It will help maintain your connection with the stars on this side of the world,' she said with tears in her eyes. My parents were happy that I had been selected for the trip, but they were also worried about my absentmindedness. Mama had sewn a calico money holder into the lining of my jeans for the trip, and tied a red silk ribbon around my right wrist. 'It will help you remember where you are, and who you are,' she said. I nodded.

The darkness of the night closed in on us as we headed to the airport. I felt as if an eclipse in my heart had turned my emotions pitch black. At the airport, Mama and I hugged for a long while, and we both tuned our hearts to beat in unison, so one would always know when the other was in trouble. I suspected that a spectre of sadness would be escorting me for a long time. I walked to the plane, hit by a pang of separation. In my soul, I must have known I would not return for a long time. And not to stay. I turned around to take a last look at my family, and their image became printed on my mind. Mama stood behind the metal fence on the observation deck, holding Papa's hand, her gaze focused on the path of my journey; his eyes glazed with the crystals of his own emotions. From the air, I saw my land moving away from me, locked beneath the clouds of time. And it hurt.

Three days later, I arrived in Sydney – without my scarlet bag containing my most treasured possessions. I had left it in Tahiti, where we had a stopover. When we were about to take off from Tahiti airport, I saw my bag sitting in the middle of the tarmac. I tried to run off the plane, screaming that I had left my life behind, but one of the flight attendants managed to convince me that the bag would meet me in Sydney. A miracle would have to happen to recover my bag, I thought. For the rest of the journey, I fought hard against the voice of self-recrimination. Could Mama be so right, so soon?

In the new land, I was immediately dazzled by the light in the sky, and the fresh air. The sun seemed to be happier, spreading warm smiles around. I felt I was some kind of pioneer who had landed on the other side of the horizon, thousands of miles away from home. I boarded a bus that would take me to the hostel where I would be staying. On the journey, I noticed factories and eucalyptus trees and, unlike Lima, most of the cars on the road were new and shiny – no honking or beeping, and no dents or scratches. It all looked very clean, very organised, very serious.

I was one of a group of thirteen Peruvian women, each of us with a good reason for the journey. Some wanted to fall in love; others wanted to save money to help their families, then go back and marry well; and some wanted a dose of adventure. Most of us wanted a bit of all three.

The bus stopped outside a large heritage building with arched doors and bay windows, and two tall palm trees outside. It was on a busy road, facing a huge park. It was a women's hostel, where we would be instructed in the ways of the country. The entrance hall was impregnated with a hospital smell; the windows were dressed with mournful drapes; and the hallway reminded me a bit of an old Presbyterian school. The matron, a woman of stern appearance, greeted us at the door. I immediately sensed that she was not the type of woman one should bother with one's worries. We lined up for registration, and, like a group of school girls, were given a tour of the building. We were told to have a good shower before dinner. 'Six o'clock sharp. Do not forget.' In my tiny room, which looked more like a cell, I folded my favourite garments in the way Mama liked. Matching gowns and underwear, socks and pants and colours the way the spirits liked it. Amongst my woollen socks, I found a Saint Anthony's card that Aunt Dorita had slid into my suitcase. I kissed it and pinned it on the wall above my bed, hoping his supernatural power would bring my scarlet bag back to me. I imagined Mama's face, and sang along with her: '*Que será será*, whatever will be will be'.

During our first days in the country, we were bombarded with information about the proper way to behave, and how to avoid hassles: never walk alone after dark; always carry your address in your bag, and always keep important documents safe in the hostel. At night, I tossed and turned in my narrow bed, snuggled under my llama-wool poncho, making plans and pushing melancholic thoughts away. At times, I was besieged by fear, unable to clarify in my mind the real reasons for my trip. Anxiety crept into my heart in the eerie emptiness of the night. It was then that I pictured familiar scenes – the large dining table, and my brothers arguing over soccer clubs as Mama poured ladles of steaming minestrone soup into our bowls. Sometimes I thought of the university cafeteria, where one day, a friend had shown me an ad calling for women to work in Australia. Now, I was here, and my priority was to work, sweat and make it. All work was good work, Mama had told me. And I was prepared for anything. The immigrant stories I had heard as a child were filled with romance, dramas, mishaps, and triumphs. Just like in the soap operas Mama and I listened to. Stories about women beating all the odds to achieve their dreams, help their families, their community and themselves. Mama had been one of those women. She had not bowed down to tragedy. I would do the same, I thought during my sleepless nights. And, hopefully, one day I would find somebody like Papa, a person with whom to stay forever.

One morning about a week after our arrival, I came downstairs to find two Immigration officers were getting together a group of girls to work in a nursing home. I had not been allocated a job yet, so I put my name down. Many of the other girls were already working in factories in the nearby area, making biscuits or cigarettes. They would come home smelling of baking powder, sugar or tobacco. I had been told that one could not be too talkative in a factory, so I prayed for a job that involved a bit of communication. Perhaps I could talk to the old residents at the nursing home. I could tell them stories of colour and magic, stories about Incas, stolen gold, rivers of blood and giant bananas. After two hours' travelling, we arrived at a large white building with a huge lawn, delicate flower beds, and birds in trees. The building was grand but eerie looking. There was an unearthly silence inside.

A matron, as stern as the one in the hostel, came to take our details. We were measured and weighed, our blood was tested, our ears and eyes were examined, and our hair closely inspected for lice. We had just arrived from 'exotic' lands where it was believed insects could kill. We were told about our duties, the house rules, and the rosters; but one thing we did not talk about was money. After a few hours of touring and checking, and feeling a sense of responsibility, I offered myself to the group as a representative to discuss our wages. They agreed. Shock hit me the instant I heard the amount we would finally receive, after all living expenses, taxes and other deductions had been made. I realised that we would be lucky to have enough left to pay our fares into town. I tried to tell the matron that we were young women with needs and aspirations, but she just stared at me blankly. I could have been a piece of furniture creaking. My cheeks reddened with anger. Before consulting the group – for I was convinced they would not like the conditions either – I said, 'If we don't get more pay, we won't stay.' Because I had some experience in industrial relations, I was certain the matron would negotiate. But the egg was on my face when she thumped her fist on the desk, and said that we were a bunch of ingrates and she would call Immigration to take us back home. She pushed us out of her room unceremoniously, and I was left to tell the others what had happened. Including that we might be sent back home. 'What? Send us back home! And all because of you.' The women were angrier than the matron; I wanted to sink into the ground. If only Mama was here to advise me. Or reprimand me. I explained that all I wanted to do was get a better deal for us. I also explained that the government would not be so silly as to deport us because we did not like a job. But the women just looked at me with eyes filled with recrimination. I felt lost and isolated, and it was a rough way for me to learn that generally people will judge actions and not intentions. So I had to be sure before I took risks, particularly if it involved other people.

Finally, the bus came and we were driven home: the hostel. That was the home the matron had been referring to, the driver told us. We all hugged and yelled the moment we saw the old building, and some of the women even thanked me for getting them out of such a 'horrible' job. 'Oh, and it was so far away, and so little money.' I felt part of the group again, and I smiled. When I walked into my room I discovered that Saint Anthony had brought the scarlet suitcase back to me from Tahiti, impregnated with the scent of frangipani, valerian and lemon blossom water.

When the Immigration officers discovered what had happened at the nursing home, they thought I would be better placed in a job dealing with people. So in a way, because of my challenge to the matron, I ended up working as a salesgirl in a city department store. It was a fun job, once I learned to understand the way locals spoke English.

One day, as I walked home through a park, I asked a gardener to tell me the name of a leafy and beautiful tree with giant roots, which reminded me very much of a tree in the Colonial park in Lima. 'It is Ficus tree,' the man said. A Ficus tree. The tree became a symbol that connected me to my old world. During my lunch hour, I often sat against it with a bag of donuts, a big appetite and a bundle of letters from home. I became addicted to donuts because they reminded me of *picarones*, sweet potato dough rings soaked in sugar syrup, my favourites in Lima. Leaning against the trunk, I would gaze at the neat green lawns, the organised traffic, the politeness of pedestrians when they bumped into each other, and the pigeons squabbling over French fries. It was all very pleasant, and very different – so different that I sometimes felt tears behind my eyes. How much I missed the sound of Latin music on the buses, the raucous honking on the road, and the strutting of women in stiletto heels, red lipstick and long black hair.

One evening after a long day at work I was returning home when I noticed a great commotion outside the hostel. Someone was being lifted on a stretcher into an ambulance. I ran upstairs to find out what was going on. Maria had tried to commit suicide. My heart sank; I could not believe it. Maria was one of the women in our Peruvian group, a mature person, always quiet and composed. She had come to Australia so she could save money to help her family, and pay for her fiancé's studies. When she'd saved enough, she would return to Lima, and they would get married. She worked long hours in a bread factory, kneading dough in the heat of an industrial kitchen. But a few days before the sad episode she had received a letter from her boyfriend. In it he told her that it would be better if they went their separate ways. Unable to bear her grief, she had swallowed a whole bottle of pills.

That night, I prayed for her recovery – and for my protection. I felt as if Maria's suicide attempt was an assault on hope. Fortunately, she recovered fully, and eventually the Immigration department arranged for her to return home. I never heard from her again, but the incident left a profound dent in my psyche. Hope could be very frail, I realised; and I made a promise that I would never choose such a drastic option, no matter what happened.

I could never forget Mama's advice – when one wants something badly one has to be prepared to give something in return. Sometimes this is done willingly but at times life will just take it without asking. I had left home to discover new landscapes and design my own life, but as I took the initial steps of my journey, I realised that gods and demons wear more or less the same apparel, and are always keen to help along the way. I always had a trusting nature, which had greatly disturbed my parents. I had walked the streets with confidence, always feeling protected by something from on high. Despite being aware of the dangers on the streets of such a volatile city as Lima, deep inside I had always felt that nothing would ever happen to me. But a few weeks after my arrival, it was time for such a naive sense of trust to be challenged.

It had not taken the women in the hostel long to befriend a few men in the vicinity, mainly migrant boys. One of these men invited some of us to accompany him in his new car on a drive over the Harbour Bridge and along the northern beaches. I was thrilled at the invitation, so I brushed my hair, applied lipstick and jumped in. It was a Sunday afternoon and the sky was bright, with only a few patches of cloud far in the distance. He was a stocky guy with beady eyes who loved to wear tight leather pants and show off his hairy chest and a gold chain. We had a glorious afternoon eating ice cream and chips, wowing at the white sand, the expansive beaches, and the stunning surfer boys with their golden tans. The only problem we had was that we found no café where we could have a decent cappuccino. And an outing without a cup of coffee was not an outing for me. With the air of a know-all adolescent, I remarked that coffee was the vitamin of the soul, and what a pity the new land had not yet learned that. On the way back, our host suggested he could take me to a really nice café where the coffee was freshly roasted and the froth was genuine. I was not attracted to him, but, because he had been polite enough to show us Sydney, I felt obliged. Politeness breeds politeness, Mama always said.

Outside the hostel, the rest of the girls stepped out of the car and we drove off alone. Soon, heavy clouds crept in, and the sky darkened. Suddenly, I realised that he had driven into a large reserve, and in the looming darkness, I could see only trees, tall and intimidating. I began to feel anxious, but I didn't want to show it. He said that the café was not far, and it was easier to get there through this park. A roar of thunder interrupted my thoughts. He must have noticed the alarm in my eyes, for he tried to place his arm around my shoulder. I moved it by sharply jerking my shoulder. He stopped the car immediately, using the excuse that he wanted to have a cigarette until the storm passed. I bit my lower lip, and told him I had never experienced a storm before in my life, because it hardly even rained in my home town. He threw his cigarette out the window and rolled on top of me. A bolt of lightning flashed in the sky and my heart pounded fast, in panic. I struggled to get the guy off. First, I tried to reason with him. 'You told me we were going for coffee. Why are you doing this?' But he wouldn't listen. I pleaded for him to respect my trust. I begged and implored, and told him I was still a virgin. He did not care. He grabbed my hair and pulled my head back, then ripped the buttons off my blouse. I kicked as he tried hard to unbuckle my belt. I thanked the gods for suggesting I wear a tight pair of jeans. I fought, and screamed, but there was no one around to hear me. There were only the echoes of my pain, the pelting rain and the dark tall shadows around. His breathing was heavy; his mind seemed to be in a trance. Outside the car the lightning looked like iridescent spider legs, and I invoked all my guides to help me protect my innocence. He had nearly succeeded in undoing my belt when I noticed the gold chain with a cross dangling from his neck. I grabbed it, and with tears in my eyes, I screamed, 'I could be your mother. Or your sister. Please leave me alone!' My words pierced him like a dagger. He froze for a second then rolled off me, and looked at me with fury. I was shaking like a leaf, trying to close my blouse over my naked breasts. He slapped my face twice, and kicked me out of his car in the pouring rain. My body hit the hard ground. I lay on the wet bitumen until he drove off. For a while I tried to convince myself that it was a nightmare, that I would soon wake up.

Gradually, the rain washed away my tears and I picked myself up, wrapped my blouse around me and tucked it into my jeans, and made my way out of what seemed to me a cold-hearted forest. Eventually I reached the hostel by taxi. There, I hid in my room, feeling far too embarrassed to tell anyone. I should have known better, I said to myself. For some time I would not go out with a man on my own. And ever since then, a few days before a storm is due, my whole body tenses.

I, and many of the other migrant girls, became like working machines. We enjoyed watching our savings soar, and became niggardly. After Maria's sad departure, I decided I wanted to get out of the hostel, and I moved into a tiny flat with a couple of girls from Peru. It was the first time I had lived by my own rules. As the only daughter in my family, I was very territorial and did not like it one bit when my flatmates wore my clothes without my permission. And I annoyed them when I forgot to lock the front door or take the laundry off the line before it rained. But we also enjoyed each other's company, and our evenings of music, spicy cooking, romantic memories and La Bamba sessions at a Latino club. In time I decided to get myself a job in a restaurant because it paid more. Perhaps I could save enough to travel to Europe at the end of my two-year visa, and later, perhaps enrol at university and do psychology. Perhaps, if I worked hard enough.

I began to serve steak and chips, and pop bottles of cheap champagne, and work longer hours. I did not mind the longer hours, because I felt more alive. The mad rush of food-making and serving tables made the time pass quickly. The more often I had to run in and out of the kitchen carrying four plates in my hands, while balancing on high heels, the more energy I got. The job of course had a down side. Whilst there were many more people to meet, there was a lot of alcohol too, and lots of indecent whispers, lewd gestures and groping. At first I would blush, or would tell them off in the way we used to at home: with a stern look or a soft reproach. But I soon learned that such ways did not work in my new land; in fact, rejection seemed to nurture lewdness. Moving jobs I started work in a pizza restaurant, where the cook seemed to believe that sexual advances were included on the menu. Every time he walked behind me at the counter, he would wiggle his crotch and make a wicked gesture with his lips. Sometimes he even shoved his pelvis into me. How much I hated his tobacco breath and his olive-and-cheese odour behind my shoulder. I spent sleepless nights tormented by his gestures, questioning whether I was encouraging his approaches. But I could not bring myself to leave – defeated.

The next time he did it I said, 'Excuse me. I don't like what you do.' But the cook did not care, and went on swirling his pizza dough up in the air. So I complained to the boss, hoping he would put a stop to the nonsense. He laughed at me and said, 'Who do you think you are, the Queen of Sheba? We migrants have to understand one another.' I felt humiliated, ridiculed. To him, migrants had to lick the floor before they could earn any respect. Migrant women? We came at our own peril, according to him. I would not go that far. I had other options, I told myself.

The next night, I went to work armed with my invisible weapons: courage and determination. It was all I needed. I acted naturally, cleaning the glass counter and replenishing the trays of pizza toppings, humming a friendly tune. Then the cook approached sneakily to stand behind me. I breathed deeply and waited, delivering myself to the plan. I reassured myself that this time, whatever will be, will have to be fast and effective. The instant I smelled his odour close to me and felt his crotch pushing forward, I turned around and launched my right knee forward, hitting him where it hurt. Within seconds, his face turned from the white of shock to the red of pain. Before the boss had a chance to say anything, I picked up my belongings and walked out. There were no laws to punish harassment at the time, and I lost a whole week's pay. But I had earned my self-respect, and that was the most important thing.

DEAR MAMA

Dear Mama,

There is so much to see, so much to do, so much to say.

After weeks of knocking on doors, I finally got a job in an office. I walked for hours, tripping on cobblestones, skipping on grass, stomping on hard cement, until I found one. The more I live here, the more I like it, Mama, lots of trees and flowers, and dreams. My job is to pay all the bills for a firm that imports chocolates and mini-cucumbers soaked in spiced vinegar and garlic. The food is really nice here. You would not believe the things I taste, the biscuits I nibble. Some of the bonbons are filled with cinnamon and almonds, cream and liqueur. I am sure Aunt Dorita would go nuts about them — a good complement for the afternoon aperitif we used to have in the old house. Every time I eat a truffle I smell the old house and the chocolates Papa used to bring home.

Today, I saw the most beautiful red flower, crimson red. It is called a waratah, and instead of petals it has pins like spider legs. I saw this flower in the Blue Mountains. It stood alone, like a woman forever waiting for her soul mate. A friend told me the story of this flower. Long long ago, in the era of the In-between, there was a young and beautiful princess who every afternoon sat in a clearing waiting for her lover who had gone into battle. She sat there, clad in a kangaroo skin, and with red feathers in her hair. Sad, sad for the princess of the red feathers — her beloved never came back. She was heartbroken. So much so, that her pain turned her into a flower so the spirit of her lover could find her one day. Here, the world of the In-between is called the Dreamtime. I met a local Aboriginal girl the other day. Her name is Justine and she is a model, and an actress. Her looks are stunning, very much like our women: cinnamon skin, black hair and deep black eyes, deeper than wisdom. We talked a bit and exchanged phone numbers. I hope I see her again.

The mountains here are not as high as the mountains at home, but they are blue and haunting. Behind me in the photo are the Three Sisters. I am sure there is a story behind them too. The guy next to me is Francesco, a good friend. He is teaching me the art of silver service.

I am sure Sydney has a lot of potential; I can breathe it in the air. My English is a lot better now, and I can understand a bit more. I am sorry things are getting tougher at home, and that all the prices keep going up. Don't worry, I will always send you whatever dollars I can save. Tell my aunts that I miss them very much. Remember that you are my inspiration. Thank you for your daily prayers, I am sure they are protecting me. I beg you to stay healthy so you can visit me here if I decide to stay. My new flat is nice. Not a lot bigger than my old bedroom, but it has everything I need. There are posters on the walls, family photos on my dresser and green leaves in a vase, for good fortune. My bed is small and my poncho is now a blanket. I have a formica table and four chairs for dinner parties, and a television, not that I have much time to watch it. No dust here, Mama. It's a joy. I am sending you a money order and a bag of goodies for the family. Hope you receive the parcel in good order.

Lots of love,
Emilia

Behind these lines lived the story of the first romance in my new land. A few months after the tears and tribulations of my arrival, I met the boy who transformed me into a woman in full bloom. It was not quite love at first sight, but almost. I was not even nineteen and he was a couple of years older. He was a flamboyant Italian with an enchanting smile and deep blue eyes. I met him on an afternoon when the air was scented with sweet black coffee, and vanilla. I was working in a café and trying to learn how to make cappuccinos. 'The whirling is all wrong,' he said. 'You have to hold it like this.' His name was Francesco and he came from Trieste, a city of mystery, dim lanterns and strong winds. I let him show me how to make a good cappuccino. How to hold the jug, where to position myself next to the espresso machine, how to produce a decent froth, and the precise swing of the wrist necessary to sprinkle the chocolate on properly. 'It's all in the swing, my dear, in the swing of life.'

We got to know each other, exploring parks, looking at flowers, and listening to songbirds. Under my Ficus tree I asked him to share my bag of donuts while I translated Mama's letters. I liked the rhythmical way he spoke and his animated gestures.

Francesco brought back into my life a spark of adventure. The days of gloom, when I had felt the strain of being separated from love, from my family, from the voice of wisdom of the women's circle, were gone. The void I had felt inside me began to disappear, fuelled by Francesco's attention. I learned to taste an array of life's different flavours. He worked in a top Italian restaurant with starched tablecloths, silver cutlery and fresh flowers. He knew how to carry a plate the way a matador knows how to flick his cape before a bull charges. Such graces were part of the training he'd received when he had worked in Switzerland. 'I can teach you all there is to know,' he assured me.

I had planned to take a job on a cruise liner, but eventually he made me forget about that. Being with Francesco made me feel protected, as if I had been returned to the cradle of my family, as if I had my brothers around. Being far from home and walking the new path I had traced for myself alone had been tough. Before I met Francesco,

I used to go to the movies alone so I could cry as much as I liked in the darkness. Together we compared our dreams and intertwined illusions about life. He wanted to have a restaurant of his own one day. I told him I wanted to be a psychologist, to help the weak and confused. 'One day,' he said. 'One day we'll have what we want. One day.' Over polenta and veal parmigiana, we spent our free time discovering what made each other tick – what provoked our anger and our passion. A real bolognese sauce, he said, has to be made with pork sausages and chicken liver of the best kind. 'And not ordinary pepper, oh no,' he would stress. 'It has to be freshly ground.' I was bedazzled by his flair and the way he wore his designer jeans. Life became bright again for he assured me that with him I did not need a guardian angel.

After this promise to give my guardian angel a break we moved in together. I began to wake up with butterflies in my stomach, always searching for Francesco in the room. He nurtured the woman in me, rediscovered the girl in the migrant worker, and introduced a new role to my life: that of the housewife. I became the longing woman who waited until late for her beloved to come home. I played the de facto wife with pride and the best of intentions, and I placed my academic aspirations on the back burner in the name of love. Perhaps owning a restaurant could be fun. I discovered I liked waiting on people, teasing them a bit, telling them about the Incas, making their meal a special moment. I spent my spare time cleaning the house, washing his white shirts by hand, and ironing them with starch on the cuffs and collar. I took up sewing, and made my own frocks and uniforms. I refined my cooking skills. 'The love of a man is always found in his after-dinner grin,' Mama claimed. She would know. Like my father, Francesco liked boasting a bit about the things he knew, particularly when he won in poker.

Some Sunday afternoons we would leave his old Humber at home

and stroll in the park, under the jacaranda trees discussing our unfolding dreams. 'You can feed your clients and I can treat my patients,' I
told him the day I bought my first book on psychology, *The Will to
Happiness*. And Francesco listened. He said that for a man to love a
woman was scary because 'the closer you look at a woman, the more
you discover that there are other women under her skin, women you
have never met before'.

Months went by and letters from home grew fewer and grimmer. My
heart would quiver every time I opened one. I longed for news, but
most of the news I got was shrouded in pessimism. At home, a new
general had taken power and raised prices even more. Loretta's husband had died by shooting himself in the head one lonely night; he
had been unable to conquer his addiction to cocaine. Mama was having new liver tests, but she was fighting her karma by making more
spiritual home visits. There were rumours in the south that a rebellion was about to be mounted. News of an emerging indigenous
leader, seen as a local Messiah by the Indians had spread throughout
the countryside. This was forcing the military to consider holding
elections. Military dictatorships had begun sprouting in other parts of
the continent, and young people were disappearing without a trace.

With Francesco's tuition, I moved quickly from working in coffee
lounges to trattorias, wine bars, clubs and, finally, five-star hotels. I
learned to mix cocktails to the beat of a rumba, bone fish with flair,
and flambé strawberries in brandy. After a while, though, the whole
scene became monotonous, despite the flowing vodka, clandestine
casino life, smoking and drinking. I decided that getting a daytime job
would help me focus more clearly on my real goals. Now that returning to Peru did not seem too appealing, I had to review my options.

While jobs in waitressing came by the dozen, proving my ability in the corporate world was extremely tough. 'Not only can I add,' I found myself repeating when my patience ran low, 'I can also balance your books, determine your profit and loss, draw statistical charts, and make good cappuccinos.' Months of knocking on doors paid off. A Russian lady took the plunge and gave me my first job in an Australian office. I was a clerk for a smallgoods importer, and I kept my waitressing job on weekends.

Francesco began to invite his friends over to play poker. I learned to play well – and bluff even better – but I never understood how people could take the game so seriously. Then one day Francesco said he would not be able to make it to the movies with me that night because he had to play poker.

I could not tell Mama I was living with my boyfriend. She would have preferred me not to have followed her path of living with a man outside of marriage. At home, a girl could only surrender her most precious possession to the man she would share the rest of her life with. Everything was going well, until one day I received a letter that burnt my fingers, because it carried Mama's seal of reproach. The wasps of mischief had carried my secret all the way to Peru, and Mama was in a serious state of shock. Shame overtook me, as I felt I had committed my first act of betrayal. I had promised myself I would never upset Mama in such a way after I saw how distressed she became when one of my brothers married in a rush, to save the honour of his girlfriend. How could I explain to Mama that living together with a man was part of the sexual revolution in the age of flower power? How could I convince her that in the new western generation, to which I now belonged, it was an unwritten requisite for a woman to live with a man before getting married?

In an outburst of wild spontaneity, I thought of a possible solution: to get married. Perhaps that would please Mama. Was Francesco the man of my dreams? Or at least, was he the sort of man with whom I could realise my dreams? I could not answer either of those questions. All I knew was that I did not want to upset my mother, nor did I want to part from Francesco. 'If it doesn't work, we'll get divorced,' I suggested to him. Francesco agreed to the wedding, giving the divorce option little attention.

A couple of months later, wrapped in innocent illusions, we married in the park. I wore flowers in my hair and a handmade white satin dress, and there were twelve guests. At the party afterwards, we had the Thousand Leaves wedding cake, made with brandy blancmange filling and fine pastry. My family, after recovering from the shock and the spontaneous marriage announcement, threw a big party at home in Lima for all relatives and friends, with a live band and a multi-tiered cake adorned with Chantilly lace and silk ribbons.

I knew I was taking a huge risk. The night before the wedding, Francesco had skipped the party thrown by his friends. When I returned home, I discovered our shared piggy bank had been opened and all the money had gone. His friends went looking for him and brought him back in tears. He had lost our honeymoon money. We sat up all night in bed, weighing up our circumstances, and decided to give it a go. We agreed to skip the honeymoon, work even harder, introduce some austerity into our lives, and build up a financial base again, so long as he could to learn to handle money. Unfortunately, Francesco had problems holding on to a job for long. He would walk out in a fluster every time somebody pointed out even a small flaw in his work. In a bid to show off, I'd told my family that Francesco was a restaurant manager, but in fact he was a head waiter. He could have been a manager, for he was charismatic and full of flair, but his weakness and lack of responsibility often sabotaged his chances. Perhaps a family would instil in him that responsibility, said an older friend of his. Perhaps I could give him a couple of *bambini* soon, he suggested. 'Don't people in your country like having children?' I am sure they did, but that option was not in my book. The thought of having children terrified me, apart from Francesco, I was all alone.

Francesco and I spent two years doing our best to keep our pledges of love, support and mutual understanding. Unfortunately, when life showed him a face he did not want to see, he fled, moving from restaurant to restaurant and even from city to city. One day, I came home to find a note on our neatly made bed. He had gone to find himself. A week later, he rang to tell me he had found a golden city. I followed him north, and settled down with him in a large house on stilts. I even bought myself a Dalmatian dog, which I called Belinda. But soon after we had begun to settle down, he flew away like a disgruntled hummingbird, this time to the south. He had found a winter city that reminded him of his beloved Italy. With a pang in my heart, I returned Belinda and went back to Sydney. My young husband seemed to have an aversion to steady ground and I had a need for security. But the promises to love each other forever which we made at our wedding ceremony pulled on my psyche stronger than an anchor every time I considered leaving him. And there was also the issue of a failed marriage, which at the time was quite a burden for women of my culture. To redeem my sense of guilt for the marriage fiasco, I decided to go home and visit my parents, to give myself some breathing space. Francesco thought it was a good idea, because he did not want to divorce.

I arrived in Peru loaded with presents and souvenirs. I had scripted this moment in my mind for years, with musical accompaniment, glittering lights, and sentimentality. The return. I had dashed across every restaurant floor and balanced every business account thinking of this day, picturing how I would enter the airport smiling triumphantly. And I did, although reality was not quite the same as my rehearsals. It was strange to be addressed as *la Señora*, instead of *Señorita*. Mama was proud showing off her married daughter – and married overseas, which was even better. Her little girl had been transformed into a woman, with the responsibilities of a spouse. But the truth was different. The girl who left home had been buried, her dreams squashed in the name of duty. I could not admire myself, instead I felt beaten, overcome with grief. I had put so many dreams on hold and felt I had achieved little. A marriage had not given me satisfaction; a ring on my finger had not made me a more interesting person. But I hid my emotions and celebrated with my friends and family.

'Oh yes, the kangaroos are cute. No, not as big as llamas.'

'No, the koalas are not cuddly bears. They might look like it, but one could rip your ear lobe off if you tried to kiss it.'

I got inebriated on cakes and fried sweet potatoes, picked up old tracks and traces, visited aunts, and took flowers to the cemetery. Mama took me to her Buddhist temple and, out of respect for her faith, I prayed with her. Prayers were not part of my life anymore. The search for my spirit had ceased, together with my ambitions. When I had delivered all my gifts and had tea with everyone, I confessed to Mama I did not want to be married anymore. In tears, I explained that Francesco and I had different dreams. He was not ready; we had married too soon. I dropped to my knees and sobbed on Mama's lap. I knew my confession hurt her deeply, as she had already made plans for future grandchildren. But she dried my tears with typical tenderness, and said, 'Do what you must do.'

A few days after my confession something terrified me. My period was late. When test results showed I was pregnant I had mixed feelings. In a way I was happy because I was in touch with my creative womanhood, but fear stood right by my side. It was too early for the commitment of having kids. Alone. I knew Mama would not be with me, for she did not want to come and live in Australia, not yet. She felt safe in Peru with her familiar medical specialists, with Papa. As for me, I was very scared, because in the last six months Francesco had shown little sign of acting on our renewed vow to make the marriage work. Mama did not want to give any opinion on the alternative to going through with the pregnancy. Her faith presented her with a conflict. It would have to be my decision. After long deliberations

288 THE RAW SCENT OF VANILLA

with my conscience, and without giving anybody a chance to change my mind, I opted for a termination. All Mama said was that my decision was my own karma; I would have to deal with it when the time came and in the best way I could.

I found myself lying on a table covered by a white sheet, with my mother by my side. It was the saddest moment in my life. The surgical procedure did not go smoothly and there were complications. I was hospitalised four times before I finally healed. First, the doctors discovered that I had a retroverted uterus; then that the scraping had only taken half the contents; then that the suction tools had caused an infection. I had to go for a more serious surgical intervention to clear my womb of the polluted debris.

For many years, I carried a sense of guilt, a lump stuck like an oyster on the bedrock of my feelings, causing chronic grief and self-condemnation. When I finally returned to Australia, Francesco said, 'How could you do a thing like that? Without telling me!' He was furious that I had let go of the pregnancy. There was little I could say, for despite loving him I knew for sure his dreams were not mine. Dark circles had settled around my eyes, and I felt old and confused. The dreamer in my heart had been put to rest, buried next to the bundle of tissues the doctor had pulled out of my body on the darkest day of my life. Quietly, I packed my bags and left Francesco for good. I would have to start again. The grief was, at times, unbearable, turning my world greyer than the sky at home.

I stopped eating donuts, but I made time to visit my Ficus tree and stare at the passers-by, although their images were often blurred by my tears. My days began and ended in a lethargic ceremony of inertia and pessimism. One day after I picked myself up from under the Ficus tree with great difficulty – for I was physically feeling a weight on my back – I crossed the road and walked into a hall where people were talking about the Brotherhood of the Light, a Christian esoteric fraternity. A lady with a sweet face took me by the arm and sat me down to hear a verse being read. I listened for a while, letting my heart be soothed by hope. Good also exists behind the bad, that's all I can remember. After listening for about an hour, I decided to store my guilt somewhere deep inside, where no one would ever enter, not even me until the day I die. On the day when I will answer for my deeds. From then on the weight eased and the circles around my eyes disappeared. But I discovered that guilt can never really be locked away. It haunts me every so often, shape-shifting like a trickster, turning into a migraine, or inertia, or self-doubt.

I came to appreciate my skills in accounting, because although it was a science lacking in glamour, there was never a shortage of finance jobs. My sadness lifted gradually and I put on high heels, lipstick and a silk scarf, and marched into the business world.

In time, I moved from accounts to share investments, and then became the personal assistant for a shrewd investor. His name was Rudolph and he had an eye for mineral resources – and a healthy interest in the history of the Incas. I told him that the Incas had known the secret of modifying atom vibrations, could change the weight of matter and had been able to transport giant slabs to build large temples. He was a cultivated man, astute and courteous with his employees, always making sure we felt appreciated. I discovered how much a person can produce when they are shown praise and encouragement. I felt as if I had found myself a new family, for whom I was prepared to put in long hours, work on weekends and even prepare traditional Peruvian dishes for special functions.

Through Rudolph, I met older migrant families who had arrived on boats from Eastern Europe with only a bag of hopes, like my grandfather. During consulting sessions I spiced our clients' financial reports with political chats and grim details of Peru's post-Inca era. 'Oh I hope it never gets like that here,' they used to sigh, carefully storing their dividend cheques in their pockets. Glad to be in the lucky country. Like his friends, Rudolph had done extremely well in

Australia. And like his friends, he was a staunch defender of capital-ism, branding anyone who felt differently a rampant communist. I used to get into serious arguments with him, defending homeless and unemployed people's rights to welfare. As I grew to know him better I got less upset about his views, as I realised that his experiences had traumatised him. His country had been taken by force and his family had lost its fortune, so he hated anyone who dared speak of the redis-tribution of wealth. Rudolph had arrived by ship with other refugees, some of whom ended up in positions of great power and respectabil-ity in their new nation. Since coming to Australia, he had driven taxis, sold houses, explored for oil and minerals, and owned a string of companies, including a liquor warehouse and a holiday resort in Fiji. I became very fond of him and found in him the fatherly attention I had been missing. He encouraged his staff to work harder with after-hours dinners, share benefits and birthday celebrations. Although he preferred to keep wages down. I had stepped into a different niche of Australian society and I realised that no matter what a person's colour, cash flow opened any doors.

As the company's portfolios were doing so well, and everyone was counting their gains, Rudolph suggested I take up business studies again and complete the course I had started in Peru. The company would pick up all the bills. The invitation filled my head with enor-mous pride, and my heart with unparalleled gratitude. Whilst I did not want to imagine a future as an accountant, I said yes in the name of financial security, aware that money would make the process of weaving my dreams a lot more pleasurable. I enrolled immediately, setting aside my plan to study psychology. My new studies allowed me to explore the intricacies of currency fluctuations, compare share indexes, observe market forecasts and cash in the benefits of my own dealings. In a short time, I learned the tricks of the trade, and my well-guided transactions allowed me to replace my homemade frocks with designer suits, and gave me the key to my first apartment.

No matter how protected I felt by my financial gains, I never stopped being terrified by tempestuous weather. A storm never failed to clench my heart with intense fear. Deep inside I heard Doña Panchita's rumblings about the riders of the Apocalypse, which 'would come as the sky darkens'. One day, as I left the office, heavy rain began to pelt down on the streets. The sky was grey and mournful, and a thick shroud tightened around my heart. I felt very uneasy – I sensed something terrible had happened. I dashed through the streets drenched to the bones because I was never in tune with weather forecasts, so was never prepared with an umbrella. I ran inside my apartment and noticed there was mail for me. Despite the usual pessimism which most home correspondence carried, a letter always made my heart beat with exhilaration. I longed to know whether Mama was happy and well. I recognised her handwriting: round and steady, aesthetically pleasing. The sky turned black outside the window and I opened the letter. Mama's handwriting began to speak, riding dauntingly across the white page conveying very, very sad news. Aunt Dorita had died. Her death was so unexpected, so terribly devastating for me, that I crushed the letter in my palm. A sudden gust of wind tipped a vase off the table, and it crashed on the floor. Green leaves floated in a pool of malodorous water. It was not fair. My favourite aunt had been suffering from breast cancer, and I had never known. Mama assured me she had not suffered too much in the end. She wrote that Aunt Dorita had completed her cycle here. I wanted to believe her so much that I dropped to my knees and wept for hours, in complicity with the rain. I thought of the day that I went to see her after the termination of my pregnancy. 'Well,' she had said, 'cheer up, perhaps Nona Emilia already filled up your quota.' I had told her I would have babies, one day. 'But if you don't, it will be by the grace of God. That's fine too. Some do, some don't. That's all there is,' she had replied.

Aunt Dorita had been a sacred example of tolerance and acceptance. I made myself a glass of water with orange blossom that Mama had packed into my bag when I left Peru on my last trip, and drank it in the name of Aunt Dorita. Then I put on a Peruvian record, prepared a cup of black coffee, and sat on the floor to invoke her memory. I wanted to give her exuberant stories life, to hear her chuckles again. Oh Aunt Dorita, the woman of the round hips, kinky hair, and the white pearl laughter. Her wicked words of wisdom had brought much laughter into my life. Now, I was so far away, in the land of eucalyptus, unable to attend her funeral. The room filled with her stories, which had fed my young imagination. Perhaps I could call on the angels to guide her on her journey to heaven, I thought, as I lit special candles. Mama said that when a person dies, one thousand Buddhas emerge to welcome the soul and guide it on its journey to the final retreat, Nirvana. It is a journey of one hundred days, I am told. I imagined Aunt Dorita dressed in white chiffon, being greeted by her mother and all the people for whom she lit candles back in the old neighbourhood. Now she was another star in the firmament. Her death reminded me it could happen to anyone in my family. My parents could die, and I would be so far away. The thought became a nightmare. I was living three days away from home by plane, for there were no direct flights to South America at the time. I dreaded the moment, the letter, the telegram or the phone call with the tragic news. There was always enough money in my bank account for such emergencies. That Friday afternoon I took a pen and wrote a reply letter. I begged my family to let me know well in advance should a sign of death approach our home. But Doña Panchita had once told me that death has a way of appearing unannounced. I wondered whether the Blue Cat would be polite to us.

The death of Aunt Dorita forced me to reassess my priorities and look inside myself, at my emotional deficits and possibilities. Was I really happy with my life? Was I really happy with the job I did? Was money my best friend? Three weeks later, at an office party, I met one of Rudolph's friends, a man who worked for the country's national broadcaster. He was overseeing an experimental radio station that would broadcast in more than thirty languages. He had noticed how much I loved talking about current affairs as well as my ability to tell stories, particularly about my ancient culture. So he asked me whether I would like to be part of the team that produced the radio programs for the Spanish-speaking community. His request flattered me, but brought with it a tinge of fear. My flaws would be exposed on air. What if I made a mistake? I said I would think about it. At home, I looked at myself in the mirror and I saw the face of incompetence. What did I know about radio anyway? My doubts spoke loudly: I did not have a good voice, let alone any ability to write a script. A whisper from deep inside reminded me of a successful play I had written and staged at school. It was funny and very popular. But those were the days of Walter; he had done the writing. Was I going mad? No, I could tell the time. A doctor in Peru had once said, 'As long as you can tell the time, no one will lock you away for being mad.' When the man rang, I declined his invitation. I said that media production was an area about which I had no idea, nor could I make it up.

Besides, I did not want to dissolve my childhood illusions that radio was indeed a box in which little people acted out the dramas of life.

I offered to introduce the radio man to my friend Manuel, a Spanish journalist with a handsome voice and a healthy ego. He was a close friend and a source of inspiration; I admired his passion for reading and writing. With him, I learned all about Karl Marx and the doctrine of socialism, the Spanish Civil War, and the need for a revolution when discussion did not work. Rudolph did not like Manuel at all because he was sure he was trying to 'brainwash me with twisted ideas about bludgers who would take from the rich and give to the poor'. Rudolph exaggerated grossly, for Manuel was not a communist. A champagne socialist perhaps, a smart and debonair Spaniard with a taste for good literature, spicy women, red wine and current affairs. In his library, I discovered James Joyce, Ernest Hemingway, Gore Vidal and other classics like the works of Jean Paul Sartre,

Hermann Hesse and Albert Camus. Of all of them I found Heming-way the most accessible, and Kafka the most fascinating.

Christmas came and following it restlessness, the child of boredom, appeared. I found my job repetitive, the clients tedious, and the con-versations banal. In the afternoons, I began to imagine butterflies fluttering off the pages of the ledger, darting out of the window. I drank cup after cup of coffee to prevent my falling into daydreams again. If I were to take up something other than business at univer-sity, it would mean leaving my job, and being poor. Had I come to Australia to be poor? What about Mama's eternal mortgages?

An invitation from my boss to a new restaurant interrupted my self-analysis. He told us that this restaurant had a certain peculiarity, and that only those with an open mind and a penchant for adventure were welcome. Sure that the peculiarity lay in the food, many of the staff declined the invitation, for they did not want to venture into more unfamiliar flavours. I agreed, sure that I had what it took. Those of us who accepted the challenge dolled ourselves up with frosty lip-stick and pastel eye shadow, closed the share books, locked the filing cabinets, checked the water in the plants, fed the pigeons that nested outside the window, and strutted out on high platform shoes. There were seven of us. We rode in two taxis, although the mysterious restaurant was located only a few blocks away. Rudolph's companies were doing very well, and transport was tax deductible. Indeed, in Rudolph's life, everything was tax deductible.

The restaurant had an unassuming facade. We went down a set of stairs in semi-darkness. 'I wonder what's so unique about this joint. It can't be the decor,' I said as we descended into the unknown. A recep-tionist behind a veneer desk greeted us politely and asked for our names. 'Names?' I cried out loud. 'What for?' It was for her to write them on our name tags. I immediately refused, because Loretta had once warned that only people who are for sale wore name tags.

'No thank you,' I said, 'I am not for sale.' Rudolph grinned, and all the girls followed my trend. Inside, we found a poorly carpeted floor and dimmed red lights, giving the place a sombre atmosphere. My intuition suggested that the uniqueness of the place had nothing to do with food. Rudolph's friend, a ragged man in his twilight years, came to welcome us. He affably boasted that the place was his latest investment, and something new in Sydney. The proprietor ordered champagne, telling the waiter to extend special care to our table. When the champagne arrived, we all made a toast, and the men proceeded to talk business. My eyes travelled around and noticed a few couples chatting and drinking. The conversations at our table stopped when a young woman loomed out of the darkness and approached our group. She was wearing a tiny miniskirt that looked more like an accessory than a whole garment. Her looks, and the name on her tag, suggested she was of Latin American background, but her accent did not. She stood there in her high heels trying to utter words that did not seem to want to come out. She had long, thick hair, and an air of acquiescence but her gaze was sad. Her attitude and her presence made me feel strange. I asked her what she wanted.

'My husband would like to meet you,' she said.

'I beg your pardon?' I replied, sure I had misheard her.

On the other side of the dance floor I noticed an older man looking at our table. The invitation left me speechless. One of the men at our table snapped, 'Her husband wants to meet you. He must like you.' In a flash I understood the peculiarity of the place. I looked at the woman and felt a profound sadness. Had she been given another option in life? I replied that perhaps I might not like to meet her husband. Explaining that I had found her request quite strange, and totally out of order, I assured her I was not interested in games. She looked embarrassed, and I was immediately assailed by guilt. After all, she was like me, a guest in this strange place. The men at my table asked her to sit with us and have a drink, but she smiled timidly and tiptoed back to her table, trying hard to keep her balance, feeling vulnerable under the heated gaze of my companions. So this was the uniqueness of the place. I searched for an explanation from Rudolph, but he just cleared his throat. Without apologies he said that his friend was introducing a swinging place to Sydney. The culmination of the sexual revolution.

'A swinging place!' I exclaimed with reproach. 'How could you?'

'I am not pushing you to do anything,' Rudolph insisted, explaining that we were all there to see how it worked, in case somebody wanted to come back later. This restaurant was a window onto a life I had not seen before. I felt sorry for the girl, for she looked fragile and worn out, a destitute soul. Probably she was paying a debt, recompensing somebody for having shown her a new world, for having pulled her out of misery.

Downstairs, another party was going on. I went down there, in the name of healthy exploration. Crouched behind the stairs, I saw a scene not much different from the erotic pictures I had seen in my early years. Although this one was much more surrealistic. The protagonists of the uninhibited theatrics looked hungry, keen to plunge into each other, to possess each other. Desperate to numb their senses and satiate their cravings. I retreated with astonishment, adding more guilt to my soul, but reassuring myself that I knew now what I did not want. I realised that everything was up for auction. What was once offered to the gods in sacrifice was now traded and consumed by human predators. I returned to the table, muttering under my breath, 'Is that all there is?' To my surprise a little voice seemed to answer, 'No, there is more. A lot more.'

THE EDGE OF DESTINY

GONE WITH THE seventies was flower power and the call for social, and transcendental, change. With the eighties, came a craving for material abundance. I was truly astonished at how many people turned into millionaires overnight, at how much champagne flowed along the corridors of business. It was all very surreal, because while some people were driving their flashy cars down the main streets another group in society was wearing safety pins in their noses and threadbare jeans, in solidarity with the poor and the natives on the other side of the world. At least that's what I thought. I too earned my few dollars on the stock merry-go-round. Mama would be so proud. I invited her to come and enjoy it while it lasted, before the bottom fell out of my coffers. My money was not going to last long because I was about to take a big leap towards the next stage of my dreams. After much deliberation, I realised that a career in business would not make my heart happy, despite the material comfort. I conveyed my decision to Rudolph with a touch of trepidation, because he had invested a good deal of money in my studies. He thought I was mad, and was sure I would eventually learn from my 'huge mistake'.

I had enrolled at university to study Communications, a course that included psychology. It was all thanks to a Hungarian Jewish woman called Erika, whom I had met while attending women's meetings in the late seventies. 'You should become a journalist,' she said one afternoon after noting my interest in the appalling conditions of migrant women working in sweat shops. These were women whose fear was abused, who like myself had come from countries where feudal regimes and exploitation had been the rule for centuries. Up until then, the thought of becoming a journalist had never entered my mind.

I felt that journalists were people born with a vocation, not made by circumstances. Was it the right path towards my dreams? Marriage had not offered the bliss I sought. If a husband and children were not my ultimate dream, though the idea of a partner had always made me happy, what was the answer to my longings? The certainty in Erika's voice, the fire in her eyes and the assurance that my future lay in the area of communications, not business, gave me a glimpse of my destiny. A few weeks after our conversation, I found myself at the dean's office speaking with passion about the need for multilingual journalists. I called for the voice of multicultural Australia to be heard, knowing that 'multiculturalism' was the key word at the time. Immigration was changing the face of Australia and there was a resistance against cultural integration.

Meanwhile in Peru, terror loomed in the mountains and peasants were slaughtered if they refused to join the ranks of the revolutionary army. Armed youth persecuted terrified Indians who were still practising the old crafts, and planting potatoes and corn. They were told that a new Inca messiah had appeared in the south, a saviour who would return the glory into their lives and would lead them to a new life, free of injustice and ruthless consumerism. This messiah, known as *El Presidente*, was a professor in a regional university. Influenced by Chairman Mao's ideology, *El Presidente* had spread such terror across the country that the notion that he was the messiah was hard to swallow for most villagers. Peasants descended from the hills to the capital, abandoning their elders, their land and their animals, desperate for protection. There was daily carnage all over the country; and a group of Peruvian journalists had disappeared in the highlands while trying to expose a link between local authorities and terrorist forces. Local authorities and religious leaders fell victim to both sides of the conflict. And the government had deployed its own counter revolutionary forces to kill, kill, kill.

My family locked the doors, put bars on windows, and hardly ever saw the night sky. Old Aunt Lucinda, Aunt Lisa's mother, used to come to visit, aided by her walking stick, and forecast the Book of Revelations and the time of gloom: Lima would burn, to be purified, and the sins of the colonisers would be forgiven. Mama listened while sauteing potatoes and beef, reminding Aunt Lucinda of the causes of universal suffering because her new faith spoke more of an era of peace.

In such a climate, Mama prepared for her trip to Australia. She left Papa with a pantry full of food, and guidelines for making a good minestrone soup. 'Not too much basil, Alberto, not too much. It will be bad for your liver,' she said as Papa bade his farewells at the airport, reassuring her that all would be well. She arrived in Sydney in a happy mood, despite the thirty-six-hour journey. Although exhausted she was still the same beautiful woman with rosy cheeks and tenderness in her eyes. It was a moment I had spent endless evenings visualising in bed by candle light, relishing every detail and expanding the thrill in my heart. I had always wanted to show Mama how bright the sky was in my new city. 'Mama, welcome to Australia!' I cried as I ran to meet her, showering her with rose petals and tears. I hugged her firmly, expressing the love I had for so long not been able to show her tangibly. As I kissed her I felt the scent of her breath, from where so many memories soared; and in her kisses I tasted the feminine essence of her heart, filtering into mine. It was bliss.

We swept Sydney's streets, visiting all the cultural nooks and historical alleys, and piling stuffed koalas on top of fluffy kangaroos. She was in awe of all the beauty, comparing it to the island of the

In-between. I took her to watch the buskers at the quay, whom she found evocative of her childhood when she danced the charleston to her father's clarinet, when she counted her coins to buy vanilla bars and touch her own memories. We huddled under the leafy branches of my old Ficus tree, which had sheltered me for so many years, and we listened to the bells from the cathedral tolling in the distance. She found it all very pretty and pristine. I wanted to introduce her to my favourite donuts, but she was living under the guidelines of a liver-restoring diet. It turned out that most of her previous ailments had been due to cirrhosis of the liver, which she developed from Hepatitis B, contracted at the Bethlehem markets in Iquitos when she was young. She began to watch what she ate, banning fats and spices from her plate, and drank as much *boldo* herbal tea as she could. We fed the donuts to the pigeons, and talked like two old friends.

Mama told me that Loretta was now a priestess. She had started this new life after her eldest son had drowned, just a week after her father had passed away. Now she sold food for the soul with tarot cards made out of symbols from her former mystery schools. With the money she earned she was sending her second son to the seminary. Uncle Arnaldo had died from prostate cancer, but he had taken his last breath while lying next to Aunt Renatta. Seizing the opportunity to have the man she loved next to her, without ever having to send him back to his official wife, Aunt Renatta had 'kidnapped' his corpse, stating her right to hold the funeral in her house. A family scandal had ensued. Uncle Arnaldo's legitimate children could not convince Aunt Renatta to release the body, so the police were called. In the end, the funeral was held on neutral ground with a special guard present. The two women sat side-by-side, embarrassing family members when they approached to offer their condolences. We giggled, and wondered how Mama's life would have been had she become Martin Lozano's mistress. She replied that the best decision she made in her life was to marry Papa. 'Despite his foibles, darling, he has proven to be a good man, a good support,' she said. I longed to experience such a love, which, like my Ficus tree, was always reliable and embracing.

When Mama told me that she had given my old doll, the one who had been baptised, to Aunt Techa's first grand-daughter, I felt a tinge of sadness; and I detected an omen when she said, 'The universe only knows if you will ever have a child.'

Mama's visit unleashed a turmoil of emotions inside me that I found hard to interpret at the time. She criticised my lifestyle – single, and too idealist. 'You must find a good man.' she said. I was sharing a house with a friend who was experimenting with lesbianism. The house was divine, with marble floors and many art pieces, some of which celebrated women's sensual embraces and would make me blush. The day Mama arrived, I ran around pulling all the nude paintings down and dressing some of the controversial sculptures with cheesecloth shawls, which Mama found hilarious. She did not seem to mind the artwork, and became quite fond of my flatmate whom she found sweet and generous.

Papa sent a letter describing Peru as a nation in flames, and saying that he missed her very much. He also said that one of Aunt Dorita's sons was joining the secret service to fight terrorism, while our childhood neighbour had joined the revolution; worse even, that toilet paper had become unavailable. As she folded the letter, I sensed her nostalgia for the things she missed – her home visits and daily afternoon strolls in the local park, breathing the scent of petunias, and holding Papa's hand. I tried to compensate the best way I could by taking her to my favourite café opposite Bondi Beach. She took the plunge and dared to taste a *caffè latte* again, and a piece of the house speciality – apple strudel. We watched the sea, the giant waves framed by sparkling sand and deep blue sky. Reminiscing about her early days in Lima, she gazed at the swell that ebbed and flowed in a perennial dance of aquamarine hills exploding dots of white into the air.

She said the sky was the colour of goodness, the hue of our heart's true expression, as harboured in our dreams. Our lives were separated by the strip of ocean that lay before us.

Her proximity revived my soul. In the tone of her voice, I could hear the enchanting hum of the jungle; smell the chili in the air, and the oregano in the chicken soup; and taste my favourite ice cream, Lucuma, and cinnamon in my tea. Fanned by the wind of love we discussed the secrets of life and the makings of spirit; the deeds of successful relationships, and about the things that were changing in us.

'Do you remember my dream about a temple in the mountains?' Mama said. She had been on a pilgrimage to Japan to visit a Buddhist temple a couple of years before. She described the monks in their starched robes and the giant gongs that marked the beat of their chanting meditation. She was still the colourful raconteur, and her words reverberated with the sacred energy of the grand temple at the foot of Mount Fuji. I realised in that moment that my mother had become my goddess.

During her pilgrimage, she had discovered that her liver condition was one of the causes of her unresolved anger. She prayed, invoking universal forgiveness for her past shortcomings, for her impatience, and for her frustration. For having buried her pain when she had no time to cry because she had to sell bananas in the market. The trip to Japan helped her dissolve some of her anger. She developed an even stronger determination to succeed in life, to keep a vigil on her liver until she decided it was time to go. I bowed to her wisdom, like an initiate does to a master. Reassured by her strength and courage, I confessed that I, on the other hand, was filled with insecurities. 'My life seems to have lost its route,' I cried.

I was going through a rough patch, exhausted from fighting my demons – my doubts and my fear of failure. I felt very alone, and not even romantic liaisons gave my heart a spark. 'Don't worry, my sweetheart,' she whispered, 'you are not alone. Fear is part of the process. Knowing you are not alone helps.' As she spoke about the need to fulfil one's dreams, and her belief that nothing is impossible, my fears settled. The woman I had before my eyes was not the Mama of my early adolescence, with her tensions and her apprehensions, but a woman giving birth to her own power. I knew it was not just her prayers that had transformed her, but her will to change, and live longer – longer than the gypsy had forecast. Helped by healthy food and herbal tea, her smile had returned, along with her ability to tell tales, although these no longer came from the green In-between, but from a shining heart. It did not take Mama long to persuade me to take up her spiritual practice. It was her example that had persuaded me, more than her words. She was so happy and at ease, while I, in contrast, was shaking with fatigue and an unhealthy trepidation.

Mama's trip came to an end and she boarded a plane bound for the other side of the ocean, leaving me with the taste of ripe papaya and an incomparable sadness – but with a new layer of inner strength. With her guidance, I established a daily meditation routine designed to invigorate my spirit, cleanse my karma, and find the cause of my suffering. Perhaps I would see my dream more clearly, if I could dissolve suffering?

At university I discovered the heart of Australia, a space I had not found in ethnic clubs or in posh restaurants. I felt supported and stimulated, and most importantly I felt free. It was as if I had found a piece of myself that fitted. But as my life had been an ongoing road of tests and trials at university I also suffered. My drive to prove I had not made a mistake in choosing a new career often led me to despair. Mama had warned me that some karmic mud might rise as I began to meditate and chant. I did experience a series of dramatic episodes, one of which nearly took my flat away. I had moved to a smaller studio to meet the mortgages. The tenant who had rented my apartment claimed protected tenancy. An old legislation, now repealed, gave her the right to stay in the flat forever. As odd as it sounds it was true. There seemed to be some strange karma in my family about owning houses with unfinished business attached to them. I felt cheated by life but I decided to fight it. For a while I thought I was being punished – my old Catholic fears had come to the fore. Eventually the penumbra lifted and the wheel of life turned. I saw the bright side of life the day I got my first job in the media, a week before I was due to finish my degree. It was no coincidence that it was at the multicultural radio station where I had once been asked to broadcast. It was true: life does offer us chances.

The day I finished my last university paper I ran to visit my Ficus tree at sunrise, carrying a bottle of champagne. 'Here, old boy,' I said. 'We made it.' I skipped across the park barefoot, happy as a bird saluting the birth of a new day, my heart about to burst. Never mind the heavy bags under my eyes or aching kidneys, I had finally made it. The first door of my dream had opened. I sat under my tree and drank the whole bottle, pouring some onto the roots, for it is our tradition to offer the land our best brew when prosperity visits.

In my new job, I began an affair with the spirit of my creativity. I discovered another world creating sound effects and mixing them with dramatic text. I captured the magician who enlivened the dramas inside the radio set. My creativity burst forth like water out of a crumbling dam. For a while, the void in my heart was filled. Working in Spanish was a cultural renaissance for me. My life became filled with colourful vests, pan flutes, congas and *charangos,* the Indian guitar. On the airwaves we talked about social injustice in poor countries and painted a better world with our intentions. I regained the connection with my home land, and realised how much the cultural isolation I had imposed on myself had caused my fatigue. Leaving one's land is like abandoning a dear lover for whom the heart still throbs. Listening to my music in the morning after meditating made me feel loved again.

At the radio station we lived in a kind of multilingual village within a cluster of sounds and egos that often defied description. I created programs for people from regions as diverse as the jungles of Central America, the plains of Argentina, and the Catalonian region of Spain. I fell in love with everything Latin American, including touring singers who, like my Grandad Desiderio, expressed Latin America's soul. I learned to use melodies, tones and sound effects to invoke feelings, colours and sensations on air. I saw my job as a task with a purpose and in it I found a piece of my true self.

Mama's health deteriorated gradually while I was at university, and in my first years as a journalist. I visited her in Peru as often as I could, because despite my belief in reincarnation, I dreaded the final moment. Mama, on the other hand, approached death with calmness. The question of where her soul would rest was of no concern to her – what was important to her was that it would return to its source. There was little difference between the Blue Cat and the soul's journey to the In-between, and the teachings of Buddhism.

Sensing Mama's death began to affect me. I was assaulted by migraines and fatigue, and I dreaded the experience of transition. I went back to using herbs, poultices and tinctures, the way we did at home, to treat my problems. At this time I was diagnosed with a muscle injury that affected the tendons in my arm, limiting the amount of typing I could do. My left hand had become almost limp, with tingling nerves and cramped muscles. I froze in fear. It was the last problem I needed if I was going to earn my living as a journalist. A friend took me to the gym, where I learned to work with weights to develop stronger muscles in my shoulders. Eventually the pain subsided. As a sign of my gratitude to the universe, I promised myself that I would always try to maintain a global perspective in my work.

Not long after this, I was leaving a union meeting at work when a man with a kind face approached me and said that he liked the way I promoted my ideas. 'You could convince a lemming not to jump,' he joked. His face was clear, his smile comforting, and his words empowering. I was so moved that I told him he reminded me of my Ficus tree, 'a comforting old boy who likes champagne'. We began a friendship based on mutual respect and admiration, and eventually he introduced me to the world of television, a world I had never imagined I would enter. The day I was told that I had a job with the television news I rang home to tell Mama. I wanted so much to share my successes with her, to give her one more reason for optimism, so she would stay with us a little bit longer. In Sydney, my brother Roy's family made a cake in the shape of a television screen, and on it we wrote 'Thanks' in big letters, so the cosmos could read it. Roy had immigrated to Australia a couple of years after I left Peru.

Life spares no one bad news, and, as expected, I began to hear the rustle of the Blue Cat as it approached our home in Lima. The phone rang in the middle of the night; the voice of my brother Luis from Peru announced that Mama could go any moment. She was not in a coma yet, but it would be good if I came home to be with her. One is never prepared for such a call. I was just about to leave for Europe, to take my first holiday in a very long time. I changed my ticket, and flew to Peru to see my Mama. The future seemed grey to me the day I arrived in Lima. The atmosphere was dark, as if the bells in my hometown tolled for nobody any more. In my heart I could hear the wind carrying the wails of grief from the other side of the mountains, vibrations that joined the echoes of my pain. At the airport, I sniffed the scent of mistrust, fear and suspicion that filled the air. The country was in a state of civil war. The sound of bullets and explosions jolted the city most evenings.

Mama was much thinner than I had ever seen her, but still possessed all her abilities and senses. I hugged her, showering her with as much attention as I could, while trying to rekindle the memories of a colourful past, of strength and courage, of humour and music. There was a dull ring around her former glow. My aunts Techa and Lisa came to see her often, bringing bowls of fat-free chicken soup and boiled vegetables, and news of their children and grandchildren.

'Now, Rosita, your daughter is here and you are going to get better,' said Aunt Lisa.

A film of dust now covered the altar my mother had built with such care and devotion. Mama and I lit candles, cleansed the corners of the room with incense, and talked about the advice from her friend Bufeo, about the middle way and finding the right measure in life. I rested my head against her heart and heard the rumblings of her deeply rooted fears, the echo of the call from the other side, the rustle of the leaves as the Blue Cat moved through the forest. But we still had time to giggle, and perhaps taste one more slice of vanilla cake together.

One balmy afternoon when the clouds parted, allowing the sky to reveal its true colours, Mama felt strong enough to take a stroll across the park. Slowly and with care we walked around the park, reminiscing, and admiring the begonias, petunias and impatiens. I asked someone to take a photograph of the two of us standing by the side of a pine tree that I had passed every day on the way home from school. It now framed one of the final moments between Mama and me. It was one of the most heart-wrenching moments in my life. We sauntered home down a flower-rimmed path, gingerly taking one step after another, me supporting her, as a mother holds a toddler taking its first steps.

Mama fell into a coma, and I thought it was the end. I cradled her limp body and wept, feeling totally lost. I begged for her forgiveness for the times I had hurt her; for having gone and not come back. I felt for Papa, who had loyally supported Mama for years, even kneeling by her side in the prayer room, though he hardly understood the prayers. 'Alberto, wake up. It's time for our morning meditation,' she had called to him each day for more than two decades. And he had always been there – dusting the shrine, lighting the candles and humming mantras with her. Now he wanted to do everything possible to ease her pain, and to keep her with us a bit longer, perhaps long enough to celebrate another birthday. She was now sixty-six.

Secretly, too, I wanted my father to help me deal with the pain, to wipe my tears at night and tell me there was nothing to fear. By the kitchen table, we drank coffee and held hands in silence. He was still the good-looking man I had always watched with pride dancing with Mama at parties in the old neighbourhood. Time had bent his distinguished frame a little, creased his brown skin, and added some weight to his walk. But time and suffering had also added a rim of compassion to his eyes. With the help of doctors, Mama came out of her coma, though she was still gravely ill.

My dreams of living in an Australian garden flat with my parents had disintegrated. A little voice inside told me that I was a failure, for my parents were still living in a house that they did not have property titles to. Mama's most important mission had not been completed, and she was dying. I helped her bathe in the same green tub in which she had so often bathed me. After pouring in some lavender oil, whilst singing childhood melodies, I softly massaged her back and rinsed her hair with special Amazon flower shampoo that her cousin Rosa the pianist had sent from Iquitos. Although she had the looks and the strength of a little bird, she asked me to spray French cologne all over her body before she went to bed. 'If I'm going to enter the next life, it is better that I smell good,' she giggled softly, remembering how Doña Panchita had rubbed her body with rose water before she died in her sleep.

I spent a couple of months with Mama, not knowing how long she would last. One night a week before I left home, I carried her in my arms and placed her on a chair by my side in front of her shrine. I chanted in her name, asking the universe to guide her in this most difficult period. My sobs took my voice away, and she held my hand feebly. She had transferred her soft power to me. The light in her heart was very dull now, and I could feel the life force trickling out of her.

A heavy fog shrouded my feelings, and at night I began to dream of waves of sand suffocating me. Roy arrived from Australia to see Mama, and his visit gave her renewed zest. And I had to return to Sydney, and my job.

Late one night, after I had been home in Lima for three months, I came downstairs with my small suitcase; around my neck I wore a gold chain and a pendant of the Virgin and the Sacred Child. It was a family heirloom that Mama had passed on to me during my visit. At the bottom of the stairs, I saw Mama curled up on the blue couch, which still had the clear plastic cover on it from the day we bought it. She was wearing a pastel pink robe; she looked like a frail rose. I was used to saying goodbye, but this time I feared I would collapse. I wished I could stay with her until she took her last breath. I squeezed her against my chest – our last embrace. The girl inside me kicked in rebellion, wanting to stay, but the woman in me picked up my suitcase and walked to the door. I turned around for a last glimpse of Mama, who had risen, and now stood by the door, held up by Papa's arms. The light above the door caught the pink of her robe, and I remembered her words: 'As long as the colours of the rainbow appear in the sky after a storm, we will always be together.'

Mama lived for several months more but we knew she could go any time. When my brother Roy conveyed the news, I ran out to the garden, hoping to catch a glimpse of a falling star. A loud scream from inside my chest shattered the silence. I felt as if a silver thread that had always linked me to her sparkling life had snapped. Her passing was the biggest loss I had ever experienced. She was my mother, and my goddess, and now she was gone.

THE RITUAL

ALTHOUGH MAMA WAS no longer living on this planet, her spirit had moved into my heart. Her face appeared in my mind every time I felt a tapping behind my chest. I began writing letters to her on my computer, hoping that this device would carry my messages beyond space and time. Sometimes I wrote at night, with a candle on one side of the computer, and her sepia photograph on the other. If the soul lived eternally, I was sure that Mama would get my messages. In a way, I felt she understood me more now that she had crossed to the other side, from where she watched and helped, without judgment. Her funeral had been Christian, because with Mama gone, Papa went back to Christianity. It was easier, he thought. So the local priest was asked to give Mama the spiritual farewell. I did not mind.

Mama's death encouraged me to look deeper into the mysterious and the metaphysical. I read books on the occult, spending many a weekend snuggled in the library, soaking up ancient knowledge and superstition. The last decade of the century was upon us, and indige-nous wisdom was being accorded a renewed respect. I began to listen to the call of the Indian within me.

One Sunday in August 1987, I walked into the newsroom and found a note pinned above my desk from my boss. It said that 'some loonies were gathering at Bronte Beach for a convergence of sorts. It was an international event with good pictures. Perhaps a good story for colours.' He wanted me to cover it. How strange, I thought. My boss had always been a champion skeptic. I went and did the story, using my best resource: my optimism. It was the day of the Harmonic Convergence. According to a Mayan prophesy, it was the beginning of the Aquarian age – the door to a more humanistic era. People from all over the world gathered at key spots around the planet; in Australia, these included Uluru, Mount Warning and Bronte Beach. Their aim was to meditate 'to create good vibrations at this crucial moment'. I was curious about it. The event predicted huge changes. By sheer coincidence, a week later, the stock market crashed.

To maintain my credibility, I made sure I kept my interest in metaphysics and spiritual development separate from my work in political affairs. Sometimes I preferred to work on assignments with less analysis and more humanistic feeling. My boss did not like 'stories of colour', 'the touchy feely ones' and he sometimes called me the 'Ethnic Crusader'. During an interview with an important politician I asked the question: 'What would you change should you be given the power to change the world?' He became flustered and asked me to come down to earth. 'You are a silly girl,' he said, 'of course I would never have this power. Where are you coming from?' I enjoyed playing the 'good guy' as often as I could, trying to expose racism, discrimination, homelessness, unemployment, domestic violence, child abuse and other social bacteria. After nearly a decade in journalism, I felt little had changed. The world continued to have the same ills, and victims were still disempowered. The stories of tragedies and tribulations repeated themselves. The only difference was that the most recent disaster always seemed to be bigger than the last. 'Could I be doing more?' I often asked myself.

Not far from the park where my Ficus tree stood there was a second-hand book shop packed with publications about ancient knowledge; about the things Loretta and Doña Santitos had talked about. I spent incalculable hours on my knees, covered in dust, searching, until I found a book that really filled my heart with curiosity. It was *The Secret of the Andes*, and it spoke of a Golden Disk that lay under a monastery in Cusco, in Peru. It was believed that the Golden Disk held the secrets of nature, and that the person who came in contact with it would discover their true mission in life. It had the power to attune discordant energies, and impart clarity and wisdom.

I decided that I would search for the Golden Disk. Somehow I had a feeling that it was not really a metal disk, but perhaps a point of light, a source of the divine spark. I managed to convince the television station to support my research so that I could possibly make a documentary on it, and left for Peru.

When I arrived home, I found Papa immersed in the echoes of the past. He looked as if he was trying to summon the Grim Reaper. We drank coffee together in the empty kitchen where he sat with glazed eyes. He agreed that I should go and find my Golden Disk; perhaps it would help me find a husband, too.

I travelled to Cusco, where the snow was melting, running like milk down the ragged mountains. The sun cast orange beams of light over the city of the ancient Incas. From a window in the house where I was staying, I looked at the view with wonder, and with reverence. The next day, I set out, looking for clues. In the square, Indian kids sold colourful artifacts. 'One little souvenir, please, mister, to make you sexy.' And each of us visitors bought that one little souvenir, to feel less guilty for the things we had and they did not. But as soon as the guilt had been purged, the next little Indian child would pop out of nowhere with a bag of pretty wares. The sound of pan flutes filled the air, and I sat in the middle of the plaza, wondering what my next step should be. I pulled a note pad out of my bag and wrote a few lines. Then suddenly my eye caught a box of shining jewellery. 'Would you like some, miss?' said the jewellery seller, a man with eyes as bright as his pieces of silver and precious crystals. I was so impressed with his jewellery that I promised I would buy all my presents from him before I left town. He nodded, and reassured me that he would definitely find me before I left, because he knew what I was looking for.

The next morning, I had breakfast in a cafeteria and asked the waitress whether she knew of any agency that dealt with mystic rituals. Most waitresses were tourism students or graduates, and the girl knew exactly what I wanted and pointed me in the right direction. I strode quickly along the cobbled streets, tripping over sleeping dogs, crossing puddles, and greeting women on their way to the markets. I turned a corner and bumped into the man with the box of jewellery. He smiled and said, 'Hey aren't you the lady who's going to take my earrings to Australia?' I explained why I was in a rush and told him that I was interested in mystical journeys. 'Me too,' he replied. I heard a chuckle from the sky. 'I am a Buddhist of the Nam Miojo Renge Kio,' he added. It could not be. I had found a Buddhist, named Angel, in the heart of a Catholic enclave. Cusco has more churches per capita than any other city in the world, and is also the capital of Indian mysticism. Angel was one of the few Buddhists in the area, and lived with his wife and three children not far from the main square. To test his honesty, I went to his home and kneeled before his altar, offering my respects – and silently apologising for my lack of trust. It was the same altar that my parents and I had at home. After exchanging traditional greetings and having a few refreshments, I confessed that I was searching for the Golden Disk. Did it exist? Angel did not answer straight away, but after several minutes, and a few *empanadas*, he spoke with the wisdom of those who are connected to their souls. 'Certain things are only visible to those who can see them,' he whispered, and with gleaming eyes, he added that he knew the person who could help me find my missing link. She was known as the Godmother.

We headed up through the hills to the Godmother's mudbrick shack, where we found her sitting on an old rattan rocking chair, knitting a red shawl and humming a local tune. It was as if she knew I was coming, because her eyes greeted me with a flash of recognition. She scooped some *chicha* out of a large earthenware jug and poured it into a mug with little llamas painted on it, and handed it to me. In the backyard a few chickens ran wild and picked at corn on the ground, while a mournful-looking dog stared at the clouds on the horizon. Angel left me alone with the Godmother, and I felt as if I had entered a familiar chamber, where the spirits of my ancestors dwelt. I told her of my search for the Golden Disk, and how I no longer knew my identity. 'Each morning, the mirror reveals a person I no longer know,' I said. Since Mama had died I had stopped wishing. I worked hard as a journalist to report other people's identities but I was confused about my own. I told her that I had never stopped loving Peru, that I still believed in Jesus and in the Incas, and that I found a lot of wisdom in Buddhism. I wanted to be an Australian, but sometimes I did not know whether I had the right. Perhaps finding the Golden Disk would help. The Godmother smiled and listened to every word. Then she got up from her rocking chair and slowly ambled over to a large chest of drawers which contained crystals of every colour, and feathers and stones from all over the world. She picked out a piece of turquoise and handed it to me. 'Take it and place it under your bed tonight,' she instructed me in a slow and husky voice. 'What is important is that you want to find the disk. It is up to you when and how you find it. I can only help you take the first step. Tonight, sit up all night and meditate on your life. It will help open your heart. Tomorrow, before dawn, we go to Tambomachay.' I wept deeply with a sadness that had sprung from unfathomable depths within me. A sadness that had been my constant companion. After I finished sobbing, I brought my hands together and bowed my head before her. I remembered Tambomachay from my school days – a shrine where the waters from the Great Fountain of Life washed away all the impurities of the girls who served in the Incan temples. I felt honoured.

That night, I thought of Mama's death, and how much I would have liked to have been with her when she took her last breath. I decided to recreate in my mind her last moments – only this time, I was there to take her to the final gateway by the hand, in the way she had guided me into this life one purple midnight. Lying under my poncho, I reconstructed her last moments, with love in my heart and clarity in my mind. Tears flooded down my cheeks as I visualised her life dripping away, discreetly vanishing. I imagined myself kneeling by her side under the flickering stars. Calmly, I watched as a host of sparks danced across the sky, and formed the outline of the Blue Cat, waiting patiently to carry out his sacred mission. I held her hand and kissed her forehead, as she exhaled her last gasp. Her life force soared into the sky like a thousand incandescent petals. The Blue Cat, with glowing whiskers and gleaming eyes, turned and carried Mama into the ocean of universal life. Her story is written in the lives of her children, and those who were touched by her imagination and courage.

I headed to the Godmother's place at dawn. She was already waiting for me, dressed in her shamanic gear of tunic, beads and feathers to greet the Inca gods. She held out a mug of herbal tea and a hot roll. 'Drink this. It will warm your memories and keep you going,' she said. The green valleys looked crisper than ever, and a string of multi-coloured skirts and shawls descended from the hills like a river of happiness. The Godmother loaded herself with backpacks full of crystals, rocks, small drums and wind instruments. She asked me to carry a set of multicoloured little balls, feathers, sticks and stones.

She carefully packed an empty ceramic bowl into her shoulder bag. 'It is for drinking the crystalline waters of Heaven, so you can rinse the heart of toxins,' she explained solemnly. A taxi took us close to Tambomachay, about eight kilometres from the main square, and we walked the remainder of the way because the pilgrimage of purification has to be done by foot. I knew the site very well, but that morning it felt special, and different. The time had come for me to uncover the secrets of life. Tambomachay is a stone structure made up of terraces ascending on its four sides. The Incas had built it in balance with the sacred cosmogony of their science. Inset on the back wall are four human-size alcoves, believed to be used by the Inca elders during their rites. Here, the story says, they communicated with their gods, or higher energies from other planets. Every wall is linked and a crystalline waterfall springs out from within a terrace naturally formed on top of the second wall. The icy waters fall into a natural pool in which the initiate is meant to bathe. The Godmother placed all the artifacts we had brought on top of the front terrace and asked me to go into one of the alcoves and meditate. I invoked the Inca gods for guidance. In my mind, the ceremony marked a turning point in my life as a woman who had chosen to live outside her homeland and its traditions, and now sought integration and recognition. I climbed into one of the alcoves, and prayed cross-legged, connecting my heart with the cosmic beat of life. After a few minutes of meditation, the Godmother asked me to come down, undress to a bare minimum, and wash myself under the spring, so that the water could cleanse me of all impurities. Under the icy stream that gushed out from the depths of the mountain and burst through nozzles on the stone walls, my skin froze and turned purple, but I felt invigorated. The Godmother played her drums and did a traditional shamanic dance, singing songs that seemed like melodies from the sky. In a quasi-trance, I let my arms sway. She stopped singing and filled the bowl she had brought specially with water from the spring. I drank from it, and the pure water cleared all my confusions, and left a refreshing taste in my mouth. For a moment, my rational mind questioned what I was doing taking part in this bizarre circus of sorts. But my heart pushed the thought away. The early morning heat soon dried my body, and we placed the fruit and drinks we had brought at the foot of the terrace, for no ritual is ever complete without an offering from the heart. I kneeled before the sun and promised I would live a life of honesty and courage, always in harmony with the universal law of life. I would tread the path of equilibrium and stability as much as I could; to me, achieving balance has always been an effort.

'What will happen now?' I asked, not sure what to expect.

'The doors of your true path are now open,' said the Godmother. 'You will integrate all the issues that have been nagging you.' We sat down on the grass, and she clasped my hands and asked me to listen carefully. 'Observe everything that happens from now on with the eyes of a condor, and listen to the voice of life with the ears of a puma, for you have been unblocked, and will see right through people with the wisdom of the snake. The veils over your eyes have been removed.' In Inca times, the condor was a symbol of freedom, the puma of strength, and the snake of wisdom.

We ambled slowly back to the city, drums over my shoulders and feathers on my head. I was euphoric, keen to start my new adventure, and totally unaware of what lay ahead. What the Godmother did not tell me was that in the process of true cleansing, I would meet my fears and demons face to face.

After lunch, while enjoying the serene sun of the afternoon, I asked the Godmother to describe the steps of a sacred journey – a journey of the soul. To start a sacred journey, she said, one has to go back home, to one's centre. The next step is to follow the heart. The third is to let go of all that is unnecessary. The fourth is to face one's own demons – one's own darkness, which comes in the form of doubts and persecution. The final step, once the journey is completed, is to review your progress and share your story with others.

GOING HOME

I ARRIVED BACK in Sydney feeling like a maid under a golden spell. It was now easier for me to look inside my heart, to peer through the veils of sadness, and let the sun warm the dark corners of my soul. I could smell the essence of real love coming my way, and tasted a different flavour of happiness, one free of the rush of expectation. I realise now that the significance of the ritual correlated to the seriousness with which I took it. Who knows how many rituals were held that day, and how many lives were transformed. Mine certainly was. My soul had sat by the river of life to receive the final word from Bufeo Colorado. I began to weave dreams again, dreams of having children, a big house and a husband; perhaps write a book. Of this I had never thought myself capable. Instead, I had fallen in love with people who wanted to write books, because they complemented my longings. My inner eye had become a lot sharper, and the outline of my future began to appear. It was all going to be up to me.

I had developed a special friendship with a Peruvian-born woman living in Sydney. Her name was Zoyla, and she was like a mother to me, but a mother whose emotional turmoil I had not inherited. I met her while rehearsing to appear in a Spanish play in Sydney. I was to play a funeral mistress, a woman in a village in Spain in the nineteenth century who was tormented by loneliness and death all around, and driven to alcohol. But my voice had not been able to reproduce the nature of her pain and her misery. No matter how much I rehearsed. My reporter's voice, which I had worked so hard to obtain with elocution lessons, kept creeping in during rehearsals, driving the director mad. Zoyla came to the rescue: 'Take yourself down to the core of your guts. Imagine yourself drenched in the clotted mud of your sorrows. Feel the weight of the shovel as you dig deep – deep into your own loneliness. Feel the burning alcohol down your throat, feel the pain of being an outcast, feel the anger, and then speak.' The voice came out in the end and I delivered my best, although my learned reporting voice suffered a bit.

I became close to Zoyla, with whom I spent evenings by candle light rehearsing and discussing the meaning of life. She was a Catholic and a Rosicrucian, a woman who believed that the way to find God inside was to live in the spirit of service. 'You must always have a smile to give, for it is the window of our feelings. It's your best gift,' she said. In Peru, Zoyla had been a friend of Aunt Arnaldo's official wife, and therefore knew of the Bresciani family. Whenever she went back there, she visited my family, and my mother had been very fond of her. By the grace of the universe, she had been in Lima during Mama's final days and had visited her frequently, to give her massages and because she knew it would fill my heart with comfort. On her death bed, Mama asked Zoyla to guide me, to hold the torch above my head when life lost its colour, to counsel me if ever my heart was besieged by darkness. And Zoyla had promised.

I had a habit of letting my apartment out and moving in with other people in order to never lose the experience of sharing. It helped bring back the memories of my childhood in the old block.

When I returned from Peru, Zoyla and I shared an old Spanish-style house not too far from the city. We had Fijian neighbours living downstairs who kept ducks, chickens and a small goat on the lawn at the back of the house. I was not sure whether this was legal in an urban zone, but I did not mind at all; on the contrary, I loved the crowing of the rooster in the morning and the squabbling of the ducklings as they were fed. The scene conjured up a memory of Papa bringing down fresh hen's eggs from the coop on our roof, not far from Doña Panchita's duck cage.

On my first night back from Peru, I showered Zoyla with presents and anecdotes about the Godmother and my search for the Golden Disk. 'This is the vessel of happiness,' I said giving her the bowl the Godmother had used for the ritual. We talked, and cooked duck with coriander sauce and rice with green peas – our own evening ritual. Zoyla chortled as I told her how a group of Japanese tourists had clicked away with their cameras when the Godmother beat on a drum during the ritual. Zoyla always cheered my heart. My kitchen sessions with her were evocative of my aunts' visits; I loved watching her mix herbs and pound garlic in a black mortar she had brought from Peru, to keep the flavour of the land. She was a grandmother, but despite the generational difference, I liked to think that Zoyla and I were peas from the same pod. Zoyla pounded the garlic and ground herbs with such passion that the chickens got a bit restless, and the dogs howled. Outside the moon shone like a sugar-iced cake and the whole room seemed to lift above the ground. I spoke to her about the Pleiades, which according to the Godmother, was the star constellation from where the Inca gods had descended. The more I talked to Zoyla the more I felt the ritual had loosened blocks within myself.

My nieces sent letters with news that Papa was getting better, and going out a lot more. I had hoped that he would find a companion, but he preferred to live in the castle of his memories. Perhaps if he came to live in Australia? Perhaps if Zoyla was willing, they could be friends and rear chickens together in the backyard? But who was I to persuade him to change his mind? I had not attracted the type of man with whom I wanted to settle down, despite already being past thirty. To my family, I was becoming a spinster. Sometimes, I felt that it would have been easier to stay in Peru. The family would have recommended the best suitor – a respectable accountant – while my peers would have convinced me to have three children. At least. But moving to Australia seemed to have crossed the wiring of my heart, and I was on my own. I had become a modern woman, focused on her career, with long-term singlehood a deleterious side effect, and a lifestyle that left no time to analyse why I had attracted so many Mr Unsuitables. While my senses were satisfied with the onset of passion, there always came the dreaded emptiness. Despite physical closeness I always felt alone. I spent my free time practising yoga or reading politics or metaphysics. In Sydney, women were experiencing a severe scarcity of men who would make ideal partners. So much had changed since the seventies. The idea of such a shortage terrified me, for I thought I would keep on attracting Mr Big Ego, Mr Anxious, or Mr Know-all. There had to be some who were different, I told myself when I lit my candles at night. I had seen some happy women around, with very nice men by their side. There had to be one for me, I hoped, invoking the forces of the universe and scattering rose petals under my bed. Zoyla bathed me with sugar and lemon, and covered me with a pack of special aromatic herbs that would attract a good man.

Convinced that things would change, and following the first of the five steps given by the Godmother – to return home – I left Zoyla and went back to rip up the carpets, sand off the paint, and refurbish my whole apartment. In a show of cultural faithfulness, I sprinkled salt in all four corners to purify the ambience, dabbed a few drops of a herbal essence at the front door to invite protection, and splashed one wall in the kitchen with magenta paint to invoke the spirits of love and affection. Perhaps, in the renovating, I was also expressing some internal change. I felt that I was rediscovering some of my native self; my indigenous identity now went beyond falling for South

American musicians, or siding with the rebels. I was preparing the ground to plant new seeds, and I had faith that the old ways of my homeland would work. My motto became 'Rebuild, renovate, and revive'. Gone was the old brown carpet, in order to stop my dreams of being suffocated by a sand storm. The salmon-coloured walls were now all shades of blue. Blue would help my expression. I felt as if my house was turning into an ocean vessel to let my feelings sail. I wanted to start again, all over again.

Charged with this attitude, I returned to work with an added edge to my stories. I searched for meaning and feeling, rather than the sort of quantitative comparisons that often reduced humans to units of production in stories. I covered Sydney's increasing interest in spiritual exploration – whether it was yoga or tai-chi to release pent-up feelings, or left-hand writing to draw the inner child from the depths of the subconscious. The topics of suicide, depression and reconciliation were also high on my research list, and I began to look at the reasons why people had lost their spirit of motivation. Inside me there was a call to help restore and reconcile growing rifts in a changing society. I presented my proposal for a documentary about Cusco and the search for the Golden Disk, and it was accepted. In the words of the South American writer Paulo Coelho, the universe had conspired to help my initial enterprise, and I was thrilled. The Golden Disk had become a metaphor for my searches, and it led me into a space I had perhaps been far too scared to enter. A space of intimacy and vulnerability.

Sydney was looking even prettier to me. One afternoon, as I crossed the Harbour Bridge on my way to work, it seemed that the water sparkled more brightly than ever before, as if a giant opal had suddenly come alive. Boats swayed lazily, in a siesta mood, their sails like South American flutes intoning melodies in the wind. I was so glad to be alive, and in Sydney, the favourite child of nature. On this day my senses had acquired a peculiar sharpness. I arrived at work in sparkling spirits, and stood before the lift, watching how the receptionist smiled every time the phone rang – it gave the voice an added appeal, I had been told. A couple of girls with tanned legs and miniskirts stood next to me. There was slender man in a dark suit waiting too. A suit I had not seen before at the station, a conservative but elegant suit. And I watched him, in the way I often did, without people noticing me, with the eyes of a transparent butterfly. I watched his air of calmness, his body swaying from side to side subtly, his gaze clear as he explored his surroundings with innocent curiosity. I wondered who he was, what he was doing here. Inside the lift, my eyes met his – blue and mysterious, like fathomless pools. A buzz of recognition shot through my body, but I could not explain the feeling. I wanted to know who this man was. Urgently. But Mama used to say, 'Don't ever make a move without certainty.' So I stood next to him, silently, invisibly. His proximity took me to a very deep, very personal space where I felt comfortable. And then a voice came out of my mouth.

'Hi, I am Emilia,' I said. 'I haven't seen you here before.'

'My name is Richard Diack,' he replied. He had just started working at the station.

'Perhaps we should have coffee soon,' I suggested, and he said it would be a good idea.

He looked at me again. It was the moment that linked my fate to the big roller coaster of life. It was the beginning of a journey that raised my feelings to unbelievable peaks and also dragged them to unimaginable lows.

Instead of coffee, we met at the local Thai restaurant, from which we could see a slice of the harbour, and the pillars that held up the bridge. A view that had always made me appreciate the life I had in my new land. It was my favourite eatery, where journalists discussed media gossip, and professional secrets were rinsed in chardonnay. At a table dressed with a pink cloth and little silk flowers, we sat and got to know each other. He was a handsome man in an individual sort of way, with a red beard and long hair which contrasted with his conservative suit. He was Scottish, but had lived in Australia for some years – enough to grow to like the warm weather and the bush. He had just moved to Sydney from Melbourne; his favourite dish was Thai noodles; and he had a collection of Bob Marley records. I liked the way he spoke softly, but with confidence – though he talked much less than I did. 'Are you here with your family?' I asked, to avoid disappointment, and he said he had no family. He believed in Buddhism, but he did not meditate, for he felt that living fully was one form of meditation. He appeared very cultivated, and had a good knowledge of most of the developing world, the ancient gods of South America, and our writers, like Gabriel García Márquez. He had studied Spanish at school because he knew that one day he would be taken to South America 'to climb a big mountain'. Everything about him fascinated me – even the things I did not like so much, such as his old-fashioned suit with two vents at the back. It was the British style, he pointed out.

'But aren't you Scottish?' I asked, naively.

'Oh, yes,' he said, 'Scottish, and also *British*.' The 'British' stressed in a tone that told me I should never forget it. I apologised for my mistake; to a South American, Scottish people appeared to have a very separate identity from the English.

To smooth things over, I laughed and said, 'Well, I am an Inca princess on a rebirth mission.' He grinned. I explained that my first name was Sara, which means princess, but I much preferred to be called Emilia because it was synonymous with hard work. His eyes were always wide open as I spoke and that made me feel good. He told me he was in awe of the Machu Pichu mountains, and made me promise that one day I would take him there.

The day I met him, I joked with a colleague that I had seen an extra-terrestrial in the lift, for 'his gaze was out of this world!' The same colleague later came to tell me that my 'extraterrestrial friend' was the new chief. And that was not good. He had been brought in to fill a new position, which our union had found controversial. We had fought tooth and nail against it because we wanted the money to make more programs, as the station operated on a shoestring budget. His role was to transform our station into a self-reliant enterprise.

'Oh no. There must be a mistake,' I said.

'No mistake, my dear. You've been having lunch with the new axe man.'

I had told myself he could not be that bad if he liked Thai peasant food, Incas, and reggae. No chief talked about meditation and reggae, not in my experience. I staggered back to my desk, doubts stabbing at my romantic aspirations. Then I remembered that at lunch, in the tradition of an ardent unionist, I had spoken about our frustration with management. For a few days, the echoes of our conversation haunted me.

'You have no idea what management is like,' I had whispered across the table, staring into his blue eyes.

'No, I don't.'

'Well, let me tell you, they are a bunch of buffoons,' I had said, with the passion of a warrior.

'Really?' He had looked troubled.

My only solace was being able to tell Zoyla how I had blown my chances. She recommended valerian at night. The sun kept rising every day; the sky was still blue; and at least I'd had an opportunity to air my frustration. I continued with my research, my reports, and my renovations at home, pondering the mystery guy, who I could not take my mind off. He had been so very pleasant, so unassuming – there had to be a catch, I said to myself. If he called me at home I would find out more. If not, I would remember our lunch together as a nice gift. A week later, he did call and asked me out again. I said yes, and my life changed forever.

Richard and I spent endless evenings on the phone, talking about his background in social work and psychology, his work with West Indian youth in London, and his transfer to the realm of economics. He did not find his job at the station too difficult, because he had a strong will and did not focus on barriers. I was in awe of his resolve, because for me the path had been sprinkled with a few sharp thorns, many of which I had scattered myself. He confessed that he envied my job, for he too wanted to make a documentary one day. At home, he had a collection of cameras, some of them ancient representatives of better times, which he had collected from adolescence. We kept our meetings secret to avoid gossip. I spent a great deal of time show-ing him the treasures of the city; eating vanilla ice cream on the beach; and talking about trees, bark and pebbles at the Botanic Gar-dens. There was a cool serenity about him, a gentleness that conquered the stubbornness of my feelings. I could only surrender all my insecurities, and follow the call of my heart. The anxiety I used to feel every day had lulled; I had no more palpitations, or feelings of emotional dislocation. Real love had knocked on the door, and I could no longer refuse the call. It was as though he was the mirror of my soul; and in his gaze, I felt I had found the other side of myself. For the first time in my life, I realised how much I had masked the loneliness of my evenings with obsessive work and entertainment.

Our romance flourished, mainly during weekends at the Blue Mountains, where the firmament embraced a ragged horizon. We would sit on a small ridge, listening to the murmur of a waterfall that flowed like a curtain of fluid crystal. There, I would pour my heart out to him. His response was always tender, and in him I found gen-uine support. During these interludes, I felt like a maid who had found herself in some enchanted place. Love had attuned my heart to the In-between, and the tree-covered mountains became my luminous forest where I saw transparent butterflies. The glowing waterfalls became rushes of exuberant life bursting out of cracks in inhibitions, cascading down into hollows of apathy, breeding pools of fertility below. Lost in the thick of love, we would make up stories about the origin of the Blue Mountains, meander through the rainforest, and compare the hues of the mountain flowers. He knew about flowers, more than I did. He told me about the forest fungi, the geebungs and the grass trees, as well as the sundews, boronias and sunshine wattles. Each of them represented an emotion. Oh, there was one I did know: the waratah.

'See, I know this one, this red one, crimson, the colour of Latin passion,' I said with a twinkle in my eye. He fluttered his long and curly eyelashes, and gave me a cocky smile.

'Oh, yeah, and what do you think the colour of Scottish passion is?'

'Well, you tell me,' I replied. I had entered into a glistening world of scents and colours; I had discovered that the little girl with the pink ribbon was very much alive in my heart.

Embraced by the amber hue of autumn, we rolled into each other's hugs, blessing the angelic moment that had touched our lives. Richard became my best friend, my confidant, the face I had seen for years beyond the horizon. With total surrender, I spoke to him about my childhood, my sadness, my worshipping of my mother, and the sense of duty I had always felt towards her. I told him about my hidden resentment too, how I had masked my anger with aloofness when she became hysterical and flogged us in frustration because she could not flagellate the villains of her past. I cried on his shoulder, telling him how I had always felt like the odd one out, the bent rod in need of straightening, the warped creature that had to be reshaped. He laughed the day I told him how I had deliberately shocked the family at the age of nine, when I told my aunts that when Mocho, my dog, died I would much prefer to eat him, rather than burying him for the worms to eat. I only wanted to shock them out of their stuffiness, but they branded me a 'pet muncher', and a 'heathen from the Amazon', Mama did not understand my reasons for saying it, and my back bore the consequences. I was releasing memories, as if I had placed myself under a kind of therapy. Sipping port on my new blue floral couch, which I realised was in keeping with family tradition, I confessed to Richard about my abortion and the scar it had left: an indescribable sense of loss I had not yet reconciled. I had not felt a strong urge for motherhood since, perhaps because I still had this guilt. He listened, and nodded, like a perfect counsellor.

On the other hand, he found it hard to talk about his past, except to say that he always had a soft spot for Joni Mitchell, and had spent a lot of his adolescence bike riding and bush walking. I felt as if he had a pain locked inside, a pain he did not know was there. I suspected he too had his secrets, but I understood that men found it more difficult to talk about themselves. It had taken a long time for my father to open up to Mama, to cry on her shoulder and release his sorrows. It would take some time for Richard, too. We grew closer, and I thanked life for this gift, acknowledging that it had been worth the long period of celibacy to which I had subjected myself.

But as Richard and I satisfied our yearning for closeness in a land where neither of us had family, a ghost hovered, a mysterious force that affected our complete intimacy. His work was so intense that it absorbed most of his energy, leaving his life force at its lowest ebb during our evenings of passion. But Richard preferred to ignore it. We were very different people, with very different traditions and expectations. Richard was too shy to admit there was something in him that needed fixing. I was too. We were both fatigued and trying to impress each other. We tried lots of soothing meditation, massages, herbal concoctions and sessions with a specialist counsellor and when we did connect, when we touched our raw essence, we felt we were part of each other. With him I also learned to make love with the

heart. I loved him for the essence my soul had sensed inside him –
although my mind often questioned it. My heart always melted when
I received the bunch of long-stemmed red roses he sent to the station
every month to celebrate our first meeting. His first gift to me was a
beautiful pictorial book about the Blue Mountains, in which he had
inscribed, '*Para Emilita con amor,* To Emilia with love'.

Richard had been a loner and a rebel in his youth, and he had refused
to cut his hair above shoulder-length for forty years. He was born one
winter morning under the sign of Aquarius, on a cold day when the
trees were dressed in snow. His birthplace was the granite city of
Aberdeen, in the north of Scotland. As time went by, I managed to
persuade him to tell me his favourite childhood memories. I visualised
him in the woodlands, where the Merlin of his mythical past had sauntered about the forests picking magic leaves and spreading ancient
wisdom. He would ride his bike for hours, he said, past the inquisitive
gaze of sheep, rolling over green plains, past pine trees and misty hills.
He said his Mama always wanted him to cut his hair, and would have
preferred it if he'd been born blond, like his younger sister. He was
glad he had red hair – lots of it – and he let it flow in the wind as he
rode, accompanied by his thoughts, wrapped in layers of wool, battling
his teenage anxieties. He was partial to Zen philosophy, and wanted to
learn to launch an arrow with his eyes closed, and hit the target. In the
silence of the woodlands, he developed his own telepathic language
with nature; he was captivated by the sounds, the shades and the texture of the trees, and perhaps aware of the invisible thread that linked
him with the cosmic web. He had a stutter when he was young, but
had cured himself, although he never told me that. He did not like
imperfections. His sister told me when I saw her in London, years
later.

Richard's favourite pastime was to ride along a winding road,
guided by the cool wind from the North Sea – the same icy current

that had brought his ancestors, the Diack clan, from Scandinavia in the eighteenth century. His mother was twice widowed, and had worked hard to provide well for her five children, with private school education but little time for demonstrations of affection. We were both products of strong women who had struggled, and who had projected their insecurities onto us. Women of strong fabric, who were intolerant of failings, fiascos and handicaps; queens of safety and control, rulers at home, and eager for attention. And we both carried these blueprints in our cells.

Eventually, the cat got out of the bag, dragging our secret affair into the open. In a flash, the news was carried to every corner of the network. We had tried in vain to hide it, meeting clandestinely under the Harbour Bridge before driving home together after work, hiding like school kids or adulterous lovers. I now realised how silly it had been to build excuses about our relationship. Perhaps I did it because I did not believe it myself, or because I was embarrassed to admit I was going out with the boss who was shaking the foundations of the station that provided our living. Richard's proposed changes to the station were for the best, but despite our brief to promote social change in society, change was the thing that scared us the most.

Some of our colleagues celebrated our relationship, but others described me as a social climber and a gold digger. I was surprised, for Richard was no aristocrat, nor did he have money. Their gossip hit a nerve, and my insecurities came galloping back. The first challenge – to combat my need for outside approval – had appeared in my search for the Golden Disk, and I did not know how to handle it. But Richard was not worried; he could handle anything with a velvet glove. Every time he found my confidence wavering, he would say, 'Don't worry, happiness is the best revenge.'

In Peru, the 'Rebel Messiah' had taken the city of Cusco hostage with a concerted campaign of attacks. The population was riddled with fear and frustration, and the attacks had hit the tourism industry. It was almost 1992, and controversy had erupted about the planned celebration of the discovery of the American continent by Christopher Columbus 500 years earlier. Amongst other things, indigenous people resented the name given to the celebrations: 'A Meeting of Two Worlds'. To them, there had been no meeting of worlds – it was more like one had swallowed the other. Their rage and resentment ignited more rebellions across the southern continent. My plan to make a documentary on Cusco fell through due to lack of money, and I realised that reaching my goals was not going to be easy. I blamed the executive decision not to fund it on my affair with Richard, because I had noticed that people's attitudes towards me had changed. I feared that they no longer liked me. At times I asked myself whether my romance with Richard was worth pursuing, or whether it was going to take away all that I had worked so hard to achieve. But my heart would sulk every time I planned to put an end to it. The Godmother had taught me that the second stage of the journey was to follow my heart, no matter what happened.

I had begun to feel something stirring inside, something like an omen. 'There is something tight in my heart,' I confided to Zoyla. 'Something that says "No".' She soothed me, saying that real love was always frightening, and that she would continue to hold the torch above my head so I could see the path of this relationship more clearly. My fear would come and go, but when I looked into Richard's eyes, my self doubts dissolved. On the bright side, my friends outside work were fond of him, admiring his quiet poise and unassuming nature. They joked that we were like chalk and cheese. One day I gave him a bright ochre shirt as a gift, and he looked at it suspiciously. 'Do you expect me to wear this?' he said, and frowned. I told him that I knew colours had power, and that Mama had won battles with the right combination of hues. To my surprise, he put on the shirt, and liked what he saw in the mirror. Opportunity was all that he had been waiting for, I discovered. He gradually revealed a side of himself that was bright and chic. We spent time with friends, who were a mixed bunch of Iranians, Jews, Italians, Latinos, Asians and Anglo-Australians. Most of them lived on the eastern side of Sydney and loved philosophy, hot salami and coconut milk. Richard knew how to mix his own curry, and preferred to cook it himself, inspecting every ingredient for its quality. He surprised me with his ability to handle more chili than I could, and he adored raw fish with lime juice. Our romance was fertilised by pungent flavours and rich aromas on our table, and new colours in his wardrobe. He even cut his hair, and began to wear bright silk shirts, pleated gaberdine pants and suede shoes. But he never abandoned his fine wool double-vented jackets, his British trademark.

The Golden Disk was still in the back of my mind, but I decided to let my search rest for a while. The renovations to my house were complete, and Richard had bought a little house for himself not far from the city. His job had given him dark circles around his eyes, and sometimes we got into heated debates about work issues. Despite our concerted efforts, it was very difficult to leave work behind when we were at home. Staff complaints about the changes at the station were always reverberating around me, and to block them out, I buried my nose in my work. I was working on a weekly program called *Vox Populi*, 'The Voice of the People', which championed the cause of the underdog. We fought constantly for better budgets, and the lack of funding forced us to be versatile and creative in the extreme. I never lost an opportunity to tell Richard how important our work was, and that he must make sure that commercialisation did not crush our ideals and vision. And he always listened with attention.

FOLLOWING THE HEART

THERE IS A ceramic bowl on my shrine, a beautiful vessel that holds my prayer beads and other ritual accessories. There is a love story hidden in the clay, a story that weaves with another of a similar tone in the maternal lineage of my family. Three months after meeting Richard, I found myself in South Australia filming a profile of a Chilean-Australian artist whose work was impregnated with an aura of agelessness and magic. She had lived in Australia for a few years and I'd been told that her art pieces evoked the mystery of Inca lands, for she felt that the soil of this land spoke to her. Her work was ebullient, as if the shapes and images conveyed the force of every element, revealing the secrets held in the essence of its particles. Vases, urns and plates so alive. I watched her work, the cameras capturing the magic that oozed from her fingers as she kneaded and shaped her clay, then baked and purified it in the heat of life, in a process guided by her higher spirit. I called her 'The Weaver of Life'. One particular piece, a brown-and-bone-coloured bowl with a silver bird etched in the bottom, led me back to a familiar space in my heart. Where had I seen this bowl before?

'I see you can relate to it,' she said, standing next to me. I could sense her presence in the bowl.

'I don't know. It reminds me of something.'

'Something from home?' she probed. 'A ceremony?'

'I know. It's a wedding bowl.' The words just came out. I had not consciously remembered; the words had just drawn themselves on my lips and rolled out. The little bird etched inside had stirred something in me.

We filmed all of her art, asked every question that came to my mind, and later sat with her family to share a sumptuous meal. A job perk I had always enjoyed. We talked about the meaning of being multicultural, the painful process of our original roots coming together with our new environment, and the reward in seeing the emerging product. As the weaver of cultures, she kneaded and painted her own Dreaming, mixing Latin American soul with Australian soil. Mesmerised by her work, we headed home with a pile of well-wrapped vases, bowls and figurines. I deliberately did not select the bowl that had caught my attention, for a reason I could not explain, but as we left for the airport, her daughter handed me a parcel. It was the bowl, the wedding bowl. I touched it, and it seemed to greet me with the type of recognition that only comes from a breath exhaled at the beginning of time.

On my return, I found Richard more affectionate than ever. We had missed each other terribly. Although we had only known each other for a short time, a very deep bond had been established during my absence. I stretched out my arms, holding the bowl in both hands.

'This is a gift for you,' I said. His eyes gleamed with surprise.

He unwrapped it with genuine curiosity. 'It is a ritual wedding bowl,' I explained, showing him the painting inside. He took the bowl and gazed at it with admiration, tracing the outline of the bird with his fingers. He looked at me and said, 'We should use it then.' I was stunned. A proposal had not been my intention, at least not consciously. In retrospect, I realise how life repeats itself until we can make sense of it. The feathery prince on the island of Manaos had once handed Sarinha the bowl of life, and then he had vanished, pulling the maiden into the In-between. Sarita Davila handed a bowl of *masato paco* to Desiderio, and she had transcended to become the muse that inspired his music. Had I sensed the parallel at the time, I would have placed the bowl on my book case and given him a bottle of good red wine instead. But no, I did not place it on a shelf.

'Oh yes, we should use the bowl. But only when you say the magic word,' I replied.

One hour later he asked me to marry him, and I said yes. He had never been married before, so his proposal carried some weight. We opened a bottle of South Australian red wine and drank it out of the bowl. Inside it, the sleek, dark liquid seemed to change its texture; and it acquired a hypnotic bouquet and alluring appearance. We drank out of it in turns meeting each other's gaze, trying to find in the depth of our souls the origin of our story. The wine's tantalising warmth travelled through my body, soothing me, and incensing my memories. The red liquid slithered down like a serpent river moistening old nooks and arid territories. Soon, we fell to the floor, inebriated by our own impulses. Later, I told him I had seen a feline inside his eyes. A dark feline.

'It must be wedding jitters,' he teased.

'Perhaps,' I replied. We giggled.

I wanted to marry in 1992. To me, the ceremony would be symbolic of the encounter between two worlds, only this time, one world did not have to swallow the other. We were to be married in Antigua, where Richard's brother owned a large house; all of Richard's family would gather there. It was in the Caribbean, close to where Columbus had first set foot on American land. The news of the wedding made my family in Peru joyously happy. I wrote a letter to Mama on the computer, telling her how sad I was that she would not be there, and of my need for her to choose the colour of my wedding dress. Even though I could feel her presence inside me, I wanted to hug her round and soft body, snuggle against her bosom, shop with her for fabric for my gown, and have coffee and cake together once again. I swallowed my tears and listened to my heart for her answer. She suggested that I wear the gold chain and Mary and Jesus medallion, for protection. I had kept the chain in a box, waiting for a special moment. This was such a moment. Not by coincidence – for I do not believe in coincidences – my family had been planning a reunion at the end of the year, so Richard and I would travel to Peru, before heading to Antigua to be married. Richard would have the chance not only to meet my family, but also to climb Machu Pichu mountain, which he had dreamed about for so long. We would even have a ritual marriage there, at the top.

Everything seemed so perfect. The congratulations, the preparations, even the palpitations at four in the afternoon seemed to be exactly what a bride has to go through before a wedding. Richard bought me a beautiful ring that would serve as both an engagement and a wedding ring, as I wished. The band was thick, representing eternity. On the front, a delicate woven basket of gold held a large, dark garnet, the colour of recognition. I told him that the ring made me feel like a queen, and that one day I could even engrave my initials on the stone and use it as a seal. He was getting used to my whimsy, which at the beginning he had described as 'Banana syndrome'.

My dilemma was the kind of dress I should wear, as we would be marrying during the day in a hot country, and I wanted it to be practical. I remembered a story from my past. It was about a happy cicada, who one day found a coin under a leaf in the forest. The cicada wanted to get the best value for her money. She concluded that if she bought chocolate, it would soon be eaten; if she bought a new house, the envy of her friends would destroy it; and if she bought a trip somewhere in another jungle, her life would be at risk. After much consideration, the glamour bug decided on a dress – a red dress, in the green forest. Dolled up like a bug Barbie, she sat at the window of her tiny leaf house, to attract good fortune. The God of Time came past. Because her dress was new and glowing, he admired her, and granted her years of good health. The God of the Land saw how beautiful her tiny green house looked against her dress, and instructed nature to shield her well. Then came a wonderful minstrel bug that brought the magic of love to her heart. The happy cicada realised that her decision had been right, for all she needed was love. I decided that red would be the colour of my dress, for all I needed was love. I chose waratah red fabric, to ground myself in the land where I had come of age and had begun to manifest my dreams. Perhaps the waratah in the bush would not be lonely any more, I thought.

When we arrived in Lima a couple of weeks before Christmas, the whole family, buzzing with emotion and curiosity, met us at the airport. My brother and his family had made the trip from Australia with us. The wedding announcement had been so sudden, and I had such a reputation for being unpredictable, that my family had its doubts. Richard was closely, but discreetly, examined in accordance with our tradition. My sister-in-law observed the shade of his skin, the colour of his eyes, how he smiled, the texture of his teeth, the colour of his hair, his manners, what he wore, and how he wore it. My father gave him a fatherly embrace, and that was what was important to me.

We revelled in engagement parties and *pisco* sours. Richard felt good being called Ricardo, for it gave him a cavalier's aura. He was treated like a king, pampered by all the women of the clan; fed with dried fruit, nuts and spices; and honoured with the best of meats and the freshest of vegetables. I showed him my old city, intoxicated by the smell of history and red carnations, which became the symbol of our relationship, for the flower's down-to-earth quality and irresistible scent. On our first day we were taken in by petty swindlers while exchanging currency.

A couple of hours later, two young rascals snatched Richard's watch as we made our way back home. For the first time, I saw

Richard livid with anger. He was eager to chase the bandits, but I stopped him, for I knew such boys carried arms. To calm him down, I took him to the park near Aunt Renatta's house, in which I had played as a child with my cousin, Tato. We strolled silently, admiring the old-fashioned lamp posts and the winged cherubs; the trees all around us soothed his anger. Later, we bought his wedding ring – a gold band with Inca engravings on it. It pleased him greatly, but my family wondered why we would marry with different rings. 'It is to keep our individuality intact,' we said.

Richard was happy to take salsa lessons from my nieces. We stuffed ourselves on sautéed tripe with mint sauce, suckling pig with nut stuffing, beans with smoked bacon, and minestrone soup, for Papa insisted that Richard had to try our family's version. In the end, Richard became very ill. Not from overeating, but because he had picked up rubella from my niece during the flight to Australia. At first, we thought the red spots were insect bites, and confused his weakness with work fatigue. He lay limp on the bed in my former bedroom. The room was no longer pink, as I had painted it once, but yellow. The blinds were still there, the same ones that had kept my adolescent secrets. I could no longer see the park from the window because a house had gone up on the vacant lot. I could still look at the horizon, though, at the place where the face of Walter had so often loomed, beckoning and smiling. I looked into Richard's eyes and made a comparison. Was it possible that I had seen him in my childhood dreams? Anything was possible.

We waited a week before braving the mystic citadel of Machu Pichu, sanctuary of ancient civilisations. We climbed to the crest of Huay-napichu mountain to hold our private ceremony. It was symbolic of the heights we aimed to reach together, despite all odds, despite all troubles. We were aware of our differences, and had promised to build on our strengths together. When we made it to the top, he stretched his arms out to help me cross over. He had always said he was in my life 'to help me'. Feeling close to the firmament, we promised we would love each other forever, and that we would stand firm against adversity. We bowed to the presence of divine love, yielding to our soul-inscribed providence. We knew that the bond we linked on that mountain would never be broken, no matter what happened – perhaps because we were already one in soul.

In Antigua, I shook hands with my new relatives, instead of the kissing greeting traditional at home. They checked me out, wondering where I got my golden tan and my colourful clothes. A few days into the New Year, in 1992, we married under the glowing Caribbean sun before a local magistrate and eighteen guests. I crossed a green field towards the shrine we had set up for the wedding, my heart beating furiously, and tears in my eyes. Around my neck the gold medallion hung for protection. Deep in my heart I felt a strange sadness. I said, 'Yes', and we hugged, were toasted, and danced for twelve hours, until the moon reminded us there was honey in our cot: a traditional way of saying love was waiting for us in bed. We were staying in a four-storey apartment inside a windmill, which Richard's brother had refurbished for our honeymoon. On that night I had woken up thirsty in the middle of the night, and climbed down the spiral stair case to get a drink. As I came down a single drop of blood fell out of my body and stained one of the wooden steps with a dark red dot.

'My womb cried last night,' I said to Richard the next morning. 'I wonder why?'

My marriage to Richard lasted a short time on this earth, but has continued to be meaningful in the unfolding of my life. I had no idea that in symbolising our union as the meeting of two worlds, I was marking a period in which the two sides of myself would come together, face to face – where my resistance would be challenged by my will to find true happiness. We returned from Antigua to a world of accelerated activity, marked transition and urgent needs. As a married couple, we lived in my apartment. Some of Richard's English antique furniture blended harmoniously with the contemporary pieces I had acquired over the years. Life seemed to be determined to show us the doors to its different stages. Two of our close friends got married, a young friend died of AIDS, and another had a baby. The stress at work intensified; the changes to the station had pushed the staff to rebellion, and I felt caught in the firing line. I was torn between my loyalties to my union colleagues, and my support as a wife. Sometimes, as Richard's wife, I too was exposed to attacks. One day, in frustration, I resigned from the union, although I maintained my support for its principles. It was obvious, even to us, that in each other, we saw reflected a side we perhaps did not want to accept in ourselves. We would argue, but then we made up, and hugged and kissed; and then argued some more.

One morning, I got up and noticed a lump in my right cheek. It was a lump on a gland but the specialist recommended an operation, in case. There was a fifty per cent chance that my nerves might be affected and I would suffer Bell's palsy, where half my face would sag downwards. The specialist did not know whether the lump was a malignant tumour. Richard was as devastated as I was, and we cried together. It was rare for Richard to let me see his tears, but this time he did not care. My doctor suggested I seek a second opinion, and the next specialist recommended a biopsy. It hurt when they put the needle under my skin, but the pain was worth enduring as it prevented dangerous exploratory surgery. The week we spent waiting for the results brought us closer together, and the demands of his twelve-hour job took second place. Finally, the results revealed nothing worth worrying about. I had an inflammation of one of my facial glands, probably a product of undue anxiety. I sighed in relief and came out of hiding; I had been terrified that the loss of my facial muscles would be a test in my search for the Golden Disk.

Mental and emotional exhaustion assaulted Richard, too; he was tired of trying to justify himself and prove he was not the bad guy. He often collapsed into bed early at night so he could be ready to start early the next the morning. I resented his commitment to his job, and reminded him we were newlyweds. He said that his hectic lifestyle would last only until the end of the year. Then we would go to live abroad, somewhere in Southeast Asia. We would have babies, make a documentary, and write a book together. Zoyla counselled me as a South American elder would, recommending that I respect and honour Richard's devotion to performing his duties. When the rebel in me soared up from the depths of my frustration, I would cry inconsolably. To calm my nerves, I joined my girlfriends for coffee and let go of my disappointments. Sometimes Richard would go for a long drive or a bush walk alone, and come home revived. Sometimes we went together, or hugged in the blue couch and watched videos.

One day, while filming a story, I met a family counsellor and asked him to give us some tips on how best to handle work stress and family relations. He suggested that we stop communicating verbally for a period of time to see whether we could separate the world of resentment from the world of love, although he did not put it quite like that. We began to write notes to each other and cultivate silence around us. It was so very new to me, and so very relaxing. Embraced by silent peace, we began to enjoy the essence of ourselves in all its purity; we walked through the park in tranquillity, caressed by the scent of stillness, disentangling the demands of our busy lives. The period revived the happy moments, and fuelled our emotional and sexual intimacy. We were never as happy as when we let our hearts do the talking. But in a world where silence is not the norm, we were forced to go back to verbal mode after a week. Perhaps the sores of the past, and the burdens of the present, are carried on the crest of our verbal interactions. Perhaps the distortion of our lives is reflected in the vibration of our voices, which, like an invisible lance, pierce the other at their most vulnerable spot. Weeks later Richard agreed to have special tests done to measure his blood flow, because as the job demands intensified his problem with keeping an erection for long returned. The day he got the results he said everything was fine. All we had to do was wait until the end of the year. Then it would all be different. Oh, how I looked forward to that moment.

LETTING GO

SEVEN MONTHS AFTER our wedding, I found myself driving along a peaceful, tree-lined road to visit a spiritual healer. I had met her only a week before, at a televised forum on the topic of chance and coincidence. The audience included members of esoteric circles, students of metaphysics, clairvoyants, Buddhists, and of course the sceptics needed to fuel passionate debate in the name of good television. I spent most of the session fascinated by the radiance of a white stone ring worn by the woman sitting next to me, because the forum was disappointingly boring. Afterwards, I introduced myself, and told her I had a healthy interest in things beyond the boundaries of conventional reality. Her name was Dawn, and she was a clairvoyant with a long-established practice and her own radio program. We soon got into a hearty discussion about the spiritual awakening of the pre-millennium decade. Amongst many things Dawn said that the soul knew everything, including the time of one's death. The key is to get close to it and listen. I asked her whether I could see her again to continue our talk, and she kindly offered a complimentary past life regression session, a look behind the veils of the past.

That was how I came to be driving to her place one Saturday afternoon. I wanted to ask her about my soul connection with Richard. I wanted to know the source of my deep and strange familiarity with him, which I felt went beyond our present lives. I knew by then that no matter what happened, an aspect of our souls was joined. I intuited with great certainty that, despite our initial hurdles, we would always stick together through thick and thin. I felt he had come into my life to show me something I needed to learn, and the process of yielding to this awareness was at times filled with friction. I was not sure whether Dawn would be able to help, but I wanted to give it a chance. Despite my passionate attraction to all things mystical, I also had a touch of scepticism about those who claimed they were psychics, so when I left Richard that afternoon, I joked about the possibility of bringing home 'mystic gossip for dinner'.

At the end of a two-hour journey, I arrived at a beautiful white house with pastel louvre windows, colourful creepers on the wall and a harmonious atmosphere. I felt at ease, so when she offered me a session to penetrate my past, I said yes. She led me to a high-backed armchair. I rested my head against a soft floral cushion and closed my eyes. Gently, she guided me into a deep meditative state, which made it easy for me to enter the chamber of awareness that lay beneath my conscious mind. There was nothing to lose, I thought. As Dawn guided my breathing, I entered into a frame of mind similar to a dream state. Very relaxed, very tranquil, very liberating. My awareness began to go deeper and deeper, until images came into my head as clear as a movie on a huge screen. Then Dawn asked me to go to where my connection with Richard was, and I obeyed. Images appeared in slow motion. I felt I was underwater, swimming deep in the ocean, like a fish. I experienced the coolness of the water on my body. A part of me was enraptured by the feeling; the other observed the scene from the armchair. I saw colourful fish darting in and around a beautiful underwater garden. Suddenly, a dolphin appeared. It came my way, frolicking in the water. Then I realised I was one of its kind too. We played, whirling and jumping in unison. I felt very happy, so happy that tears welled up and rolled down my cheeks. Sitting in the armchair, I could feel the tears on my face, but could not, or did not want to, move my hands to wipe them off. My heart was in bliss, and I wanted to hold on to the moment a little longer. I described what I saw, and Dawn took notes. Suddenly my ecstasy was shattered by an enormous blast from somewhere deep in the ocean. I jolted in my seat. The sea became turbulent, a huge whirlpool formed, and then, a tidal wave crashed over me, followed by an eerie stillness. I felt something throw me out of the sea. The ocean disappeared, and a dried-up basin, surrounded by desert, was all that remained. My playmate had gone with the sea, and I felt a profound sense of loss and sadness. So intense was this feeling that I burst into sobs. Dawn asked me to open my eyes, and gave me a tissue to clean the mess that my eye make-up had made on my face. I felt profoundly sad, and very shy – and somehow apologetic for having experienced something so vividly.

Dawn explained later that perhaps I had touched a deep source of sadness. I might previously have lost touch with the deeply stored emotions that the sea represents. She explained that in some way Richard and I had experienced previous lives together, but had been violently separated. I listened with an open mind and then we had a cup of tea. Whether it had been under the sea or deep inside our hearts I knew I had seen Richard before. I said my farewells, thanking her for the gift. On the way home, I remembered an episode that had brought out intense fear and discomfort in Richard's expression, something I had rarely seen before. It had happened during our honeymoon in Antigua, when I followed him into the water. His eyes filled with panic when he noticed me trailing behind him. Annoyed, he ordered me to leave the water, or play in the shallows. He had never spoken to me like that before, and I was astonished. He warned me that the Caribbean waters could be treacherous. I went back to the shore, head down, feeling dejected and somehow embarrassed. After all, I had never been a good swimmer.

That night, over a succulent Thai dinner, I told Richard about my dream vision – the dolphins and the tidal wave.

'It's strange to have made this connection. The only dolphin I am familiar with is Mama's Bufeo Colorado,' I said to him.

'Perhaps it is trying to tell you something,' he said, then joked that it was better to have appeared as a dolphin than as a feathered prince.

The incident fortified the link between our hearts, and we talked about our plans – the house we would buy, the job he wanted to move to by the end of the year, the child we wanted to have. However, there was a cloud of melancholy in his gaze. When I asked him to tell me what had happened that day while I was away, he said he was just suffering from work overload. My heart felt warmer than ever before, and as we walked to the video shop, I held his hand tightly, thanking the spirits for giving us a renewed chance. Perhaps this moment will be meaningful for us, I thought. So meaningful that we will reorganise our priorities once and for all. Perhaps the counsellor who suggested I have a child and leave the station was right. At home, we snuggled in our favourite spot, the blue couch, and watched a video of Bob Marley, Richard's favourite. With the intuition that emerges from the most hidden of places, I picked up a notebook which I had titled *The Book of Life*, for it contained our reflections on life. I asked him to write some affirmations, as a seventh-month anniversary celebration. It would be like renewing our vows of love for each other. He gently complied, and we signed guided by our hearts, yet unconscious of what was to follow. We wrote the words: 'I believe in love. I believe in my higher self. I am open to love.'

In bed, I hugged him tight and we went to sleep, entwined as one.

No matter how fierce were the winds that blew the earlier pages of my life, it still hurts when I think of that episode. It hurts because I wish I knew at the time a little bit of what I know now. It hurts because I wish I had given a little bit more of myself to the relationship. It hurts, even when I know that I did my best under the circumstances; even then, I wish I had known a bit more at the time.

The next morning Richard woke up bright and early and got dressed to go bush walking. 'You are meeting your higher self today,' I said, naively referring to the vows we had signed. I was not going with him; I knew he needed a day of fresh air and silent meditation. He called it a day of regrouping.

A close friend, Ann Marie, who studied Spanish with Richard, came to have breakfast with me. I told her that we would be celebrating Mama's seventieth birthday the next day – even though she was dead – and that Richard would be cooking the curry that night. She left around midday, and I tidied up the house and went to a party with people from my old theatre group, where I had met Zoyla. After a paella session, and a few glasses of wine, someone discovered that my husband was bush walking alone and joked, 'Make sure he does not find a Red Riding Hood in the woods.' I replied that I was the only Red Riding Hood who mattered, and we all laughed. I drove Zoyla to a friend's place around sunset, then rushed home because Richard had been due around five. We were going to watch a report I had produced about two Latin American refugee women. When I got home, Richard was not there, so I prepared tea, placed two cups on the table, and sat by the window, eager to see his white car appear. He had always been punctual, and it was past six. I counted the white sedans that passed my window; I searched for his reddish-blond hair in every driver's seat; I surrendered to my anxiety and lit a cigarette. Then a second one, and a third, but his car did not appear. I waited with apprehension. I waited with my chest feeling tight and my eyes focused on the ticking of the clock. I waited until my eyes met the darkness in the sky, and the cars were reduced to headlights.

I waited for three hours, then I phoned my friend Cleo to tell her

I was worried. She worked at a Sydney radio station and promised to come as soon as she finished her broadcast. Around nine, I called the police. I waited by the window as the pounding in my chest accelerated, until I ached from fear, my muscles cramped. I lit candles for his protection. Two policemen came at around ten, took notes, and told me to wait twenty-four hours before beginning a search operation. I was outraged, because I was sure Richard was hurt somewhere. I phoned Richard's colleagues. I tried to visualise him in the bush. Then I prayed for his soul. Cleo arrived and waited with me. Panic charged through my whole body as the sun rose. No matter how long I waited, Richard would never come back. But still I waited, until a voice on the phone told me he was dead. It was four in the afternoon.

I kneeled on the floor, unable to understand the voice at the other end of the line. He was talking about a body found in the bush.

'Are you alone?' asked the policemen from the mountains. 'Can you come to identify the body?'

I shivered, and refused to accept that it was Richard's body. I could no longer feel the beating of my heart. There was a bitter taste in my mouth, very bitter. Cleo held me as I felt myself about to collapse. I wanted to sink into the ground, erase this moment of my life. I wanted to scream until the planet exploded. I felt terribly alone. In shock, feeling and acting like a zombie, I called my brother and told him that something horrible had happened. Brian, the station's managing director, was on his way to take me to the mountains. Cleo made cups of hot tea laced with drops of herbal medicine.

Two hours later, I sat in a long, white limousine bound for the mountains – my brother Roy on one side, Brian on the other. None of us wanted to believe that the body found lying by a tree was that of Richard Diack. We hoped there had been a mistake, a case of confused identity. With small talk, we tried to push away the looming reality that awaited us in the mountains. We remembered Richard – his jokes, his ideals, his patience. I prayed in silence, wishing that my reaction, once we got there, would be dignified. Richard had often accused me of being 'too emotional, too bananas'.

When we arrived at the Katoomba police station, the homicide detectives had not yet arrived, so we had to wait two hours before the body was shown to us. It was icy cold outside, and I felt the chill in every cell of my body. Roy stood by my side. All he said was, 'Be brave if it is him.' I was not sure I could be brave, so I asked Brian to identify the body on my behalf. When Brian came out of the room, I read the news on his face. It was Richard's body lying inside. He had been killed by a blow to the head. The mountains had taken him forever.

'No! *No!*' I screamed. I hugged my brother, choking on my sobs. I asked God, 'Why?' Roy held me tight. I wanted to disappear. Then I composed myself. An inner voice told me to be courageous; to be serene and dignified, for I was now Richard's widow. With a level of poise that surprised me, I gave the police a statement about my whereabouts on the day he was murdered. The police offered me the option to come back later to give my statement, but all I wanted was to be away from that scene, and dissolve into my pain. I did not want ever to return to the mountains. I felt they had stolen Richard from me, sucked his blood into the ground, drained his life forever. I blamed the mountains and the trees: how could they have let it happen when Richard had been so faithful to them? He had captured their beauty in the photographs that adorned our lounge room. How could they have watched silently as his killer took his last breath away?

Outside, shivering in the cold night, I looked up at the sky, and pledged that the goodness of my husband would never fade. Our love would live forever, even if I had to connect with him across dimensions. I promised I would honour his memory, and would never stop seeking to know the truth. There was nothing else I could do.

Over the following days, my mind felt like an autumn leaf, blown about by a cruel blizzard, lost in the rumble of people's exclamations of horror and sympathy. Every time a person uttered, 'Oh my God, how horrible!' the dagger of my grief pushed deeper into the wound. All I wanted was silence, and a hug. To protect myself, I grew an invisible bubble around me, which always made me feel cold. I was always freezing, with a bitter taste in my mouth. Friends and family came and went, bringing herbal potions and soothing pills to help me cry, to help me accept the blow, to help me walk again. Outside my home, journalists hovered, waiting for a shot, for a word, for a tear. I felt trapped and terrified; and I wished that everyone would leave and let me cry alone, until I had no more tears to cry.

The police came too, loaded with questions. Questions about Richard's life, my life. I told them as much as I could. Three days later Richard's car was recovered from a town two hours away from the death scene. His backpack was found a week later in between these two locations. The police had no inkling about what had happened, no clues, no fingerprints, no traces. They had ruled out the possibility of a mugging gone wrong, although his wallet and one of his cameras had been stolen. They said that the killing had the appearance of a conspiracy. They would not give me any more details, because, as his partner, I was under suspicion. At first I recoiled with horror at the suggestion, but I understood that it was procedure. I had no idea who would have wanted to kill Richard. The idea of a conspiracy made me think of secret agents, or secret information. I stopped myself from thinking about it, because such a line of thought only led me to the place where I worked – or to some much larger operation, of which I knew nothing.

Zoyla moved into my apartment for a while. At night, I stared at the ceiling, wondering how painful Richard's death had been, how much suffering he had undergone. Zoyla reassured me that 'his soul had left his body peacefully, because he had been under the stars, with no one pulling him back'. Whether I believed her or not, such words gave me peace. Lovingly, she reminded me that our time together, no matter how brief, had been of great value. Keeping her word to Mama, Zoyla waited until my heart was ready to understand that our souls had connected before our bodies had been separated again. 'Your souls knew,' she said, 'but it will take time for your mind to accept that.' I longed to see him walking through the door. I needed an explanation – how could he have gone so suddenly, so unexpectedly? I wanted to scream, but my rage was gagged by my own fear and remorse. I blamed myself for not being at the mountains with him, and for not having been happier during our marriage. I longed to see him in my dreams, to tap the memories of our eternal romance. I recalled the details of our last night together, the atmosphere in the Thai restaurant, the sound of his giggles, the scent of his breath when he kissed me goodnight before we went to bed.

One day he came back just before dawn and took me gliding to the spot where we had met, to the ascending lift of the station. There we had fused in one loving embrace. He had come to say goodbye from the other side of life. And I had accepted his farewell.

I dealt with my grief as it came. I felt burnt out inside. But my sense of duty had returned.

I had aged all of a sudden. At times, I felt nostalgia for the woman who had lived inside me before I met Richard, but it was impossible to go back. I felt one hundred years old, and buried in exhaustion. At night, I caressed his clothes and wore his silk shirts to bed. I played his music and began to write letters to him. I begged him to help me deal with my grief, with my emptiness, and my indignation.

Three weeks after Richard's death I returned to work. I wanted to appear as strong as I could. Brian had described my reaction as courageous, and I decided I would live up to those words. Anything less than that would be undignified, I had concluded, and Richard deserved my utter respect. I began to see his image in every corner of the building, and hear his voice on the phone, calling from his extension. Sometimes, I even saw his shadow waiting for me in the car park. I retraced our steps together under the bridge, silently observing the harbour through his eyes. I had entered a phantom world. The lump on my cheek returned, but I did not care any more. I was aware it had come to let me know my heart had been torn. The only needle that would mend such a tear was time. It would take time, and I would wait. If healing meant that I had to learn to endure my losses, then I would. I had to learn to let go.

Entering my office one day, I found a box full of Richard's belongings on my desk – his pens, his urgent work files, and a few computer disks, one of which was labelled 'Personal'. Looking at the urgent files, I thought how insignificant it all appeared in the light of my current reality. All the urgency that had stolen our time together lay in a few files that other people would now peruse when they got a chance. I flipped through his papers with nostalgia and scribbled his name on my note pad with his gold fountain pen. I checked the computer disks, hoping to find clues that would shed light on his death. In one of the disks labelled 'Personal' I found a few files, one of which had his and my name on it. They were notes to himself. Notes about me, and our relationship. Some were good, some not so good. It was some kind of sporadic diary, a sympathetic ear for when he felt frustrated. Some of the lines saddened me, lines keyed in anger.

I am sure she is crackers . . . she is a stranger in a world of western logic . . . she is irrational. She sometimes reminds me of a wasp or a nettle. Bright, colourful, exotic, but stingy.

He had told his computer the sort of things I would tell my girl-friends about him. But the diary was not all bad and my eyes moistened as I read other lines.

I do love her. It has been terribly hard for her to make it in another country. I could not have become a TV presenter in Peru. Her motivation appears unfailingly positive.

I felt moved, but my heart sank when I came across his notes about the results of his blood test. A shot of pain went through me as I read that he indeed had some problems with his circulation – something to do with arterial spasms. Why had he denied that he had a medical problem? I was so hurt that I did not want to read any more. A voice inside told me to let go, to let the universe dissolve the painful record. A subtle force guided my finger to the keyboard, and I pressed 'Delete'. There was no point in keeping these negative feelings alive, for I knew that whatever was left unresolved could fester. He was dead, he could not explain. He could not confirm or deny the writings on the disk. I gave it to one of his former secretaries to check the remaining files on it, business matters that I did not fully understand. And then I chose to let the whole affair rest. Time would heal.

I would have preferred to swallow a set of knives than to tell my father of Richard's death. My brother Roy phoned the news to the family, and they were devastated. Papa sobbed over the phone, sharing his pain with me – the excruciating loneliness of losing a loved one. I could feel his anguish from the other side of the ocean, and his astonishment at the type of death to which Richard had been subjected. In Australia of all places – a country he believed was safe and peaceful. The whole family in Peru came to console him, reassuring Papa that I had Mama's courage to pull through. Did I? I often wondered. Aunt Techa placed an image of the Purple Christ on a small shelf in my old bedroom, next to a photograph of me as a child. 'He saved her once, and he will save her now,' she said. She and Papa lit seven tea candles, one for every month of my marriage, sprayed my photo with holy water, and said a few prayers for protection. Papa took a bunch of red carnations to Mama's grave and asked her soul to guide me. He had placed the flowers around the marble plaque engraved with the Buddhist mantra she had chanted for years. I had had the plaque made during my last visit to Lima, to compensate for her Christian funeral. All gods would be happy now, Papa thought. With Mama gone, Papa had taken refuge in an Anglican group, where he learned to sing hymns of peace and glory.

One hundred days after his passing, I held a Buddhist ritual for Richard, as I believed his soul was about to enter his next destination, guided by the one thousand Buddhas. Around my shrine, my Buddhist and non-Buddhist friends kneeled in meditation; together we visualised the end of his journey into the light. The ceremony fortified my endurance, and helped me summon the courage to go on. What was important for me was to endow Richard's passage through this world with genuine significance, honouring the transient nature of his life and the eternity of his soul. The following weekend, despite my anguish about entering tainted grounds, I went to the mountains to scatter half of his ashes near the spot where he died. I placed them in the same bowl we had drunk wine from the day he asked me to marry him. I mixed the white dust with rose petals, and, with Ann Marie and two other friends, scattered his ashes. One by one, we held the grains of white dust in our hands, then let go, evoking his memory and sending the best of our wishes for his new life. As I held the bowl above my head to offer the earth the fragments of his physical life, a bolt of lightning rent the sky. Our eyes widened, but we made no comment, as there was no comment to be made. The universe had accepted our offering, and in the pouring rain, we ran to the spot where the local park ranger had prepared a native seedling for us to plant in Richard's name. Next to the seedling, a small plaque had been erected at my request. It read: 'This tree is nurtured by the spirit of Choclino.' That was Richard's nickname, which, in Inca language, means 'food for the gods'.

As I lived from ritual to ritual, in the back of my mind, Richard's killers haunted me. Theories abounded at work, theories that shed an ambiguous light on his memory. Some rumours claimed that his death was a crime of gay passion, while another concluded that he had made a secret discovery at work that had to with fraudulent operations and missing money. I did not know what to make of it all. Together with a colleague, I put together a feature article for one of the weekend papers. It was a whodunnit, produced in response to a series of strange happenings around me. Over a period of several months, an unknown person had been purchasing mail order items on my behalf, which were delivered to my house. Some of these items were plainly cruel, such as a baby's story book, or an insurance policy made out in favour of Richard, in the case of my death. Through this period, I forced myself to remain stoic. But at times I would burst into fits of anger, particularly when the detective in charge of Richard's murder investigation rang to seek more and more intimate details about me. On one occasion I felt so insulted that I rang his boss to complain. It was as if a time bomb had been planted inside me.

What kept me going was the new truth I had discovered now that Richard was on the other side. My sensitivity had been sharpened, and I began to experience meaning in everything around me, particularly things that reminded me of him. I sensed him in the rain tapping on the window, or the rustle of the wind at night, calling me to write letters to him on the computer. I knew he was always there, with a knowing I discovered in the depth of my suffering. Suffering had acquired a new dimension, and I was learning to see the other side of it. Sometimes I felt the vibrations of his soul around the house when I returned home from work. I would feel his presence across the table when I dined alone; and the essence of his love wiped my tears every time I looked at the photos of our wedding in Antigua, he wearing his blue tartan kilt and I the red waratah dress in flamenco style. Richard died one week after I had completed our wedding album. The copies I had made for our families still lay on top of the mahogany sideboard, next to the crystal decanters we had received as wedding gifts. One evening, when I came into the apartment at midnight, the sound system switched itself on and played the tune I had used at his funeral. I could not explain the incident rationally, for I had never programmed my sound system. There was no point in analysing it in the light of logic, because on the subject of death, there are still many unexplainable things.

I became drawn to people who suffered, for I found refuge in their pain. I felt as if I could read their emotions, sense their anger, smell their fear. If madness was part of grief, then I was grieving fully. But I told myself that as long as I could tell the time, nobody would lock me away. I felt that it was essential that no one doubted my psychological stability. I felt my job was at stake. If the evil spirits had taken Richard, I was not going to let them take any more. On my birthday, a single red rose was delivered to my desk, and I was sure Richard had sent it from the other side. The sender was a friend of mine. 'Well,' I said to myself, 'a dead person cannot buy flowers, so they use other people to do it.' Sometimes I'd wake up feeling as if a rain of feathers was pouring down from the sky above my head, but they never actually touched me.

To numb my pain, I acquired a renewed sense of purpose at work. I carried out my productions with increased devotion and a sharper edge. I felt as if my life was now dedicated exclusively to the spirit of human development, and I thrived in the feeling of cooperating to build a new society. My mission was to help society recognise itself. But in my obsession, I did not realise that my body was simply exhausted. I was not aware of the damage I was causing it. Most mornings began with huge health shakes that contained herbal stimulants, vitamins, and other wonder nutrients advertised as God's gift to energy. I took regular shots of vitamin B12, and had acupuncture needles placed in most energy-rousing spots. I became very creative in designing excuses to get out of social engagements, in order to save energy. Life seemed difficult for me until I ran into an old woman I had once interviewed for a program on nursing homes. When she saw me, she suggested I drink chicken soup and make offerings in the name of loved ones who had passed away. I did this and began to feel a little better.

Not all was tragedy, a few months after Richard's death I received an award for a report dealing with youth and sex, which had quite a bit of input from Richard, as he had been a youth counsellor in his earlier days. I felt the universe had smiled. Then followed another award for a story on youth and drugs, which asked parents to share the responsibility. I felt that Richard was working with me from the other side; a new window had been opened in my life, from where ideas poured out. The following year, I dusted off my wedding dress, and wore it to another awards ceremony. A documentary I had produced, which presented the dreams and visions of nine different Australians for the world they wanted to live in during the third millennium, had won a national media award. The ceremony was held on Australia Day. Dazzled by the lights at the posh hotel, I delivered my thank-you speech before a distinguished audience which sensed the heartbeat of the young woman who had arrived in Sydney two decades before with a hundred dollars in her pocket and a pouch soaked in dreams. I knew that the spirits of my ancestors watched from the other side as I received the honours for my contribution to my new home.

One evening, after I had shut down my computer and watered the wall of plants around my desk – which had earned me the nickname 'The jungle queen' – I went home feeling somehow different. At peace. I picked up a takeaway dinner, a bunch of red carnations to place by the wedding photo of Richard and me, and a video called *Fried Green Tomatoes*. The name had attracted me, though I had no idea what the movie was about. All I knew was that Aunt Dorita would have liked it too. Anything that had food in it had to be a good story, she used to say. The movie was about friendship and death, and I went through a box of tissues as I watched. It brought back memories of our local serenades, the smell of freshly baked biscuits, the incense, the procession of the Purple Christ, and my father, who was alone at home. I remembered the most recent conversation we had had. He told me about a disabled girl who came to his house for lunch every so often. She had no arms and could not speak, and he had to spoon-feed her, as if she were a baby. I had implored him to be careful. Papa had become a sweet old man, and emotionally vulnerable. When the movie finished, I hugged my pillow, shut my puffy eyes, and said a prayer of protection for my father. I felt closer to him than ever before, and I thanked all the gods for the richness of my life. A soft feeling entered the room as I switched the lights off, and I fell asleep snuggled in the memory of my father's embrace.

The next day, my brother Roy came to tell me that Papa had passed away. He had died in his sleep. His heart had given up, and his soul had moved into the next life, to join his eternal sweetheart. I bit my lip until it bled, for I could no longer cry. All I wanted was to lift my gaze to the sky and scream. I was being stripped of everything I loved. I was too scared to scream, in case the wrath of the universe intensified against me. I wept for not having been with him in his last moment but I thanked the universe that Papa had not suffered. He was seventy-three. It had been a year since Richard had died. Within five years, I had lost three of my closest loved ones. All I wanted to do now was surrender to the universal will, and avoid more suffering. Everyone seemed to be leaving me and I had to let go.

FACING THE DEMONS

YEARS OF GRIEVING peeled away many layers of my heart. Wherever I was, I found myself a step closer to the suffering of others. I began to write down my thoughts, and I liked what I read. I managed to integrate the essence of Walter into myself and I began to understand what his presence had meant in my life. Now, in my widowhood, I wrote and wrote, inspired by the people who had filled my life with meaning and who now watched over me from beyond the horizon. Eventually, time began to heal my emotional wounds, and bowls of chicken soup gave me the energy I needed to review my role in life. Only one event cast a shadow over my plans. I longed for the inquest into Richard's death to begin. I wanted to know the truth. Once the truth was in the open, I would be able to start again. Nearly three years had passed since his death, and I was no closer to finding out what had happened that Sunday afternoon in the Blue Mountains.

The last stage in sealing Richard's life in this world was to take the other half of his ashes to his homeland. I felt that he had to be taken

back to the home of his ancestors for his soul to be fully renewed. I
flew to London, then made my way by train to Aberdeen, in northern Scotland. I clutched tightly a small urn that held the tiny granules
of Richard's material life. The scenery outside was the most enchanting I had ever seen. The sun cast an iridescent glow over the lakes,
and the open fields whispered to the winds tales of ancient castles,
damsels and wise dragons. I felt connected to the sense of wonder
Richard had experienced when we travelled to Machu Pichu by train
all the way from Cusco. When the train arrived in Aberdeen, I
stretched my arms up and took a deep breath, crisp air from the Arctic Circle welcoming me. I was in one of the most northern points
on the map; I looked down and waved to my home in Sydney. I was
definitely a southerner – the instant the sun disappeared behind the
mountains, I felt as though I would freeze to death. Like a messenger
with a sacred mission, I walked along the same road that had seen
Richard blossom in adolescence, and I was overwhelmed by the
magic of the rolling hills that had inspired his dreams. I walked
through the grey city made of granite, accompanied by the ethereal
nature of his being, the ghosts of our past, and the angels of my
dreams; and with each step I took on the cobble stones, I realised that
our journey was drawing to a close.

I visited Richard's family, and they took me to his favourite places
– the movie house, his school and his university. His eldest brother
helped me find a befitting spot for the final ceremony, on the side of
the mountain Richard used to wander on when he needed to find
peace. With traditional reverence and a Christian prayer, we offered
our last farewell, scattering his ashes to the mountainside. 'Thank you
for being part of our lives,' I whispered and a breath of wind took his
soul to join his ancestors.

The city of Edinburgh appeared like an enormous castle, dressed in
beautiful brocade, and fanning medieval tales in the afternoon air. I felt
compelled to spend a few days there and reflect; I had begun to hear
a call from within my heart. I explored all the historic nooks and cran-
nies of the city – the lofty buildings, the medieval architecture. It

looked just like the setting for many of the stories I had read in my childhood, tales of love and treachery, stone castles, precious jewels, and embroidered gowns. I sat in a castle for hours, searching for the young woman who still lived in my heart. I thought about my life, and the paths I had taken. I thought about the driving force behind my steps – my purpose. I was far from both of my homes, and at that distance, it was as if I could see my life projected on a screen in the sky. I asked myself whether I had ever been truly happy. I felt satisfied that I had pleased my mother, my bosses, my friends and the people whom I had assisted through my work, but deep inside I realised that something was missing. I had never taken time off to clarify my own dreams. Over several hours, I came to the conclusion that I had to take that time; that I had to honour the promises I had made to myself when I was a child. I would never see the face of my true spirit if I did not listen to the deep whispers of my heart. I rubbed a ring I had bought at the castle that afternoon, and invoked clarity. The idea of leaving my job loomed in my mind, and a strange feeling came over me. Yes, that was what I wanted. I needed to leave the safety of a large organisation and follow my own path. It was time for a change. But to change, I would need courage. I was asking myself to leave a job that had given me so many rewards, that had filled my life with exhilaration, that had allowed me to meet, be inspired by and assist so many people. The more I thought about it, the faster my heart beat. Clarity was not a big flash of light, I realised, but a long process. The more I developed my plans, the stronger became my conviction to act. The business name 'Courage Communications' sprung forth, and I liked it. It would be a reminder to keep going, no matter what happened. From the top of the castle, I gazed at the immensity of life before me, and stretched my arms out. 'Yes,' a little voice said. 'Yes.'

To save me from wavering on my decision, the universe gave me a blatant reminder. A few days after my return, I filmed a story about refugees and trauma. One of the people around the filming snapped and became involved in a vicious brawl with my cameraman. I think he felt that we were persecuting him. Blows were exchanged, and the cameraman was left with a broken bone. I found myself at the police station, pressing charges against a man whose mental health I was unsure of. I realised that I had reached my boundaries. I would hand in my resignation as soon as the TV season was over.

Early the next summer, when most of my colleagues were on holidays, I carefully took down my framed awards from our unit's hall of fame, packed them into a cardboard box with my other mementoes, and walked out through the glass doors of the large white building which Richard had helped to establish years earlier. My mood was sombre, for I was leaving a huge slice of my life behind. I felt as if I was leaving home again, for at the station I had experienced a range of emotions: the ecstasy of the creative process; the indignation at social prejudices; boundless love; and devastating heartbreak. I had learned from every line I had written, every person I had met, and every scandal I had caused. Outside, a new beginning awaited me. I loaded my car and drove off, without looking back.

In a corner of my house I created a cosy space for my office. On top of a large antique table I set out all the necessary equipment for my media production business – a new fax–phone, computer, and business cards. The bowl that had held Richard's ashes was now a container for paper clips. On the wall, I hung the awards I had won and pictures I had collected during my years at the station. I toasted my business with champagne, friends and a few potential clients. Courage Communications would produce media for the new millennium. Whether it was a pamphlet, a corporate video or a documentary, it would reflect my vision: a language of the heart.

On top of the pile of incoming mail was a letter from the coroner's court advising me of the date of Richard's inquest – only a few days after I had opened for business. While I felt relieved, I also felt anxious. My brother Roy and his family had gone to live in Peru for a year, so I thought I would have to go to the court on my own. I wanted to ask Zoyla to come with me, but I felt she would get lost in the legal language, so when Dawn called to ask whether I needed company, I said yes.

I put on a cream suit for serenity, rubbed my wedding ring for good luck, and picked up a Buddhist book to hold against my heart in case of shock. I feared that during the proceedings I might discover some unpleasant truths. I had no idea who the other suspects were; all I knew from the police was that I was not the only one. When I asked a lawyer friend whether I should take a solicitor with me, he asked me whether my notice had requested that I do so. I said, 'No.' Then I had nothing to worry about, he replied.

Dawn and I entered the court and sat in the front row. As we waited for the magistrate, I heard a few reporters whispering behind me. I had been inside the court before, full of confidence, in the company of my crew; but this time I felt vulnerable. I reminded myself that it would all be over soon. It was a two-day process, and I was to appear as a witness on the second day. Apart from the senior detective who had headed the investigation, and who would be giving his brief at the beginning, I did not know any other names on the list of witnesses. I looked at the yellow walls around me, and at the walnut furniture, trying to curb the rising beat of my heart.

The hearing started solemnly, as we rose while the magistrate entered the room. The senior detective was called to the witness box. Now I will know, I thought. And I waited. The beat of my heart grew faster as the man in the booth narrated the particulars of the case. The words pounded on my ears. The whispers behind my seat grew louder, and Dawn, who was sitting nearby, suddenly appeared to me to be miles away. The police detective had come to his conclusion: I was the only person who could have killed Richard. He added that he could not prove this because there was no evidence. I could not contain my shock, and I screamed. The magistrate told me to calm down. I felt trapped, unable to move. I was asked whether I had a legal representative who could question the detective, and as I had none, I was asked to do the questioning myself. I felt totally lost. I was in no state to rationally question a police officer, let alone challenge him in legal terms. I burst into tears, and asked him why he hated me, why he had never given me the chance to grieve, why he had always seen me as a killer, right from the beginning of the investigation.

After getting hold of the disk, the police had made a copy of the deleted file which they had managed to retrieve and the detective had read his journal. He had found the deleting of the file suspicious, and blamed me for it. What I had seen as an innocent computer disk had become a weapon. I tried to explain that I had erased the file to clear sad memories. The magistrate again told me to calm down, and said that I would have my turn to explain later. I felt ambushed and betrayed. I left the court late that afternoon, crushed by a feeling of defeat. I could not understand why this had happened.

At home, a huge bunch of white lilies was waiting for me; they were from a Buddhist friend. My emotions had turned my face as white as their petals. I knew that the blow I had received would either kill any hint of emotional recovery in me, or force me to stand up and fight for my right to a fair go. I spent the night desperately trying to find a solicitor to represent me the next day. As I phoned, I looked at my new business cards on my desk and a line from an old Peruvian song came into my mind: 'Courage breeds courage'. I felt as if the universe was calling me to honour the name I had chosen to represent me in business. To win this struggle, I needed courage.

After much phoning and imploring, I found a solicitor. Before the hearing started the next day, he presented me with two options. I could either let this inquest run its course, refuse to answer any questions and let the world judge me. Or, I could launch a legal challenge, which would be long, anxiety-ridden and expensive. I had five minutes to make up my mind. The words 'Defend! Defend!' echoed in my head, and I chose the second option. Poison can sometimes be turned into medicine. The court's failure to advise me of my right to legal representation became a ground to have the inquest cancelled and a new one called. The law had come to my rescue.

Indeed, the process was long, anxiety-ridden and expensive. I engaged a female lawyer, and, together, we launched our own review and investigation of the reasons behind the police accusation. Damage had already been done. After the first day of the aborted inquest, the media had carried the news of the accusation to the four corners of the universe. Conclusions had been made in splashy headlines that I wanted to kill my husband because he was abandoning me. Rumours grew more and more bloated by the day. Richard soon became the dead rich businessman with a dark streak. I was the mad Latin woman ready to kill. At night, I would cower in the corner of my bedroom, shaking, fuming at those who I felt wanted to see me go down, and wondering how all the rumours could have started. In a way, I had become the first client of Courage Communications. I was learning what it meant to act with a humane approach, that is, without resentment.

In the first few weeks I had to deal with a range of emotions, particularly anger and frustration. I felt my rights as a widow had been violated, that my pain was continually being assaulted. I could not understand how a person could be dragged through the mud without there being any evidence. The situation forced me to look at reality as it really was. Screaming 'It's not fair' or 'It's not true' did not help. I would have to prove my innocence according to the law. I would wake up in a cold sweat and spend the rest of the night peering through the bars on my windows, fearful of intruders. I imagined my phone was tapped and feared evidence could be planted. The phone rang continually with requests for interviews, or assurances from well-wishers that they did not believe I had killed my husband. There were also the weirdos who had already judged and condemned me, and left obscene messages or spat insults down the line, telling me to go back home. I began to give the option some thought. But I would not do that until my name had been cleared. I rang Roy in Peru, seeking his support and asking the family to pray for me.

The police had compiled a blue book containing all the reports upon which they had based their accusation. It contained heartbreaking descriptions of Richard's last moments, according to the pathologist who had conducted the autopsy. I could no longer avoid the ugliness of the truth, so I read every line, and became fully aware of the brutality of his murder. The more I read the more the echoes of my pain reverberated as if my wound had been stamped with fire. The blue book included testimonies from my colleagues about my character, and my relationship with Richard. Two of these testimonies seemed to me to be the products of wild imaginations, but they had become the basis for the police accusation. One woman, who stated that she was Richard's closest confidante, said that he had secretly told her he was leaving me because we had sexual problems. A second claimed that I used to beat Richard up. I knew these women, and, at first, I refused to believe that they had written these extravagant statements. But their names on the page struck me in the face. I was deeply hurt. Their betrayal was the hardest thing I had to deal with in the whole legal process.

The blue book also contained a report by a doctor – who I had never met – which dealt with my psychological state. It explained in great detail how a person of my background could kill when faced with abandonment by somebody of Richard's position. It was a long document, which the doctor had based on carefully selected testimonies, extracts from Richard's computer journal, and the opinion of the senior detective. The doctor questioned the genuineness of my grief, comparing the way I grieved with that of others. He assumed that the vitamin pills I took every day were drugs that had been prescribed to suppress my rage.

To me, the most disturbing aspect of the report was that the doctor had also assumed that the notes on Richard's computer disk were a true and complete reflection of our relationship. For some strange reason, this document had a sinister power over me. The more I read it, the more I felt trapped by its contents. I became obsessed with it. The statements and theories contained in it acquired demonic dimensions, as if they were the ghosts of my innermost fears. At night, I placed the blue book under my pillow, fearful that the words would escape on their own, and make their way into the public arena. Indeed my fears were facing me in bold writing for I had become the victim of my own sad story. And it was my reality so I had to deal with it the best way I could. In a way, the whole legal process was forcing me to face what I feared most in life – public judgment.

Something that puzzled me about the blue book was that it did not contain any statement by Ann Marie or Cleo, or any of my friends from the theatre group who I had been with on the day Richard was killed.

As the weeks passed, with Zoyla reminding me constantly that courage meant acting despite my fears, the blue book began to lose its power over me. The more I immersed myself in it, the clearer it became that there was a way out. I had no work, for no client was prepared to hire me until my name was cleared, so I dedicated myself to working on my case. In the morning, I would take a long stroll, meditating and trying to transform negativity into energy to help me find a solution. Watching the waves smash against the rocks, I let my shame dissolve. There was no reason to feel shame, Zoyla said, but I did. Perhaps because I strived for perfection in myself, while the computer disk had brought my imperfect private life out into the open. I felt the whole world was pointing its finger at me. I was caught between wishing that I did not care what other people thought, and the reality that I needed to prove I wasn't involved in my husband's death. I felt as if I had been called upon to swim through a sea of sludge in order to discover the raw scent of life. According to my ancestors the raw scent of life integrates both its intoxicating perfume and its stench. It is in the balance of these scents that one finds the perfect fragrance. Mama often reminded me that the lotus flower grows up out of swamps. I had a strong premonition that something fragrant had to come out of all this muck.

While an inquest is a legal hearing, it is not an official trial. Nevertheless, the crude reality was that in the eyes of the public, and the press, I was being tried. And if I lost my challenge to the police accusation, I could be arrested. I knew that if we could destroy the doctor's report point by point – and there were twenty-two points in total – we could quash the accusation. We waited six long months until we were given a date for the new inquest. I worked full time on gathering evidence to support my case. What scared me was that I knew that the detective and his team would, at the same time, be doing everything to prove their point.

To help put my mind at ease, and to fortify my spirit, members of my Buddhist group, mainly women, came on Monday nights to meditate and chant. Their aim was to help boost my life force, and reinforce my faith that there was light at the end of the tunnel. After our meditation sessions, we drank tea and analysed the whole affair in the light of spiritual clarity. We decided to see the process as a test of my courage, and of my ability to forgive and let go of resentment. I was reminded that everyone has a role to play in life, and the detective was simply playing his. He was doing his job in the only way he knew. If he, or the doctor, hurt me, it might be because they carried wounds too. Monday nights were the only source of solace I had during that period. Sometimes I felt I was being punished for trying to understand life, for daring to search the face of my real spirit.

After many Monday nights of meditation, and sessions at my solicitor's office, the day of the inquest arrived. After six months, I had finally surrendered to the dictates of life. I did not feel the need to point the finger at my accusers, or to blame anybody for causing my hurt. I had gone as far as accepting that if I had to go to jail, then so be it. Perhaps my destiny determined that I would have to make a stopover in a real prison – I had been in a mind prison already. Such acceptance was one of the hardest things I had ever done in my life, for it meant rising above my need to prove my innocence. I knew my truth, and I trusted that if I radiated it fully, from the depths of my heart, without the interference of negative emotions, one day the outside world would accept it.

This unconditional surrender saved my heart from being poisoned. I had fought against bitterness when Richard was killed; I had even publicly expressed my forgiveness of his attacker, or attackers, in a naive bid to attract their confession. It was exceptionally hard to fight against negativity, again. The barrister quashed one by one, the points raised in the doctor's report, removing one of the key bases to the accusation. My alibi was heard, and my name was cleared. Four years after Richard died, I sat in the witness box of the coroner's court holding on to nothing else but the certainty that life had given me this test – and I had passed it. When the magistrate asked me whether I had killed my husband, or caused his killing, I answered, 'No', and the court accepted my word. It was the voice of my heart that had spoken, and they had heard it. My faith in humanity returned and with it my faith in myself.

EPILOGUE

ONE SUNNY AFTERNOON, three weeks after the end of the inquest, I arrived at the foot of the Inca shrine, Tambomachay, to tell my story; and the wind was there to listen. The Godmother who had opened the gates of Inca spirituality for me, was no longer living in Cusco. My Buddhist friend Angel had also moved on in search for work. On this visit I found there was a healthier pride in the population. The indigenous Peruvians now recognised their own dignity instead of feeling shame and resentment. Something had changed in their attitude but it was difficult to pinpoint precisely what it was or what had caused it. I was coming back after six years, with many emotional sores but feeling at peace, as if a debt had finally been paid.

I stood humbly before the stone altar, mesmerised by the murmur of the sacred spring that carried echoes of the earth's spirit. I felt grounded, wholly connected to a side of myself I had not acknowledged before. Staring at the sparkling waters of the spring I felt as if chunks of pain were being washed from the depth of my soul – anger and hostilities that had tugged at me for many years. I had gone to Tambomachay to say thank you and claim my reward. I had suffered what I needed to suffer; now I wanted to enjoy what was to come.

I arrived in Cusco with a group of travellers who were attending an international conference on indigenous Peruvian spirituality. Anthropologists, scientists, shamans and healers of all sorts were gathering in Urubamba, the Sacred Valley of the Incas, to discuss millennium prophesies. After the inquest, this exceptional conference offered the extreme alternative I needed to help me forget recent events so I joined the group. That it was held in Cusco, three weeks after the inquest, was a blessed coincidence. The delegates were required to visit Tambomachay before attending the conference. Tradition dictated that a visitor should first cleanse in the waters of the sacred spring before entering mystic grounds. Around us the sun shone with added radiance, painting the sky with hues of Calypso blue and hugging the mountains.

The ceremony began with a Japanese Buddhist monk robed in a stiff white gown, who made sharp and elegant movements with his arm, calling for nature's blessings to the land. It was Spring Equinox in the Southern Hemisphere and, I was told, an important day for the cosmic energies. Perhaps enthralled by the transcendental nature of the ceremony – and feeling the effects of an empty stomach – my awareness brought down the boundaries of my perception and my eyes captured a flock of clouds cruising across the sky like angels. Then, the Indian children who watched the ceremony with curiosity and laughter, turned into flowers. I blinked twice and in my mind I joined in their giggles. What was very real, however, were the thirty Australians who had come here in search of a spiritual boost. Dressed in white robes and mesmerised by the air of the Andes they too waited for their turn to be anointed with the spring that rose from the belly of Inca land.

As I splashed my face with the ice waters of the spring, a little voice inside me asked what on earth was I doing there again? Hadn't I had enough with the outcome of my previous visit? Why did I insist in turning my life into a ritual? I was so dizzy I could not reason with my own doubts. Instead I stood there to honour the indigenous in me, the side of myself that had held me together through thick and thin, that had found meaning in prayers and messages, and even in a misguided accusation. Watching the circle of people around me and the line of spiritual healers, I understood that the drama in my life had been beyond my control.

A few days before the end of the conference, I had the chance to share a meal with three very special men. One was a great Zulu healer, the other was the Buddhist monk, and the third, an English writer, an exponent of modern Christian discourse. Over beers, potato balls in cheese sauce and barbecued heart, which the monk blessed before eating, they discussed the power of people to manifest their destiny. It was a privilege for me be with them and listen to their words. It was as if that moment, too, was a prize for the harsh times I had gone through. The African healer, a large man of dignified bearing, spoke about the need to connect with one's own ancestral story in order to be able to read the signs of life. He laughed with loud guffaws as he told us his own story, while relishing every bite of the magnificent food. Next to him I felt as if I had touched the essence of the earth. The Buddhist monk, on the other hand, with his compassionate and practical attitude which led him to bless everything he ate, mirrored the influences that had shaped my parents' lives in their last years, persuading them to let my destiny unfold in a new land. Completing this distinguished triad was the English writer, the voice of modern reason, who interpreted Christian tales with new meaning and singular clarity. In his opinion, the prophesied second coming of Christ is reflected in the shift in spiritual awareness the world is now experiencing; a more humane approach to life.

I was not sure I wanted to go back to Australia. I felt the new land did not want me. Or did I not want the new land any more? I knew that staying in Peru was not an option, not at the time. I had changed so much in twenty years that I felt a foreigner in my own country, alien to some of its traditions. I did not have the energy to pursue a new business, nor did I feel I could go back to a media job. Not for a while. A breath of wind whispered in my ears, telling me that rewards are stored in the folds of a single moment. I could start by relishing my time there.

While I was in Cusco I heard a distant call from the Amazon, a place I had never visited despite my hitchhiking tours in the countryside. I felt I needed to breathe my mother's earliest memories and anoint myself with the essence of her exotic tales. I packed my red poncho neatly at the bottom of my suitcase and tied a knot around the pouch of recent experiences. Then I flew into the rainbow that waited on the other side of the mountains, to the land where the pink dolphins serenaded the souls at night before a dark feline escorted them to the Other Side when it was time to depart.

I stepped off the plane and walked into Iquitos as if I was stepping into the pages of a fairytale. The presence of nature and the colours in the sky were as exuberant as the smiles with which people greeted each other. I felt at home immediately, a home of the heart where there was no need to explain who I was or what I was doing there. I felt that I had penetrated the source of my good feelings. I searched for Mama's spirit in every corner of the tropical town, in every leaf that fell from the trees, and in every musical note that danced out of the bar windows. Then I was able to smell the fresh spring of her imagination.

My senses came alive, for Mama had not exaggerated at all when she had spoken of the colours of the rainbow so tangible and alive, of the giant palm trees that seemed to converse with each other; the sagacious reptiles and the inebriating fragrance of ripened fruit. Everything seemed larger than life, everything was larger than life. I looked around and I tried to visualise her image behind the counter in a fabric shop, the smile that greeted her customers, and her lullabies around the rolls of silk and taffeta in Don Ramon's fabric department. I felt her soul was still there, and I realised that the Amazon was a place where magic and reality lived in harmony. But inside it I felt tiny, even smaller than a blade of grass. As I walked along the streets edged by walnut trees, I met children with infectious laughs and gleaming skin. In their gaze I found the living soul of the Amazon.

At the Bethlehem markets little had changed from Mama's descriptions. It was still an extravagant place pulsating with life; where you could find your way to heaven, or an orifice to hell. My niece, Jessica, my brother Luis' daughter, had come with me to see it all, and together we explored the colourful thread that had woven our family tapestry. Despite my eating from the fruit of Amazon life I felt a sense of detachment, something did not allow me to get close to my family. A fear of sorts. As I walked through the narrow alleys bumping into pet monkeys and fruit carts, one of the stall holders, a woman with a broad smile, called out to me.

'You look lost,' she said, and I nodded. The woman was a local healer and was interested in my story about Australia and how my destiny was unfolding. A daughter of the Amazon in Australia. She wanted to know how I managed.

She offered me a native drink that was meant to align my memories. Into a small glass – which I preferred not to scrutinise for cleanliness – she poured a dark potion. And with a blend of curiosity and reverence I drank the whole lot in one go. 'Well,' she said, 'you are certainly into extremes.' The thick potion slithered down my throat like a stream of fire, turning my organs inside out and warming any icy spots in my memory.

'Yes,' I replied. 'I must learn to be measured.'

A few days later I attended a traditional purifying session with the same woman to help restore my health. I stepped into a large tin bath with rose petals floating on the water. For a long while she massaged my skin with a brush made of snakeskin and wild-cat whiskers. She brushed and hummed in rhythm, and her lullaby brought me close to my mother. My eyes moistened as I realised that Mama had appeared to me in the gaze of most of the women who had come to my help. With every stroke of the brush I felt that layers of pain were being removed. I was another link in the family chain of short-lived happiness followed by tragedy. The woman hummed and brushed and I burst in to sobs, feeling that I had sacrificed my heart for a career. I told her that I felt guilty for having abandoned Mama to search for a dream I still could not name. But she replied that I did know what it was; I had known it all along. My dream had been the search for my own happiness. Happiness for me had always been the thrill of motion, change, progress, the beauty of diversity. I needed to move like the wind, look at the world with the eyes of a condor and tell stories about life. The session concluded with a vigorous rub with a lotion made of the belly fat of a lizard to fertilise my spirit and a layer of nut oil to awaken my sensuality.

In the local library at Iquitos I discovered that Yurimaguas, the name of the village where my ancestors came from, meant 'City of women'. That explained why Mama and I were like trees that refused to break. The discovery rattled my subconscious and brought me to the river to smell the silver cod which Mama had told me carried the perfume of women's fertility. I sat there for hours pondering the existence of the Other Side, the In-between; where the purpose of life was said to be written. As my mind floated I noticed a little girl playing not far from where I was sitting. She was barefoot and long legged with a floral skirt, a scarf on her head and an air of sweet innocence. She was carefully picking up pebbles from the river bank and throwing them into the water, jumping and giggling as she did so. It seemed as if she was playing with an invisible spirit, so much so that I was not sure whether the girl was real or was a sliver of my longings. But my cousin Rosa walked over to me and saw the girl too. With a wicked smile she said that the girl was probably talking to Bufeo Colorado, the Pink Dolphin that appeared to those who still believed in the spirits.

Three months later I was back in Australia, unable to make a decision about what to do or where to go. I decided to get a job but I felt lost. A few days after my arrival in Sydney, I felt the effects of the bark syrup of the Bethlehem market and the cat-whisker brushes in my heart, for I found myself connected to Mama's storytelling ability. With vivid detail I wrote an article about the essence of a café society, describing the story of Caffiro, a love-sick prince who turned into a coffee bean in order to be reunited with his lover. The tale had flowed so easily from my mind that I was certain a surge of answers would follow. But as bubbles of memories began to rise from the depth of my subconscious I fell into a deep depression; my grief was emerging too.

One morning I woke up and everything around me was dark, even the sun outside my window had turned into a circular shadow. I was suffering a personal eclipse and I panicked. I called an agency that helped victims of crime and begged for support. Through them it was eventually recommended that I see a psychologist. Her name was Caroline, she specialised in trauma counselling, and she was from Latin America.

Three years later, on the eve of the third millennium, I tied the knot on a neat parcel that contained the story of my family life. It was a story I had written to heal the wounds of my tragedies and losses. It was a story filled with tears and laughter, with fears and euphoria, and with pain, both emotional and physical. Travelling to the past had helped me understand and accept life as it was, and despite my inflamed joints and cramped muscles I felt I could move again. I was no longer cold – the ice had melted from my heart.

Soothed by the essence of vanilla in the oil burner I switched off the lights and went to bed with my cat Chaska at my feet. Soon I felt my awareness gliding into a glass palace built on the skirt of a three-peak mountain. Inside, people were writing busily with phosphorescent pens. I asked the receptionist for Richard and she pointed to a room on the top floor. Somehow I knew I was gliding between two worlds. He was in there, sitting behind a large wooden desk noting down his thoughts. His face was filled with contentment as he lifted his gaze to greet me. The colour of his jacket struck my eyes. It was bright scarlet. Dazzled by it I dropped to my knees and looked down, feeling vulnerable. A stream of tears poured from my eyes, and I sobbed profoundly for a long time, unable to articulate the reasons for my surrender but forced by the intensity of my feelings. Tears washed my anguish, trying to dissolve the suffering of Richard's departure and for the shame I felt about the exposure of our private life. The dream allowed me to experience a sense of liberation and forgiveness. Richard's face had become the face of the love that lived in my heart, and the red jacket mirrored the colour of the passion I thought I had lost. As he looked at me I saw that his eyes carried the same torch of compassion I had begun to experience for myself. Then he stood up and walked towards me, gently helping me up. With his arm around my shoulders we walked out of the luminous building into the streets of life. The radiance of his jacket embraced my feelings, then I heard a roar from the depths, a familiar roar that said: 'To handle pain we must first embrace it.' I hugged him and we moved on. I woke up tickled by the light of dawn, certain that the void in my heart had now been filled. Chaska was still at my feet.

I guess I have found my Golden Disk. It is the light that bathed the episodes of my life as I looked back, the clarity that made me see beyond my pain. It is inside me, and it feels good to know I am not alone.

ACKNOWLEDGEMENTS

TO BEGIN THIS journey took a spontaneous will, to continue it took a great deal of effort; but to arrive at the end required the support and faith of my family and friends.

My deepest gratitude to all members of my extended family whose vibrant lives coloured the threads of my memory. My heartfelt thanks to Caroline Leiva, my therapist, for guiding me out of the black hole of depression and into this story; to my friend and doctor Katrin Munz, for keeping my energy going. All my loving appreciation to Zoyla Vasquez and Michael Redhill, whose parental guidance filled the vacuum of my loneliness. Special thanks to Jackie Woods, Clarita Norman, Cecilia Yeomans, Patricia Triton and all the women of my spiritual circle for being there. To Ken Marslew from Enough is Enough, for recognising the survivor in me; to my solicitor, Joan Baptie, for her drive towards justice. My heart will always be open to Selwa Anthony who read this story in the folds of my memory before I did. To my publisher Nikki Christer and editors Vanessa Mickan and Bernadette Foley, who were able to read under the jungle of my entangled emotions. And, last but not least, thanks to Life for letting my heart beat on.